Object-Oriented Design
With C++

To my mother, Peggy
— K.B.

To Michael Westcott for his wise counsel
and friendship over many years
— J.S.

Object-Oriented Design With C++

K A Barclay and W J Savage
Napier University

PRENTICE HALL

London   New York   Toronto   Sydney   Tokyo   Singapore
Madrid   Mexico City   Munich   Paris

First published 1997 by
Prentice Hall Europe
Campus 400, Maylands Avenue
Hemel Hempstead
Hertfordshire, HP2 7EZ
A division of
Simon & Schuster International Group

Typeset in 10/12pt Palatino and Courier
by Keyword Publishing Services Limited, Barking, Essex

Printed and bound in Great Britain by
T. J. International Ltd

Library of Congress Cataloging-in-Publication Data

Barclay, Kenneth A., 1947–
    Object oriented design with C+ + / K. A. Barclay and W. J. Savage.
        p.   cm.
    Includes bibliographical references and index.
    ISBN 0–13–256371–1
    1. Object-oriented methods (Computer science)   2. C+ + (Computer
program language)   I. Savage, W. J. (W. John)   II. Title.
QA76.64.B353   1996
005.1'2—dc20   96–28666
                                                                        CIP

British Library Cataloguing in Publication Data

A catalogue record for this book is available from the British Library

ISBN 0–13–256371–1

---

1   2   3   4   5   01   00   99   98   97

Contents

Preface

This book presents an introductory text to object-oriented design and C++. The target audience for the book is undergraduate students in computing science and software engineering. However, it can also be used by practising software professionals who wish to update their knowledge in this area.

The text assumes no prior knowledge on the part of the reader of either object orientation or the C++ programming language. However, experience with a high-level programming language would be an advantage. The book forms a basis for an academic course in which object-oriented design and the C++ language are jointly introduced.

Considerable effort has been taken to present the topics in a clear, concise and orderly manner. Each chapter participates in the development of the object concept from simple objects and classes through to abstract classes, dynamic binding and polymorphic behaviour. A number of object models are developed, representations are defined, and implementations are programmed from illustrative applications.

A particular feature of the book is the inclusion of a number of case studies. They are used to illustrate various aspects of design and the C++ language, and fundamental and systematic program design in a relevant context not otherwise achievable with small systems. Where appropriate, each chapter includes complete design and program listings. All are reproduced from the computer and should execute correctly on any machine supported by a standard C++ compiler.

A short list of major issues raised in each chapter are repeated as a summary at the chapter end. Most chapters include a set of exercises. The exercises include the construction of new designs as well as modifications and extensions to the given examples. Solutions to these exercises are available on request from the authors.

Many practising professionals consider C++ as the implementation language of choice for object-oriented development. This is undoubtedly a result of the success of the C language. However, both languages through their power, and in the case of C++ through its size and complexity, offer a bewildering array of functionality. The adoption of C++ as a programming language presents a number of major challenges, not the least of which is to reduce the degrees of freedom available to the programmer. This book explores some of these difficulties and their resolution, by imposing on the language the use of an object model. It is expressed in the design language LOOM (Language for Object-Oriented Modelling) which, in addition to constraining the form of the model, also removes the arcane syntax of C++ and its confusing semantics.

The emergence of a number of object-oriented methods offers the opportunity to impose object-oriented modelling and designs on the development process from the beginning, ahead of any implementation concerns. LOOM reinforces the holistic nature of the object model where there is less division between the phases of the software life cycle. It also provides the balance between the power and flexibility of the C++ programming language and the control required in its usage. In this way LOOM reduces the risk involved in the adoption of C++ as an object-oriented implementation language.

As the modelling activity, we need some means of capturing details of the principal abstractions of the problem domain (classes), their architectural relationship with other abstractions (associations, aggregations and specialisations), and a definition for the effect of the related operations. We achieve this with the high-level object modelling language referred to as LOOM.

LOOM permits developers to capture the detail of their design without the need to embrace the C++ language. It has sufficient expressive power to record the classes, their basic properties, relationships with other classes, and the behaviour of their operations. The latter are specified with structured English-like sentences with, where appropriate, constructs to emphasise object-oriented concepts such as message passing.

The benefits from the approach is that there is a significant shift of emphasis away from detailed programming difficulties on to the higher ground of analysing the meaning and accuracy of the model. Further, as the mappings from the model to the implementation develop, we recognise emerging and repeated patterns and consequently the programming collapses into a coding chore.

LOOM provides most of the characteristics of object orientation – objects, classes, message passing, single and multiple inheritance, choice of method binding, and genericity. Abstract and concrete classes are carefully distinguished, and deferred and polymorphic operations are explicitly stated. Inter-object relations through aggregations and associations are explicitly documented in the class specifications. Similarly, class relations are presented through specialisation and inheritance clauses.

Chapter 1 gives an account of the fundamental concepts of object orientation and presents an introduction to topics discussed in more detail later in the book. It describes software development as a modelling activity with objects as the main building blocks and outlines the properties of objects, encapsulation, information hiding, abstraction, the class, message passing, inheritance and polymorphism. Chapter 1 presents the essentials and the vocabulary of object orientation which we detail in subsequent chapters.

Chapter 2 gives an account of the fundamental features of an object-oriented analysis and design (OOAD). A discussion of the identification of objects, the classes to which they belong, their operations and representation starts in this chapter. It includes the architectural relationships of association and aggregation that may exist between classes. The object model arising from the design is presented diagramatically. At this point the reader may care to review Chapter 10 which acts as a user guide for the ROME tool presented along with the book. ROME, in addition to other services detailed later, may be used to create and maintain these object models.

Chapter 3 presents a description of a language for object-oriented modelling (LOOM) developed by the authors. For the remainder of the book, LOOM acts as the main vehicle for discussing and capturing the details of an OOAD. The LOOM language has all the characteristics of an object-oriented language, including class specifications, method definitions, object creation and message sending, class specialisation, polymorphism and dynamic binding. The fundamental types of LOOM include, among others, string and date. Containers are also used extensively. Their LOOM specifications as well as the LOOM base types are given in Appendix B. A formal definition of LOOM is to be found in Appendix A.

Chapter 4 is a case study intended to consolidate the points made in the preceding chapters. A relatively simple lending library is modelled with LOOM. Emphasis is placed upon using the principles of good software engineering within the context of an OOAD. The case study presents a strategy for delivering an OOAD, through identification of problem classes, the architectural design, the main design including public services and private properties associated with the problem classes, and finally the detailed design of the class operations.

Chapter 5 shows how a dynamic model of a complete system can be developed. In keeping with the aim of the book, a straightforward approach is taken. State transition diagrams (STDs) are used to describe the dynamic behaviour of a system. The automatic nature of the mapping from an STD to LOOM control code is emphasised.

Chapter 6 gives a detailed account of the implementation in C++ of object-oriented systems. Great care is taken to use best practice so as to avoid opaque or confusing code. The bulk of the code developed can be traced back to LOOM scripts of Chapters 3, 4 and 5. C++ concerns such as class declaration, data and function member definition, message passing, argument-passing strategies, scope and duration of objects and flow control, are now readily accessible through their early presentation in the object model and the matching LOOM scripts. Appendix C gives an overview of classes in C++.

Chapter 7 completes the discussion of OOAD with the specialisation of classes, the redefinition of methods, and the use of the polymorphic effect. The notion of abstract base classes and deferred methods is also presented. Other issues including public and protected properties, private operations and inheritance for implementation are also addressed.

Chapter 8 is a case study that revisits the library system of Chapter 4. As before it consolidates the most important issues raised in earlier chapters. Incremental development through a series of versions is offered as a variation of the development method adopted in Chapter 4. Specialisation of classes and the use of the polymorphic effect is highlighted in the context of this application.

Chapter 9 is an account of the C++ implementation issues raised in Chapters 7 and 8. As in Chapter 6, the C++ developed maps directly from the LOOM scripts. The implementation concerns include class derivation, function member redefinition, virtual functions, abstract base classes and pure virtual functions, polymorphism and dynamic binding.

Chapter 10 completes the book with a tutorial on the ROME modelling tool. This chapter may be read at any point where the reader wishes to use tool support for the development of the object models presented throghout the book. The disk supplied with the book contains the ROME tool and includes all the sample models presented in the book.

Tool support

Using LOOM means that modellers can readily communicate their designs to others. With the mappings between LOOM and C++ defined, the programming activity now finds its proper place as a simple coding activity.

LOOM has been incorporated into a graphical design tool called ROME operating under Microsoft Windows. This object modelling environment permits the user to present the object model graphically, with dialog boxes to complete the LOOM class specifications. The dialogs are backed by a compiler to validate the user input. An underlying parse tree is constructed by the tool to generate the LOOM scripts and the resulting C++ code.

The generated C++ code is further supported by a class library. This library presents C++ support for the fundamental and container classes used throughout the text. The sources for these classes have been supplied so that the reader may gain additional insight into their construction.

The ROME tool is offered on an as-is basis to the reader without express or implied warranty. It is a fully functional modelling tool and code generator, by which the reader can follow the presentation of this book. It has been used extensively by the authors for the past two years in their teaching programmes. The authors have taken every precaution to ensure the robustness of this distribution. The product is offered in good faith to the readers of the book. The authors, however, cannot accept any liability for any computer system fault resulting while using the software. Equally, the authors imply no warranties of merchantability or fitness for a particular purpose. The authors shall not be liable for any damages suffered by a licensee as a result of using any generated code from the ROME software.

The increasing number of ROME users is matched by an ever-increasing wish list of new features. Many are being incorporated into new releases actively under development. In addition the authors are exploring other related tools/ capabilities, briefly outlined in Chapter 10.

Acknowledgements

The authors recognise the stimulation to this project given by their colleagues. Their gratitude is offered to the Computer Studies Department, Napier University, Edinburgh. We thank the students of this Department who actively participated in the development of LOOM, both as guinea-pigs while LOOM was being formulated and as contributors as it evolved into its present form. Some 500+ undergraduate and postgraduate students of the Department have had direct experience of LOOM. Most acted as unofficial beta-test sites for the ROME tool. The authors also benefited from the experiences and insights offered by the practitioners who attended their professional development programmes.

The authors would wish to record their deepest thanks to Richard McMahon who undertook the development of the ROME modelling tool used throughout this book as his final year Honours' project. This considerable undertaking made concrete what would otherwise have remained at the concept stage. The students of the Department now benefit from its availability both for program design and generation and for the numerous projects it has spawned.

K A Barclay

W J Savage

April 1996

Chapter 1

Object technology

This chapter presents the essence of object-oriented computing. It is intended to provide the necessary background for the material in the remainder of the book. The chapter examines the fundamental characteristics of object oriented computing including abstraction, classes, information hiding and specialisation. The concepts are framed around everyday illustrations, in which we concentrate on introducing the vocabulary of object oriented systems. Formal definitions are deferred until later chapters.

Computer technology has developed extremely quickly since its inception. Today, computer based systems impact much of our lives in many spheres including banking, medical, flight reservation, educational and military applications. They are distinguished by having large amounts of software at their core. The capabilities of these systems is derived from the complex computer programs which control them.

Although we better understand the process of developing computer software, we still deliver it late and over budget. Often the software fails to do what the user requires and is difficult to maintain and modify. These cliched remarks have always applied to the computer software industry, and while we have improved the technologies to support the development process, it has not fully matched the size and complexity of contemporary systems.

1.1 Objects: combined services and data

The concept of software objects arose to model real-world complex objects in computer programs. An *object* describes an entity that is a collection of procedures and data, related by their common support of a single abstraction. *Abstraction* is the process of formulating generalised concepts by extracting common qualities from specific examples. In object oriented software systems the first principle is that of *data abstraction*, the essence of which is that a level of abstraction over the data and the algorithms required to manipulate that data is established. In the object oriented approach algorithms are realised in the implementation of the *operations* and the data elements are referred to as *properties* (or *attributes*).

1

For example, if we are developing an airline reservation system, then one of the principal abstractions in the application is the `Airplane`. The properties of this abstraction might include the passenger capacity and current location. A possible operation is to set the destination of the next flight to be taken by the plane. We refer to the data abstraction `Airplane` as the *class* for the object type. A class specifies the characteristics of the abstraction, including the operations and the properties. Collectively, the operations define the *behaviour* of the abstraction defined in terms of the properties.

A class is effectively a blueprint or template describing an arbitrary number of such objects. The `Airplane` class will describe any number of such objects. The class `Paragraph` could be used to describe any of the paragraphs in this text. Operations associated with the `Paragraph` class might include the accessor operation to count the number of words in the paragraph. Equally, we might have a `Student` class to represent the students attending a university course. A student may change course or inform us of his place of residence. These are the `Student` class operations.

Figure 1.1 shows diagramatically how we present an *object instance*, a particular example of an object from some named class. The upper region names the class to which the object instance belongs (e.g. `Airplane` or `Paragraph` or `Student`). The operations in the right margin list the publicised operations on that object type. The greyed lower region refers to the property values maintained by the instance.

In the figure the operations project from the right margin and denote a collection of public services. Since these operations are public they represent the range of services associated with that object. For example, a vending machine will have an operation by which we select whether tea or coffee is dispensed. An automated bank teller will have an operation which allows us to obtain the balance of our account.

In Figure 1.1 the properties are shown in the greyed region enclosed by the boundary of the rounded rectangle. This arrangement connotes the fact that the properties are not directly accessible. In fact, the key idea with data abstraction is that the properties are hidden or private, and they are only manipulated by the operations. Hence, for example, if a `Student` object has a property which

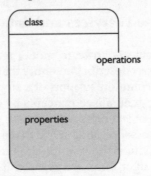

Figure 1.1   *An object instance*

names the course attended by that student, we only find that information if there is an accompanying operation. If there is no such operation then we cannot access that information, even when it is a property value maintained by such instances.

Consider how we might model a bank account. An account can exhibit a variety of behaviours such as debiting some amount from the account, or crediting some amount to the account, or requesting the account's current balance. These behaviours give rise to some of the likely account operations. Debit and credit transactions will document the amount involved and the date of the action. Each of these details, along with the account number and the account balance, must be maintained by each account instance. Every example of a bank account will carry its own data values for these characteristics. All bank account instances will, of course, be subject to the same behaviours as specified by the collection of operations.

To represent an account as an object we describe its behaviours as operations and its characteristics with properties. During the execution of a system, the object is requested to carry out its various operations, changing its properties as needed to reflect the effect of its actions. For example, in Figure 1.2, a debit operation applied to such an account object will result in a change to `theBalance` property.

Some operations give information about the object, while others have some effect on the object. For example, a debit transaction on a bank account changes the current balance. This category of operation we describe as *transformer operations*. A transformer operation changes one or more of the object instance property values. Some operations only give information and are referred to as *accessor operations* and are distinguished with a query symbol suffix. The operation to obtain a statement about an account's balance is of this latter type. Both operations refer to the values of the object's properties. Collectively, these property values are called the *state* of the object. Transformer operations result in a state change, while accessor operations do not usually affect the state of the instance.

Figure 1.2 *A bank account instance*

1.2 Objects as software modules

The concept of an object is both simple and powerful. Objects make ideal software modules because they can be defined and maintained independently of one another, with each object instance forming a self-contained entity. Everything an object knows is expressed in terms of its properties, and everything it can perform is expressed by its operations.

Consider the class of `Television` objects. A television has a set of controls which are the public operations associated with the class. Transformer operations include the channel selection buttons which select the viewing channel. On some televisions there is a button labelled `Tv` which presents in the bottom right corner of the screen a small number giving the current channel being viewed. This information is shown for a few seconds then disappears. This button corresponds to a query operation.

The state of the television is implemented by the many electronic components contained within the case of the television set. This plastic or wooden carcass isolates the viewer from the internals. Since the viewer has no direct contact with these components there is no likelihood that he will damage himself or the set. Consider the position where instead of a volume control button the viewer controlled the volume by using a screwdriver on some internal control screw. The volume control button would usually have some restricted amount of movement, limiting the viewer to a certain maximum of sound. Without this restriction it is possible that adjustments made directly to the control screw may set the volume above its maximum working level and consequently damage vital components.

Equally, by isolating the viewer from the internals and only permitting a trained engineer access to the components, a second benefit is obtained. If the television tube produces a poor quality picture then an engineer may replace that component and improve the service to the viewer. The change has, however, been effected without any operational change. The viewer still selects the channel and controls the volume level as before. Only the improved quality of the picture has changed.

In software, these ideas are referred to as *encapsulation* or *information hiding*. They give the same benefits to software as to television sets. In a software object the properties are hidden from a user but may be replaced without affecting user software which relies on that object abstraction. In a software object behaviour is defined by the public operations and not by the private representation. The public operations govern what we can ask a software object to perform. If we give the wrong value to an operation, then the effect can be denied, ensuring the correct state of the object. For example, a debit operation applied to a bank account might only be permitted if sufficient funds are available.

Since object properties and operations only define their own abstraction and no other abstraction, they usually exhibit *loose coupling* with other objects. This is highly desirable because strong coupling makes software components harder to understand, change or correct. Typically, when defining an object's operation we need not concern ourselves with the requester (client) of that operation. Only the effect of that operation on the object properties need be considered. Equally, the client requesting a service need not concern himself with how that request is achieved and what properties are involved. Objects are also *highly cohesive* since all the elements of an object are present to provide some well-bounded behaviour for the particular abstraction they represent.

1.3 Object interaction is expressed as messages

Objects interact with each other by sending messages requesting the recipient to carry out one of its advertised operations. For example, a bank customer may send his account a credit operation. Here, the customer is the sending object and the account is the receiving object. A *message* is composed of an identification of the recipient object and the name for the message. The message name represents one of the public operations of the class to which the recipient belongs. If the operation requires any further details they are given as *message parameters*.

For example, to make a bank account engage in a transaction to debit it by some monetary amount, some sending object such as an automated teller machine (ATM) might send it the message:

```
account123 debit 50
```

Here, *account123* is the name of the receiver, *debit* is the operation it is being asked to execute, and 50 is the parameter telling the receiver the amount involved in the transaction (Figure 1.3).

When a message is received by some recipient an action is performed. This action usually involves some or all of the the values of the properties representing the state of the receiving object and is usually also influenced by any message parameters. The logic associated with this action is described by the method. The *method* refers to the algorithm which is applied when an operation is executed.

We have noted how transformer operations usually result in a state change

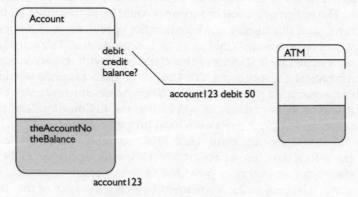

Figure 1.3 *Message to* account123

to the receiving object, while accessor operations merely request information from the recipient. The only means of communication is a message sent from a sender to a receiver. In the case of an accessor operation a secondary information flow is observed. Here, the sender is expecting a response from the receiver in the form of a *return value*. Occasionally, transformer operations also supply return values, perhaps, to report that they have successfully carried out their designated task.

Observe the asymmetry of the messaging concept. The recipient object, when defining its operation, does not concern itself with the object that is sending the message. Equally, the sender need not be concerned with how the operation is implemented. As noted in the preceding section this greatly assists the production of quality software systems.

1.4 Classes: sets of similar objects

It is common to have more than one object of each kind. For example, a bank will certainly hold a number of customer accounts. A *class* is a template or blueprint that defines the operations and properties for a particular kind of object. The descriptions of the operations and properties are included only once in the definition of the class. The objects that belong to a class, called *instances* of the class, contain only their particular values for the properties representing the current state of that object. The instances share the same behaviour through their common operations. Henceforth, we shall omit the operation list from each instance since it will be defined once in the class template and the instance will name the class to which it belongs.

A class is introduced using the same notation as that for an instance. The latter is presented using a rectangle with round corners (sometimes known as a soft box, or rountangle), while the former uses a rectangle. Once again, the publicised operations appear in the right margin, while the properties are listed in the lower third of the figure (Figure 1.4).

For example, a modern banking system will contain many bank accounts, each of which will carry out the same actions and maintain the same kind of information. The entire collection of accounts could be represented by the single class Account, and that class would contain the specification of its operations, the definitions of its operations (methods) and its properties. The actual accounts would be represented by instances of this class, each with its own unique name (say, accountABC123, accountXYZ456, . . .). Each instance would contain data which represents its particular state. When an account receives a message to carry out one of its operations, it would use the definition of the operation given in its class and apply it to its own local property values.

Figure 1.5 shows the Account class and two instances of that class. The instances are referred to as accountABC123 and accountXYZ456. The Account class has three services provided by the operations debit, credit and balance?. The properties maintained by every instance of this class have their own values for the two properties theAccountNo and theBalance. For

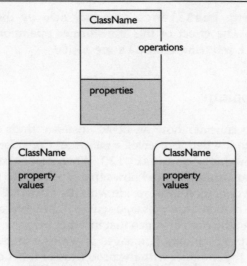

Figure 1.4　*A class and two instances*

example, in the first instance these properties are respectively ABC123 and 150. The message:

```
accountABC123 debit 50
```

results in the execution of the method for the debit operation. This might be defined in terms of subtracting the value of the message parameter 50 from the

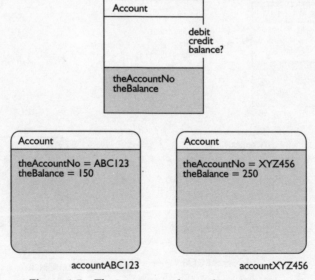

Figure 1.5　*The* Account *class and two instances*

value of the property `theBalance` presently held by the `Account` object `accountABC123`. The effect of this transformer operation produces a state change in the object, reducing `theBalance` to 100.

1.5 Method lookup

It is appropriate to consider how an object instance finds the code for some operation applied to it when it receives a message. Consider an instance of the `Account` class known as `accountABC123`. When it is sent the message to debit the sum of 50 pounds, this instance knows that it belongs to the class `Account` so the code for that operation must reside with the class (Figure 1.6).

For an object to respond to a message sent to it, the corresponding operation must be looked up in the class to which that instance belongs. This is no different from conventional programming languages in which a *procedure call* or *function call* is associated by the compiler with the procedure or function definition which provides the necessary logic. This process is known as *binding*. When the binding is done at compile time we refer to it as *static binding*.

Under static binding, the system converts a message into an activation of the operation method defined in the class of the instance. Where appropriate, any actual parameters given in the message are also transmitted to the method.

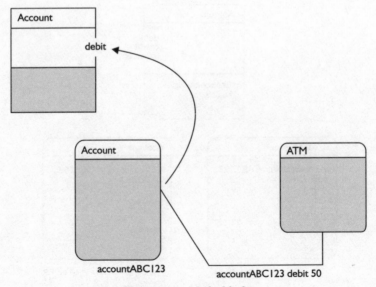

Figure 1.6 *Method lookup*

1.6 Specialisation

Large object oriented models can give rise to many classes. Such complex models may be rationalised and simplified by arranging the classes into hierarchies starting from the general and leading to the more specific. This categorisation of knowledge is applied in many science and engineering disciplines and greatly assists in simplifying complex information. For example, many thousands of species of animals are classified as mammals. All mammals, whatever their particular kind, share common characteristics. Mammals may be further detailed into the particular kind, e.g. human, which in addition to all the mammalian features has additional characteristics peculiar to it. Everything that applies to mammals also applies to humans and every instance of a human is implicitly an instance of a mammal.

The Human class is a *specialisation* of the Mammal class. Conversely, the class Mammal is a *generalisation* of the class Human. The specialised class Human is said to *inherit* all the features of its generalisation class Mammal. We say that the class Human *isA* specialisation of the class Mammal. Any operation that may be applied to a Mammal instance may also be applied to a Human instance. The converse, however, is not true. A Human may have properties and operations peculiar to it. Since a Mammal is a generalisation of a Human, only those general common characteristics are applicable to Mammals.

Specialisation is the mechanism where one class is defined as a special case of another class. The specialised class includes all the operations and properties of the general class. The specialised class may also include additional operations and properties peculiar to it. In addition to the operations inherited, the specialised class may choose to redefine the behaviour of any one of these. The specialised class is known as the *subclass* and the general class is known by the term *superclass* (Figure 1.7).

For example, in a banking application the class Account could be specialised into two subclasses CurrentAccount and Deposit Account. Each inherits the general characteristics of its common superclass. Either subclass may add to the list of operations and properties of the superclass, or override the behaviour of one or more inherited operations.

In Figure 1.8 any instance of the class CurrentAccount will have the properties theAccountNo, theBalance and theOverdraftLimit. The latter property is introduced in the CurrentAccount class itself, while the other properties are inherited from the Account superclass. Equally, any instance of CurrentAccount will respond to the messages debit, credit, balance? and limit?. Again, the first three operations are inherited from the superclass and the last is defined for the CurrentAccount class. A similar story applies to the DepositAccount class in which the properties are theAccountNo, theBalance (both inherited) and theInterestRate, and the operations are debit and credit (inherited) and interest? and balance? (overridden).

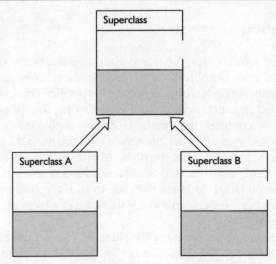

Figure 1.7   *Two specialised versions of subclasses of a single superclass*

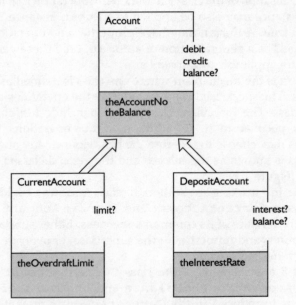

Figure 1.8   *Two subclasses of bank account*

Overriding the definition of an operation in a subclass permits a specialised implementation of the method. For example, the operation `balance?` in the `Account` class may be defined to simply return the present value of the property `theBalance`. In the subclass `DepositAccount` the reappearance of the operation `balance?` indicates a redefinition which might, for example, deal with any interest accruing.

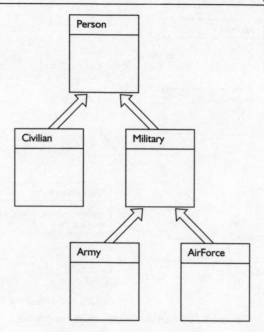

Figure 1.9 *A class hierarchy*

1.7 **Hierarchies of classes**

Class specialisation is transitive across any number of levels, giving rise to a structure known as a *class hierarchy*. From Figure 1.9, superclass Person is specialised into the subclasses Civilian and Military. Class Army and class AirForce are subclasses of class Military.

1.8 **Method lookup under inheritance**

It is worth considering again method lookup through static binding when, this time, inheritance is involved (Figure 1.10). When an instance of class DepositAccount is sent the interest? message, we first look for that operation definition in the class to which the object belongs. Since the method is defined there, the static binding is to that operation code. When the instance is sent the message debit, once again we look for the operation definition in the class DepositAccount. If it is not defined there, we look for it in the immediate superclass and so on up the class hierarchy. Here, operation debit is defined in the superclass Account and the static binding is to that implementation.

If no such operation is defined, the message is an error since an object of the given class cannot respond to such a message.

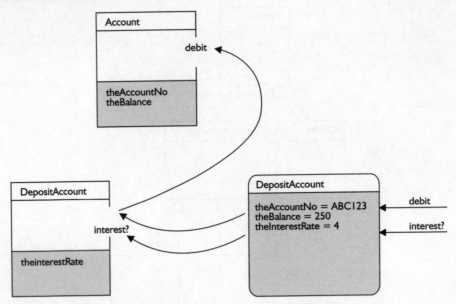

Figure 1.10   *Method lookup under inheritance*

The method lookup under specialisation emphasises the inheritance of features from the superclass. If the subclass `DepositAccount` chooses not to redefine the `balance?` operation, it is still valid to send this message to an instance of the class `DepositAccount` since that operation is inherited into the subclass.

1.9 Defining operations at multiple levels

Generally an operation is defined at one class level in a class hierarchy. There is nothing to prevent operations from being defined at both a general level and a specific level. In this case, since objects search for the definition for an operation up through the hierarchy from the specific to the general, the most specific version would be found first and that version executed.

Suppose we have the class hierarchy shown in Figure 1.11 and the root class `Account` defines an operation `balance?`. For an ordinary `Account` instance this operation may simply accumulate all the debit and credit transactions and the original amount brought forward. In the subclass `DepositAccount` we wish to *redefine* this operation so that any interest which accrues is included.

The solution benefits us since we do not alter the class `Account`. Any instance of the class `DepositAccount` when sent the `balance?` message will incorporate the interest into the final amount. The technique is called

1.13 Exercises

1. Give a diagrammatic presentation for the class `Person` with `theName` and `theDateOfBirth` properties, and with the operations `name?`, `age?` and `changeName`.

    Show two instances of class `Person` representing yourself and someone in your family.

    Suggest other plausible properties and operations for the `Person` class.

2. The `Account` class in Figure 1.5 shows two properties and three operations. The accessor operation `balance?` interrogates an `Account` object for part of its state. Which property value will be returned by this operation? How will this value be used when implementing the additional operation `isOverdrawn?` which indicates the state of an `Account` object?

    When we debit or credit an account, which property value is affected? By what amount is it changed? How is this change value introduced with the `debit` and `credit` operations?

3. How is a class operation invoked? What are the three principal components? Which component is optional? When missing, what category of operation do we typically then have?

4. Figure 1.8 shows three kinds of bank account. The operations `debit`, `credit` and `balance?` of the `Account` class will operate on which properties? What property will operation `limit?` in the `CurrentAccount` class use? How will the redefined operation `balance?` of class `DepositAccount` operate? What properties are involved and to which class do they belong?

5. Figure 1.9 gives a class hierarchy for five related classes. If the `Person` class is described as in exercise 1 above, does a `Civilian` object have a name property? Does an `Army` object have a name property?

    If the `Military` class is given a property representing a rank and serial number, list all the properties of the class `AirForce`. Why does `Civilian` not have a rank?

    Is an instance of class `Army` also an implicit instance of class `Military`? Is the same `Army` instance also implicitly an instance of class `Person`? Explain your reasoning. Can an instance of class `Person` substitute for an instance of class `Civilian`? Give reasons for your answer.

6. If the `CurrentAccount` class of Figure 1.12 redefines the `balance?` operation and a `Bank` instance holds a collection of either `DepositAccount` objects or `CurrentAccount` objects, and sends the `balance?` message to all, which versions of this operation are executed? How is this selection determined?

    What then is the purpose of the operation `balance?` from the `Account` class in this new arrangement? Do we need to define this operation for class `Account`? If not, what kind of class is the `Account` class?

    If an `InterestBearingCurrentAccount` is introduced into Figure 1.12 as a specialisation of `CurrentAccount`, what changes have to be made to the `Bank` class? Explain. Why would we choose to redefine the `balance?` operation in this new class?

Chapter 2

Object-oriented analysis and design

The previous chapter introduced an object-oriented system as one composed of software objects co-operating with each other to achieve a common goal. Clearly it is of paramount importance that objects and their relationships are correctly identified. Unfortunately, it is difficult to give hard and fast rules as to how this can be accomplished in all cases.

The reason is that problem solving is a human activity that as yet cannot be completely formulated as a generally applicable method. However, over the past few years several *object oriented analysis and design* (OOAD) methods have become popular (Booch, 1991; Coad and Yourdon, 1990; Rumbaugh et al., 1991; Shlaer and Mellor, 1992). Although they differ in some important respects each has at its core the belief that humans naturally think in terms of objects and therefore by modelling systems with objects we can make problem solving as easy as possible.

2.1 Fundamentals of an OOAD

Any software system is actually a model of a problem that exists in our real (or imagined) world. It follows that the more closely a software model corresponds to the actual problem, the more effective it will be. OOAD methods recognise this fact and use key abstractions (objects) taken from the problem domain as the fundamental building blocks of software systems.

With this approach there is only one model of the system no matter what stage of development it is at. System development is a process that progressively adds more detail to the model until such time that it can be executed on a computer (see Section 3.8 for a fuller discussion).

2.1.1 Identifying objects and classes

Before attempting to identify the objects that can be used to model a particular problem, it is important that we identify the kind of application that we are dealing with (Yourdon, 1994). Many applications are dominated by either the data they contain, their functionality, or the way in which they behave when stimulated by external events.

Systems that are dominated by data usually carry out relatively little processing but contain data elements that are complex. Commercial applications such as those found in the banking and insurance sector belong to this category of problem. By way of contrast, systems that are dominated by their functionality usually carry out complex processing on data that is relatively simple. Many scientific applications fall into this category. Lastly, systems that are dominated by their behaviour must respond in real time to external events. Engineering applications that control, or are controlled by, computer hardware devices are typical examples.

When considering a system from a data perspective we can discover candidate objects by consideration of the major data elements it contains. For example, a bank application would almost certainly lead us to nominate an account as an object. Underlining nouns in a textual description of the problem is often a good place to start. With care and some experience, sentences such as:

> *Each customer has an <u>account</u> that he may pay into, debit from or enquire as to the current balance.*

can be surprisingly useful. As object orientation has a strong element of data orientation, this approach is considered by many practitioners as one of the best ways to identify candidate objects (Coad and Yourdon, 1990).

If we consider a system from a functional perspective, we can identify candidate objects by asking what responsibility an object needs to have. In other words we must identify the operations an object must perform in order to discharge its responsibilities. As functions are concerned with doing something, an examination of the verbs (and verb phrases) in the problem description can often be useful for operation identification just as nouns were with object identification. For example, the sentence taken from the specification of an electronic mail system:

> *Mail items may be <u>edited</u>, <u>sent</u> or <u>received</u>.*

viewed from a functional perspective would lead us to identify an object with operations that allow a client to edit, send or receive a mail item. This would lead us to nominate a mail item as an object.

Although this approach can be very useful, it must be treated with care. If it is taken too far, it can lead to a system view that is not object-oriented but functional. In the extreme case objects could become just an arbitrary collection of operations. It is vitally important that any object must represent a well-defined data abstraction with a definite role. It is not just a way of packaging unrelated operations.

From a behavioural perspective the important objects that make up a system can usually be identified by examination of a list of the events (requests from objects that are external to the system) that stimulate it. They can then be partitioned in a manner that makes sense within the context of the problem at hand and an object made responsible for dealing with each partition. For example, the software used to control a nuclear reactor might have to respond to events that originate from sensors. Typically sensors measure many kinds of physical data such as pressures, flow rates and temperatures. However, we could partition all of the events caused by any sensor going outside its specified temperature range. This would lead us to identify an object that responds to this kind of event, perhaps by sounding an alarm or by taking corrective action.

With this approach role-playing is often a good place to start. Each player represents an object that responds to events as they occur in the real world. Clearly, if an event is not handled by one of the players then it must be allocated to an existing object or a new object must be created. As we shall see later in this chapter this approach can be extended to help with the construction of any object-oriented system.

Unfortunately, it is a common occurrence that the application we have to analyse is not so clear-cut as the examples we have used to illustrate each approach. Typically it will have some of the attributes of a data, functional or behavioural system. In this case we may decide to let one view dominate or adopt each view as appropriate at different stages in the OOAD. For example, a text processing system presents a user with a graphical user interface (GUI) that allows him to make complex manipulations of textual data. Consideration of the GUI from a behavioural perspective might lead to the identification of a mouse object responsible for monitoring mouse events and a keyboard object responsible for monitoring keyboard events. Each stimulates other objects, e.g. text objects, upon receipt of a mouse or a keyboard event. To view it as a functional or data-dominated system is possible but it would not be as effective in identifying the objects that must respond to events.

Similarly text manipulations are best considered from a functional perspective, and might lead to the identification of an editor object responsible for editing operations such as cut and paste. Lastly, the text that is manipulated could be considered from a data perspective and might lead to the identification of paragraphs, pages, lines and words as objects. To view it from a behavioural or functional perspective would again not be as effective and could even lead to a system composed of inappropriate objects.

Before we leave this section we should discuss the identification of the class to which an object belongs. To identify an object is not enough as this information is usually far too specific. It is much more useful to be able to identify the class to which it belongs so that more general relationships can be established.

In some cases the textual description of the problem may describe all the objects that belong to a class and so make class identification rather easy. For example, the sentence

> *Each customer has an account that he may pay into, debit from or enquire as to the current balance.*

indicates that we should nominate `Account` as the class of which each account object is an instance. Similarly the sentence

Mail items may be edited, sent or received.

indicates that we should nominate `Mail` as the class of which each item of mail is an instance.

Note that as there is only one class we always use a singular noun to identify it. For example, there might be a temptation to name a class as `Accounts` to indicate that there are several objects of the class `Account`. However, this is clearly a mistake as the identifier refers to the class and not its instances.

In some cases we may have to invent an identifier for a class if the textual description of the problem only describes objects. For example, the sentence

John and Ken are employed by Napier University.

might lead us to identify a class `Employee` of which John and Ken are instances. Clearly the name of the class depends on context but should always give a strong indication of the nature of the objects that are instances of it.

2.1.2 *Identifying operations*

When the objects that make up a system have been identified it is relatively easy to identify their associated operations. This apparently simple statement often comes as a surprise to novice designers but it is a major benefit of using object orientation. Further, once identified it is also relatively easy to change the operations associated with each object. However, the designer must always bear in mind that the overriding aim is to produce a class interface that makes sense within the context of the problem at hand. It should have a minimum but complete functional interface. Over-elaborate or duplicate operations inevitably result in a cluttered class interface that can be difficult to use and understand.

A good source of candidate operations is the verbs or verb phrases that are found in a textual description of the problem. For example, for an `Account` object the operations `credit`, `debit` and `balance?` (the query symbol implies that a value is returned to the client, see Section 3.2) could have been identified from the text:

Each customer has an account that he may <u>credit into</u>, <u>debit from</u> or <u>enquire as to the current balance</u>.

Consideration of the operations that can be reasonably associated with an object is also very useful. For example, an `Account` object would almost certainly have the operation `close` associated with it even though it may not be explicitly stated. As we shall see in Chapter 6 this approach can be taken further so that some operations are mandatory for all objects.

These strategies can be combined with role-playing where each player (real or imaginary) pretends that he is an object responding to messages sent by other objects (Beck and Cunningham, 1989). Details of each object (actually its class) are recorded on a card and each of the system functions is considered in turn. The responsibilities implied by the function are broken down and assigned to objects as appropriate and the system *executed*. An object can only respond to requests to execute operations on its interface and only has direct access to its own state information so deficiencies in its design can be quickly identified and rectified. If necessary the behaviour of an object's operation can be modified, new operations can be added to an object's interface or new objects (and of course their class) can be nominated.

2.1.3 *Representation of objects*

In order that an object can support the operations available on its interface it must maintain an internal state. Typically, an object's internal state represents the private data elements encapsulated by an object. Collectively we refer to the private data elements as the *properties* of the object. Their identification is usually quite straightforward as they are normally constructed from standard classes for commonly occurring objects such as strings (a sequence of characters) and numerics.

In general, objects are significant coarse-grained elements within the context of the problem under consideration, while their properties are much finer-grained and therefore do not merit an independent object existence. For example, the class Employee might have properties that represent the name, address, age, sex, employee number and salary of each employee. On its own each property has no relevance. It is only of importance if it is seen as part of the representation of something larger, i.e. an Employee. This is an important point to understand as it is common for novice designers to identify too many objects in a system. Although it is difficult to give hard and fast rules, between six and ten objects would be a reasonable maximum when a system is viewed from a particular level of abstraction.

2.1.4 *Association between objects*

As objects usually need to co-operate in order to achieve their effect, they commonly enter into relationships with each other. One of the most important relationships is *association*. Objects that are associates co-operate by sending messages. Association should be used where two objects are not conceptually related but, within the context of the problem at hand, need to make use of each other's interface. For example, we can imagine a scenario in which an Employee object is employed by a Company object. They are associates in the sense that the Company object adopts the role of the employer while the Employee object adopts the role of the employee. Typically, as part of the run-time behaviour of the system, an employee could request the name of the

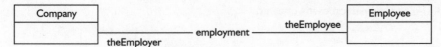

Figure 2.1   *Associations*

employer while the employer could request the job title or salary of an employee. Figure 2.1 is a *class diagram* describing this relationship.

A rectangular box represents a named class and the line between class boxes represents an optionally named association between them. Each class (and therefore each instance) may adopt a named *role* in the association. In our case we show that an employment relationship exists between a Company class whose instances act as the employer, and an Employee class whose instances act as the employee. The employment association implies that Employee objects and Company objects may make use of each other's interface by sending messages.

Note that the class diagrams of Chapter 1 were decorated with the names of the associated class operations. Although they can be included we shall omit these details in order to avoid unnecessary clutter. Similarly in order that explanatory text is more readable we will often refer to objects by their class name. For example, we might refer to an Employee, or an Employee object. In either case the context should make it clear that we mean an object and not the class to which it belongs.

Obviously, a Company may employ more than one Employee and an Employee may work for more than one Company. This leads to the classes taking part in the association having a *multiplicity* which documents the number of objects involved. Frequently occurring possibilities are shown in Figure 2.2 in which the multiplicity denoted by N represents none or more objects.

The default multiplicity for an association is one and is usually omitted from the class diagrams. Roles and the name of the association may also be omitted if the designer feels that they are clear from the context. The role names do, however, provide the means whereby an instance of one class can refer to an instance of the associated class. For example, in the second illustration of Figure 2.2 an instance of the Employee class would refer to the Company object by which it is employed through the role name theEmployer.

The third illustration of Figure 2.2 shows a many-to-many association. A Tutor teaches many Students and one Student will be taught by many Tutors. In effect we have two related yet distinct associations operating simultaneously: a one-to-many association between a Tutor and the Students he teaches, and a one-to-many association between the Student and his Tutors.

We sometimes find an association between the same class. For example, every person is the child of some other person, their mother. This is expressed in the fourth illustration of Figure 2.2 in which every Person is the child of some mother. Such an association is described as a *recursive association*. Observe

one-to-one: One person owns one car.

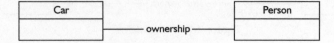

one-to-many: One company employs many employees.

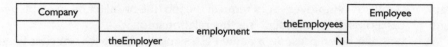

many-to-many: A tutor teaches many students; one student is taught by many tutors.

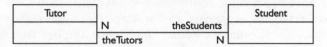

recursive association: A child person has one mother person.

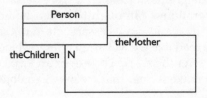

Figure 2.2   *Associations and multiplicities*

how for this example the role names are vital so that we can clarify the usage of the class `Person`.

Before we leave the association relationship between classes, it is very important that we realise that a class diagram does not describe a particular implementation. It is a general description of the relationship between two classes.

Figure 2.3 shows that one `Company` object will act as the employer for many `Employee` objects that act as the employees in the employment relationship that exists between them. It most certainly does not specify which `Company` object or which `Employee` object will enter into this association. This is the point about a class diagram that must be understood.

In order to show the architecture of a real system with real objects, and not just descriptions of objects, instances of the classes must be established with links

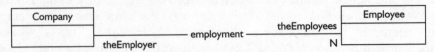

Figure 2.3   *Class diagram*

formed between them. Just as an object is an instance of a class, a *link* is an instance of an association and there must be a link between each object taking part in the association. For example, the *instance diagram* in Figure 2.4 uses rounded rectangles (soft boxes) to represent instances of classes and shows a Company object c1 with links to three Employee objects e1, e2 and e3.

The important point to understand about this diagram is that it represents a concrete architecture and is not abstract in the way that a class diagram is. It represents a particular implementation that conforms to the general description embodied in the corresponding class diagram of Figure 2.3.

Each instance of a class often has a unique identifier so that it can be distinguished from other instances. Where there are several instances of a class we normally make the choice of identifier as straightforward as possible by using the first letter of the class name followed by a suitable number. If only one object is required we can relax this rule and allow the possibility of choosing an identifier based on context. For example, the Employee object identifiers are e1, e2 and e3. However, we could have used theCompany as an identifier for the single Company class object.

Note that there may be some confusion between the use of the phrases *the name of an object* and *the identifier for an object*. As an object only has a name if that is one of its properties, they are not the same. For example, an Employee object could have an identifier e1 and a name "Ken". Strictly we should always use *the identifier for an object* if we are referring to object identity as opposed to an object with a name property. In similar vein the phrase *the object e1* is not strictly correct. It should actually be *the object with an identifier of e1*. However, to enhance readability we normally do not make this distinction.

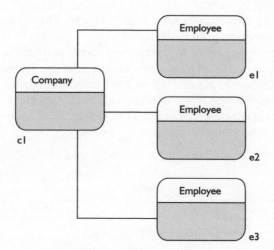

Figure 2.4   *Instance diagram*

2.1.5 *Aggregate components of objects*

A second important relationship between objects is *aggregation*. It is sometimes referred to as the *has-a* or *part-of* relationship as it indicates that an object is composed of another object. With aggregation, the relationship between objects is much stronger than with association in that the whole could not exist without its parts. Therefore, it should only be used where an object is considered to be part of another object and not just a casual associate with an independent existence. The aggregate component must be for the exclusive use of the object of which it is part and is completely encapsulated by it. This means that an aggregate component is not visible outside its containing object and has no direct visibility of other aggregate components or the whole of which it is part. Messages received by the whole can be relayed to its aggregate components if necessary but messages cannot be sent directly to aggregate components.

Clearly, aggregate components are very like properties. The difference is that the former are important enough in the context of the problem under consideration to be considered as objects in their own right, and not just ordinary property items. For example, a mailbox can be considered as an assembly consisting of items of mail. A typical scenario is that a message to display all the mail items in the mailbox is received by the `MailBox` object. In response to this message the `MailBox` object sends a message to each `Mail` object in the assembly to display itself. This kind of execution behaviour is common in object-oriented systems and is referred to as *message propagation*.

The class diagram in Figure 2.5 describes a class `MailBox` and its `Mail` class aggregate components. A line terminating with a diamond indicates the aggregation relationship. The diamond symbol is placed against the whole in the whole–part relationship.

Although there is only ever one whole the parts in the aggregation relationship have a multiplicity with a default of one. The relationship may also be recursive. The notation used is the same as for association. As before, a class diagram showing aggregation is completely general but the corresponding instance diagram is specific. An instance diagram for a specific `MailBox`, mb, with three `Mail` items m1, m2 and m3 in it is shown in Figure 2.6.

We normally refer to the representation, aggregations and associations of an object as its *features* or as its *characteristics*. They represent all aspects of the object's class including both its properties and its operations.

Figure 2.5   *Aggregation*

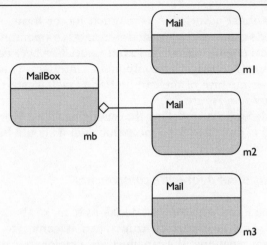

Figure 2.6 `MailBox` *instance diagram*

2.1.6 *Aggregation versus association*

Aggregation requires that there is a whole–part relationship between the objects concerned. It is implicit in the relationship that a client has access only to the interface of the whole and cannot access any of the parts directly. For example, a car engine could have an aggregation relationship with components such as cylinders and a carburettor. This means that users of the engine can only indirectly access the engine parts through a limited set of operations such as start and stop advertised by the engine. They are blissfully unaware of the existence of any of the parts as they are under the exclusive control of the whole. Figure 2.7 illustrates these relationships.

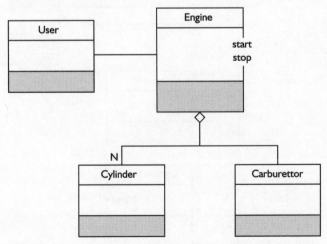

Figure 2.7 *An engine modelled as an aggregation of its parts*

By way of contrast association is a much looser form of dependency or *coupling*. The objects concerned are casual associates co-operating to achieve some overall effect. If a car engine is modelled as an association between its components then users have direct access to each component's interface. This means that users could adjust the air mixture of the carburettor as well as starting and stopping the engine, as shown in Figure 2.8.

Clearly if the designer is modelling the car engine for a driver then aggregation is in order but if it is modelled for a mechanic then it should be an association.

2.1.7 *Association of aggregate components*

Designers are often faced with difficult decisions to make about the relationships between objects. This is especially true when it comes to combinations of associations and aggregations. We can illustrate a major source of difficulty if we consider the construction of a simple electronic mailbox.

During the execution of the mail system a mail item can be edited and then added to a mailbox for onward transmission. An initial analysis might lead us to identify the classes `Editor`, `MailBox` and `Mail`. Clearly `Mail` objects are an integral part of the `MailBox` and should be modelled as aggregation components. However, we might decide that an `Editor` object and a `Mail` object are loosely coupled and so they should be modelled as associates. As an `Editor` object needs to add a `Mail` object to a `MailBox`, the `Editor` and `MailBox` should also be associates. The class diagram of Figure 2.9 captures these relationships.

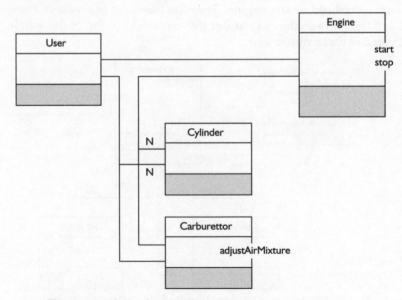

Figure 2.8   *An engine modelled as an association of its parts*

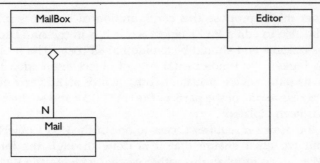

Figure 2.9 *A class diagram of a mail system*

Recall from Section 2.1.4 that a class diagram is a general description and does not describe a particular implementation. This means that we should also construct an instance diagram for the mail system, as shown in Figure 2.10.

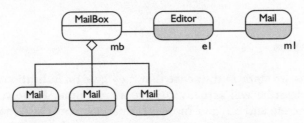

Figure 2.10 *An instance diagram for a mail system*

It shows clearly that the Editor object e1 does not have an association relationship with any of the Mail objects that are aggregate components of the MailBox. This means that they cannot communicate with each other. However, the Editor object e1 does have association relationships with the MailBox object mb and the Mail object m1. This means that they can communicate with each other. This mirrors our intention that a Mail object (m1) should be edited by an Editor (e1) then added to the MailBox (mb).

However, there is another instance diagram that can be legally drawn, as is shown in Figure 2.11. It shows that an Editor object has an association relationship with a Mail item that is an aggregate component of the MailBox.

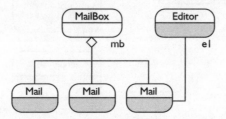

Figure 2.11 *Another instance diagram of a mail system*

A designer might propose this configuration of instances if he wants the `Editor` to be able to edit a `Mail` object while it is in the `MailBox`. However, it is a serious mistake and should be avoided at all costs. The reason is that the designer has broken the fundamental rule of object orientation that an object encapsulates its state, i.e. it is private. In other words an `Editor` object has been given direct access to one of the parts of the `MailBox` and so the integrity of the `MailBox` has been violated.

Clearly, the designer requires access to one of the `Mail` objects held by the `MailBox` but we must ensure that it is done through the interface of the `MailBox`. We can accomplish this rather easily by giving the `MailBox` class a public operation that delivers a `Mail` object to a client just as it could deliver a private property. The detail of how this is achieved is discussed in later chapters. For the moment all we need to do is to recognise that the configuration of instances illustrated in Figure 2.11 should not be part of our designs. It is extremely bad practice and should not be allowed.

2.2 Scenarios

Class diagrams are static in the sense that they give no indication about how the system they describe will actually behave at run time. However, an instance diagram is concrete and can give more information about the dynamic behaviour of objects. For example, we can annotate messages with an integer to signify the order in which messages are sent. In this way, it is possible to give a snapshot, or *scenario*, of the run-time behaviour of all or part of a system. Data flows may be added if they are considered necessary. Figure 2.12 shows that a `Company`

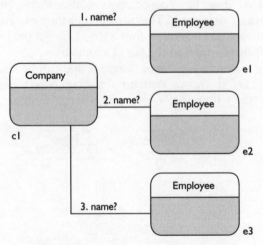

Figure 2.12 *Instance diagram scenarios*

object c1 requests the name of the Employee objects e1, e2 and e3 in sequence.

Similarly, a *message trace* or *interaction* diagram may be used as part of the description of a scenario. Instances are shown in the top row and subsequent rows represent the sequence in which messages are sent between objects. Time increases from the top of the diagram to the bottom. A fat vertical line indicates that the object in that column is executing a method while a thin vertical line indicates that it is inactive. The sender and receiver of a message are shown by placing an annotated directed arrow between them. The arrow may be from right to left or left to right. In this way, we have a clear account of all or part of the execution profile of the system.

For example, Figure 2.13 records the same information as in Figure 2.12: a message name? is sent from the instance c1 to the instance e1, then from the instance c1 to the instance e2, and finally from the instance c1 to the instance e3. In addition it is clear that the instance c1 is at least in principle (in practice its execution may be suspended) executing during the time that the three messages are sent but the instances e1, e2 and e3 execute only when they are responding to the message name?.

Note that in order to describe the main elements of the execution of a system, several scenarios may be required. Typically, they would be selected as being representative of the normal execution of the system or as being particularly problematic.

When establishing scenarios it is important to understand two important points so as to avoid confusion. The first is that just because an object could request any operation advertised on another object's public interface it does not follow that it will actually do so. Only a subset may be required. The second is that messages may be sent between objects on each side of a relationship or only from an object on one side. In other words, the relationship may be traversed bi-directionally or uni-directionally.

For example, Figure 2.14 shows that an Employee object e1 makes a request to the Company object c1 for its name. There is a data flow of the name

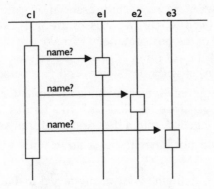

Figure 2.13 *Message traces*

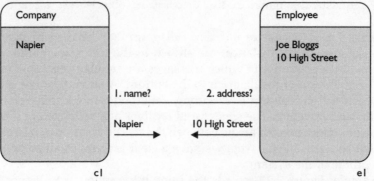

Figure 2.14   *Scenarios and data flows*

"Napier" from the Company to the Employee object. It also shows that a Company object c1 then makes a request address? to an Employee object e1. There is a data flow representing the *return value* of the address "10 High Street" from the Employee object to the Company object.

Note that there are other ways to achieve the same effect. For example, an Employee object may have no need to request the name of its employer from the corresponding Company object if this information is held in each Employee object as a property. In this case, no message to the Company object need be sent and the association is traversed in one direction only (see Section 3.7).

2.3 Summary

1.   Objects and their associated operations can be identified by a combination of textual analysis of the problem, role-playing and scenarios.

2.   A class diagram records the classes identified in the problem domain together with the architectural relationships that exist between them. An instance diagram represents instances of the classes appearing in the class diagram.

3.   Relationships between classes include associations and aggregations. Associations should be used where two classes are not conceptually related but, within the context of the problem, need to make use of each other's interface. With aggregation, the coupling between the classes is much stronger since the whole cannot exist without its parts and vice versa.

4.   Associations and aggregations may have multiplicities recorded in the class diagram. Both may also be labelled with role names. Optionally, an association may also be labelled with a description of that association.

5.   An instance should not have an association with an associate's aggregate component.

6.   Scenarios present a dynamic view of the object instances. They offer a run-time view of the behaviour for all or part of the system.

2.4 Exercises

For each of the following problem definitions:

- Identify the major classes present.
- Identify their most important operations and properties.
- Construct a class diagram showing any associations or aggregations.
- Construct suitable instance diagrams.
- Construct message trace diagrams showing interactions between objects.

For the moment do not concern yourself with how operations are actually implemented.

1. A person, identified by a unique identification number and a surname, can own one vehicle at any given time. A vehicle is given a maker's name and a registration number. In addition a person must also be able to disown a vehicle and should be able to display details of the vehicle owned.
   Show how a person could own a vehicle, display its details and then disown it. Similarly show how the same person could own a different vehicle and then display its details.

2. A country has as many cities. Each city has a name and a population, while a country has a name and a capital city. It is a requirement that a country should display, on request, its capital city through the operation displayCapital? as well as the names of all its cities through the operation displayCities?. In addition, it should display the total population of the country through the operation display TotalPopulation?, and the average city population through the operation displayAveragePopulation?.
   Model this system showing how the capital city, the names of the cities and the average city population of a country could be ascertained.

3. A bank has a name and a number of accounts each of which has the name and reference number of the account holder as well as the current balance. An account holder can make a deposit to a specified account or withdraw a specified amount.

   - making a deposit
   - making a withdrawal without a check that sufficient funds are available
   - displaying account details
   - making a withdrawal with a check that sufficient funds are available
   - making a withdrawal with an overdraft facility available.

4. A teaching block consists of several rooms each with a unique room number and specified seating capacity. Rooms may be booked on a particular day for lectures. Each booking must start on the hour and can be of any duration. It must be possible to book a room in the teaching block if it is free and generate a display of the status of each room in the teaching block for a particular day.
   Construct a model showing how a room in the teaching block could be booked.

5. University lecturers may obtain from a library a loan of textbooks. Every lecturer has a name and every book a title. Construct a model of this system showing how a lecturer could ask for a display of books in the library, borrow a book or return a book. Lecturers should also be able to display books out on loan.

6. Diving competitions are scored as follows:

    -   Each competitor is given a mark out of 10 for a dive by each of five judges.
    -   The score for a dive is calculated by discarding the highest and lowest mark,
    -   determining the average, and then
    -   multiplying it by a difficulty factor (a number in the range 0.1 to 1.0 in increments of 0.1).

    All competitors complete three dives. Their overall score is the sum of the marks for each dive. The winner is the competitor with the highest score. You are required to construct a system to automate this scoring process.

7. A computer game consists of several players who compete with each other to build a beetle. A complete beetle has two antennae, a head, a neck, a body, six legs and a tail. When a player's beetle is complete that player's name is displayed and he leaves the game. The game continues until each player's beetle is completed.
    The rules of the game are that a beetle:

    -   cannot have an antenna unless it has a head
    -   cannot have a head unless it has a neck
    -   cannot have a neck until it has a body
    -   cannot have a leg unless it has a body, and
    -   cannot have a tail until it has a body.

    During the game, each player takes it in turn to be given a random number representing the throw of a die, with which to construct his beetle. An integer in the range 1 to 6 represents an antenna, head, neck, body, leg and tail, respectively. There should also be a display of the configuration of a player's beetle before and after his turn.
    Construct a model for the game.

Chapter 3

A language for object-oriented modelling

Many important decisions are made as part of an OOAD. Clearly, all of them must be recorded in an unambiguous manner so that the analyst or designer can produce accurate documentation. In order to achieve this objective we have developed a language that describes the interface, representation, architectural relationships and interactions between objects. It is named a Language for Object-Oriented Modelling (LOOM). As we shall see in Chapter 6 it can be easily mapped to C++, and in Chapter 10 we show that it can be produced automatically from a class diagram.

3.1 The role of LOOM

During a typical object-oriented analysis the main source of information is a requirements document. It is intended to give a clear description of the system to be constructed but inevitably, for all but the simplest systems, it is often incomplete and informal. The role of the analyst is to make it more precise and internally consistent so that the essential features of the system it describes can be accurately modelled. The analysis model defines the static structure of objects as well as their dynamic behaviours and the data transformations they carry out. However, it gives no indication of implementation details and refers exclusively to objects directly traceable to a requirements document or its equivalent.

The main thrust of an object-oriented design is to elaborate the analysis model so as to provide the basis for its implementation. It represents a shift from the real world in which the problem at hand is defined, to the computer world in which its solution will be executed. As such it may contain objects that are not present in the analysis model but are necessary for its implementation. However, objects and their relationships identified during analysis must still be present in the design.

LOOM has many features that are important to developers but for the moment the most important ones are:

- It is independent of the system implementation language but maps easily and consistently to a variety of object oriented programming languages (OOPLs).

- It has an obvious well-defined object-oriented syntax that is easy to read and understand.

- LOOM encourages the developer to adopt the object-oriented paradigm even if the system implementation language is not a pure OOPL.

- It accurately describes decisions made during an OOAD but also permits translation to the implementation language.

As we progress through the following chapters other important features of LOOM will become apparent.

3.2 The basic LOOM script for a class

A LOOM specification of a class has its reserved words in upper case, while user-defined names (identifiers) are in lower case or are capitalised. All user-defined identifiers are case sensitive and of arbitrary length. In addition they must start with a letter, but may be followed by letters, digits or underscores (_). Comments start with // and continue to the end of the line on which they occur. The basic LOOM description of a class is:

```
CLASS className
WITH
PUBLIC INTERFACE
  // Features available to clients.
PRIVATE IMPLEMENTATION
  REPRESENTATION
    // Features not available to clients.
DEFINITIONS
  // One method for each operation of the form:
  METHOD operationName AS
    // Detailed logic.
  ENDMETHOD operationName

ENDCLASS className
```

It shows that a class must have a name with mandatory PUBLIC INTERFACE, PRIVATE IMPLEMENTATION, REPRESENTATION and DEFINITIONS clauses.

- The PUBLIC INTERFACE clause is a list of the features associated with a class.

- The PRIVATE IMPLEMENTATION clause contains REPRESENTATION and DEFINITIONS sub-clauses that are hidden from clients.

- The REPRESENTATION clause is a list of private features. They are not available to clients but may be accessed from within the class after their declaration.

- The DEFINITIONS clause contains the detailed logic for each operation introduced in the PUBLIC INTERFACE clause. It is this logic that defines the effect of the operation and is often referred to as the *method*.

The reserved words METHOD and ENDMETHOD define the scope of a method definition and the reserved words CLASS and ENDCLASS define the scope of a class.

LOOM also has the reserved word NONE. If there is no entry for any of the mandatory clauses then this fact must be recorded by the use of this reserved word. This rule is intended to help remove ambiguity from a LOOM script and is typical of the LOOM approach. Clarity and precision are the main goals of a LOOM script even at the cost of apparent verbosity.

For example, a class Employee can be described in LOOM as:

```
CLASS Employee
WITH
PUBLIC INTERFACE
  Employee(aName :String, aDateOfBirth :Date)
  changeName(aName :String)
  name? -> String
  age? -> Integer

PRIVATE IMPLEMENTATION
  REPRESENTATION
    theName :String
    theDateOfBirth :Date
  DEFINITIONS
    METHOD Employee(aName :String, aDateOfBirth :Date)
    AS
      // Detailed logic to construct an Employee object
    ENDMETHOD Employee

    METHOD changeName(aName :String)
    AS
      // Detailed logic to change the name of an Employee object.
    ENDMETHOD changeName

    METHOD name? -> String
    AS
      // Detailed logic to deliver the name of an Employee object.
    ENDMETHOD name?

    METHOD age? -> Integer
    AS
      // Detailed logic to deliver the age of an Employee object.
    ENDMETHOD age?

ENDCLASS Employee
```

Conventionally, class names start with a capital letter and operation names are capitalised on the second and subsequent component, e.g. the operation

changeName. In addition, a property name begins with *the*, to show that it is
particular to an instance of the class. In this specification the class names `String`,
`Date` and `Integer` are assumed to be fundamental LOOM classes. These and
other basic classes are detailed in Appendix B.

The LOOM script shows that:

- The class `Employee` has four public operations, two private properties for
  its representation and four method definitions.

- Its properties consist of a `String` object `theName` and a `Date` object
  `theDateOfBirth`.

- The operation `name?` returns a `String` object. The ? symbol is appended,
  by convention, to the operation identifier in order to indicate that it is an
  accessor operation. In addition, the symbol -> indicates the class of value that
  is returned. Similarly, the operation `age?` is an accessor operation returning
  an `Integer` object.

- The operation `changeName` is a *transformer operation*. It is supplied with a
  `String` object `aName` as a formal parameter.

- The operation `Employee` has the same identifier as the class and is referred
  to as a *constructor*. It allows an instance of the class `Employee` to be created
  and initialised with its two formal parameters, of which `aName` is a `String`
  value, and `aDateOfBirth` is a `Date` value.

In a similar way the class `Company` can be described in LOOM as:

```
CLASS Company
WITH
PUBLIC INTERFACE
  Company (aName : String)
  changeName (aName : String)
  name? -> String
PRIVATE IMPLEMENTATION
  REPRESENTATION
    theName : String
DEFINITIONS
  METHOD Company (aName : String)
  AS
    // Detailed logic to construct a Company object
  ENDMETHOD Company

  METHOD changeName (aName : String)
  AS
    // Detailed logic to change the name property of a
    // Company object
  ENDMETHOD changeName

  METHOD name? -> String
  AS
    // Detailed logic to deliver the name of a Company object
  ENDMETHOD name?

ENDCLASS Company
```

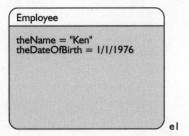

Figure 3.1 *Initialised* Employee *instance*

3.2.1 *Object creation*

Objects are created with the LOOM sentence:

    INSTANCE instanceName :ConstructorName(actual parameters)

For example:

    INSTANCE e1 :Employee("Ken", Date(1,1,1976))

This instantiation uses the constructor explicitly defined in the class:

    Employee(aName :String, aDateOfBirth :Date)

As is shown in Figure 3.1, it has the effect of creating an object e1 of class Employee with the property theName set to the String "Ken", and the property theDateOfBirth set to the Date value representing the first day of 1976. Note the form of a Date object supplied as a day, month and year invoking its standard constructor, and that the literal value for a String is enclosed in double quotes.

3.2.2 *Sending messages*

Messages are sent between objects by the LOOM sentence:

    SEND instanceName THE MESSAGE
    operationName (actual parameters)

For example:

    SEND e1 THE MESSAGE changeName("John")

is a request from a client to the Employee object e1 to execute its public operation changeName. An actual parameter "John" is supplied by the sender of the message. The receiving object e1 maps the actual parameter to its formal parameter in the method defined for the operation. In this case it changes the private property theName to "John" as shown in Figure 3.2.

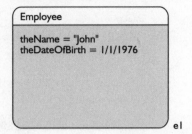

Figure 3.2   *Effect of the operation* changeName *on an* Employee *instance*

The special LOOM message assign is used to give a new value to an existing object. For example, the changeName operation of the Company class assigns the parameter value to the property theName in the receiving object:

```
METHOD changeName(aName :String) AS
  SEND theName THE MESSAGE assign(aName)
ENDMETHOD changeName
```

Equally, the message initialise is reserved to give the initial values to the properties of some class when instances of that class are created. Specifically, this message is reserved for use with constructor operations:

```
METHOD Company(aName :String) AS
  SEND theName THE MESSAGE initialise(aName)
ENDMETHOD Company
```

3.3 The behaviour of an operation

As discussed previously, each operation has a definition for its behaviour, referred to as a *method*, in its class specification. The detailed logic in the method normally consists of *sentences* that:

- create objects for the private use of the method;
- send messages to other objects in sequence;
- send messages to other objects that are conditional on an expression evaluating to TRUE or FALSE;
- send messages in turn to each member of a collection;
- process data.

Since a method is within the scope of its class, enclosed by the reserved words CLASS and ENDCLASS, it can access all the features of the class defined in its PUBLIC INTERFACE and its PRIVATE IMPLEMENTATION clauses.

A method also defines its own scope, delimited by the reserved words METHOD and ENDMETHOD, so it may have objects for its exclusive use. For example, in the class Employee the method defining the operation age? ->

Integer constructs its own object today of class Date used to compare with the object's private property theDateOfBirth:

```
METHOD age? -> Integer AS
  INSTANCE today :Date
  // Other sentences may follow.
ENDMETHOD age?
```

The object today is private to the method. Note that there is a possibility that an object today of class Date may be a property of the Employee class. In this case, it is the most local object that is selected, i.e. the definition in the method.

Information flow into a method is normally through its formal parameter list. An actual parameter supplied by the sender of a message maps to the formal parameter in the method definition. The association between actual and formal parameters is achieved by their relative position in a message. In other words actual parameters must match the order of their corresponding formal parameters. A formal parameter may only be used in the method body for which it is declared. Just as a property name is prefixed by *the* to imply that it is particular, a formal parameter name usually begins with *a* or *an* to imply that it is general. For example:

```
changeName (aName :String)
```

and

```
METHOD changeName (aName :String) AS
  // Detail of the METHOD
ENDMETHOD changeName
```

Information flow from a method to the object sending the message is usually by a RETURN sentence. For example:

```
METHOD name? -> String AS
  RETURN theName
ENDMETHOD name?
```

will return to the sender a copy of the property theName of the instance that receives the message.

Commonly RETURN sentences may be more complex, so that the value returned by a method may be the return value of another message. For example:

```
METHOD companyName? -> String AS
  RETURN (SEND theEmployer THE MESSAGE name?)
ENDMETHOD companyName?
```

returns the return value of the message name? sent to the object theEmployer.

LOOM also permits arithmetic, relational and logical expressions to be evaluated. The operators used in these expressions have the normal meanings as used in procedural languages such as Fortran, Pascal, C and Ada. They are as follows:

```
+ - * / %                    for arithmetic expressions
> >= < <= == !=              for relational expressions
AND OR NOT                   for logical expressions
```

For example, consider the following INSTANCE sentences illustrating these operators:

```
INSTANCE one : Integer(1)
INSTANCE two : Integer(1 + one)        // Arithmetic addition.
INSTANCE fourteen : Integer(2 + 3 * 4)// Multiplication has
                                       // precedence.
INSTANCE remainder : Integer(27 % two)
                                       // Remaindering operator.
INSTANCE isBetween : Boolean(1 <= fourteen AND
fourteen <= 27)                        // Logical connective.
```

In the third illustration, the multiplication operator (*) has precedence over the addition operator (+), meaning that the values 3 and 4 are first multiplied before the value 2 is added to the outcome. In the fourth example, the modulus operator (%) obtains the remainder upon dividing the first operand (27) by the second operand (two), producing the value 1. The Boolean instance isBetween is initialised with one of the two Boolean values TRUE or FALSE. The logical initialiser determines that fourteen is between 1 and 27 inclusive and sets isBetween to the logical value TRUE.

In LOOM, assignment is carried out with a predefined operation:

```
assign(expression)
```

For example, the sentence:

```
SEND theAge THE MESSAGE
assign(todayYear - dateOfBirthYear)
```

has the effect of evaluating the integer expression:

```
todayYear - dateOfBirthYear
```

by using the arithmetic operator - on the Integer operands todayYear and dateOfBirthYear, then assigning the result to the existing Integer object theAge.

In order to describe the detailed logic contained in a method, LOOM adopts control sentences for *sequence*, *selection* and *repetition* typically found in traditional procedural programming languages.

3.3.1 *Messages in sequence*

The default control sentence sends messages in sequence so that during the execution of the sentences:

```
SEND p1 THE MESSAGE changeName("John")
SEND p2 THE MESSAGE changeName("Jim")
```

the object p1 is sent the message changeName("John") and then the object
p2 is sent the message changeName("Jim").

3.3.2 *Paragraph selection*

Selection requires the evaluation of a Boolean expression at run time to
determine the paragraph that is executed. Note that a paragraph is defined as a
sequence of sentences. The form of control sentence for selection is:

```
IF aBooleanExpression THEN paragraph
{ELSEIF aBooleanExpression THEN paragraph}
[ELSE paragraph]
ENDIF
```

The braces {. . .} indicate zero or more repetitions of the subclause, while the
brackets [. . .] indicate zero or one occurrences.

Assuming the instantiations:

```
INSTANCE theAdult               :Boolean(FALSE)
INSTANCE theOldAgePensioner     :Boolean(FALSE)
INSTANCE theJuvenile            :Boolean(FALSE)
INSTANCE theAge                 :Integer(16)
```

some examples are:

```
IF theAge > 21 THEN
   SEND theAdult THE MESSAGE assign(TRUE)
ENDIF
```

If the value of the Integer object theAge is greater than 21 then assign the
Boolean value of TRUE to the Boolean object theAdult.

```
IF theAge > 21 THEN
   SEND theAdult THE MESSAGE assign(TRUE)
ELSE
   SEND theAdult THE MESSAGE assign(FALSE)
ENDIF
```

If the value of the Integer object theAge is greater than 21 then assign the
Boolean value of TRUE to the Boolean object theAdult. However, if it is
not greater then 21 then assign the Boolean value of FALSE to theAdult.

```
IF theAge > 65 THEN
   SEND theOldAgePensioner THE MESSAGE
   assign(TRUE)
ELSEIF theAge > 21 THEN
   SEND theAdult THE MESSAGE assign(TRUE)
ELSE
   SEND theJuvenile THE MESSAGE assign(TRUE)
ENDIF
```

The Integer object theAge is tested for having a value greater than 65 and if
so the Boolean object theOldAgePensioner is assigned the Boolean value

TRUE and the control sentence is exited. Otherwise `theAge` is tested for having a value greater than 21 and if so the `Boolean` object `theAdult` is assigned the value TRUE and the control sentence is exited. If both tests fail then a value of TRUE is assigned to the `Boolean` object `theJuvenile`.

3.3.3 *Paragraph repetition*

Repetition also involves the evaluation of a `Boolean` expression. While the expression has the value of TRUE a paragraph is repeated. Its form is:

```
WHILE aBooleanExpression DO
  paragraph
ENDWHILE
```

Assuming the instantiation with initialisation:

```
INSTANCE theCounter : Integer (1)
```

the sentence:

```
WHILE theCounter <= 10  DO
  SEND theCounter THE MESSAGE assign(theCounter + 1)
ENDWHILE
```

tests the object `theCounter` for having a value that is less than or equal to 10. While the `Boolean` expression evaluates to TRUE a value of 1 is added to the `Integer` object `theCounter`.

Control sentences may also be nested as in:

```
SEND theCounter THE MESSAGE assign(1)
SEND theAdult THE MESSAGE assign(FALSE)
// ...

WHILE theCounter <= 10  DO
  // ...

  IF theAge > 21 THEN
    SEND theAdult THE MESSAGE assign(TRUE)
  ENDIF

  // ...
  SEND theCounter THE MESSAGE assign(theCounter + 1)
ENDWHILE
```

which repeats the sentences between DO and ENDWHILE (including a test for the `Integer` object `theAge` having a value greater than 21) ten times.

The previous control sentences are frequently found in procedural programming but there is an additional control sentence available in LOOM that is particularly useful with object oriented models. It assumes that objects are stored in a specially constructed object referred to as a *container*. An example of a container is a Set that holds objects in no prescribed order and does not allow duplicates. The form of the control construct is:

```
FOREACH anObjectIdentifier :aClassName IN
aContainerName DO
  paragraph
ENDFOREACH
```

When it executes, each member of the container specified is visited and the paragraph executed. Termination occurs when all members have been visited once. For example, if the object theEmployees is a set of Employee instances then in the sentence:

```
FOREACH anEmployee :Employee IN theEmployees DO
  SEND anEmployee THE MESSAGE display?
END FOREACH
```

the object anEmployee assumes the identity of every member of the container object theEmployees in turn, and on each occasion sends the message:

```
SEND anEmployee THE MESSAGE display?
```

In this way a message is sent to each member of the container. When all members have been visited the control sentence terminates automatically and control is passed to the next sentence in sequence.

Note that the operation display? does not return a value but it still gives a client access to the private state of an Employee. For this reason it has the query symbol in its name to indicate that it is an accessor operation. We adopt this convention throughout the remainder of the book.

3.4 Architectural relationships

So far we have considered only LOOM scripts for isolated objects. However, as we have seen objects form aggregations and associations with each other. LOOM uses an AGGREGATIONS and an ASSOCIATIONS clause to describe these architectural relationships. Although the properties of an object are application independent, aggregation and association relationships depend on the particular configuration of objects and so they may change from application to application.

In order that an object has an *aggregation* relationship with one or more objects it must act as an assembly of its aggregate components. This is easily accomplished by designating each component of the aggregate as part of the AGGREGATIONS clause of the containing object. For example, we can extend the Company–Employee scenario so that a Company object has several Department objects. Figure 3.3 is a class diagram which describes the relationships between the classes.

As there are many Department objects in the aggregation, a suitable container is required to hold them. A DOrderedCollection has been chosen based on two assumptions. The first is that there is no requirement for

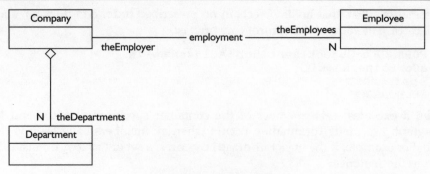

Figure 3.3   *Aggregation*

the Department objects to be held in some specified order, e.g. alphabetic. As a DOrderedCollection holds objects in the order in which they are added to it, it is a suitable container for our purposes. The second is that it should hold a complete copy of each Department object. It may seem strange that we would want to hold anything other than a complete copy but in fact it is very common in object oriented systems to have the choice of having a complete object available or just a reference to it. In the former case the object can be accessed directly (hence the D in DOrderedCollection) but in the latter case it must be accessed indirectly.

The DOrderedCollection is one of the fundamental container classes available in LOOM and is detailed in Appendix B. All that we need do is to instantiate it with the appropriate class of the objects it contains. For example, the declaration:

```
theDepartments :DOrderedCollection [Department]
```

declares the object theDepartments as a container of the class DOrdered-Collection that holds complete Department objects in the order in which they are added.

Although containers are extremely useful they do have a small cost associated with them. As a container is completely general purpose in that it may contain any class of object it follows that the container can have no prior knowledge of how to compare the objects it may contain. Unfortunately as part of their inner workings all containers must have this ability. Clearly comparison of simple objects such as two Integers is straightforward but the comparison of two Employees or two Departments is not. Therefore the responsibility for providing a public operation to compare two objects must lie with the class that defines the objects that are compared, i.e. the classes Integer, Employee and Department.

This means that when a container is instantiated it assumes that the actual class of object it contains has a public operation that allows two objects of the class to be compared. In LOOM we have standardised the comparison operation to be:

```
lessThan?(anObjectName :ClassName) -> Boolean
```

It allows a container (or any other object) to send the message `lessThan?` to one of its members to determine if it is less than another similar kind of object supplied as an actual parameter. For example, this would be necessary when adding objects in some sorted manner to a container.

For this reason we need to add the operation

```
lessThan?(aDepartment :Department) -> Boolean
```

to the public interface of the class `Department` if we are to have a container holding `Department` objects. Its method in this case is:

```
METHOD lessThan?(aDepartment :Department) -> Boolean
AS
  IF theName < (SEND aDepartment THE MESSAGE name?) THEN
    RETURN TRUE
  ELSE
    RETURN FALSE
  ENDIF
ENDMETHOD lessThan?
```

In effect we have decided that comparison of two `Department` objects is actually a comparison of their respective names using the operator < that is defined for `Strings`. The basis for the comparison is not really important and is at the discretion of the class designer. All that matters as far as the container is concerned is that a `Boolean` value is returned.

Partial LOOM scripts for the `Company` and `Department` classes are:

```
CLASS Company
WITH
PUBLIC INTERFACE
  Company(aName :String)
  changeName(aName :String)
  name? -> String
PRIVATE IMPLEMENTATION
  REPRESENTATION
    theName :String
  AGGREGATIONS
    theDepartments :DOrderedCollection [Department]
  ASSOCIATIONS NONE
  DEFINITIONS
    // Suitable method definitions ...

ENDCLASS Company


CLASS Department
WITH
PUBLIC INTERFACE
  Department(aName :String)
  lessThan?(aDepartment :Department) -> Boolean
```

```
  name? -> String
PRIVATE IMPLEMENTATION
  REPRESENTATION
    theName : String
  AGGREGATIONS NONE
  ASSOCIATIONS NONE
  DEFINITIONS
  // Suitable method definitions ...
```

```
ENDCLASS Department
```

It is important to understand the implications of these LOOM scripts. They state that:

- The aggregate component `theDepartments` contains a full copy of each `Department` object in the relation and not just a reference to it.

- It is assumed that the class `Company` has an operation to create `Department` objects and adds them to the property `theDepartments`.

- Only a `Company` object has visibility to the `PUBLIC INTERFACE` of each `Department` object in the `DOrderedCollection`, `theDepartments`.

- `Department` objects have no direct visibility of each other or the `Company` object of which they are part.

In contrast to the aggregation relationship, if an association exists between two classes then they are not strongly coupled. They are associates only for the purposes of the particular application we happen to be constructing and are more or less independent of each other. The `ASSOCIATIONS` clause records this relationship and recognises that with association we need only a reference to an associate object and not a complete copy by using the LOOM reserved word `LINK`. For example, the LOOM script for the `Employee` class is:

```
CLASS Employee
WITH
PUBLIC INTERFACE
  Employee(aName : String, aDateOfBirth : Date)
  changeName(aName : String)
  name? -> String
  age? -> Integer
PRIVATE IMPLEMENTATION
  REPRESENTATION
    theName : String
    theDateOfBirth : Date
  AGGREGATIONS NONE
  ASSOCIATIONS
    theEmployer : Company LINK
  DEFINITIONS
    // Suitable method definitions ...

ENDCLASS Employee
```

The association entry `theEmployer` holds only a reference to a `Company` object and not a complete copy of it. In other words, a Company object in this association is not contained by the Employee class, it is merely referenced by it. This implies that it has an independent existence and may, for example, have relationships with other objects in the system.

In this last example recall from Figure 3.3 that one Company object acts as the sole employer for an Employee object. Therefore the attribute the Employer is single-valued. However many Employee objects act as the employees for one Company object. In order to model this relationship, we need a container for each LINK to an Employee object. Assuming Employee objects are unsorted, a POrderedCollection is an appropriate choice for the container. The POrderedCollection is the counterpart to the DOrdered-Collection but is used to hold Employee LINKs rather than full copies of Employee instances. Access to each object it contains is indirect as it actually contains a pointer (a kind of reference) to an object (hence the P in POrderedCollection). The declaration:

```
theEmployees :POrderedCollection[Employee LINK]
```

declares the object theDepartments as a container of the class POrdered-Collection that holds pointers (references) to Employee objects in the order in which they are added.

A LOOM script for the Company class is:

```
CLASS Company
WITH
PUBLIC INTERFACE
  Company(aName :String)
  changeName(aName :String)
  name? -> String
PRIVATE IMPLEMENTATION
  REPRESENTATION
    theName :String
  AGGREGATIONS
    theDepartments :DOrderedCollection [Department]
  ASSOCIATIONS
    theEmployees :POrderedCollection [Employee LINK]
  DEFINITIONS
    // Suitable method definitions ...

ENDCLASS Company
```

3.5 Input and output

Data items are often taken from the keyboard and displayed on a computer screen. The keyboard can be viewed as an input stream with data extracted from it by objects. Similarly, the screen can be viewed as an output stream with data inserted into it by objects. Consider the class InputStream which is responsible for making available to a program data taken from the keyboard. Similarly consider the class OutputStream which is responsible for displaying on the screen data taken from a program. Partial LOOM scripts for these classes are as follows:

```
CLASS InputStream WITH
PUBLIC INTERFACE
  extract(anInteger : Integer OUT)
  extract(aDecimal : Decimal OUT)
  extract(aString : String OUT)
  extract(aDate : Date OUT)
  // ...

ENDCLASS InputStream
```

and:

```
CLASS OutputStream WITH
PUBLIC INTERFACE
  insert(anInteger : Integer IN)
  insert(aDecimal : Decimal IN)
  insert(aString : String IN)
  insert(aDate : Date IN)
  // ...

ENDCLASS OutputStream
```

Note that there is an operation for each class of data that is inserted or extracted. Although they have the same name they are distinguished by having a parameter with a different class. This is referred to as *overloading* and is very common in object oriented systems.

In addition, the formal parameter of each extract operation in the InputStream class has a mode OUT associated with it. It signifies that the actual parameter supplied by a sending object will be changed by the method for the extract operation in the receiving InputStream object. Its value in the sending object is irrelevant as it will be overwritten by the receiving InputStream object.

The use of an OUT parameter can be dangerous and it should always be used with care. The difficulty is that a message with an OUT parameter results in the sender having a state change through a change to that parameter. This can lead to much confusion especially if there are several OUT parameters in one message. If a state change is required in the sender it is usually better expressed as an explicit transformer operation advertised by the sender.

In this case we justify the use of an OUT parameter as it simplifies input of data to our programs. It allows an object to send the extract message to an InputStream object with an accompanying change in its actual parameter. The alternative of having an InputStream object sending a transformer message to the object in question is much more clumsy and does not reflect the way in which data input works in practice.

As it is most commonly used, the default mode for a parameter is IN. This signifies that the sending object supplies a parameter to the receiver object as part of the message but any changes are restricted to the receiving object and do not affect the sender. It is usually omitted from a LOOM script but is specified in the insert operations of the class `OutputStream` for clarity.

There is also a mode INOUT that signifies that a parameter associated with a message will be used to supply some initial value but will subsequently be changed by the receiver. However, the change will be dependent on its value in the sending object. For example, an operation:

```
increment(anInteger : Integer INOUT)
```

adds one to the value of an actual parameter in the sender. As with an OUT parameter its use should always be justified.

In order that we can send messages to the computer screen and keyboard we use the standard identifiers `theScreen` and `theKeyBoard`. Instances of the appropriate class are created as normal:

```
theKeyBoard      : InputStream
theScreen        : OutputStream
```

Assuming the instantiations:

```
INSTANCE i1      : Integer(0)
INSTANCE d1      : Decimal(0.0)
INSTANCE s1      : String("John")
```

example input and output messages are:

```
// Write the value of i1 on the screen.
SEND theScreen THE MESSAGE insert(i1)

// Write the value of s1 on the screen.
SEND theScreen THE MESSAGE insert(s1)

// Read the value of d1 from the keyboard.
SEND theKeyBoard THE MESSAGE extract(d1)
```

3.6 LINK instance

In the `Company–Employee` scenario we intend that a `Company` object should be able to send messages through an `Employee` LINK to an `Employee` object. This means that in order to send a message to an `Employee` object we actually require two objects. Obviously, we need the `Employee` object in question but we also need an object to hold the LINK to it. The first is an instance of the class `Employee` and the second is an instance of the class `Employee` LINK.

It is very important that we understand that these two objects are very different in nature. The `Employee` LINK object has none of the features of an

Employee object and certainly does not behave like one. All it does is to allow a message to be sent through it to an Employee object.

Returning to the Company–Employee scenario, in order to establish the LINK between a particular Company object and a particular Employee object we might have the operation:

```
hire(anEmployee :Employee LINK)
```

advertised on the interface of the Company class. Clearly the formal parameter anEmployee is of the class Employee LINK and not Employee. This means that with the instantiations:

```
INSTANCE c1 :Company("Napier")
INSTANCE e1 :Employee("Ken", Date(1,1,1976))
```

we cannot send the message:

```
SEND c1 THE MESSAGE hire(e1)
```

since the operation hire is expecting an Employee LINK object and the actual parameter we have supplied is an Employee object.

The solution is to establish an Employee object with *dynamic duration*. Here, the Employee object is created dynamically, i.e. at run time, and e1 is LINKed to that object as shown by Figure 3.4.

We obtain this effect with the modified INSTANCE sentence:

```
INSTANCE e1 :Employee LINK("Ken", Date(1,1,1976))
```

With this new instantiation we can now establish the LINK between c1 and the Employee object that e1 is LINKed to with:

```
SEND c1 THE MESSAGE hire(e1)
```

A fuller discussion of this topic is given later in Section 4.9.

A consequence of having a formal parameter that is a LINK object is that we must know if the parameter-passing mode IN, OUT or INOUT applies to the LINK object or to the object to which it is LINKed. In LOOM the situation is clear as it is always the case that the LINK object cannot be modified and the parameter-passing mode applies only to the object that is LINKed.

With this knowledge we can now consider the operation:

```
hire(anEmployee :Employee LINK)
```

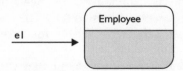

Figure 3.4   *A LINK instance*

As we have not specified a parameter-passing mode the default mode IN applies. This means that the Employee object that is the target of the Employee LINK cannot undergo a state change as a result of a message sent through that LINK. In effect the Company object making the LINK to this new staff member is not permitted to make a state change in the Employee object during execution of the hire operation. A message such as:

```
SEND anEmployee THE MESSAGE hiredBy(me)
```

(see Section 3.8) appearing in the hire method of the Company class is not legal. This is because it is a request to change the state of a constant Employee object through the Employee LINK.

Sometimes this is not the behaviour we require when there is an association relationship between classes and so we may specify a parameter-passing mode of INOUT as in:

```
hire(anEmployee :Employee LINK INOUT)
```

This means that the Employee object that anEmployee is LINKed to is no longer a constant and can be sent messages through it that can change its state. Further, as the mode is INOUT rather than OUT a state change is based on the state of the Employee object that exists before the message is received.

3.7 **Building a system**

In order that we may explore LOOM further, the operations of the Company, Employee and Department classes are extended to give a wider range of behaviours. Methods are also defined so that we may examine their behaviours in detail.

Assuming that Employee objects are hired and fired by a Company object, two operations:

```
hire(anEmployee :Employee LINK)
```

and

```
fire(anEmployee :Employee LINK)
```

are required in the Company class. In keeping with the association relationship between the Company and Employee classes the formal parameters are LINK values. We add to the Company class an operation displayEmployees? to display the details of each Employee, an operation averageAge? to deliver their average age, and an operation displayDepartments? to display the details of each Department. An updated LOOM script is:

```
CLASS Company
WITH
PUBLIC INTERFACE
  Company(aName :String)
  hire(anEmployee :Employee LINK)
```

```
fire (anEmployee :Employee LINK)
displayEmployees?
changeName (aName :String)
name? -> String
displayDepartments?
averageAge? -> Integer
PRIVATE IMPLEMENTATION
 REPRESENTATION
  theName :String
 AGGREGATIONS
  theDepartments :DOrderedCollection [Department]
 ASSOCIATIONS
  theEmployees :
POrderedCollection[Employee LINK]
 DEFINITIONS
  METHOD Company (aName :String)
  AS
  SEND theName THE MESSAGE initialise (aName)
  SEND theEmployees THE MESSAGE
  initialise (DEFAULTSIZE, UNMANAGED)
  SEND theDepartments THE MESSAGE
  initialise (DEFAULTSIZE)
ENDMETHOD Company

  METHOD hire (anEmployee :Employee LINK)
  AS
   SEND theEmployees THE MESSAGE add (anEmployee)
    // Where add is an operation advertised by the class
    // POrderedCollection.
  ENDMETHOD hire

  METHOD fire (anEmployee :Employee LINK)
  AS
   SEND theEmployees THE MESSAGE remove (anEmployee)
    // Where remove is an operation advertised by
    // the class POrderedCollection.
  ENDMETHOD fire

  METHOD displayEmployees?
  AS
   FOREACH emp :Employee LINK IN theEmployees DO
    SEND emp THE MESSAGE display?
   ENDFOREACH
  ENDMETHOD displayEmployees?

  METHOD changeName (aName :String)
  AS
   SEND theName THE MESSAGE assign (aName)
  ENDMETHOD changeName

  METHOD name? -> String
  AS
```

```
    RETURN theName
  ENDMETHOD name?

  METHOD displayDepartments?
  AS
    FOREACH aDepartment :Department IN
    theDepartments DO
      SEND aDepartment THE MESSAGE display?
    ENDFOREACH
  ENDMETHOD displayDepartments?

  METHOD averageAge? -> Integer
  AS
    INSTANCE totalAge :Integer(0)
    FOREACH anEmployee :Employee LINK IN
    theEmployees DO
      INSTANCE employeeAge :
      Integer(SEND anEmployee THE MESSAGE age?)
      SEND totalAge THE MESSAGE assign(totalAge +
        employeeAge)
    ENDFOREACH
    INSTANCE avAge :
    Integer(totalAge / SEND theEmployees THE MESSAGE
    cardinality?)
    RETURN avAge
  ENDMETHOD averageAge?
```

ENDCLASS Company

No operation is presented to add new Departments to the scheme. The reader is referred to exercise 1 at the chapter end for these details.

Note the form of the Company class constructor. The representational data theName is initialised with the parameter value. The architectural data is also initialised and as the aggregation theDepartments and the association theEmployees are both containers, they too need to be initialised. According to Appendix B the DOrderedCollection, theDepartments, needs to know its original size when it is initialised. The POrderedCollection, theEmployees also needs its original size when it is initialised and whether it has responsibility for the objects it references. If the deletion of a reference results in the object it refers to being deleted as well then it is designated as MANAGED. On the other hand, if the deletion of a reference leaves the object it refers to unchanged then it is UNMANAGED (see Section 4.9 for a fuller discussion of this point).

Similarly, the Employee class has an operation:

hiredBy(anEmployer :Company LINK)

that has a LINK to the Company object that hired it as a formal parameter and an operation:

fired

that is used to notify an Employee object that it has been fired. It has no parameter identifying the employer as the design specifies a unique employer for each Employee.

There is also an operation companyName? that delivers the name of the Company object that a Employee object is employed by and an operation display? that displays the details of an Employee. An updated LOOM script is:

```
CLASS Employee
WITH
PUBLIC INTERFACE
  Employee(aName :String, aDateOfBirth :Date)
  display?
  name? -> String
  changeName(aName :String)
  age? -> Integer
  hiredBy(anEmployer :Company LINK)
  companyName? -> String
  fired
  // ... others, including lessThan?
PRIVATE IMPLEMENTATION
  REPRESENTATION
    theName :String
    theDateOfBirth :Date
  AGGREGATIONS NONE
  ASSOCIATIONS
    theEmployer :Company LINK
  DEFINITIONS
    METHOD Employee(aName :String, aDateOfBirth :Date)
    AS
      SEND theName THE MESSAGE initialise(aName)
      SEND theDateOfBirth THE MESSAGE
      initialise (aDateOfBirth)
      SEND theEmployer THE MESSAGE
      initialise (NIL)
    ENDMETHOD Employee

    METHOD display?
    AS
      SEND theScreen THE MESSAGE insert(theName)
      SEND theScreen THE MESSAGE insert(theDateOfBirth)
    ENDMETHOD display?

    METHOD name? -> String
    AS
      RETURN theName
    ENDMETHOD name?

    METHOD changeName(aName :String)
    AS
      SEND theName THE MESSAGE assign(aName)
    ENDMETHOD changeName
    METHOD age? -> Integer
    AS
      //
```

```
        // Simplistic solution.
        //
        INSTANCE today :Date
        INSTANCE todayYear :
        Integer (SEND today THE MESSAGE year?)
        INSTANCE dateOfBirthYear :
        Integer (SEND the DateOfBirth THE MESSAGE year?)
        INSTANCE resultAge :
        Integer (todayYear − dateOfBirthYear)
        RETURN resultAge
    ENDMETHOD age?

    METHOD hiredBy (anEmployer :Company LINK )
    AS
      SEND theEmployer THE MESSAGE
      assign (anEmployer)
    ENDMETHOD hiredBy

    METHOD companyName? -> String
    AS
      RETURN (SEND theEmployer THE MESSAGE name?)
    ENDMETHOD companyName?

    METHOD fired
    AS
      SEND theEmployer THE MESSAGE assign (NIL)
    ENDMETHOD fired

  ENDCLASS Employee
```

Note once again how in the constructor the architectural data is initialised. Each
Employee object has a LINK to the organisation by which it is employed. Until
the employed takes up employment we set this value to NIL, a special value that
a LINK may have to signify that it does not reference any object.

The Department class has an operation:

```
allocateStaff (aStaffName :String)
```

that records an Employee allocated to the Department object as a staff
member. Employees' names are held in a container theStaffNames as part of
its representation. In fact the container is of the class DSortedList so that the
names are held in alphabetical order (see Appendix B). There is also an operation
display?, associated with the Department class, that displays the names of
staff members allocated to a Department object. The updated LOOM script for
the Department class is then:

```
CLASS Department
WITH
PUBLIC INTERFACE
  Department (aName :String)
  name? -> String
  allocateStaff (aName :String)
  display?
```

```
PRIVATE IMPLEMENTATION
 REPRESENTATION
  theName :String
  theStaffNames :DSortedList[String]
 AGGREGATIONS NONE
 ASSOCIATIONS NONE
 DEFINITIONS
  METHOD Department(aName :String)
  AS
    SEND theName THE MESSAGE initialise(aName)
    SEND theStaffNames THE MESSAGE
    initialise (DEFAULTSIZE, "")
  ENDMETHOD Department

  METHOD name? -> String
  AS
    RETURN theName
  ENDMETHOD name?

  METHOD allocateStaff(aName :String)
  AS
    SEND theStaffNames THE MESSAGE add(aName)
  ENDMETHOD allocateStaff

  METHOD display?
  AS
    FOREACH staff :String IN theStaffNames DO
      SEND theScreen THE MESSAGE insert(staff)
      ENDFOREACH
  ENDMETHOD display?

ENDCLASS Department
```

The Department constructor sets its underlying structure theStaffNames to some initial size and fills it with empty Strings. Note that a DSortedList container must be established with some original size and filled with a value that will be distinguishable from the actual values stored (see Appendix B). Here we have chosen the empty String as the distinguishing value.

In order that we can construct a complete system we require an object that is able to respond to a message that originates from an execution environment, e.g. an operating system. We refer to it as the Application object and export from it a public operation run that we assume can be activated externally. The corresponding method for this operation creates the major objects as well as the control logic necessary to stimulate them. Its form is:

```
CLASS Application WITH
PUBLIC INTERFACE
 run
PRIVATE INTERFACE
 REPRESENTATION NONE
 AGGREGATIONS NONE
 ASSOCIATIONS NONE
  DEFINITIONS
```

```
METHOD run AS
  // Creation of objects that make up the system.
  // Note that some objects may create their own objects
  // such as aggregation components or local objects in
  // methods.

  INSTANCE object1 : Class1
  INSTANCE object2 : Class2
  // ...

  // Messages sent to objects in the system.
  // They may be in sequence, conditional or repeated.
  // Note that if we intend that objects are associates they
  // should be instantiated as object LINKs, e.g.
  // INSTANCE object3 : Class3 LINK

    SEND object1 THE MESSAGE message1
    SEND object2 THE MESSAGE message2
    // ...
ENDMETHOD run

ENDCLASS Application
```

In principle, the LOOM sentence:

```
INSTANCE theApplication : Application
```

creates an executable program (the object theApplication), and the sentence:

```
SEND theApplication THE MESSAGE run
```

sent by an execution environment starts it running.

For a more concrete example, we can create an Application object for our Company–Employee illustration. Recall that a class diagram is a general description but an instance diagram is specific to a particular configuration of objects. Also, a message trace diagram shows the messages that are sent between objects. All three diagrams have an important part to play in the design of the method for the run operation of an Application class. The class diagram that models the system acts as the basis for the instance diagram that determines which objects are created. Hence the instance diagram in Figure 3.6 is based upon (and must conform to) the class diagram in Figure 3.5.

Note that we only consider *top-level* objects so that aggregate components are not created by the Application object but are created by the whole of which they are part (see Section 4.9 for a fuller discussion of this point).

The message trace diagram gives us the sender and receiver of each message as well as the order in which messages are sent. Hence the message traces in Figure 3.7 determine the sequence and nature of the messages in the run method of an Application object, theApplication, that are required to establish a two-way association between the Company object c1 and the three Employee objects e1, e2 and e3 (see Section 3.8 for a fuller discussion of this point).

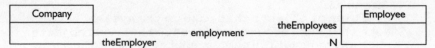

Figure 3.5   *The class diagram*

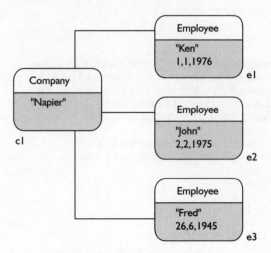

Figure 3.6   *The instance diagram*

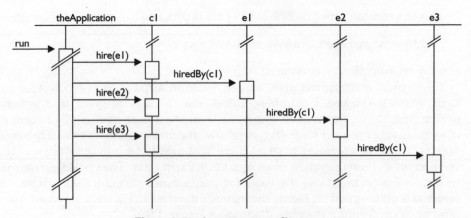

Figure 3.7   *A message trace diagram*

Note that this message trace diagram could be extended to describe other run-time behaviours of the `Application` object and hence define the nature and sequence of the other messages in its `run` method. We leave this as an exercise for the reader.

In this manner we arrive at the LOOM script for the `Application` class:

```
CLASS Application
WITH
```

```
PUBLIC INTERFACE
  run
PRIVATE IMPLEMENTATION
  REPRESENTATION NONE
  AGGREGATIONS NONE
  ASSOCIATIONS NONE
  DEFINITIONS
    METHOD run
    AS
      //
      // Create and initialise top-level objects.
      // Department objects are not included as they are
      // aggregate components of
      // the Company object and are created by it.
      //
      INSTANCE c1 :Company LINK("Napier")
      INSTANCE e1 :Employee LINK("Ken", Date(1,1,1976))
      INSTANCE e2 :Employee LINK("John", Date(2,2,1975))
      INSTANCE e3 :Employee LINK("Fred", Date(26,6,1945))
      //
      // Hire the employees.
      // Note that the employer and employee are informed by
      // the Application object of the hired object and hirer
      // respectively.
      //
      SEND c1 THE MESSAGE hire(e1)
      SEND e1 THE MESSAGE hiredBy(c1)

      SEND c1 THE MESSAGE hire(e2)
      SEND e2 THE MESSAGE hiredBy(c1)

      SEND c1 THE MESSAGE hire(e3)
      SEND e3 THE MESSAGE hiredBy(c1)
      //
      // Output the average age of the employees.
      // Note that the String "\n" is specific to C++
      // and causes the cursor to
      // appear on a new line.
      //
      SEND theScreen THE MESSAGE
      insert("Average employee age:")
      SEND theScreen THE MESSAGE
      insert(SEND c1 THE MESSAGE averageAge?)
      SEND theScreen THE MESSAGE insert("\n")
      //
      // Display details of each employee
      //
      SEND c1 THE MESSAGE displayEmployees?


      //
      // Output the employer's name for employee e2
      //
      SEND theScreen THE MESSAGE insert("Employer name:")
```

```
SEND theScreen THE MESSAGE
  insert(SEND e2 THE MESSAGE companyName?)
SEND theScreen THE MESSAGE insert("\n")

//
// Fire an employee and see the effect
//
SEND e3 THE MESSAGE fired
SEND c1 THE MESSAGE fire(e3)
SEND c1 THE MESSAGE displayEmployees?
ENDMETHOD run

ENDCLASS Application
```

3.8 Informal reasoning with LOOM

LOOM allows us to reason about a design without the distraction of the detail introduced by an implementation language. This is a major advantage and its significance should not be underestimated. For example, in the previous LOOM script, an `Application` object sends messages to `Company` and `Employee` objects when `Employees` are hired or fired. An alternative and probably better approach is to charge a `Company` object with the responsibility of informing an `Employee` object if it is hired or fired. This simplifies the `Application` object and places the responsibility where it probably should be, namely with the employer.

The only change that needs to be made to the `Company` class is to modify the `hire` and `fire` methods so that messages are sent to a corresponding `Employee` object. From our discussion in Section 3.6, here we have a situation in which the `Company` object which is the recipient of the `hire` message wishes to produce a state change in the `Employee` represented by the parameter. In this case the correct parameter mode is `INOUT`. The actual parameter me, sent as part of the message in the method `hire` for the `Company` class, is a predefined property whose value is a `LINK` to the object sending the message, here a `Company` object. It allows an object to identify itself. All class methods have me as an implicit property.

```
// Company class ...
METHOD hire(anEmployee : Employee LINK INOUT)
AS
  SEND anEmployee THE MESSAGE hiredBy(me)
  SEND theEmployees THE MESSAGE add(anEmployee)
ENDMETHOD hire

METHOD fire(anEmployee : Employee LINK INOUT)
AS
  SEND anEmployee THE MESSAGE fired
  SEND theEmployees THE MESSAGE remove(anEmployee)
ENDMETHOD fire
```

No changes are required in the Employee class.

With this amendment, the Application object messages:

```
SEND c1 THE MESSAGE hire(e1)
SEND e1 THE MESSAGE hiredBy(c1)

SEND c1 THE MESSAGE hire(e2)
SEND e2 THE MESSAGE hiredBy(c1)

SEND c1 THE MESSAGE hire(e3)
SEND e3 THE MESSAGE hiredBy(c1)

SEND c1 THE MESSAGE hire(e4)
SEND e4 THE MESSAGE hiredBy(c1)
```

simplify to:

```
SEND c1 THE MESSAGE hire(e1)
SEND c1 THE MESSAGE hire(e2)
SEND c1 THE MESSAGE hire(e3)
SEND c1 THE MESSAGE hire(e4)
```

In this example a Company object has a LINK association to several Employee objects and each Employee object has a LINK association to a single Company object. Obviously, a Company–Employee LINK and a Employee–Company LINK association are related. In a sense one is the inverse of the other. There is a clear responsibility to maintain the integrity of these relationships. For example, if an Employee LINK is added to the property theEmployees in a Company object then we must make sure that the property theEmployer of the corresponding Employee object is also updated. We can record this relationship in a LOOM script by the keywords INVERSE OF, as in:

```
theEmployees :POrderedCollection[Employee LINK]
INVERSE OF theEmployer
```

defined for the class Company, and:

```
theEmployer :Company LINK INVERSE OF theEmployees
```

defined for the Employee class.

After some deliberation, we may even decide that there is no need to traverse the association in both directions. Perhaps we consider it imposes too great a time penalty for an Employee to get the name of an employer. It is easy to prohibit the possibility of an Employee object sending messages to a Company object by the simple expedient of removing the LINK attribute theEmployer from the class Employee.

However, we may still need a way of having access to the name of the employer for an Employee object. A String property theEmployer Name for the class Employee is a suitable alternative that does not require the association to be traversed if the name of the employer is requested by a client. Obviously, there is a small storage overhead. With this new strategy, the property theEmployerName is updated by the Employee object hire method with data supplied by a Company object.

Partial LOOM scripts are as follows:

```
CLASS Company WITH
PUBLIC INTERFACE
  // ...
  hire(anEmployee :Employee LINK INOUT)
  fire(anEmployee :Employee LINK INOUT)

PRIVATE IMPLEMENTATION
  REPRESENTATION
    theName :String

AGGREGATIONS
  // ...

ASSOCIATIONS
  //Note there is no INVERSE as this is now a one-way traversal
  theEmployees :POrderedCollection[Employee LINK]

DEFINITIONS
  // ...

  METHOD hire(anEmployee :Employee LINK INOUT) AS
    SEND anEmployee THE MESSAGE hire(theName)
    //Note that a String is sent.
    SEND theEmployees THE MESSAGE add(anEmployee)
  ENDMETHOD hire

  //This method is unchanged but is included for clarity.
  METHOD fire(anEmployee :Employee LINK INOUT) AS
    SEND theEmployees THE MESSAGE remove(anEmployee)
    SEND anEmployee THE MESSAGE fired
  ENDMETHOD fire

ENDCLASS Company


CLASS Employee WITH
PUBLIC INTERFACE
  // ...
  //Note that a String parameter is now required.
  hire(aCompany :String)
  fire

PRIVATE IMPLEMENTATION
  REPRESENTATION
  // ...
  //Property to hold the name of the current employer.
  theEmployerName :String
  // ...
```

```
METHOD companyName? -> String AS
  // No traversal of the association is necessary.
    RETURN theEmployerName
ENDMETHOD companyName?

METHOD hire(aCompany :String) AS
  SEND theEmployerName THE MESSAGE assign(aCompany)
ENDMETHOD hire

ENDCLASS Employee
```

The `Application` class is unchanged.

In this case the class (and instance) diagram should also be modified with a multiplicity of zero on the Company side of the association, to show that there is no access possible from the `Employee` class, as shown in Figure 3.8. Regrettably, this nomenclature can be misleading. The intent is to emphasise that there is no `LINK` from the `Employee` class to the `Company` class, not that there are no `Company` objects!

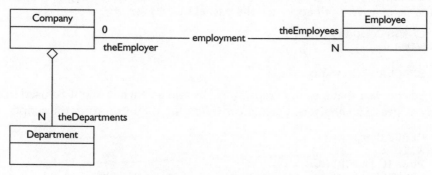

Figure 3.8   *One-way traversal of an association*

3.9   Development life cycles

Several different software development life-cycle models are widely used. For example, the traditional *waterfall* model starts with requirements capture and is followed by analysis, design, implementation and testing activities. It is based on the assumption that each activity is more or less completed before embarking on the next stage. Reuse is not a major feature of this model. At the other extreme the *prototyping model* assumes extensive libraries of classes exist and adopts an evolutionary approach to system construction. It is probably true that for real systems several models are used simultaneously. Typically one object in a system may be fully implemented very early during the analysis phase, another object may not be implemented at all but taken from a class library, while other objects may be implemented very late in the life cycle.

It is a matter of current research as to which model is best for object oriented systems development. However, no matter which model is used a fundamental point does not change. It is that objects identified in an analysis must be major components of the design. Extra detail may be added but none of the properties, aggregations and associations previously identified should be changed unless there is a very good reason for doing so, e.g. optimising a design to have a one-way association. Similarly, objects present in the design must be clearly identified in the implementation. As before, extra detail may be added but not removed. Objects not present in the original system specification may be introduced as part of the design or implementation.

Usually objects identified during analysis are major entities drawn from the problem domain. However, objects introduced during the design and implementation are relatively minor parts of the problem domain or are present in order to make a design strategy possible. Typical examples of the latter are reusable container objects such as the POrderedCollection as well as the fundamental classes String, Integer and Boolean.

LOOM is very flexible in that it may be used for any life-cycle model. For example, in a waterfall approach the partial LOOM script:

```
CLASS Company
WITH
  // ...
ENDCLASS Company
```

records the fact that a class Company exists and as such it might be used in the early stages of an analysis. Further consideration might produce the script:

```
CLASS Company
WITH
PUBLIC INTERFACE
  // To be done.
PRIVATE IMPLEMENTATION
  REPRESENTATION
  // To be done.
AGGREGATIONS
  theDepartments :DOrderedCollection [Department]
ASSOCIATIONS
  theEmployees :POrderedCollection[Employee LINK]
  INVERSE OF theEmployer
DEFINITIONS
  // To be done.

ENDCLASS Company
```

which defines the relationships between classes in an architectural design.

Later, as the design progresses, the LOOM script:

```
CLASS Company
WITH
PUBLIC INTERFACE
  Company(aName :String)
```

```
  changeName(aName :String)
  hire(anEmployee :Employee LINK)
  fire(anEmployee :Employee LINK)
  name? -> String
  averageAge? -> Integer
  displayEmployees?
PRIVATE IMPLEMENTATION
  REPRESENTATION
  theName :String
AGGREGATIONS
  theDepartments :DOrderedCollection [Department]
ASSOCIATIONS
  theEmployees :DOrderedCollection[Employee LINK]
  INVERSE OF theEmployer
DEFINITIONS
  // To be done.

ENDCLASS Company
```

defines operations and properties for the class. It would probably be the product of a main design activity. Obviously, the addition of corresponding methods leads to a detailed design and implementation.

By way of contrast, a partial LOOM script such as:

```
CLASS Company
WITH
PUBLIC INTERFACE
  Company(aName :String)
  changeName(aName :String)
  hire(anEmployee :Employee LINK)
  fire(anEmployee :Employee LINK)
  name? -> String
  averageAge? -> Integer
  displayEmployees?
// ...
ENDCLASS Company
```

could easily be used to define the interface of a `Library` class encouraging a bottom-up reusable component approach.

Alternatively, prototyped classes may be constructed by defining dummy methods and a restricted list of operations and properties. For example, the method `averageAge?` shown below is not fully implemented but it does return a reasonable value.

```
METHOD averageAge? -> Integer AS
  // Detail to be added later.
  RETURN 42
ENDMETHOD averageAge?
```

Another implementation strategy could be to indicate that a standard algorithm is to used by documenting the method body with a suitable comment. Here the parameter mode is `INOUT` since the sort operation will change the list.

```
METHOD sort(aList :POrderedCollection
[Employee LINK] INOUT) AS
  // Standard bubble sort algorithm.
  // See reference ...
ENDMETHOD sort
```

It is also possible that the detail of a method could be written in the system implementation language. This is achieved by using a comment that starts with //> rather than // in a method body.

```
METHOD displayHeading? AS
  //> cout << "\n" << "Object Oriented Design with C++"
  //<<"\n";
  //> cout << "\n" << "Barclay and Savage" << "\n";
ENDMETHOD displayHeading?
```

3.10 Modelling an association as an object

We have seen that if there is an association relationship between two classes then we may embed a LINK value in each class to allow two-way communication. For example, the association entry:

```
theEmployer :Company LINK INVERSE OF theEmployees
```

in the class Employee, and the association entry:

```
theEmployees :POrderedCollection[Employee LINK]
INVERSE OF the Employer
```

in the Company class.

Similarly, if there is an aggregation relationship between classes then we may embed a full copy of an aggregate component in it. For example, the aggregate entry:

```
theDepartments :DOrderedCollection [Department]
```

in the class Company. In this way the whole may access the interface of its parts. Note that the parts may not directly access the whole or other parts (see Section 2.2).

In general, incorporating a LINK to an associate's interface or embedding an aggregate component is good practice and is widely used. It clearly specifies the architectural relationships between classes for a particular Application. However, rather than traverse a relation (perhaps for performance reasons or to reduce message traffic), we sometimes add properties to a class that are part of an association with another class. In fact, they really have nothing to do with the class. For example, as discussed in Section 3.7 the property:

```
theEmployerName :String
```

could be in the class Employee instead of:

```
theEmployer :Company LINK
```

This avoids the necessity of traversing the association with the class Company to discover the name of the employer as the required information is held in the class Employee as a property.

However, taken to an extreme, if too many properties of this kind are added to a class then it defeats the purpose of using a class in the first place. This is because a class describes the features of all of its instances and we should not presuppose that all instances take part in a particular association. Moreover, it becomes increasingly difficult to separate properties that belong to the class, by right, and properties that derive from an association with another class.

An alternative strategy is to model an association as an object. In this way the classes taking part in an association can be decoupled from the detailed information relating to the association. Quite apart from this argument, it is possible that the association is significant enough to be modelled as a class anyway.

An association Employment modelled as a class is shown in Figure 3.9.

In this case all of the information relating to the employment association is held by the class Employment. This makes the Company and Employee classes much simpler as they now only require a relation with the Employment class to access information relating to the employment association. For a complex association this represents a considerable simplification of the classes concerned.

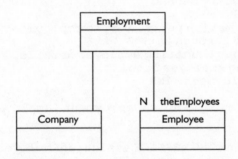

Figure 3.9   *Association modelled as a class*

```
CLASS Company
WITH
PUBLIC INTERFACE
  addEmployment(anEmployment :Employment LINK)
PRIVATE IMPLEMENTATION
  REPRESENTATION
  // As previously defined.
AGGREGATIONS
  // As previously defined.
```

```
ASSOCIATIONS
  // Any information pertaining to employment is
  // passed through this
  // LINK, e.g. requesting employee details,
  // supplying employer details.
theLink : Employment LINK
DEFINITIONS
  METHOD addEmployment (anEmployment : Employment
  LINK)
  AS
    SEND theLink THE MESSAGE assign (anEmployment)
  ENDMETHOD addEmployement

// Other suitable definitions.

ENDCLASS Company


CLASS Employee
WITH
PUBLIC INTERFACE
  addEmployment (anEmployment : Employment LINK)
PRIVATE IMPLEMENTATION
  REPRESENTATION
    // As previously defined.
AGGREGATIONS
  // As previously defined.
ASSOCIATIONS
  // Any information pertaining to employment
  // is passed through this
  // LINK, e.g. requesting employer details,
  // supplying employee details.
theLink : Employment LINK
DEFINITIONS
  METHOD addEmployment (anEmployment : Employment
  LINK)
  AS
    SEND theLink THE MESSAGE assign (anEmployment)
  ENDMETHOD addEmployment

// Other suitable definitions

ENDCLASS Employee


CLASS Employment
WITH
PUBLIC INTERFACE
  addCompany (aCompany : Company LINK)
  addEmployee (anEmployee : Employee LINK)
  theEmployerName? -> String
  theEmployeeNames? -> DOrderedCollection [String]
```

```
   totalEmployees? -> Integer
   dateHired?(theEmployeeName :String) -> Date
   dateFired?(theEmployeeName :String) -> Date
   // Other accessors pertinent to employment.
 PRIVATE IMPLEMENTATION
   REPRESENTATION
     // As previously defined
 AGGREGATIONS NONE
 ASSOCIATIONS
   theEmployer :Company LINK
   theEmployees :POrderedCollection[Employee LINK]
 DEFINITIONS
   // Suitable definitions.

 ENDCLASS Employment
```

The `LINK` values held in the `theEmployer` and `theEmployees` determine the configuration of the instances that make up an actual application. In the method definitions of class `Employment`, it may traverse the associations with the `Company` or `Employee` classes to access the information it requires or it may hold it as a property. In the latter case there is no conflict as the class only holds employment-related information, unlike the `Company` or `Employee` classes. This approach is potentially very powerful and is in keeping with the object oriented philosophy of delegating responsibility to the most appropriate classes in the system.

Note also the return type for the operation `theEmployeeNames?`. Here, a collection of `String` values is produced, giving the name for every employee.

3.11 Summary

1. A LOOM specification provides all the necessary details associated with a class, and includes the publicised services (`PUBLIC INTERFACE`) and the hidden implementation (`REPRESENTATION, AGGREGATIONS, ASSOCI-ATIONS` and `DEFINITIONS`). The `REPRESENTATION` is used for the base properties of class instances. The `AGGREGATIONS` and `ASSOCIATIONS` represent the architectural relationships the class has with other classes.

2. The `DEFINITIONS` presents the parameterised `METHOD` bodies for each of the class operations. A method body is a paragraph, consisting of one or more sentences. The sentences adopt the conventional control logic of sequence, selection and iteration. Sentences can be used to create `INSTANCEs` and `SEND` messages to objects.

3. LOOM specifications may involve base classes such as `String` and `Date`. They are part of the fundamental types supported by LOOM. The set also includes the container classes such as `POrderedCollection` and `DOrderedCollection`. LOOM specifications for these are given in Appendix B.

4. An `Application` class is used to construct the top-level object in a system. It has a public operation `run` that can be activated from an execution environment. Its method creates and sends messages to the major objects in the system.

5. LOOM permits a designer to reason informally about a system.

6. LOOM is independent of the development life cycle used, and supports the traditional waterfall approach, as well as prototyping and bottom-up strategies.

7. An association may be modelled as an object.

3.12 Exercises

For the following exercises and those in subsequent chapters we advise that you make use of the ROME object modelling environment supplied with the text. Although its use is not strictly necessary it does make the development of LOOM scripts considerably easier and more enjoyable. Sections 10.3 and 10.4 contain the information you require to use it. You should read them before proceeding.

1. Review the solutions (provided on the disk) to the `addDepartment` operation for the `Company` class of Section 3.7.

2. Complete the following LOOM specification for the class `Car` by giving implementations for the method bodies.

    ```
    CLASS Car
    WITH
    PUBLIC INTERFACE
      Car(aMake :String, aModel :String, aCapacity :Integer)
      make? -> String
      model? -> String
      capacity? -> Integer
    PRIVATE IMPLEMENTATION
      REPRESENTATION
        theMake :String
        theModel :String
        theCapacity :Integer
      AGGREGATIONS NONE
      ASSOCIATIONS NONE
      DEFINITIONS
        // Method bodies ...

    ENDCLASS Car
    ```

3. Complete the following LOOM specification for the class `Student` by giving implementations for the method bodies.

    ```
    CLASS Student
    WITH
    PUBLIC INTERFACE
      Student(aName :String, anAddress :String,
      aMatriculationNumber :String)
    ```

```
    name? -> String
    address? -> String
    matriculation? -> String
  PRIVATE IMPLEMENTATION
    REPRESENTATION
      theName : String
      theAddress : String
      theMatriculationNumber : String
    AGGREGATIONS NONE
    ASSOCIATIONS NONE
    DEFINITIONS
      // Method bodies ...

  ENDCLASS Student
```

4. Complete the following LOOM specification for the class House by giving implementations for the method bodies.

```
  CLASS House
  WITH
  PUBLIC INTERFACE
    House(anAddress : String, aNumberOfRooms : Integer)
    address? -> String
    rooms? -> Integer
    extend(aNumberOfRooms : Integer)   // Add new rooms.
  PRIVATE IMPLEMENTATION
    REPRESENTATION
      theAddress : String
      theNumberOfRooms : Integer
    AGGREGATIONS NONE
    ASSOCIATIONS NONE
    DEFINITIONS
      // Method bodies ...

  ENDCLASS House
```

When a House instance is created would it thereafter change its address? If not, under what circumstances could we consider moving the property theAddress into the public interface?

5. Complete the following LOOM specification for the class Point representing a point in the Cartesian coordinate system, by giving implementations for the method bodies. In a two-dimensional coordinate system a point may be represented by its X and Y coordinate values.

```
  CLASS Point
  WITH
  PUBLIC INTERFACE
    Point(anX : Decimal, aY : Decimal)
    xCoordinate? -> Decimal   // Obtain X coordinate.
    yCoordinate? -> Decimal   // Obtain Y coordinate.
    translate(xDistance : Decimal, yDistance
      : Decimal) // Displace by amounts.
  PRIVATE IMPLEMENTATION
    REPRESENTATION
      theXCoordinate : Decimal
```

```
        theYCoordinate :Decimal
AGGREGATIONS NONE
ASSOCIATIONS NONE
DEFINITIONS
  // Method bodies ...
```

```
ENDCLASS Point
```

Develop an Application in which a single Point object is created, then displaced
by some amount and its new position displayed.

6. Using the Point class, complete the following LOOM specification for the class
   Line by giving implementations for the method bodies. A line in a two-dimensional
   coordinate space may be represented by its start and end points.

```
CLASS Line
WITH
PUBLIC INTERFACE
  Line(aStart :Point, anEnd :Point)
  length? -> Decimal  // Length of line (Pythagoras).
  slope? -> Decimal   // Slope of line (Y difference over
                      // X difference).
  translate(xDistance :Decimal, yDistance
    :Decimal)         // Displace by amounts.
PRIVATE IMPLEMENTATION
  REPRESENTATION
    theStart :Point
    theEnd :Point
  AGGREGATIONS NONE
  ASSOCIATIONS NONE
  DEFINITIONS
    // Method bodies ...
```

```
ENDCLASS Line
```

Develop an Application in which a Line is established through two Point
values, translated through some amount, and then its length and slope are printed.

7. Using the Point class, a rectangle may be represented by two Point values
   representing, respectively, the lower left vertex and the upper right vertex. Complete
   the following LOOM specification for the Rectangle class by giving implementations for the method bodies.

```
CLASS Rectangle
WITH
PUBLIC INTERFACE
  Rectangle(aLowerLeft :Point, anUpperRight :Point)
  area? -> Decimal
  perimter? -> Decimal
  height? -> Decimal
  width? -> Decimal
  translate(xDistance :Decimal, yDistance :Decimal)
  isPointInRectangle?(aPoint :Point) -> Boolean
PRIVATE IMPLEMENTATION
  REPRESENTATION
    theLowerLeft :Point
    theUpperRight :Point
```

```
AGGREGATIONS NONE
ASSOCIATIONS NONE
DEFINITIONS
  // Method bodies ...
```

ENDCLASS Rectangle

Create a Rectangle in an Application, then test the behaviours of its operations.

8. Prepare a LOOM specification for a Store class. The Store represents some storage device that holds a single Integer value. The Store constructor has a single Integer argument used to initialise the representation. A single Integer parameter for the write operation is used to update the value of the representation. The read? operation returns a copy of the representation value. The operations up and down respectively increment and decrement by one the value of a Store object.

9. For questions 1, 2, 3 and 7 in the exercises of Chapter 2, prepare a completed LOOM script for each class and then construct a suitable run method for an Application object to test the system. Make sure that you make full use of the class, instance and message trace diagrams.

10. Section 3.2 defined the LOOM specification for a class as being composed of a PUBLIC INTERFACE that advertises operations available to clients and a PRIVATE IMPLEMENTATION. The latter is composed of a REPRESENTATION part that holds properties not available to clients and a DEFINITIONS part that defines a method for every operation advertised on the PUBLIC INTERFACE. Construct a suitable class diagram to describe a LOOM specification for a class.

Chapter 4

Case study: a simple library system

This case study is intended to highlight the fundamental elements of an object-oriented analysis and design using concepts discussed in the previous chapters. For clarity, the specification of the system has been simplified but interested readers can modify it in a variety of ways as indicated in the exercises at the end of the chapter. A more realistic specification for the application is given in the case study of Chapter 8.

In this case study the principal objects would normally consist of the Library and Book. However, we have also introduced the class User even though it is outside the scope of the library application. Its inclusion allows us to develop a full working model.

4.1 Specification

A library holds a collection of books each of which has a title, author and reference number. The library has a name. There are several users of the library, but each has a unique name and address. A user may:

- request a display of the current list of library books available
- borrow a book from the library
- return a book to the library.

The library may:

- ask each user for a display of the books they currently have out on loan.

The books held by the users are ordered with the most recent book borrowed first and the least recent book borrowed last. Similarly, the books held by the library are ordered with the most recently returned or added book first and the least recent last.

4.2 Strategy

The main deliverable of an object oriented analysis and design is a completed LOOM script for the classes describing each object. In this case study their development is based upon a traditional waterfall approach as described in Section 3.9.

The first task is an analysis that identifies the most important objects in the system and the classes to which they belong. The architectural design, which follows, establishes the relationships between the classes. Next, the main design defines the public services and private properties for each class. Parameter profiles for operations are also developed at this stage. Finally, a detailed design defines a method for each operation associated with every class.

At each stage the decisions made are recorded in the LOOM script for each class, as necessary. Note that at the end of the design every LOOM script must be complete. Class and instance diagrams as well as scenarios are used for clarification and as a documentation aid.

4.3 Analysis

The most important part of the construction of any software system is its analysis. If it is of low quality then it is very difficult, or even impossible, to deliver a high quality end-product. The analysis must identify the most important objects in the problem space. Fortunately, it is relatively easy to identify three major objects in our system as our everyday experience tells us that they are the library, the users and the books. This is not unusual and is a major strength of object orientation. Time and again we find that our real-world experience and intuition can be used to identify the most important components of our software systems. With just a little practice it becomes surprisingly straightforward.

However, we can also use the strategies discussed in the previous chapter to identify the objects. For example, a data view would identify book objects. A functional view would identify a library object that holds books, displays books and allows them to be borrowed or returned. Similarly it would identify user objects that hold loaned books, display books, borrow books from the library and return books to the library.

Clearly, we should establish the classes Library, User and Book. This decision is captured in the following partial LOOM scripts:

```
CLASS Library
  // All parts to be completed.
ENDCLASS Library


CLASS User
  // All parts to be completed.
ENDCLASS User
```

```
CLASS Book
  // All parts to be completed.
ENDCLASS Book
```

4.4 Architectural design

From the description of the problem, it is apparent that:

- one `Library` object has many `Book` objects
- many `User` objects communicate with one `Library` object
- one `Library` object communicates with many `User` objects
- the `User` object acts as the borrower
- the `Library` object acts as the lender
- one `User` object may borrow many `Book` objects.

We can model these relationships as aggregations and an association as shown in Figure 4.1. We assume that the association between the classes `User` and `Library` can be traversed in both directions.

Note that class diagrams are rather concise and may be confusing to the novice. In particular, Figure 4.1 states that a `User` has a collection of `Books` and that a `Library` also has a collection of `Books`. The collections happen to have the same name (taken from the role name). The important point is that there is no implication that they share the **same** collection. Only an instance diagram could give this information.

At this stage it is helpful to consider the nature of the containers that hold the collections of objects present in the system. So that we comply with the original specification that `Book` objects held by the `Library` and `User` are ordered, they can be collected by some form of ordered container (ordered sequentially according to the order items are placed in the container). The most recent item in the container is first and the least recent item last. Assuming that we also require a full copy of `Book` objects we might use a `DOrderedCollection` for this purpose (see Appendix B). New items can be placed in these

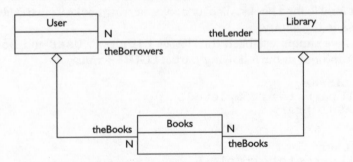

Figure 4.1 *Library system object model*

containers with the operation `addFirst` advertised by the class `DOrdered-Collection`, which implements the ordering requirements of the specification. Similiarly, items can be removed with the operation `removeLast`.

However, since there is no guidance as to the nature of the collection of `User` objects held by a `Library` object, we can assume that a simple `POrderedCollection` can be used. As there is one `Library` object associated with each `User` object, a single-valued object is all that is required in the `User` object to implement the association. Recall from Section 3.4 that we always hold a `LINK` to an associate so there is no possibility of using any of the containers that hold full copies of objects.

We can also note that at some point we must supply suitable `lessThan?` operations for the classes whose instances are to be contained (see Section 3.4). However, it is too soon to worry about this and we defer it to the detailed design.

LOOM scripts for each class with the AGGREGATIONS and ASSOCIATIONS clauses completed are:

```
CLASS Book
WITH
PUBLIC INTERFACE
  // To be completed.
PRIVATE IMPLEMENTATION
  REPRESENTATION
    // To be completed.
  AGGREGATIONS NONE
  ASSOCIATIONS NONE
  DEFINITIONS
    // To be completed.
ENDCLASS Book


CLASS Library
WITH
PUBLIC INTERFACE
  // To be completed.
PRIVATE IMPLEMENTATION
  REPRESENTATION
    // To be completed.
  AGGREGATIONS
    theBooks :DOrderedCollection[Book]
  ASSOCIATIONS
    theBorrowers :POrderedCollection[User LINK]
    INVERSE OF theLender
  DEFINITIONS
    // To be completed.
ENDCLASS Library


CLASS User
WITH
PUBLIC INTERFACE
  // To be completed.
PRIVATE IMPLEMENTATION
```

```
REPRESENTATION
  // To be completed.
AGGREGATIONS
  theBooks :DOrderedCollection[Book]
ASSOCIATIONS
  theLender :Library LINK INVERSE OF theBorrowers
DEFINITIONS
  // To be completed.
ENDCLASS User
```

Note that the language word NONE makes it obvious that there is no entry for a particular clause of a LOOM script. It is not that the entry is missing and will be added later. We have decided there is no entry and are recording this decision with the reserved word. Also, observe the two matching INVERSE OF phrases for the associations, in which we make an explicit statement that corresponding LINKs must be properly maintained. Note that we cannot enforce this in LOOM.

4.5 Main design

So far we have identified the major classes and their architectural relationships. Now we can turn our attention to the most important operations exported by each class. This should enable us to get a feel for the execution characteristics of the system so that we can review our earlier decisions and progress with the design.

Operations are all about doing something, so if we consider the required functionality of a system we should be able to arrive at a list of candidate operations and the classes with which they are associated. Clearly, a User object must be able to borrow and return a Book object. Since it is the Library object that is responsible for Book objects it is reasonable to associate the operations borrow and return with it and not with User objects.

Both the Library and User objects must be able to display the Book objects they hold so they should both have an operation displayBooks? publicly available. Following these considerations our LOOM scripts are then:

```
CLASS Library
WITH
PUBLIC INTERFACE
  borrowOneBook
  returnOneBook
  displayBooks?
PRIVATE IMPLEMENTATION
  // ...
ENDCLASS Library

CLASS User
WITH
PUBLIC INTERFACE
  displayBooks?
PRIVATE IMPLEMENTATION
  // ...
ENDCLASS User
```

Next we turn our attention to the internal representation for each class. Again, consideration of the system specification should help us with this task. A Book object will be given three properties as part of its representation: a title, author and reference number. They can be represented as two String objects and an Integer object respectively. Similarly, a User object has a name and address as properties that can be represented as String objects. The Library object has a name that can be represented by a String object.

Note that we have decided, within the context of this problem, that a title, author, reference number, name and address are properties of objects. In a different context this might not be the case. The general rule is that if an entity, taken from the problem specification, can stand alone, then it is an object. However, if it is a small part of something more significant and does not have an independent existence, then it should be considered as a property. Introducing these properties into each class gives us the following partial LOOM scripts.

```
// Class Book.
REPRESENTATION
  theAuthor : String
  theTitle : String
  theReferenceNumber : Integer

// Class Library.
REPRESENTATION
theName : String

// Class User.
REPRESENTATION
  theName : String
  theAddress : String
```

Finally, we can complete the public operations by adding any parameter lists and return values. For simplicity we can assume that:

- a User borrows the least recent Book in the Library
- a Book returned to the Library becomes the most recent item in its collection of Books
- a Book borrowed by a User becomes the most recent item in the user's list of Books
- a User returns the least recent Book to the Library held in its collection of borrowed Books.

The operation borrowOneBook? advertised by the class Library delivers a Book object from its current stock to its client. Clearly, it should be an operation returning an object of class Book. In contrast, the operation returnOneBook allows a client to deliver a Book object to a Library object, and is a transformer operation with a parameter of class Book. The operation displayBooks? in the User and Library classes displays all of the Books they contain and requires no parameters. The LOOM specifications now appear as:

```
CLASS Library
WITH
PUBLIC INTERFACE
  borrowOneBook? -> Book
  returnOneBook(aBook :Book)
  displayBooks?
PRIVATE IMPLEMENTATION
  // ...
ENDCLASS Library

CLASS User
WITH
PUBLIC INTERFACE
  displayBooks?
PRIVATE IMPLEMENTATION
  // ...
ENDCLASS User
```

4.6 Scenarios

At this point it is useful to construct a scenario diagram to help determine the messages that must be sent between objects during the execution of the system. In this way, we can confirm that the operations we have identified so far are acceptable and can also identify further operations not apparent from the original specification.

If we conduct a *what-if* experiment then it is clear that in order to display a Book object held by a Library object or borrowed by a User object, we must have a display? operation associated with the class Book:

```
CLASS Book
WITH
PUBLIC INTERFACE
  display?
PRIVATE IMPLEMENTATION
  // ...
ENDCLASS Book
```

It is also important that we consider operations that allow the Application to stimulate key objects to initiate a chain of messages. Their existence allows us to build a simulation of the complete system with the Application object sending messages to stimulate objects as appropriate. For example, the class User should have operations borrowOneBook and returnOneBook. Upon receipt by a User object they have the effect of causing it to initiate the messages that result in borrowing or returning a Book object from and to the Library.

The class Library should also have an operation displayUserBooks?. Upon receipt by a Library object it has the effect of causing it to initiate the messages that result in the Book objects held by its User object associates being displayed.

There are at least two alternatives to having the control operations borrowOneBook, returnOneBook and displayUserBooks? in the Library and User objects. The first is to have all of the control sentences necessary to borrow a Book, return a Book or display User Books in the Application object. This is clearly unacceptable as it goes against the central concept of object orientation that objects are responsible for their own behaviour. The second is to build the system such that Application, Book and Library objects have an independent thread of control. For reasons that are discussed in Chapter 5 this is impractical.

The Library and User classes with the operations displayUserBooks?, borrowOneBook and returnOneBook are now:

```
CLASS Library
WITH
PUBLIC INTERFACE
  borrowOneBook? -> Book
  returnOneBook(aBook :Book)
  displayBooks?
  displayUserBooks?
PRIVATE IMPLEMENTATION
  // ...
ENDCLASS Library
  // ...
CLASS User
WITH
PUBLIC INTERFACE
  displayBooks?
  borrowOneBook
  returnOneBook
PRIVATE IMPLEMENTATION
  // ...
ENDCLASS User
```

Figures 4.2(a), 4.2(b) and 4.2(c) are scenario diagrams that capture the most important operations that the system must perform. Note that messages can originate from any object and not just the Application object as was the case in previous scenario diagrams. They show the sequence of messages that occur between objects when:

a. a User borrows a Book

b. the Library requests a display of the Books held by a User

c. a User returns a Book to the Library.

In each of the three figures, the labels b1, b2 and b3 are used to refer to three possible Book objects. Similarly, u1 and u2 refer to two possible User objects.

Note that the message run that stimulates the Application object (Figure 4.2(a)) does not have a sender. It is assumed to originate from the operating environment or its equivalent.

At this stage we are confident that we have the design under control as we can achieve the required system functionality using only operations available on the PUBLIC INTERFACE of each class.

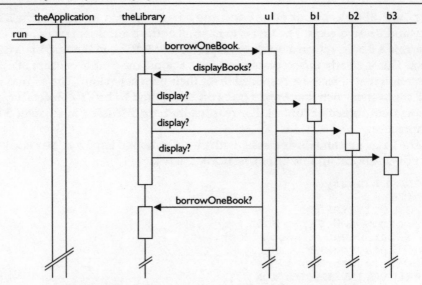

Figure 4.2(a)   *Operation scenario: a* User *borrows a* Book

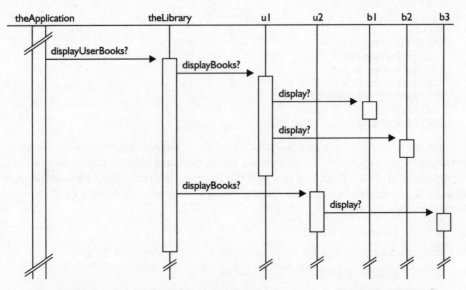

Figure 4.2(b)   *Operation scenario: the* Library *requests a display of the* Books *held by* Users

4.7 Detailed design

Finally, in order to complete the LOOM scripts for each class, we need to formalise the method definitions that support each operation. For the class Book:

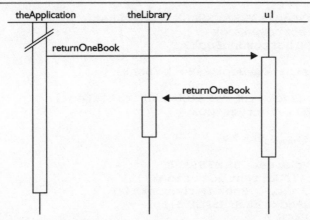

Figure 4.2(c) *Operation scenario: a* User *returns a* Book *to the* Library

- The method for the operation display? sends insert messages to the OutputStream object theScreen with its properties as parameters.

This method appears as follows:

```
// Class Book.
METHOD display? AS
  SEND theScreen THE MESSAGE insert(theAuthor)
  SEND theScreen THE MESSAGE insert(theTitle)
  SEND theScreen THE MESSAGE
  insert(theReferenceNumber)
ENDMETHOD display?
```

For the class Library:

- The method for the borrowOneBook? operation creates a local Book object, assigns to it the last entry in its collection of Book objects, removes it from the collection, then returns a copy of the local Book object to its client.

- The method for the operation returnOneBook adds the Book object supplied as a parameter by its client to its list of Book objects.

- The method for the operation displayBooks? sends the message display? to each Book in its collection of Books.

- The method for the operation displayUserBooks? sends a message displayBooks? to each User object.

The method definitions are then:

```
// Class Library.
METHOD borrowOneBook? -> Book
AS
  INSTANCE borrowedBook :Book
  SEND borrowedBook THE MESSAGE
    assign(SEND theBooks THE MESSAGE last?)
```

```
    SEND theBooks THE MESSAGE removeLast
    RETURN borrowedBook
ENDMETHOD borrowOneBook?

METHOD returnOneBook (aBook :Book)
AS
  SEND theBooks THE MESSAGE addFirst(aBook)
ENDMETHOD returnOneBook

METHOD displayBooks?
AS
  SEND theScreen THE MESSAGE
    insert("Current loan stock")
  FOREACH aBook :Book IN theBooks DO
    SEND aBook THE MESSAGE display?
  ENDFOREACH
ENDMETHOD displayBooks?

METHOD displayUserBooks?
AS
  SEND theScreen THE MESSAGE
    insert("Library user's borrowed stock")
  FOREACH aUser :User LINK IN theBorrowers DO
    SEND aUser THE MESSAGE displayBooks?
  ENDFOREACH
ENDMETHOD displayUserBooks?
```

Method displayBooks? employs a FOREACH clause to visit each Book in the
collection theBooks. At each iteration, aBook refers, in turn, to each Book in
the collection, say the three Book objects b1, b2 and b3 as shown in Figures
4.2(a), 4.2(b) and 4.2(c). The method for displayUserBooks is similar.

For the class User:

- the method for the displayBooks? operation sends messages to
  theScreen to insert its properties, theName and theAddress, then
  for each Book object in its collection of borrowed Books it sends the message
  display?.

- The method for the operation borrowOneBook sends a message to the
  Library to release one Book for borrowing, which the User object places
  in its collection of borrowed Books.

- The method for the operation returnOneBook creates a local Book object,
  assigns to it the last entry in its collection of borrowed Books, removes it from
  the collection, then sends the copy to the Library as an actual parameter
  of the message returnOneBook.

```
//Class User.
METHOD displayBooks?
AS
  SEND theScreen THE MESSAGE insert(theName)
  SEND theScreen THE MESSAGE insert(theAddress)
  FOREACH aBook :Book IN theBooks DO
```

```
      SEND aBook THE MESSAGE display?
    ENDFOREACH
  ENDMETHOD displayBooks?

  METHOD borrowOneBook
  AS
    SEND theBooks THE MESSAGE
      addFirst(SEND theLender THE MESSAGE
        borrowOneBook)
  ENDMETHOD borrowOneBook

  METHOD returnOneBook
  AS
    INSTANCE borrowedBook :Book
    SEND borrowedBook THE MESSAGE
      assign(SEND theBooks THE MESSAGE last?)
    SEND theBooks THE MESSAGE removeLast
    SEND theLender THE MESSAGE
      returnOneBook (borrowedBook)
  ENDMETHOD returnOneBook
```

The class Book needs a constructor that takes an author, title and reference number as parameters and uses them to initialise its private properties. For the class Library it is inappropriate to have a constructor with every Book it contains as a parameter. This indicates the need for an operation addBook that has a Book object as a parameter.

The Library class requires a constructor that takes a name as a parameter to initialise its private property. The Library class also has an aggregation theBooks and an association theBorrowers that need to be initialised as discussed in the previous chapter. From Appendix B we have that the POrderedCollection, theBorrowers, must be established with its initial size and management scheme, while the DOrderedCollection, theBooks, is initialised with its size.

```
  METHOD Library
  AS
    SEND theBorrowers THE MESSAGE
      initialise(DEFAULTSIZE, UNMANAGED)
    SEND theBooks THE MESSAGE initialise(DEFAULTSIZE)
  ENDMETHOD Library
```

For the class User a constructor that takes a name and an address as parameters is required. As with the class Library the container theBooks and the association theLender must also be initialised.

In general it is good practice to provide a default constructor for each class. This avoids any ambiguity that might arise later when the system is implemented (see Chapter 6).

Finally we can add the operation lessThan? to the classes Book and User so that their containers function properly (see Sections 3.4 and 4.4). In order to support the method for this operation we must also add the accessor operation title? and name? in the classes Book and User respectively.

Completed LOOM scripts for the classes `Book`, `User` and `Library` are detailed in Appendix E.

4.8 Building the system

Now that we have the three classes defined we are able to construct an `Application` object to execute the final system. As explained in the previous chapter, the method for its operation `run` creates the top-level objects and initiates the messages that control their execution.

Its first action is to use the constructors to create one `Library` object `theLibrary` and two `User` objects `u1` and `u2`. Next it establishes the association between the `Library` object and the two `User`s and vice versa to form the architecture illustrated in Figure 4.3.

The sentences that follow are based upon the scenario of Section 4.6. They result in adding `Book`s to `theLibrary`, borrowing `Book`s from `theLibrary`, returning `Book`s to `theLibrary` and displaying `Book`s held by `User`s.

An outline LOOM script for the run method of the `Application` class is as follows:

```
// Class Application.
METHOD run
AS
// Create a Library with dynamic duration.
  INSTANCE theLibrary :
   Library LINK ("Dunning Library")

// Create two Users with dynamic duration.
  INSTANCE u1 : User LINK ("John", "21 High Street")
  // ...

// Configure the architecture.
  SEND theLibrary THE MESSAGE addUser (u1)
```

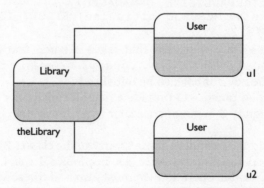

Figure 4.3 *The instance diagram for the object architecture*

```
SEND u1 THE MESSAGE addLibrary(theLibrary)
// ...

// Add some Books to the Library stock.
SEND theLibrary THE MESSAGE addBook(Book("Barclay",
  "C++: Problem Solving and Programming", 1))
// ...

// The User u1 borrows two Books.
SEND u1 THE MESSAGE borrowOneBook
SEND u1 THE MESSAGE borrowOneBook
// ...

// The Library displays Books held by its Users.
SEND theLibrary THE MESSAGE displayUserBooks?

// The User u1 returns a Book.
SEND u1 THE MESSAGE returnOneBook

// The Library displays Books held by its Users and itself.
SEND theLibrary THE MESSAGE displayUserBooks?
SEND theLibrary THE MESSAGE displayBooks?

ENDMETHOD run
```

4.9 Object lifetimes, LINKs and copies

Before we leave this case study there is an important point that must be discussed. It is concerned with the construction, ownership, copying and destruction of the Book objects in the system. Recall from Chapter 3 that for any object that is a parameter of an operation, there is a choice between passing it as a complete object or as a LINK to the object. Our justification for using a LINK to an object rather than a full copy was that we were establishing an association relationship that implied a loose form of coupling. However, there are other reasons for using a LINK to an object. For example, if an object takes up a significant amount of space then making full copies may contribute to memory overflow or unacceptably slow execution speeds. Even more important is the fact that it is inherently dangerous to have several full copies of objects present in a system as changes in one may not be reflected in the duplicates. Clearly the result could be catastrophic.

Consider the method run for the preceding Application object which uses the constructor:

```
Book(anAuthor :String, aTitle :String,
  aReferenceNumber :Integer)
```

to create a Book object as part of the message addBook sent to the Library object:

```
SEND theLibrary THE MESSAGE addBook(Book("Barclay",
  "C++: Problem Solving and Programming", 1))
```

On completion of this message, the Book object created no longer exists within the scope of the Application object. However, a full copy has been passed to the object theLibrary so all is apparently well.

A potential problem arises when a Book object is borrowed or returned by a User object as the transactions involve complete copies of the Book objects concerned. Perhaps the designer wanted this to be the case and it is intended to reflect what actually happens in the real world. Clearly, it places a responsibility upon the developer to ensure that Book objects are removed from the Library on borrowing and removed from a User on returning. Failure to discharge this responsibility would almost certainly seriously compromise the integrity of the system. For example, we could end up in a situation where a Book was returned to the Library but still held by the User.

Consider the following LOOM fragment from the run method of an Application object:

```
// Create a Library.
INSTANCE theLibrary :Library LINK("Dunning Library")

// Create a User.
INSTANCE u1 :User LINK("John", "21 High Street")

// The lifetime of this instance is the method run, i.e. the
system.
INSTANCE b1 :Book("Barclay",
  "C++: Problem Solving and Programming", 1)

// Add a full copy of a book to the Library.
// A full copy exists in the Application object and in the
// Library object !!!!
SEND theLibrary THE MESSAGE addBook(b1)
```

In contrast to the previous script, the above code creates an instance of the Book class before passing it as a parameter to a Library object. This means that after the execution of the method for the message addBook two copies of the Book object exist at the same time. One is in the Application and the other is in the Library. Further, we have no explicit mechanism for destroying either. This is not a situation that should be allowed to occur. It is just too dangerous and will inevitably lead to serious problems.

Before we propose a solution we need to understand that there are two different ways in which objects can be created in LOOM. The first allocates memory for object creation with local duration. This means that the allocated storage is released upon exit from the method body in which it appears. The second allocates memory dynamically, with the LINK having local duration. This means that the dynamic object persists until some explicit sentence relinquishes the space. It is important to realise that the two mechanisms are fundamentally different and that far-reaching consequences follow from the adoption of one rather than the other.

When we created a Book object in the method run of the Application object with the sentence:

```
INSTANCE b1 : Book ("Barclay",
  "C++: Problem Solving and Programming", 1)
```

it is said to have *local duration*. The important points for us to understand are that b1 is local to the run method in which it is created and that it can only exist during the method's execution. Clearly, a method may be executed many times and so local objects may be created and destroyed many times. When it is destroyed on the termination of the method that created it the storage associated with it is reclaimed for the creation of other local objects. This makes for an efficient use of memory by allocating and deallocating memory as objects are created and destroyed during the execution of methods.

However, if we consider the LOOM sentence:

```
INSTANCE b1 : Book LINK ("Barclay",
  "C++: Problem Solving and Programming", 1)
```

then the situation changes as b1 is now designated as a LINK to a Book object. The b1 object has local duration and is created and destroyed in the same way as any other local object. However, there is a crucial difference in that it references an anonymous Book object i.e. one with no identifier, which is created dynamically as illustrated in Figure 4.4. Such objects are said to have *dynamic duration*.

The important points for us to understand are that the anonymous dynamic object is not destroyed when b1 is destroyed and that it can be referenced by one or more objects in other methods so long they are declared as a LINK to a Book. In effect the Book object's lifetime is potentially the lifetime of the system, no matter where it is created.

As dynamic object creation is the result of a message to execute a constructor, it is appropriate that we should record this fact in a scenario diagram. A dotted line is used for this purpose. For example, Figure 4.5 shows an Application object creating a Book with dynamic duration. As in Figures 4.2(a), 4.2(b) and 4.2(c) the label b1 is used to denote the reference to the dynamic object.

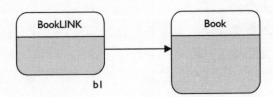

Figure 4.4 *A* LINK *to a* Book *object*

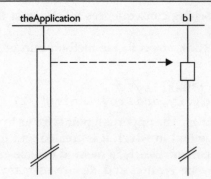

Figure 4.5   *Creation of a dynamic object shown on a scenario diagram*

Now that we have the possibility of using dynamic objects we might decide that the `Application` object of our case study should create anonymous `Book` objects dynamically and pass a `Book LINK` value to the `Library` when necessary, e.g. when adding a `Book` to the `Library`. Figure 4.6(a) captures the essence of this important modification to a scenario diagram.

Transactions between the `Library` and `Users` such as borrowing and returning a `Book` now make use of a `Book LINK`. Similarly, they hold `Book LINKs` internally in their respective containers. No changes to the class `Book` are required but the classes `Application`, `Library` and `User` require replacement of `Books` by `Book LINKs` as detailed in Appendix E. For simplicity we have assumed that a `Book` can be borrowed any number of times. In addition, a `User` must specify the title of the `Book` that is to be borrowed.

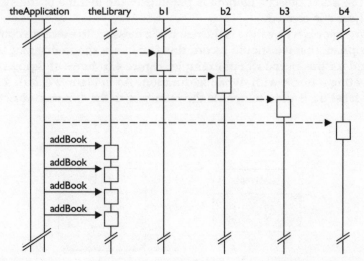

Figure 4.6(a)   *Creation of dynamic* `Book` *objects and their addition to the* `Library`

Although we will examine many of the issues relating to dynamic storage in Chapter 8, we can note in passing that great care must be exercised when using containers that hold LINKs to objects. A container can be initialised to be MANAGED or UNMANAGED. Removal of a LINK from a MANAGED container will result in the LINK value **and** the anonymous object it references being deleted. However, removal of a LINK value from an UNMANAGED container only results in the deletion of the LINK.

Two difficulties with dynamic storage commonly arise. The first occurs when there is an attempt to reference a dynamic object that no longer exists. For example, if we designate the container of Book LINKs theBooks in the User class and the container theBooks in the Library class as MANAGED, then if a Book LINK is removed from the former the Library has a LINK to a Book that no longer exists. Any attempt to reference a Book through this LINK will result in an execution-time failure. In effect the LINK is left *dangling* with nothing at the end of it!

The second difficulty occurs when we lose the ability to reference an object created dynamically. The result is *memory leakage*. Taken to an extreme it can result in a program running out of memory at execution time. For example, if we designate the container theBooks in the User class and the container theBooks in the Library class as UNMANAGED then removal of a LINK from either will not delete the Book object referenced. This means that the run method of the Application object has no mechanism for deleting a Book but only a LINK to a Book.

An instance diagram arising from this discussion is shown in Figure 4.6(b).

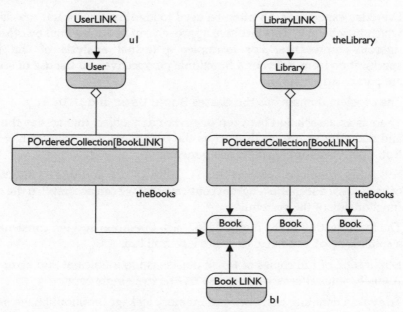

Figure 4.6(b) *Instance diagram*

In the run method of the `Application` class the `Library` object is created dynamically with the sentence:

```
INSTANCE theLibrary : Library LINK ("Dunning Library")
```

Again, we remind ourselves that the `Library` object is created dynamically, but the `Library LINK`, `theLibrary`, has local duration and is removed at the end of the run method. A similar discussion applies to the `User` and `Book` objects.

Observe how this instance diagram shows that three `Books` have been introduced into the `Library`. Since the aggregation `theBooks` in the `Library` is initialised as a `MANAGED` container, the `Library` object will remove the dynamically allocated `Book` objects for which it has ownership when it itself is deallocated. The instance diagram also shows that the first `Book` object is also shared by the aggregation `theBooks` in the `User` object. This time, the container is initialised as `UNMANAGED`, simply sharing a `LINK` to the `Book` object otherwise owned by the `Library`.

A clear rule emerges from this discussion. It is that we must have a single `MANAGED` container of `Book LINKs` if we are to avoid a dangling reference and memory leakage. We shall take up this point again when we revisit this case study in Chapter 8.

4.10 Summary

1. Everyday experience can often be used to identify objects and the classes to which they belong. This intuitive approach can be augmented by other more rigorous approaches. For example, a textual analysis of the system specification from a data or a functional perspective and the use of scenarios are particularly helpful.

2. The problem domain has the classes `Book`, `User` and `Library`.

3. There is an association between one `Library` object that acts as the lender and many `User` objects that act as the borrowers. Both classes have many `Book` objects as aggregation components.

4. Following completion of the `PUBLIC INTERFACE` and `REPRESENTATION` of each class, a scenario diagram confirms that we can accomplish the desired functionality of the system.

5. The formalisation of the methods for each operation and the construction of a suitable `Application` class are left until last.

6. Duplication of full copies of `Book` objects is too inefficient and error prone. A much better alternative is to use `LINKs` to a single copy.

7. To avoid a dangling reference and memory leakage we should have only one `MANAGED` container of `Book LINKs`.

4.11 Exercises

You should modify the system developed in the first version of the case study (the one with the full copies of the Book objects in the Library) as indicated below. Add one enhancement at a time. Do not try to do everything at once. As with the exercises of Chapter 3 we recommend that you use the object modelling environment supplied with the text which is described in Chapter 10.

1. Rather than specify the Books to be created and added to the Library in the run method of the Application object at compile time, interact at run time through the keyboard and screen. A password "Librarian" must be entered before the details of each Book to be added to the Library can be entered from the keyboard. In the first instance four Books should be created and added to the Library.
    Hint: Consider control sentences in the run method of the Application object of the form:

```
// ...
// Login the Librarian.
//
INSTANCE thePassword : String("")

WHILE thePassword != "Librarian" DO
  SEND theScreen THE MESSAGE
    insert("Password >>>>>")
  SEND theKeyboard THE MESSAGE
    extract(the Password)
ENDWHILE

//
// The Librarian creates four Books interactively and
// adds them to the Library.
//
INSTANCE theTitle : String("")
INSTANCE theAuthor : String("")
INSTANCE theReferenceNumber : Integer(0)

INSTANCE theCount : Integer(1)

WHILE theCount <= 4 DO
  SEND theScreen THE MESSAGE insert("\n Title >>>")
  SEND theKeyboard THE MESSAGE extract(theTitle)

  SEND theScreen THE MESSAGE insert("\n Author >>>")
  SEND theKeyboard THE MESSAGE extract(theAuthor)

  SEND theScreen THE MESSAGE
    insert("\n Reference Number >>>")
  SEND theKeyboard THE MESSAGE
    extract(theReferenceNumber)

  SEND theLibrary THE MESSAGE addBook(Book(theTitle,
  theAuthor, theReferenceNumber))
```

```
SEND theCount THE MESSAGE assign(theCount + 1)
ENDWHILE

// ...
```

2(a) Modify the software so that the number of Books to be added can be keyed in by the Librarian. What happens when fewer than three Books are created and added to the Library? Trace the execution of the system and try to identify the sources of the problem.

Hint: There is an implicit assumption in this case study that there are Books in the Library when a request to borrow is made by a User. Similarly, it is assumed that there are Books present when a request is made to a User to return a Book. Less seriously, it is also assumed that there are Books present when there is a request to display Books held by a User or the Library.

Consider control code in the run method of the Application object of the form:

```
// ...
// Login the Librarian.
// ...

// Determine the number of Books to be created and added
// to the Library.
//
INSTANCE theNumberOfBooks : Integer(0)

SEND theScreen THE MESSAGE
  insert("\n How many Books? >>>")

// Assume a positive number is keyed in.
SEND theKeyboard THE MESSAGE
  extract(theNumberOfBooks)
// ...

WHILE theCount <= theNumberOfBooks DO
  // ...
ENDWHILE
// ...
```

2(b) Avoid the catastrophic run-time errors of exercise 2(A) by making sure that there is a Book to borrow in the Library and a Book to return in a User before a request to borrowOneBook or returnOneBook is made. Similarly, the system should respond appropriately when there are no Books to display.

Hint: Provide an operation booksAvailable? -> Boolean supported by the Library. Its method should check that there are Books in its container theBooks with the message isEmpty? (see Appendix B).

```
// Class Library.
METHOD booksAvailable? -> Boolean
AS
  RETURN NOT(SEND theBooks THE MESSAGE isEmpty?)
ENDMETHOD booksAvailable?
```

Similarly the request to display Books in the Library should check that there are Books to display.

```
// Class Library.
METHOD displayBooks?
AS
  SEND theScreen THE MESSAGE
    insert("Current loan stock\n")
  IF (SEND theBooks THE MESSAGE
    isEmpty?) == FALSE THEN
    FOREACH aBook :Book IN theBooks DO
      SEND aBook THE MESSAGE display?
    ENDFOREACH
  ELSE
    SEND theScreen THE MESSAGE
      insert("no Books available\n")
  ENDIF
ENDMETHOD displayBooks?
```

Before a request to borrow a Book is actioned by a User it should first check that there is a Book available in the Library.

```
// Class User.
METHOD borrowOneBook
AS
  IF (SEND theLender THE MESSAGE
    books Available?) == TRUE THEN
    SEND theBooks THE MESSAGE
      addFirst(SEND theLender THE MESSAGE borrowOneBook)
  ELSE
    SEND theScreen THE MESSAGE
      insert('\nError from User')
    SEND theScreen THE MESSAGE insert(theName)
    SEND theScreen THE MESSAGE
      insert(" : cannot borrow from Library\n")
  ENDIF
ENDMETHOD borrowOneBook
```

The operations displayBooks? and returnOneBook in the class User are treated similarly.

3. Amend the class Book so that it has an International Standard Book Number (ISBN) as one of its attributes.

   Hint: Make changes to the REPRESENTATION clause as well as the constructor and display? operations for the class Book. The creation of Books in the run method of the Application object will also have to be amended.

4. Restrict a User to borrowing a maximum of five Books at any given time and make borrowing interactive.

   Hint: Give the User the Integer property theNumberOfBooks that records the number of Books on loan, and theMaximumBooks that records the maximum number of Books that can be borrowed. Incorporate their use into the methods for the constructor and the operations borrowOneBook and return OneBook.

```
// Class User.
METHOD User(aName :String, anAddress :String)
AS
  SEND theName THE MESSAGE initialise(aName)
  SEND theAddress THE MESSAGE initialise(anAddress)
```

```
      SEND theMaximumBooks THE MESSAGE initialise(5)
      SEND theNumberOfBooks THE MESSAGE initialise(0)
      // Note the actual parameter for this
      // initialisation
      SEND theBooks THE MESSAGE
      initialise(theMaximum Books)
      SEND theLender THE MESSAGE initialise(NIL)
    ENDMETHOD User

    // Class User.
    METHOD borrowOneBook
    AS
      IF (SEND theLender THE MESSAGE booksAvailable?) ==
        TRUE THEN
        IF theNumberOfBooks < theMaximumBooks THEN
          SEND theBooks THE MESSAGE
            addFirst(SEND theLender THE MESSAGE
              borrow OneBook)
          SEND theNumberOfBooks THE MESSAGE
            assign(the NumberOfBooks + 1)
        ELSE
          SEND theScreen THE MESSAGE
            insert("\nError from User")
          SEND theScreen THE MESSAGE insert(theName)
          SEND theScreen THE MESSAGE
            insert(" : cannot borrow a Book ... maximum
            Books on loan reached\n")
        ENDIF
      ELSE
        SEND theScreen THE MESSAGE
          insert("\nError from User")
        SEND theScreen THE MESSAGE insert(theName)
        SEND theScreen THE MESSAGE
          insert(" : cannot borrow from the Library\n")
      ENDIF
    ENDMETHOD borrowOneBook
```

Adopt the same strategy as in exercise 1 to elicit a response from the Users at run time. Consider the following control code for the run method of the Application object.

```
    // ...
    // The User u1 borrows at least one Book.
    //
    INSTANCE theResponse :String("YES")

    WHILE theResponse == "YES" DO
      SEND u1 THE MESSAGE borrowOneBook
      SEND theScreen THE MESSAGE
        insert("\nDoes John want to borrow any more
        Books? (YES/NO) >>>>")
      SEND theKeyboard THE MESSAGE extract(theResponse)
    ENDWHILE
    //
    // The User u2 borrows at least one Book.
    //
```

```
    SEND theResponse THE MESSAGE assign ("YES")

    WHILE theResponse == "YES" DO
      SEND u2 THE MESSAGE borrowOneBook
      SEND theScreen THE MESSAGE
        insert ("\nDoes Ken want to borrow any more Books?
          (YES/NO) >>>>")
      SEND theKeyboard THE MESSAGE extract (theResponse)
    ENDWHILE
    // ...
```

5. Permit a User to return Books interactively.

   Hint: Consider the control code for the run method of the Application object.

```
    // ...
    // The User u1 returns some Books.
    //
    SEND theScreen THE MESSAGE
        insert ("\nDoes John want to return a Book? (YES/
          NO) >>>>")
    SEND theKeyboard THE MESSAGE extract (theResponse)
    WHILE theResponse == "YES" DO
      SEND u1 THE MESSAGE returnOneBook
      SEND theScreen THE MESSAGE
      insert ("\nDoes John want to return any more Books?
        (YES/NO) >>>")
      SEND theKeyboard THE MESSAGE extract (theResponse)
    ENDWHILE
    // ...
```

6. Allow a maximum of three attempts to key in the password for the Librarian
   before prematurely terminating the program run.

   Hint: Use a RETURN sentence with no parameter if a count of the number of attempts
   is exceeded. Consider the following control code in the run method of the
   Application object.

```
    // ...
    // Login the Librarian.
    //
    INSTANCE thePassword : String ("")
    INSTANCE theAttempts : Integer (0)

    WHILE thePassword != "Librarian" DO

    SEND theScreen THE MESSAGE insert ("Password
      >>>>>")
    SEND theKeyboard THE MESSAGE extract (thePassword)
    SEND theAttempts THE MESSAGE assign (theAttempts + 1)
    IF theAttempts > 3 THEN
      SEND theScreen THE MESSAGE
        insert ("\nError : too many attempts ... program
          terminated\n")
      RETURN
    ENDIF

    ENDWHILE
```

7. Modify your solutions so that the Library holds LINKs to the Book objects.

Chapter 5

Dynamic modelling

Before we consider the construction of dynamic models we must first understand some of the characteristics of the machines on which software runs. Typically, a computer has one processor to support the execution of a program. By far the most common strategy is to implement software as a sequential program in which the ability to execute is passed from one object to another as messages are sent and received. It is implicitly assumed that when an object is executing one of its methods it has exclusive access to the single processor. No other object is able to execute one of its methods.

A good analogy is that of a football match in which the players represent objects and the ball the ability to execute (commonly referred to as the *thread of control*). In this analogy, when a message is sent between two objects the ball is passed between two players. When the associated method is completed by the receiver, the ball is automatically returned to the sender. It is only when a player has the ball that he can do any useful works, i.e. sending a message. Otherwise, the player must wait until the ball is passed to him. In principle the player could wait forever.

However, it is worth noting that some computers support multiple processors on which objects can execute. In this case objects can run in *parallel* with each other. Alternatively, even if only one processor is available, it is still possible to simulate parallel behaviour by *scheduling* objects for execution.

Unfortunately, we must restrict our discussions to the dynamic modelling of sequential programs. Systems with multiple threads of control are a specialist area that is beyond the scope of this book.

5.1 Event-driven systems

An object-oriented system consists of a collection of objects that co-operate by sending messages to each other. In this way the required behaviour of the complete system is achieved. In the examples we have considered so far, the method for the operation run defined for the Application object is the origin of the messages that stimulate the entire system. In effect, it has high-level control, and as such, determines its overall system behaviour. For example, the following sequence of LOOM sentences:

```
SEND u2 THE MESSAGE borrowOneBook
SEND theLibrary THE MESSAGE displayUserBooks?
SEND u1 THE MESSAGE returnOneBook
```

in the method for the operation `run` dictates the execution behaviour of the `Application` object in the case study of Chapter 4. These sentences force a defined sequence of requests from the `Application` object to the `User` and `Library` objects.

It is important to understand that even though an arbitrarily large number of messages may be sent or received in a sequential system there is only one thread of control. Using the football game analogy once more, the ball starts in the possession of the `Application` object and is passed to the `User` object u2 when the LOOM sentence:

```
SEND u2 THE MESSAGE borrowOneBook
```

is executed. The object u2 now has the thread of control (the ball) and is therefore able to execute its method for the operation `borrowOneBook`. On completion of the method for `borrowOneBook`, the thread of control is returned to the `Application` object which can now send the message:

```
SEND theLibrary THE MESSAGE displayUserBooks?
```

which gives the thread of control to the `Library` object `theLibrary`. On completion of the method for the operation `displayUserBooks?`, control is once again returned to the `Application` object and the message:

```
SEND u1 THE MESSAGE returnOneBook
```

is sent to the `User` object u1. On completion of the method for the operation `returnOneBook`, control is again passed back to the `Application` object.

In this example there is no interaction with a user and so the behaviour of the system is completely defined by the sequence of messages in the method for the `run` operation of the `Application` object. Once started it will execute without any external intervention. In other words the source of all messages is objects defined in the system. The LOOM control sentences for sequence, selection and repetition (see Sections 3.3.1 to 3.3.3) in the methods for their operations are all that is required to describe their *dynamic* behaviour.

However, some systems have a more complex dynamic behaviour. For example, they may interact at execution time with a user. As a consequence they must be able to respond to requests that originate in the real world. These external requests are usually referred to as *events* and systems whose behaviour is dominated by them are known as *event-driven* systems. Modelling their dynamic behaviour is an important part of OOAD.

We can illustrate some of the techniques used with the following partial system specification.

A mail system provides utilities for editing, posting and viewing items of mail held in a mailbox. In addition, accounts pertaining to the use of the system are managed. On start-up, only one user, the super-user, identified by a unique character sequence, is registered. The super-user may add other users, also identified by a unique character sequence. However, only one user is connected to the system at a time.

On successful connection to the system, a user may:

- edit or post a new mail item
- display current mail items for which he is the recipient
- display his account
- list registered users.

As part of the OOAD we can identify the classes:

UserID	A sequence of characters used to uniquely identify a user
Account	The account held for each user
UserIDList	An alphabetic list of registered users
AccountManager	The manager of the account for each user
Mail	A mail item which may be edited and posted and/or received
MailBox	The mailbox through which mail items are sent
Editor	The editor for a mail item

The architecture of the system is shown in the class diagram of Figure 5.1(a) and the instance diagram of Figure 5.1(b).

They show that the Application is composed of Editor, Mailbox, AccountManager, Mail, Account and UserIdList objects. The Mailbox object has many Mail objects while the Editor object has only one. The AccountManager object has one UserIdList and many Account objects. In addition there is an association relationship between the MailBox and the AccountManager objects.

The model is satisfactory as far as it goes, but we still need a means of allowing the Application to interact with a User. We need to make it clear how the

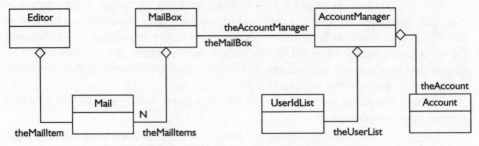

Figure 5.1(a)   *Mail system class diagram*

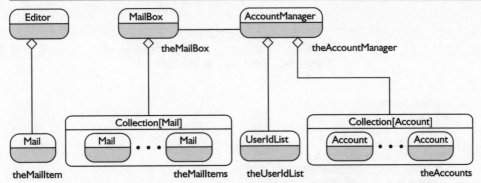

Figure 5.1(b)   *Mail system instance diagram*

system will allow the user to direct the operation of the mail system. In other words we need an object responsible for human–computer interaction (HCI).

A simple but effective solution is to have an `Hci` object present the `User` with a menu of options as shown below.

1: Edit a mail item

2: Post a mail item

3: Display mail items

4: Display an account

5: Display users

6: Add a user

7: Disconnect

Each integer elicits a different response from the system when input. Obviously, there are many different execution behaviours possible depending on the sequence of `Integers` input by the `User`. For example, the user could:

• edit a `Mail` item,

• post a `Mail` item,

• display any `Mail` items waiting for him, and then

• disconnect from the system,

by keying the sequence 1, 2, 3, 7.

Figure 5.2 captures the relationship between the `Hci` and `Menu` classes. The `Hci` object supports all communications with the `User` and has a `Menu` object, as an aggregate component, for its own use when responding to requests.

A suitable LOOM script for the `Menu` class follows. Note that it is given responsibilities compatible with a menu, i.e. a client can only request the details of the menu held (its state) to be displayed. It has no responsibility to accept input from a client or to act upon receipt of an input.

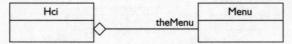

Figure 5.2 *The role of the* Hci *class*

```
CLASS Menu
WITH
PUBLIC INTERFACE
  display?
PRIVATE IMPLEMENTATION
  REPRESENTATION NONE
  AGGREGATIONS NONE
  ASSOCIATIONS NONE
  DEFINITIONS
    METHOD display?
    AS
      SEND theScreen THE MESSAGE
        insert("1: Edit a mail item")
      SEND theScreen THE MESSAGE
        insert("2: Post a mail item")
      SEND theScreen THE MESSAGE
        insert("3: Display mail items")
      SEND theScreen THE MESSAGE
        insert("4: Display account")
      SEND theScreen THE MESSAGE
        insert("5: Display users")
      SEND theScreen THE MESSAGE
        insert("6: Add a user")
      SEND theScreen THE MESSAGE
        insert("7: Disconnect")
    ENDMETHOD display
ENDCLASS Menu
```

The complete LOOM script for the Hci class follows. As with the Menu class, note that it has responsibilities compatible with an Hci object. It can only display a Menu and deliver the identifying Integer choice input by a User. It has no responsibility to take any actions that affect the behaviour of the system upon receipt of an input. This is the responsibility of the Application object.

```
CLASS Hci
WITH
PUBLIC INTERFACE
  displayMenu?
  display?(aMessage :String)
  userID? -> String
  newUserID? -> String
  choice? -> Integer
PRIVATE IMPLEMENTATION
  REPRESENTATION NONE
  AGGREGATIONS
    theMenu :Menu
  ASSOCIATIONS NONE
```

```
      DEFINITIONS
        METHOD displayMenu?
        AS
          SEND theMenu THE MESSAGE display?
        ENDMETHOD displayMenu

        METHOD display?(aMessage :String)
        AS
          SEND theScreen THE MESSAGE insert(aMessage)
        ENDMETHOD display?

        METHOD userID? -> String
        AS
          INSTANCE ID :String("")
          SEND theKeyboard THE MESSAGE extract(ID)
          RETURN ID
        ENDMETHOD userID?

        METHOD newUserID? -> String
        AS
          INSTANCE newID :String("")
          SEND theKeyboard THE MESSAGE extract(newID)
          RETURN newID
        ENDMETHOD newUserID?

        METHOD choice? -> Integer
        AS
          INSTANCE theChoice :Integer(0)
          SEND theKeyboard THE MESSAGE extract(theChoice)
          RETURN theChoice
        ENDMETHOD choice?

    ENDCLASS Hci
```

Assuming the instantiations:

```
INSTANCE theHci :Hci
INSTANCE theUserID :String("")
INSTANCE theChoice :Integer(0)
```

in the Application object, commonly occurring LOOM sentences involving the HCI object are:

```
// Elicit the user's identity.
SEND theHci THE MESSAGE display("Enter user identity")
SEND theUserID THE MESSAGE assign(SEND theHci THE MESSAGE
userId?)
```

and:

```
// Elicit the user's choice from the menu.
SEND theHci THE MESSAGE displayMenu?
SEND theChoice THE MESSAGE assign(SEND theHci THE MESSAGE
choice?)
```

5.2 State transition diagrams

Class and instance diagrams are not really suitable for modelling the dynamic behaviour of event-driven objects. Traditionally a *state transition diagram* (STD) is used for this purpose. Unfortunately, there is a conflict in the use of the word *state*. It is not used in the same sense as in object oriented technologies but is intended to mean that the object exhibits *modal* behaviour. If it is operating in a particular mode (or state) then it has a particular behaviour. If its mode (or state) changes in response to an event then its behaviour is different.

For example, the method run for the Application object that represents the mail system could be waiting for the user to input an Integer or it could be editing a Mail item. In the first case, it must wait for the user to input an Integer and cannot do anything else until an Integer is keyed. In the second case, it must edit a Mail item and cannot do anything else at that point in its execution.

In an STD, states are usually represented by rounded rectangles, annotated with a suitable description of the state, as shown in Figure 5.3.

Obviously, an object can only be in one state at a time, but it can change from one state to another, usually in response to an event. A connecting arrow between the two states together with the event (if there is one) that causes (or fires) the transition is drawn in the STD. The direction of the arrow represents the direction of the transition. Figure 5.4 shows the transition from the state waiting for input to the state editing mail item, when the Integer 1 is input by a User.

Similarly, transitions to the states:

```
posting mail item,
displaying mail items,
displaying account,
displaying users,
adding user
```

and

```
disconnecting
```

are caused by entering 2, 3, 4, 5, 6 and 7 as indicated by Figure 5.5 when the system is in the state waiting for input.

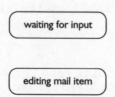

Figure 5.3 *States in an STD*

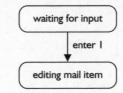

Figure 5.4 *Single state transition*

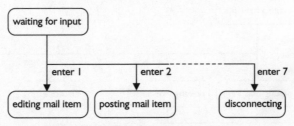

Figure 5.5 Menu *object state transitions*

It is also possible to indicate the *activities* carried out when an object is in a particular state by the use of the word DO: followed by the activity. For example, Figure 5.6 shows that when an Editor object is in the state *editing mail item* it sends the message edit to an aggregate component theMailItem.

> editing mail item
> DO: SEND theEditor THE MESSAGE edit

Figure 5.6 *Decorated state diagram*

In this simple case, it is not really necessary to add this detail and descriptions of activities are omitted so as not to clutter up the diagram. The overriding purpose of the STD is to capture the overall dynamic behaviour of the object in a clear manner. Too much detail may detract from achieving this goal. Obviously, the designer should exercise his judgement in this decision.

When the activities associated with each state have been completed the Application object changes its state automatically, i.e. no event is required. As before an arrow indicates the new state that the system adopts as shown in Figure 5.7.

It also shows the state in which the object starts by using a filled circle. Note that if an invalid ID is entered, the system will return to its initial state waiting for input. Although the mail box system is intended to run for ever, we can imagine an input of the integer 8 closing it down. A *bull's eye* symbol indicates this final state of the object. Once in this state the object has effectively terminated its execution and can no longer initiate or respond to messages.

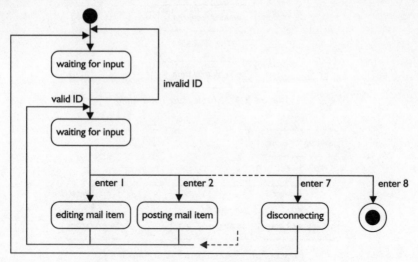

Figure 5.7   *Application object state transition*

5.3 State transition diagrams and LOOM

The purpose of a LOOM script is to record decisions made about each class in an OOAD. This includes an object's dynamic behaviour. Fortunately we can easily translate the STD describing the dynamic behaviour of event-driven objects into LOOM control sentences (Rumbaugh et al., 1991). The rules are as follows:

Rule 1
Identify the main control sequence by starting at the initial state and writing down the states in a sequence that corresponds to the normal execution of the system. This translates to a sequence of LOOM sentences.

Rule 2
Alternative backward paths that branch off the main control sequence but rejoin it earlier translate to repetition LOOM sentences. Multiple backward paths that do not cross become nested repetition sentences.

Rule 3
Alternative forward paths that branch off the main control sequence but rejoin it later translate to selection LOOM sentences. Multiple forward paths that do not cross become nested selection sentences.

Rule 4
Paths that cross should be reconsidered and replaced by non-intersecting ones. They are a strong indication that something has gone wrong with the design of the STD and map to a particularly dangerous control sentence referred to as a *GOTO*. We consider the *GOTO* (or its equivalent) unnecessary and do not implement it in LOOM.

As a first example, consider part of the library case study of Chapter 4 in which four Books are added to the Library in sequence. A suitable STD describing the dynamic behaviour of the Application object is shown in Figure 5.8.

Obviously, there are no events to stimulate the system and no branches off the single sequence of states. In each state the Application object sends a message to the Library object to add a particular Book object. The sequence of states in the STD translates directly to a sequence of LOOM control sentences as shown below:

```
// Adding b1.
SEND theLibrary THE MESSAGE
  addBook(Book("Barclay",
    "C++: Problem Solving and Programming", 1))
// Adding b2.
SEND theLibrary THE MESSAGE
  addBook(Book("Rumbaugh",
    "Object Oriented Modelling and Design", 2))
// Adding b3.
SEND theLibrary THE MESSAGE
  addBook(Book("Booch",
    "Object Oriented Design", 3))
// Adding b4.
SEND theLibrary THE MESSAGE
  addBook(Book("Yourdon",
    "Object Oriented System Design", 4))
```

If we consider the more complex example of the run method for the Application object to control the mail system then the real power of this

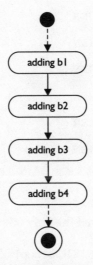

Figure 5.8 *Application object state transition*

approach becomes evident. Using our simple translation rules, we can map the control information described in Figure 5.7 to LOOM in a straightforward manner.

The nested backward branches indicate nested repetitions (rule 2). The outermost branch corresponds to the main execution loop, the next branch corresponds to the user identity input loop and the last branch to the mail system connection loop as shown below:

```
// Main execution loop.
INSTANCE terminate : Boolean (FALSE)
WHILE terminate == FALSE DO

   // User identity input loop.
   INSTANCE validId : Boolean (FALSE)
   WHILE validId == FALSE DO
    // ...
   ENDWHILE  // User identity loop

   // Mail system connection loop
   INSTANCE disconnect : Boolean (FALSE)
   WHILE disconnect == FALSE DO
    // ...
   ENDWHILE  // Mail system connection loop

ENDWHILE  // Main execution loop
```

Note the use of the Boolean objects terminate, validId and disconnect.

The forward branches indicate alternatives (rule 3) and correspond to the activity selection as shown below:

```
// Activity selection.
IF theChoice == 1 THEN
 // ...
ELSEIF theChoice == 2 THEN
 // ...
ELSEIF theChoice == 3 THEN
 // ...
ELSEIF theChoice == 4 THEN
 // ...
ELSEIF theChoice == 5 THEN
 //
ELSEIF theChoice == 6 THEN
 // ...
ELSEIF theChoice == 7 THEN
 // ...
ELSE
 // ...
ENDIF// Activity selection.
```

The final ELSE clause assumes that the only other plausible value is the selection choice 8.

In order that we complete the LOOM control sentences all that remains to do is to:

- add the detail of the messages that affect the `Boolean` objects `terminate`, `validId` and `disconnect`, and

- add the messages that need to be sent to objects in order to elicit a response from the system.

A partial LOOM script for the `run` operation of the `Application` object is as follows:

```
// Class Application.
METHOD run
AS
INSTANCE theHci :Hci
INSTANCE theEditor :Editor
INSTANCE theMailBox :MailBox LINK("Royal Mail")
INSTANCE theAccountManager :
 AccountManager ("Accounts")
// ...

// Main execution loop.
INSTANCE terminate :Boolean(FALSE)
WHILE terminate == FALSE DO

// User identity input loop.
  INSTANCE validId :Boolean(FALSE)
  WHILE validId == FALSE DO
    INSTANCE theUserId :String("")
    SEND theHci THE MESSAGE
      display("Enter user identity:")
    SEND theUserId THE MESSAGE
      assign(SEND theHci THE MESSAGE userId?)
    IF (SEND theAccountManager THE MESSAGE
    validUser?(theUserId)) THEN
    SEND validId THE MESSAGE assign(TRUE)
    ENDIF
  ENDWHILE  // User identity loop.

// Mail system connection loop
INSTANCE disconnect :Boolean(FALSE)
WHILE disconnect == FALSE DO

// Elicit a menu choice from the user
SEND theHci THE MESSAGE displayMenu?
INSTANCE theChoice :Integer(0)
SEND theChoice THE MESSAGE
assign(SEND theHci THE MESSAGE choice?)

// Activity selection.
IF theChoice == 1 THEN
  SEND theEditor THE MESSAGE edit
ELSEIF theChoice == 2 THEN
  SEND theMailBox THE MESSAGE post
ELSEIF theChoice == 3 THEN
  SEND theMailBox THE MESSAGE displayMail?
ELSEIF theChoice == 4 THEN
```

```
    SEND theAccountManager THE MESSAGE
      displayAccount?
  ELSEIF theChoice == 5 THEN
    SEND theAccountManager THE MESSAGE
      displayUsers?
  ELSEIF theChoice == 6 THEN
    SEND theAccountManager THE MESSAGE addUser
  ELSEIF theChoice == 7 THEN
    SEND theHci THE MESSAGE
      display("Mail system: disconnecting")
    SEND disconnect THE MESSAGE assign(TRUE)
  ELSE
    SEND theHci THE MESSAGE
      display("Mail system: closing down the system")
    SEND disconnect THE MESSAGE assign(TRUE)
    SEND terminate THE MESSAGE assign(TRUE)
  ENDIF

  ENDWHILE // Mail system connection loop.

ENDWHILE   // Main execution loop.

ENDMETHOD run
```

5.4 Summary

1.   A sequential system has only one thread of control.

2.   An object cannot execute without the thread of control.

3.   Message passing implies a transfer of the thread of control.

4.   An object that interacts with its environment requires a dynamic model.

5.   State transition diagrams are very useful for constructing dynamic models.

6.   For event-driven systems, events determine their overall dynamic behaviour.

7.   LOOM control sentences map directly to a state transition diagram.

a.   A sequence of states maps to a sequence of LOOM control sentences

b.   Alternative backward paths map to LOOM repetition sentences.

c.   Alternative forward paths map to LOOM selection sentences.

5.5 Exercises

1.   A computer services unit at a university offers a large number of facilities to users. These facilities are presented as a set of nested menus. The first menu a user is presented with is as follows:

      A. Applications: General Menu.
      B. Floppy Disk Service Menu.
      C. Library Reference Materials Menu.

If the user keys an A, B or C then he can select the menu indicated.

For example, the selection of the applications general menu is accomplished by keying an A and leads to the presentation of the sub-menu:

A. Word Processors
B. Databases and Spreadsheets
C. Languages
D. Return to previous menu

An input of A invites the user to select from the sub-menu:

A. WordPerfect   5.1
B. WordPerfect   6.0   Text
C. WordPerfect   6.0   Graphics
D. WordPerfect   Tutor
E. Return to previous menu

An input of A, B, C or D makes the facility indicated available. When the facility terminates the user is automatically returned to the sub-menu from which it was selected. A selection of E returns the user to the previous menu.

An input of B to the application sub-menu invites the user to select from:

A. DBase   3.0
B. Paradox   v3.0
C. Paradox   v4.0
D. Lotus123   v2.01
E. Return to previous menu

As before, an input of A, B, C or D makes a facility available and an input of E returns the user to the menu one level above.

An input of C to the application sub-menu invites the user to select from:

A. Turbo C   v2.0
B. Turbo Pascal   v5.5
C. Turbo Pascal   v6.01
D. Borland C++   v3.1
E. Return to previous menu

As before an input of A, B, C or D makes a facility available and an input of E returns the user to the menu one level above.

Finally, an input of D at the application sub-menu returns the user to the top-level menu.

From the top-level menu an input of B or C takes the user into the software that controls the provision of floppy disk utilities and library services respectively. The former offers users formatting and virus-checking utilities. The latter provides access to a wide range of library services such as keyword searches and summaries of research papers.

From the outline given, construct a suitable dynamic model described by an STD for the system.

Chapter 6

Object-oriented programming languages

In this book we use C++ exclusively as our implementation language. Many of the considerations we give can, of course, be applied to other programming languages. We do not give a complete description of C++, rather the focus is on those language features which give support for data abstraction and object-oriented programming. Appendix C presents a brief overview of the language features of C++. For a comprehensive introduction to C++ see Barclay (1994), Stroustrup (1991) and Lippman (1991).

6.1 LOOM specifications

A LOOM specification presents the details of the behaviour of objects for some user-defined class. The specification consists of a number of primary clauses enclosed within the keywords CLASS and ENDCLASS. The clauses are introduced with the keywords PUBLIC INTERFACE, PROTECTED INTERFACE (see Chapter 7) and PRIVATE IMPLEMENTATION. The latter is partitioned into minor subclauses specifying the REPRESENTATION (operations and properties), AGGREGATIONS and ASSOCIATIONS, and the DEFINITIONS (definition for the methods). The form of a LOOM specification is:

```
CLASS className
WITH
PUBLIC INTERFACE
  // ...
PRIVATE IMPLEMENTATION
REPRESENTATION
  // ...
AGGREGATIONS
  // ...
ASSOCIATIONS
  // ...
DEFINITIONS
  // ...

ENDCLASS className
```

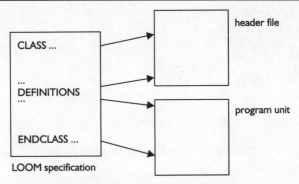

Figure 6.1   *Mappings between LOOM and C++*

A LOOM specification for one class gives rise to two C++ program files, namely, a *header file* and a *program unit file* (Figure 6.1). The header file is primarily a recasting of the PUBLIC INTERFACE clause and the PRIVATE IMPLEMENTA-TION subclauses (REPRESENTATION, AGGREGATION and ASSOCIATION) from the LOOM specification. The program unit defines the C++ *functions* corresponding to the method DEFINITIONS.

6.2   Class declarations in C++

The C++ programming language supports an aggregate type known as a *class*. The class is a composite of components which are distinct. The components of an aggregate class type can be both data items and functions.

Classes in C++ allow groups of objects to be created which share the same behaviour. This we achieve by providing class definitions for the creation of objects in the application. The class is a definition for the operations (functions) on objects of the class, and the representation (data). Generally, the representation is hidden from the user of objects of the class. Access to an object is controlled through the external interface consisting of functions.

Consider the class Employee introduced in Chapter 3. Each Employee instance has a name and a date of birth, recorded in the REPRESENTATION clause of the LOOM specification. In addition to the Employee constructor for the class, there are a number of publicised operations. The operations name? and age? are accessor operations used to enquire about the state of instances, while the operation changeName is a transformer operation used to set an instance with a new name value. An extract of the LOOM specification is:

```
CLASS Employee
WITH
PUBLIC INTERFACE
  Employee(aName :String, aDateOfBirth :Date)
  name? -> String
```

```
age? -> Integer
  changeName(aName:String)
PRIVATE IMPLEMENTATION
  REPRESENTATION
    theName           :String
    theDateOfBirth :Date
// ...

ENDCLASS Employee
```

Here is the C++ *class declaration* for `Employee` which would be given in the header file `employee.h`:

```
class Employee{
public:        //PUBLIC INTERFACE
  Employee(const CString& aName, const CDate&
    aDateOfBirth);                       //constructor
  CString  name(void) const;            //enquiry
  int  age(void) const;
  void  changeName(const CString& aName);
                                         //transformation

private:       //REPRESENTATION
  CString  theName;
  CDate    theDateOfBirth;
};
```

The reserved keyword `class` introduces a C++ class declaration consisting of the class head and the class body. The *class head* consists of the keyword `class` and the *class tag name*. The tag name serves as the type specifier for the user-defined class. Here, the tag name `Employee` has been introduced. The *class body* is enclosed with a pair of matching braces and followed by a semicolon. The class body introduces the *members* of the class and specifies the levels of information hiding. The keyword `public:` declares the subsequent members to have *public access*. The keyword `private:` declares the subsequent members to be private to that class and inaccessible to users of the class. The members of the class can be either *data members* – the representation for the class, or *function members* – the set of operations that may be applied to objects of that class.

6.2.1 *Data members*

The `REPRESENTATION` clause of a LOOM class specification introduces the basic properties of the class. This is presented as a list of property names and corresponding property types. In C++ these properties are given as *class data members*. Like their LOOM counterparts they list the data members and their types. In C++ the type name prefixes the data member name and the semicolon symbol terminates each data member declaration. Hence for class `Employee` we have:

```
#include "ccstring.h"
#include "ccdate.h"

class Employee {
  // ...
private:          //REPRESENTATION
  CString  theName;
  CDate    theDateOfBirth;
};
```

The LOOM classes `String`, `Date`, `Integer`, etc. have all been presented as fundamental LOOM classes. The LOOM class `Integer`, for example, readily translates into the equivalent fundamental C++ type (see below). The classes `String`, `Date`, `Time` have no direct C++ correspondence, but can be provided as a user-defined C++ class. For this example the type names `CString` and `CDate` are themselves user-defined C++ classes set out in their own respective header files. Hence the header file for class `Employee` will need to make this information known to the C++ compiler through the *preprocessor directive* `#include "ccstring.h"`. Here the compiler replaces the directive with the content of the header file `ccstring.h` in which the class declaration is given. For class `CString` we have a header file containing:

```
class CString {
  // ...
};
```

We have chosen to make these C++ class names different from their LOOM counterparts so that we can distinguish which we are referring to. It also avoids any name clashes with classes provided by future versions of the C++ language or versions offered by compiler vendors.

The simple classes such as `Integer` and `Decimal` are simply mapped into their corresponding C++ fundamental types, respectively `int` and `double` allowing either to be used interchangeably. This equivalencing is achieved by `typedef` statements in C++:

```
typedef int     Integer;
typedef double  Decimal;
```

The LOOM classes `String`, `Date` and `Time` are, respectively, the C++ class types `CString`, `CDate` and `CTime`. The class declarations are to be found in the corresponding header files (see Appendix D). The `Boolean` class in LOOM with the values `FALSE` and `TRUE` is expressed by the C++enumeration declaration:

```
enum Logical { LFALSE, LTRUE };
```

The type name `Logical` and the values `LFALSE` and `LTRUE` were introduced to avoid possible name clashes with compiler-supplied names such as `TRUE` and `FALSE`. The emerging ANSI standard for C++ will actually provide a language type for this purpose.

6.2.2 *Function members*

The public section of the Employee class declaration introduces the operations from the class in the form of C++ *function prototypes*. A function prototype presents the *signature* for the function giving the specification of the *formal argument types* and the function *return type*. Here, for example, the function changeName expects a CString argument and returns no value.

```
class Employee {
public:
  void    changeName(const CString& aName);
  CString name(void) const;
  // ...
};
```

The formal argument to the function is referred to as aName. The return type is introduced by the keyword void and denotes no value is returned by the function. Equally, the enquiry function name expects no arguments and returns a CString value. Since this function and the function age simply enquire of the state of an Employee object but do not modify it, the functions are qualified with the keyword const. The keyword will ensure that the function definition will not change any of the class data members.

Function names in C++ must take the form of an *identifier* which is a letter–digit combination starting with a letter. In C++ the underscore symbol '_' is considered a letter. However, an identifier cannot include a query symbol. Hence the LOOM operation name? has the query symbol removed when translated into C++.

As in LOOM, the C++ *constructor function* is used to properly initialise a class object when it is created. The constructor function is distinguished by having the same name as the class. In the Employee class the constructor requires two parameters to properly initialise the object, respectively a CString value for the employee's name and a CDate value for the date of birth.

When a class function is invoked, the actual arguments replace the corresponding formal arguments. For example, the Employee object created with:

```
Employee("John Savage", ...)  //incomplete
```

presents "John Savage" as the actual CString argument is used to initialise the corresponding formal argument aName. C++ supports three parameter-passing mechanisms and we must match these to the LOOM parameter specification.

Consider the constructor operation and the operation changeName from the LOOM class Employee:

```
Employee(aName :String, aDateOfBirth :Date)
changeName(aName :String)
```

For each parameter we could deploy the C++ argument-passing mechanism known as *pass by value*. The value of the actual argument is used to initialise the corresponding formal argument. Thereafter, the C++ function operates with that value for the formal argument. Such an arrangement would be presented with the C++ function prototypes:

```
Employee(CString aName, CDate aDateOfBirth);
  //constructor
void  changeName(CString aName);
  //transformation
```

For simple C++ types such as int this argument-passing strategy is quite appropriate. However, for class types such as CString, large amounts of memory may have to be copied and an alternative mechanism is required.

C++ also supports *pass by reference* semantics in which the formal argument acts as an alias for the actual argument. This aliasing means that any reference to the formal argument in the body of the function associates with the corresponding actual argument. The pass by reference argument passing allows the formal argument to access the value of the actual argument without the cost of making a copy, as is done through pass by value semantics. However, the pass by reference also allows the formal argument to modify the value of the actual argument, and since this is not normally what we require we further qualify the formal reference argument as const. Hence formal arguments aName and aDateOfBirth of the Employee class constructor are presented as constant reference parameter types. Similarly for the formal argument of function changeName:

```
Employee(const CString& aName, const CDate&
  aDateOfBirth);
  //constructor
void  changeName(const CString& aName);
  //transformation
```

In LOOM, formal parameters may be qualified with the mode keywords IN, OUT or INOUT. Parameters qualified as OUT or INOUT indicate that the actual parameter will be modified upon return from the operation. If no mode indication is presented, then IN is assumed. The modes OUT or INOUT give rise to reference arguments in C++, while IN results in constant references.

LOOM operation signatures carry the operation name, the return value if any, and any argument types. A C++ function is similarly described with a *function prototype*. In C++ the return type is named first. When the function has no return value, the keyword void is used. The arguments are presented in a similar fashion to LOOM but with the name and type reversed. If no arguments are present then either () or (void) is used as the formal argument list. Hence, for example, the LOOM operation signature:

```
changeName(aName :String)
```

is presented as the C++ function prototype:

```
void  changeName(const CString& aName);
```

in the class declaration. Note once more the use of pass by reference and the const qualifier. Clearly, changeName is a transformer operation changing the state of the receiving Employee object. On the other hand, name? and age? are both accessor operations. In LOOM we denote them with the query symbol as part of their name. This emphasis is repeated in C++ by the suffix const in the function prototypes. This keyword denotes that the operations leave the recipient object unchanged. Hence we have:

```
CString  name(void) const;
int  age(void) const;
```

LOOM parameters may also be specified as LINK parameters. A LINK parameter translates to a C++ pointer argument. A pointer in C++ is a variable that has the address of some other object. Consider the class Company which associates with one or more Employee objects through LINKs to these objects. The Company class has the operation hire by which a new Employee object is associated with the organisation:

```
CLASS Company
WITH
PUBLIC INTERFACE
  hire(anEmployee :Employee LINK)
  // ...
  ASSOCIATION
    theEmployees :POrderedCollection[Employee LINK]
  // ...
ENDCLASS Company
```

The C++ function prototype for hire would appear as:

```
void      hire(Employee* anEmployee);
```

with the pointer indicated by Employee*. When this function is called, the formal argument anEmployee is set to the value of the actual argument (which is an address).

6.3 Object declarations

In LOOM, instances of a class are presented using INSTANCE sentences of the form:

```
INSTANCE name :String("John Savage")
INSTANCE dob :Date(1, 1, 1973)
INSTANCE emp :Employee(name, dob)
INSTANCE pEmp :Employee LINK(name, dob)
```

The instances introduced with the identifiers name and dob are simple objects of classes String and Date respectively. The two objects are initialised with suitable values through the invocation of the corresponding constructor. These two values are then used to initialise two Employee objects. The distinction between the final two INSTANCE sentences is that the third introduces an

Employee instance, emp, in which the language system reserves the necessary memory. In the last example the identifier pEmp references a region of memory dynamically allocated at run time (see Section 4.9). The memory, in turn, is suitably initialised as an Employee object through its constructor call.

In C++ the corresponding *statements* are:

```
CString     name("John Savage");
CDate       dob(1, 1, 1973);
Employee    emp(name, dob);
Employee*   pEmp = new Employee(name, dob);
```

The statements are known as *declaration statements*. A declaration statement introducing an object instance is similar to defining a variable in a conventional programming language. Here, the variable dob refers to an object of type CDate, where the class name acts as the type name. When the object is created a region of memory is allocated by the language compiler sufficient to hold the values of its data members. The same logic applies to the variables name and emp.

In the final declaration statement the variable pEmp is introduced as a *pointer* to an Employee object. A pointer variable does not hold the object itself but rather the memory address of the object. The object's address is returned by the storage allocator new. The new operator is applied to a class name with appropriate constructor actual arguments. The pointer type delivered by the new operator corresponds to the instance type given. For example, new Employee (...) allocates storage for an Employee object. The type returned is an Employee pointer, denoted in C++ as Employee*. Similarly, new CDate (...) allocates storage for a CDate object and returns the address as a CDate* value.

Variables have an existence at run time. The duration of these objects is the period for which storage is allocated to them. Variables such as name, dob and emp are known as *local variables* (sometimes also known as *automatic* variables) – their definition occurs within a certain *scope* (such as a function body). The lifetime of these objects is that for which the scope is active. When the scope is exited, the storage space for the objects is automatically released (hence the descriptor automatic) and the variable is no longer accessible.

The variable pEmp is also subject to the same rules of scoping and duration. However, is the duration of the region of memory assigned by the storage allocator new is significant. Such dynamically created objects remain in existence until they are explicitly deallocated by a program statement or until the program terminates. The operator delete applied to a pointer variable returns the allocated space to the memory manager for subsequent recycling. The form of this statement is:

```
delete pEmp;
```

Once a region of memory has been freed, it should no longer be used by the program. The storage manager recycles the memory for use with subsequent calls to new.

6.4 **Mandatory profiles**

The C++ class declaration for `Employee` includes a constructor member for proper initialisation of objects of this type:

```
class Employee{
public:        //PUBLIC INTERFACE
  Employee(const CString& aName, const CDate&
    aDateOfBirth);
  //constructor
  // ...
};
```

We must, of course, provide two actual arguments to this constructor when creating objects of this type. It is sometimes useful to be able to create such an object and subsequently update one or more of its properties. Creating objects which are not properly initialised usually leads to many difficult programming problems. To ensure that an object is safely initialised we may provide a *default constructor* which is called if no initialising actual arguments are supplied by the user.

This can be expressed in one of two ways in C++. Either a constructor with no arguments is introduced into the class declaration, or a constructor with all its arguments given default values is specified. The latter could be incorporated into the `Employee` class above with:

```
class Employee {
public:        //PUBLIC INTERFACE
  Employee(const  CString& aName = "",
    const CDate& aDateOfBirth = CDate(1, 1, 1900));
  //constructor
  // ...
};
```

Here, if no arguments are given when an instance of type `Employee` is created, the name is assumed to be the empty string, and the date of birth is set to the beginning of the century. Hence we might have:

```
Employee john("John Savage", CDate(1, 1, 1973));
                                      //stack based
Employee* pKen = new Employee;
                                      //heap based ..
                                      //.. default values
```

Alternatively, the original class declaration may be augmented with a second (overloaded) class constructor with no arguments to deal with the declaration for pKen:

```
class Employee {
public:        //PUBLIC INTERFACE
  Employee(void);                        //default constructor
  Employee(const CString& aName, const CDate&
    aDateOfBirth);                       //constructor
  // ...
};
```

The default constructor for this class will require an appropriate behaviour. Here we might consider initialising the name of the `Employee` object to the empty string and the date of birth to, say, the beginning of the century. Whatever the default behaviour, this will have to be defined for users of the class. In a similar fashion the predefined `CString` class also has a default constructor. The behaviour is to initialise the new object with the empty string. By analogy, the default `CDate` constructor obtains the computer system date.

Either way we are now assured that a constructor is executed which guarantees that the data members of a class object are properly initialised. The corresponding LOOM constructs are:

```
CLASS Employee
WITH
PUBLIC INTERFACE
  Employee
  Employee(aName :String, aDateOfBirth :Date)
  // ...

ENDCLASS Employee
```

We noted in the previous section that to recover the space occupied by a dynamic object we must explicitly apply the `delete` operator. In fact, when an object with local duration goes out of scope or a dynamic object is explicitly deleted, then before the storage space is removed a class member function called the *destructor* is executed. The destructor complements the role of the constructor, performing any tidying up before the space for the object is destroyed.

If the author of the C++ class `Employee` does not specify a destructor function, then the compiler supplies one for free. This supplied destructor has no action. For simple user-defined types such as `Employee` this is exactly the behaviour we require, and we can accept the compiler-supplied destructor. However, as our class types become more complex we shall ultimately have cleaning-up tasks for the destructor.

In fact, to ensure that there is no ambiguity between the developer and the client for some class we will include into our class declaration a user-defined destructor, even when it imitates that supplied by the compiler. A destructor is introduced as a function with no arguments and, like the constructor, with no return type specified. Only one destructor may be given for a class and it has the class name prefixed with the tilde symbol (˜) as its name. This strange naming is used to connote the complementary action of the destructor with respect to the constructor.

```
class Employee {
public:     //PUBLIC INTERFACE
  Employee(void);                          //default constructor
  Employee(const CString& aName, const CDate&
    aDateOfBirth);                         //constructor
  ~Employee(void);                         //destructor
  // ...
};
```

Constructors, default constructors and destructors now form obligatory parts of our class declaration. That way users of the class are assured that there are no hidden special cases of which they have to be aware. This threesome form part of what we shall refer to as the *mandatory profile* of the class.

Where we wish to create a new object initialised with the values of an existing object we use a *copy constructor*. When a class has no such constructor defined, the compiler supplies one for free. The default behaviour for this constructor is to copy the data members of the existing object into the corresponding data members of the new object. Similarly, where we wish to assign to one object the values of another from the same class, we use the assignment operator. Again, the version automatically supplied by the compiler employs member-wise copying. Since all our classes, such as the Company and Employee classes, have simple data members, these simple shallow copy mechanisms are sufficient for our needs (see Section 8.8).

6.5 Message sending

Central to object oriented systems is the concept of message sending. In a world of objects, a sender requests some service from another object by sending that object a message. The object initiating the request is known as the sender while the object receiving the message is called the recipient. A message is dispatched by identifying the recipient object and the nominated message. Of course, an object is only prepared to engage in message passing if the message sent to it is one from the list of publicised operations. In LOOM this message sending is captured by the sentence:

```
SEND recipient THE MESSAGE message (expression, ...)
```

where recipient is the name of the object receiving the message. The expression list and associated parentheses are omitted when there are no message parameters. To send the Employee object emp the message requesting its age we write in LOOM:

```
SEND emp THE MESSAGE age?
```

To change the name of the Employee object, we write:

```
SEND emp THE MESSAGE changeName ("Joe Bloggs")
```

The transfer of these LOOM sentences into C++ statements is described by Figure 6.2 where the italicised *expression* is the C++ translation for the equivalent LOOM text. The recipient object and the message name are separated by the

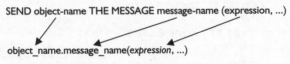

Figure 6.2 *Message passing transcription*

period symbol called the *class member selection operator*. For example, to change the name of the Employee object emp and to request its age we have:

```
emp.changeName("Joe Bloggs")
emp.age()
```

Notice, where no actual arguments are required as in the age? message we must still present the parentheses in C++. The latter message will return a value which will be used in some context by the sender. For example, we might capture the value as some initialised Integer in:

```
INSTANCE empAge :Integer(SEND emp THE MESSAGE age?)
```

which readily translates into the C++ code:

```
int empAge(emp.age());
```

If the LOOM object referenced in a SEND sentence represents an object LINK then, as we have seen, we have a C++ pointer. In the following two SEND sentences the recipient object will ultimately map to a C++ pointer variable.

```
INSTANCE pEmp :Employee LINK("Ken", Date(1, 1, 1970))
// ...
SEND pEmp THE MESSAGE age?
SEND pEmp THE MESSAGE changeName("Joe Bloggs")
```

Where the recipient object is a pointer variable, we replace the class member selection operator with the *pointer to class member selection operator* ->:

```
pEmp->age()
pEmp->changeName("Joe Bloggs")
```

When we send the assign message, the expectation is that the single message expression will be assigned to the recipient object. For example, following the execution of the sentences:

```
INSTANCE count :Integer(0)
SEND count THE MESSAGE assign(1 + count)
```

the count variable will have the value 1. In C++ we write:

```
int count(0);
count = 1 + count;
```

with the assignment represented by the *assignment operator* =. In C++ the expression to the right of the assignment operator is evaluated and the result assigned to the variable on the left. Here the expression 1 + count delivers the value 1 which is then assigned to the variable count overwriting its original value. When two pointers are assigned, both refer to the same object. Following:

```
qEmp = pEmp;
```

the pointer variable qEmp refers to the same region of memory referenced by pEmp. The messages:

```
pEmp->changeName("Jim Murray")
qEmp->changeName("Jim Murray")
```

then achieve the same effect.

Where the objects being assigned are class instances as in:

```
INSTANCE e1 : Employee("John Savage", CDate(1, 1, 1973))
INSTANCE e2 : Employee("Ken Barclay", CDate(2, 2, 1973))
SEND e2 THE MESSAGE assign(e1)
```

the assignment is performed by *member-wise copying* of the data members of the source object into the corresponding data members of the destination object. Hence if we send the message:

```
SEND e2 THE MESSAGE name?
```

the result is the string "John Savage".

The messages to display values on the output device and receive data from the input device are of the form:

```
SEND theScreen THE MESSAGE insert(expression)
SEND theKeyboard THE MESSAGE extract(anObject)
```

which from the above discussion would convert to:

```
theScreen.insert(expression)
theKeyboard.extract(anObject)
```

A C++ program including the header file iostream.h has access to two predefined stream objects called cout and cin, respectively, for output and input. These stream objects support the extraction and insertion operators, denoted as operator<< and operator>>. These overloaded operator symbols convert our LOOM sentences into:

```
cout.operator<<(expression)
cin.operator>>(anObject)
```

with the added convenience of presenting the statements as:

```
cout << expression
cin >> anObject
```

The latter form is far more common.

6.6 Method lookup

Consider the class Company described by:

```
CLASS Company
WITH
  PUBLIC INTERFACE
```

```
Company(aName :String)
name? -> String
// . . . . .
```

```
ENDCLASS Company
```

and the class `Employee` from Section 6.2. If we have the instances:

```
INSTANCE c1 :Company("Napier")
INSTANCE e1 :Employee("John Savage",
  CDate(1, 1, 1973))
```

then when we send the messages:

```
SEND c1 THE MESSAGE name?
SEND e1 THE MESSAGE name?
```

the recipient object knows to which class it belongs and hence which method is to be executed. Since `e1` is an instance of the `Employee` class, the method `name?` defined for that class is executed. Equally, since `c1` is a `Company` object, the method `name?` for that class is obeyed. For an object to respond to a message it has to look up the appropriate method. In conventional programming languages this is similar to the compiler binding a function call to the function body. Since the binding is performed by the compiler we describe the process as *static binding*.

For example, consider the message `name?` sent to the `Company` object `c1`. The compiler determines that there is an operation `name?` from the class `Company` and generates the appropriate program to execute the code for that method.

6.7 Method bodies

A method body describes the computational processes involved in the method. The processing may involve any local objects, the formal parameters of the method, and the features of the class specified in the `PUBLIC INTERFACE` and `PRIVATE IMPLEMENTATION` clauses. The local objects of the method are introduced by `INSTANCE` sentences. The formal parameters are named in the formal parameter list of the method definition. Like local objects, formal parameters have local scope. Since the method body is introduced as part of the class declaration, the class attributes detailed in the `PUBLIC INTERFACE` and `PRIVATE IMPLEMENTATION` clauses are accessible to the sentences of the method body.

A method in LOOM is converted to a C++ *function definition* consisting of a function header and a function body. A function body is presented in C++ as a program *block*, enclosed by the brace pair { and } acting for the function body. The block is prefixed by the function prototype as described earlier, giving the function header. Hence an outline for the method `changeName` of class `Employee` is:

```
void Employee::changeName(const CString& aName)
```

```
{
  // ...
}
```

Observe how the function name is prefixed by `Employee::`. The symbol `::` is known as the *scope resolution operator* and specifies in this case that the function belongs to the `Employee` class. This notation is necessary since there may exist in some other class (such as `Company`) another function with the same name.

A function with the same name appearing in different classes is known as *overloading*. This offers the convenience of reusing the name rather than inventing distinct names for what is essentially the same task. Hence we might send the message `changeName` to both an `Employee` instance and a `Company` instance. Overloading also applies to member functions of the same class provided that their signatures are distinct. In class `Employee` we might have a second version for the constructor member function provided that the number or type of formal arguments is different from that already given, e.g. the parameterised and default constructors introduced earlier.

A method body consists of a number of sentences. These are translated into their C++ statement equivalents. For example, the method to determine the age of an `Employee` object is given below. To simplify the discussion the algorithm has been kept minimal.

```
METHOD age? -> Integer AS
  INSTANCE today : Date
  INSTANCE todayYear :
    Integer (SEND today THE MESSAGE year?)
  INSTANCE dobYear : Integer (SEND
    theDateOfBirth THE MESSAGE year?)
  RETURN todayYear - dobYear
ENDMETHOD age?
```

Converting the `INSTANCE` sentences as above and the `RETURN` sentence into its C++ equivalent gives:

```
int Employee::age(void) const
{
  CDate today;
  int todayYear(today.year());
  int dobYear(theDateOfBirth.year());
  return (todayYear - dobYear);
}
```

When an object is created it is good practice to initialise the data member values. In LOOM and C++ we provide this through a constructor. In C++, when an object is created the constructor function for the class is invoked to perform the necessary initialisation. All constructor functions of a class are distinguished by having the class name. The method body for the LOOM constructor might (incorrectly) copy the argument values into the corresponding REPRESENTA-TION values through the `assign` message:

```
METHOD Employee(aName :String, aDateOfBirth :Date)
AS
  SEND theName THE MESSAGE assign(aName)
  SEND theDateOfBirth THE MESSAGE
    assign(aDateOfBirth)
ENDMETHOD Employee
```

The C++ constructor derived from this specification is:

```
Employee::Employee(const CString& aName,
  const CDate& aDateOfBirth)
{
  theName        =aName;
  theDateOfBirth =aDateOfBirth;
}
```

A C++ constructor function has a particular role as a class member function. Syntactically it is distinguished by carrying the class name and by not having a return value specified. Further, when we consider its execution we recognise that the data members `theName` and `theDateOfBirth` must first exist before values can be assigned to them. Effectively INSTANCE sentences for both `theName` and `theDateOfBirth` have been first established with, presumably, some initial values given. These initial values are then overwritten with the assigned values. We can bypass some of this process by specifying that the initial values will be those given by the argument values. This is done in a *member initialisation list*, peculiar to a C++ constructor function. The list names the data members and their initial values (given in parentheses), and is set off from the function header by a colon symbol. The function body is then empty since all the work is done by the initialisation phase.

```
Employee::Employee(const CString& aName,
  const CDate& aDateOfBirth)
  :theName(aName),
  theDateOfBirth(aDateOfBirth)
{}
```

To specify this special processing in LOOM we use the standard message `initialise` in place of `assign`. This message is only appropriate for constructor methods and is the message sent to class properties.

```
METHOD Employee(aName :String, aDateOfBirth :Date)
AS
  SEND theName THE MESSAGE initialise(aName)
  SEND theDateOfBirth THE MESSAGE
    initialise(aDateOfBirth)
ENDMETHOD Employee
```

In Section 6.4 we identified that the mandatory profile of a C++ class should include a default constructor. The default constructor must ensure that the data members have valid values. For example, we might choose to initialise the data members to an empty string for the name and the current system date for the date of birth:

```
Employee::Employee(void)
 :theName(""),
 theDateOfBirth()    //note implicit call of
 // default Date constructor
 {}
```

This code is derived from the LOOM script:

```
METHOD Employee
 SEND theName THE MESSAGE initialise("")
 SEND thedateOfBirth THE MESSAGE initialise
ENDMETHOD Employee
```

The destructor has no action to perform. Generally we only find user-defined tasks for the destructor when one of the data members is a pointer.

```
Employee::~Employee(void)
{}
```

Program 6.1 unites all these concepts. The header file employee.h presents the specification for class Employee. Since the Employee class uses the types CString and CDate, also defined as C++ classes, these header files are incorporated into the program files by the language #include mechanism. Here, the named files are read by the compiler and replace the #include statement.

The corresponding program unit employee.cpp is the code file giving the method bodies as C++ functions. Since these functions are in the scope of their corresponding class the file must also #include its own header file.

The program creates two Employee objects, respectively e1 and e2. The object known as e2 is sent the message to change its name. The name and age of each object is then displayed. The program objects are established in the run method of class Application. The Employee object e2 is a local instance which the run-time system implicitly deallocates at the end of the method (C++ function). For illustrative purposes, the second object e1 is a dynamically allocated object for which the function takes responsibility for its deletion. The program run produces the output:

```
Kenneth Barclay, 22
John Savage, 23
```

The LOOM specification for this Application class is given below. The listings for it and the C++ code were produced by the design tool ROME introduced in Chapter 10. In particular note the method body for run:

```
METHOD run
AS
 //
 // Create two instances, one local, one dynamic
 //
 INSTANCE e1 :
  Employee LINK("John Savage", Date(2, 2, 1972))
 INSTANCE e2 :
```

```
Employee("Ken Barclay", Date(1, 1, 1973))
//
// Change one name
//
SEND e2 THE MESSAGE changeName("Kenneth Barclay")
//
// ... and see the effects
//
SEND theScreen THE MESSAGE
  insert(SEND e2 THE MESSAGE name?)
SEND theScreen THE MESSAGE insert(", ")
SEND theScreen THE MESSAGE
  insert(SEND e2 THE MESSAGE age?)
SEND theScreen THE MESSAGE insert("\n")
SEND theScreen THE MESSAGE
  insert(SEND e1 THE MESSAGE name?)
SEND theScreen THE MESSAGE insert(", ")
SEND theScreen THE MESSAGE
  insert(SEND e1 THE MESSAGE age?)
SEND theScreen THE MESSAGE insert("\n")
//
// Clean up the storage with a C++ code insert
//
//> delete e1;
ENDMETHOD run
```

The final LOOM sentence in this method is a marked-up comment. Any comment consisting of the leading //> is identified by ROME as a comment which is to be translated into C++. Since ROME has no sentence to remove a dynamically allocated object from memory, we rely on the appropriate C++ code.

Program 6.1

```
#include "application.h"

int main()
{
  Application app;
  app.run();

  return 0;
}
```

For the Application class we have the following two listings. In the header file the class declaration is enclosed within the text:

```
#ifndef APPLICATION
  #define APPLICATION

#endif
```

These are known as *preprocessor directives*. They indicate that when the compiler is compiling a code file and is instructed to read this header file application.h for the first time, the compiler should note that the symbolic name APPLICATION has been defined (#define directive). If during the compilation of the same code file the compiler is asked to read the header file for a second time, then since APPLICATION is already defined, the compiler should skip around the class declaration surrounded by this *conditional compilation* logic. All other header files are treated in a similar manner.

The preprocessor directives #include "loom.h" and #include "ccstring.h" specify that the content of the named header files (here, loom.h and ccstring.h) be read. The file loom.h contains the typedefs for Integer and Decimal (see Section 6.2.1). Header file ccstring.h contains the C++ class declaration for the CString class.

```
/////////////////////////////////////////////////////
//
//  application.h
// ROME Copyright (c) Richard McMahon. 1993, 1994.
// ROME Copyright (c) Ken Barclay 1995.
// Generated On December 28, 1995 At 6:23:31.52 pm
//
/////////////////////////////////////////////////////

#ifndef APPLICATION
  #define APPLICATION

  #include "loom.h"
  #include "ccstring.h"

  class Application {
  public:     // PUBLIC INTERFACE
                             Application(void);
    void                     run(void);

};

#endif

//-- End Specification ----------------------


/////////////////////////////////////////////////////
//
//  application.cpp
// ROME Copyright (c) Richard McMahon. 1993, 1994.
// ROME Copyright (c) Ken Barclay 1995.
// Generated On December 28, 1995 At 6:23:31.52 pm
//
/////////////////////////////////////////////////////

#include "Employee.h"
#include "Employee.h"
#include "Application.h"
```

```
Application::Application(void)
{
}

void
Application::run(void)
{
  //
  // Create two instances, one local, one dynamic
  //
  Employee* e1 = new Employee("John Savage",
    CDate(2, 2, 1972));
  Employee e2("Ken Barclay", CDate(1, 1, 1973));
  //
  // Change one name
  //
  e2.changeName("Kenneth Barclay");
  //
  // ... and see the effects
  //
  cout << e2.name();
  cout << ", ";
  cout << e2.age();
  cout << "\n";
  cout << e1->name();
  cout << ", ";
  cout << e1->age();
  cout << "\n";
  //
  //Clean up the storage
  //
  delete e1;
}


//-- End Implementation --------------------
```

The code file for the Application class uses the preprocessor to include the content of the two header files application.h and employee.h. The former is required since the code file contains the function definitions from the Application class. The latter is needed since the run method introduces two instances of the Employee class.

```
/////////////////////////////////////////////////////
//
//  employee.h
// ROME Copyright (c) Richard McMahon. 1993, 1994.
// ROME Copyright (c) Ken Barclay 1995.
// Generated On December 28, 1995 At 6:23:31.58 pm
//
/////////////////////////////////////////////////////

#ifndef EMPLOYEE
```

```
    #define EMPLOYEE

#include "loom.h"
#include "ccstring.h"
#include "ccdate.h"


class Employee {
public:  // PUBLIC INTERFACE
  Employee(const CString& aName, const CDate&
    aDateOfBirth);
  Employee(void);
  CString  name(void) const;
  Integer  age(void) const;
  void  changeName(const CString& aName);

private:  // REPRESENTATION
  CString  theName;
  CDate  theDateOfBirth;

};
#endif

//-- End Specification ----------------------


///////////////////////////////////////////////////
//
//  employee.cpp
// ROME Copyright (c) Richard McMahon. 1993, 1994.
// ROME Copyright (c) Ken Barclay 1995.
// Generated On December 28, 1995 At 6:23:31.58 pm
//
///////////////////////////////////////////////////

#include "Employee.h"

Employee::Employee(const CString& aName,
  const CDate& aDateOfBirth)
  :theName(aName),
    theDateOfBirth(aDateOfBirth)
{

}

Employee::Employee(void)
  :theName(""),
    theDateOfBirth()
{

}
CString
Employee::name(void) const
```

```
{
    return theName;
}

Integer
Employee::age(void) const
{
    CDate today;
    Integer todayYear = today.year();
    Integer dobYear = theDateOfBirth.year();
    return todayYear - dobYear;
}
void
Employee::changeName(const CString& aName)
{
    theName = aName;
}
```

```
//-- End Implementation --------------------
```

The `Employee` class header file uses the preprocessor to include the class declarations for `CString` and `CDate`. These headers are necessary since the `Employee` class includes a `CString` and a `CDate` data member. The code file, once again, needs to include its own header file.

Note again the C++ `delete` statement in the `run` function of the `Application` class. This is the complement of the new operation, and takes a pointer as an argument. The object referenced by this pointer is removed from memory and may be recycled by the storage allocator. When the object is deleted, the destructor function is executed. A program which allocates memory through the new operation must ensure that that space is ultimately removed. Further, when the space is no longer required by a program it should be removed, otherwise sections of memory accumulate as garbage, consuming memory which could be reassigned by the memory manager.

6.7.1 *Flow of control*

Sections 3.3.1 to 3.3.3 introduced the flow of control primitives of LOOM (sequence, selection and iteration). Selection is given by the `IF` sentence and iteration by the `WHILE` sentence.

As we have already shown, LOOM sentences translate to C++ statements. Sequential LOOM sentences map on to sequential C++ statements. C++ requires an explicit statement terminator, the semicolon " ; " symbol.

The `IF` sentence in LOOM has a basic form and a number of extensions to that form. At its simplest we have:

```
IF condition THEN
    sentence1
```

```
    sentence2
    ...
ENDIF
```

The corresponding C++ code is:

```
if(condition){
  statement1;
  statement2;
  ...
}
```

where *condition, statement1, statement2* are the C++ equivalents for the respective LOOM code. Note how the C++ keyword if is given in lowercase; how the condition is enclosed in parentheses " (" and ") "; and how the group of statements is compounded by the braces "{" and "}". In particular, observe that there is no terminating semicolon following the final brace symbol.

In LOOM if only one sentence was given between THEN and ENDIF this would give rise to the following C++:

```
if(condition){
  statement1;
}
```

which we are permitted in C++ to simplify to:

```
if(condition)
  statement1;
```

The ELSE clause in an IF sentence is introduced to offer an alternative logical path:

```
IF condition THEN
  sentence1a
  sentence1b
  ...
ELSE
  sentence2a
  sentence2b
  ...
ENDIF
```

The C++ arising from this code is much as we might expect:

```
if(condition){
  statement1a;
  statement1b;
  ...
}else{
  statement2a;
  statement2b;
  ...
}
```

The final extension to the IF sentence in LOOM is the ELSEIF clause which may be repeated any number of times. Its corresponding C++ is:

```
IF condition1 THEN              if(condition1) {
  sentence1a                      statement1a;
  sentence1b                      statement1b;
  ...                             ...
ELSEIF condition2 THEN          } else if(condition2) {
  sentence2a                      statement2a;
  sentence2b                      statement2b;
  ...                             ...
ELSEIF condition3 THEN          } else if(condition3) {
  sentence3a                      statement3a;
  sentence3b                      statement3b;
  ...                             ...
ELSE                            } else {
  sentence9a                      statement9a;
  sentence9b                      statement9b;
  ...                             ...
ENDIF                           }
```

As a full example we might consider the activity selection logic appearing in the run method of the Application class at the end of Section 5.3. It appeared as:

```
// Activity selection
IF theChoice == 1 THEN
  SEND theEditor THE MESSAGE edit
ELSEIF theChoice == 2 THEN
  SEND theMailBox THE MESSAGE post
ELSEIF theChoice == 3 THEN
  SEND theMailBox THE MESSAGE displayMail?
ELSEIF theChoice == 4 THEN
  SEND theAccountManager THE MESSAGE display Account?
ELSEIF theChoice == 5 THEN
  SEND theAccountManager THE MESSAGE
    displayUsers?
ELSEIF theChoice == 6 THEN
  SEND theAccountManager THE MESSAGE addUser
ELSEIF theChoice == 7 THEN
  SEND theHci THE MESSAGE
    display("Mail system: disconnecting")
  SEND disconnect THE MESSAGE assign(TRUE)
ELSE
  SEND theHci THE MESSAGE
    display("Mail system: closing down the system")
  SEND disconnect THE MESSAGE assign(TRUE)
  SEND terminate THE MESSAGE assign(TRUE)
ENDIF
```

The resulting C++ code is:

```
if(theChoice == 1) {
  theEditor.edit();
} else if(theChoice == 2) {
  theMailBox.post();
```

```
    } else if (theChoice == 3) {
      theMailBox.displayMail();
    } else if (theChoice == 4) {
      theAccountManager.displayAccount();
    } else if (theChoice == 5) {
      theAccountManager.displayUsers();
    } else if (theChoice == 6) {
      theAccountManager.addUser();
    } else if (theChoice == 7) {
      theHci.display("Mail system: disconnecting");
      disconnect = LTRUE;
    } else {
      theHci.display('Mail system: closing down the
        system');
      disconnect = LTRUE;
      terminate = LTRUE;
    }
```

The WHILE sentence in LOOM realises the iteration flow of control primitive. Its structure and that of its corresponding C++ is:

```
WHILE condition DO                while(condition) {
  sentence1                         statement1;
  sentence2                         statement2;
  ...                               ...
ENDWHILE                          }
```

Again, borrowing the control logic from Section 5.3:

```
// User identity input loop.
INSTANCE validId : Boolean (FALSE)
WHILE validId == FALSE DO
  INSTANCE theUserId : String("")
  SEND theHci THE MESSAGE display("Enter user identity: ")
  SEND theUserId THE MESSAGE
  assign(SEND theHci THE MESSAGE userId?)
  IF (SEND theAccountManager THE MESSAGE
    validUser?(theUserId)) THEN
  SEND validId THE MESSAGE assign(TRUE)
  ENDIF
ENDWHILE  // User identity loop.
```

we have the following C++:

```
Logical  validId(LFALSE);
while(validId == LFALSE) {
  CString theUserId("");
  theHci.display("Enter user identity: ");
  theUserId = theHci.userId();
  if(theAccountManager.validUser())
    validId = LTRUE;
}
```

6.8 Associations

We have already identified (Chapter 2) that objects do not exist in isolation but enter into relationships with each other and that they co-operate with each other by message passing. For example, car ownership between a `Person` object and a `Car` object would be represented by the class diagram given in Figure 6.3.

Figure 6.3 *Person/Car association*

If the execution scenarios determine that traversal across the association is always from the `Person` object to the `Car` object then we include in the `Person` class a `LINK` to the associated `Car`. The LOOM specifications might appear as:

```
CLASS Car
WITH
PUBLIC INTERFACE
  Car(aMake :String, aModel :String)
  make? -> String
  model? -> String
PRIVATE IMPLEMENTATION
  REPRESENTATION
  theMake :String
  theModel :String
AGGREGATIONS
  NONE
ASSOCIATIONS
  NONE
DEFINITIONS
  METHOD Car(aMake :String, aModel :String)
  AS
    SEND theMake THE MESSAGE initialise(aMake)
    SEND theModel THE MESSAGE initialise(aModel)
  ENDMETHOD Car

  METHOD make? -> String AS
    RETURN theMake
  ENDMETHOD make?

  METHOD model? -> String AS
    RETURN theModel
  ENDMETHOD make?

ENDCLASS Car


CLASS Person
WITH
```

```
PUBLIC INTERFACE
  Person(aName :String)
  name? -> String
  carMake? -> String
  setVehicleLink(aCar :Car LINK)
PRIVATE IMPLEMENTATION
  REPRESENTATION
    theName :String
  AGGREGATIONS
    NONE
  ASSOCIATION
    theVehicle :Car LINK
  DEFINITIONS
    METHOD Person(aName :String)
    AS
      SEND theName THE MESSAGE initialise(aName)
      SEND theVehicle THE MESSAGE initialise(NIL)
    ENDMETHOD Person

    METHOD name? -> String AS
      RETURN theName
    ENDMETHOD name?

    METHOD carMake? -> String AS
      RETURN SEND theVehicle THE MESSAGE make?
    ENDMETHOD carMake?

    METHOD setVehicleLink(aCar :Car LINK) AS
      SEND theVehicle THE MESSAGE assign(aCar)
    ENDMETHOD setVehicleLink

ENDCLASS Person
```

In the `Person` class, the `ASSOCIATION` field `theVehicle` provides the `LINK` to the single `Car` object that represents the vehicle owned by the `Person` object. The field name used is taken from the corresponding role name on the association in the class diagram. Since any `Person` object will have such a `LINK`, any operation supported by the `Car` class may be sent through that `LINK`. Hence the implementation for the operation `carMake?` of the `Person` class, which asks a `Person` object which make of car it owns, is readily implemented by sending the appropriate message to the `Car`.

A LOOM LINK is realised as a C++ pointer. A `Car` pointer is expressed in C++ as `Car*`. A variable defined as a `Car*` holds the address of a `Car` object. The `Car` object may be any existing instance, either created on the run-time stack or on the heap:

```
Car  c1("Renault", "Safrane");
  // current vehicle
Car*  c2 = new Car("Daimler", "Sovereign");
  //heap object
Car*  c3 = &c1;  // address of another
```

Note how in the final definition the pointer c3 is given the address of an existing

Car object, and is described in C++ by prefixing the object c1 with the *address operator* &. Our designs do not permit this construction in order to make our programs more robust.

To send a message to the object referenced in a program by a pointer involves dereferencing the pointer to obtain the object and then applying the member access operator. This is expressed as:

```
(*c3).make()
```

The class pointer operator simplifies the syntax of this message sending. The operator, denoted as ->, is used with:

```
c3->make()
```

Finally, observe how the LOOM signature for the operation setVehicle-Link has the signature setVehicleLink(aCar : Car LINK). The parameter aCar is an IN parameter suggesting that the object it is pointing to is not subject to modification. When we translate this operation into its C++ function member we arrive at:

```
void Person::setVehicleLink(Car* aCar)
{
  theVehicle = aCar;
}
```

Now had we used the parameter type Car LINK as the mapping for the C++ argument const Car*, the C++ compiler would have complained that we were assigning a constant object pointer (aCar) to a non-constant object pointer (theVehicle), potentially bypassing the security offered by using the const qualifier. Assuming the declarations:

```
Car c4 = new Car("Renault", "Safrane");
Person p1 = new Person("Ken Barclay");
```

in an application, the we might establish a link with:

```
p1->setVehicle(c4);
```

We express this solution in Program 6.2. Here, a Person object and a Car object are created, with the latter associated with the former by setting the LINK through the message setVehicleLink. The program's output is:

```
Ken Barclay owns: Renault
```

The listing for this program and others from this chapter are given in Appendix F.

The Person class holds a data member which is the address of a Car object. To use this class name when introducing the pointer, either we need to include the header file declaring this class or we give a forward reference to the class. We choose to do the latter to avoid having to read this file when only the class name is required. A forward reference does not permit objects of the class to be introduced. We are, however, permitted to use both pointers and reference types to the named class. An extract of the Person class header file is:

```
#ifndef PERSON
#define PERSON

#include "loom.h"
#include "ccstring.h"

class Car;  //forward references

class Person {
public:  //PUBLIC INTERFACE
// ...
private:  //REPRESENTATION
  CString  theName;

private:  //ASSOCIATION
  Car*  theVehicle;

};

#endif

//-- End Specification -----------------------
```

The `Person` class has a pointer member and this demands a fully defined mandatory profile to ensure the pointer is correctly initialised. Here, we must decide what the constructors, the destructor and the assignment operator should do with this value. Since the class `Person` has a method `setVehicle-Link` to set a value into this pointer, we have the constructors give this member a suitable default value which in LOOM is the value `NIL` and in C++ is the null pointer `NULL`. Since the constructors are not responsible for creating the `Car` object to which the data member `theVehicle` is set to point, correspondingly the destructor does not delete the object. In fact, the `Car` object is both created and deleted in the `Application` method `run`.

6.9 Associations and aggregations

Consider, now, the `Company–Employee` relationship illustrated in Chapter 2. Here, there is a one-to-many relationship between a `Company` object and the `Employee` objects. The arrangement is shown in Figure 6.4. A `Company` object can be asked for its name, sent the message to hire an `Employee` object, and asked if an `Employee` with some given name is employed by the company.

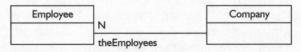

Figure 6.4 *Association*

The following LOOM specification for the Company class gives the necessary details.

```
CLASS Company
WITH
PUBLIC INTERFACE
  Company(aName :String)
  hire(anEmployee :Employee LINK INOUT)
  fire(anEmployee :Employee LINK INOUT)
  displayEmployees?
  changeName(aName :String)
  name? -> String
  averageAge? -> Integer
PRIVATE IMPLEMENTATION
  REPRESENTATION
    theName :String
  AGGREGATIONS NONE
  ASSOCIATIONS
    theEmployees :POrderedCollection[Employee LINK]
      INVERSE OF theEmployer
  DEFINITIONS
    METHOD Company(aName :String)
    AS
      SEND theName THE MESSAGE initialise(aName)
      SEND theEmployees THE MESSAGE
        initialise (DEFAULTSIZE, UNMANAGED)
    ENDMETHOD Company

    METHOD hire(anEmployee :Employee LINK INOUT)
    AS
      SEND anEmployee THE MESSAGE hiredBy(me)
      SEND theEmployees THE MESSAGE add(anEmployee)
    ENDMETHOD hire

    METHOD fire(anEmployee :Employee LINK INOUT)
    AS
      SEND anEmployee THE MESSAGE fired
      SEND theEmployees THE MESSAGE remove(anEmployee)
    ENDMETHOD fire

    METHOD displayEmployees?
    AS
      SEND theScreen THE MESSAGE insert("Company: ")
      SEND theScreen THE MESSAGE insert(theName)
      SEND theScreen THE MESSAGE insert("\n")
      FOREACH emp :Employee LINK IN theEmployees DO
        SEND emp THE MESSAGE display?
      ENDFOREACH
    ENDMETHOD displayEmployees?

    METHOD changeName(aName :String)
    AS
      SEND theName THE MESSAGE assign(aName)
```

```
ENDMETHOD changeName

METHOD name? -> String
AS
  RETURN theName
ENDMETHOD name?

METHOD averageAge? -> Integer
AS
INSTANCE totalAge : Integer(0)
FOREACH anEmployee : Employee LINK IN
  theEmployees DO
 INSTANCE employeeAge :
  Integer(SEND anEmployee THE MESSAGE age?)
 SEND totalAge THE MESSAGE
  assign(totalAge + employeeAge)
ENDFOREACH
 INSTANCE avAge :
  Integer(totalAge / SEND theEmployees THE MESSAGE
  cardinality?)
 RETURN avAge
ENDMETHOD averageAge?
```

ENDCLASS Company

The ASSOCIATION clause manages the one-to-many relationship with the Employee class. This association is a collection of Employee LINKs, linking the Company object to many Employee objects. The collection may be chosen as an appropriate container. Where, for example, the Employee objects are required in alphabetical order, a PSortedList might be used. Here, no special ordering is required other than the order the elements are entered into the container, and so a POrderedCollection is used (the P prefix reminds us that C++ pointers are involved).

Effectively we can view the container POrderedCollection (see Appendix B) as a LOOM specification of the form:

```
CLASS POrderedCollection[TYPE]
WITH
OPERATIONS
 POrderedCollection(anInitialSize : Integer,
 aManagementScheme : Integer)
 add(anElement : TYPE)
 // ...

ENDCLASS POrderedCollection
```

The notation POrderedCollection[TYPE] introduces a class specification for the class POrderedCollection which is generalised to handle any type of element. Rather than describe a collection of Employees and a collection of Companies and a collection of Integers, etc., we describe a collection in terms of some arbitrary type named TYPE. The class POrderedCollection is a template for a family of collection containers. The specification is *generic* since it is not defined in terms of any particular type of element in the collection. A particular version is described by any one of:

```
POrderedCollection[Employee LINK]
POrderedCollection[Company LINK]
POrderedCollection[Integer LINK]
```

The `POrderedCollection` container supports an operation `add` which incorporates a new element into the collection. This operation's signature specifies that some `TYPE` value is required. When we *instantiate* the `POrdered-Collection` container to, say, a `POrderedCollection [Employee LINK]` with `TYPE` replaced with `Employee LINK`, the version of operation `add` we arrive at after instantiation is:

```
add(anElement : Employee LINK)
```

The `POrderedCollection` constructor requires two `Integer` parameters. The first specifies the initial size for the container. If we add one more item over this size, the container automatically resizes itself to make room for the new incoming element. That way, we need not concern ourselves with the storage management of the container. Like any good class specification we have objects fully responsible for their behaviour. The second `Integer` parameter is one of the symbolic values MANAGED or UNMANAGED. The value MANAGED specifies that when the `POrderedCollection` instance is removed from memory, then so too must be the elements maintained by the container. The value UNMANAGED determines that the container is to have no responsibility for the elements under its care (see Appendix B).

The choice of UNMANAGED for the second `POrderedCollection` constructor parameter is a result of the association relationship between the `Company` object and the many `Employee` objects. With an association two independent objects are related but neither is responsible for the creation and deletion of the other. In this case the `POrderedCollection` container takes no responsibility for ensuring that the `Employee` objects for which it is given responsibility are removed when it is itself deleted.

In C++ the corresponding class declaration for the generic `POrdered-Collection` container is:

```
template <class TYPE>
class POrderedCollection {
public:
  POrderedCollection(int, int);
  void  add(TYPE anElement);
  // ...
};
```

where the arbitrary type name `TYPE` is introduced in the *template* clause.

The C++ header file arising from the specification from the `Company` class is:

```
class Company {
public:  // PUBLIC INTERFACE
  Company(const CString& aName);
  void hire(Employee* anEmployee);
```

```
void fire(Employee* anEmployee);
void displayEmployees(void) const;
void changeName(const String& aName);
CString name(void) const;
Integer averageAge(void) const;

private: // REPRESENTATION
CString theName;

private: // ASSOCIATIONS
POrderedCollection<Employee*> theEmployees;

// ...

};
```

The constructor for class Company must initialise both the property theName and the aggregation theEmployees. In LOOM we describe this by the code at the start of this section. In C++ this gives rise to:

```
Company::Company(const CString& aName)
 : theName(aName),
 theEmployees(DEFAULTSIZE, UNMANAGED)
{}
```

The LOOM specification for the method displayEmployees? is given above. In a sense, the FOREACH sentence is another abstraction which we call an *iterator abstraction* or simply *iterator*. An iterator permits us to visit all the members of some container without knowledge of the container's representation. Such iterators are necessary since the container types exhibit information hiding by concealing their implementation. The FOREACH clause is effectively an abbreviation for the following (using the FOREACH sentence in method display-Employees?):

```
INSTANCE empIterator :
 PIterator[Employee LINK](theEmployees)
WHILE (SEND empIterator THE MESSAGE isExhausted?) == FALSE DO
 INSTANCE emp :
  Employee LINK(SEND empIterator THE MESSAGE selection?)
 SEND emp THE MESSAGE display?
 SEND empIterator THE MESSAGE advance
ENDWHILE
```

The first sentence creates an instance of type PIterator[Employee LINK] which is an iterator to visit all the Employee LINKs in some container. The iterator is introduced with the name empIterator, and iterates across the elements in the container theEmployees. The WHILE sentence terminates when the iterator object empIterator is sent the message isExhausted? and gets the TRUE value. While isExhausted? returns the value FALSE, then there are more elements to process. At the end of the WHILE loop the iterator empIterator is requested to advance to the next item in the container. At the start of the loop we introduce an Employee LINK object emp initialised by the value obtained by sending `empIterator` the message to fetch the next `selection?` from the collection.

In C++ this translates into:

```
void Company::displayEmployees(void) const
{
  cout << "Company: ";
  cout << theName;
  cout << "\n";
  PIterator< Employee* > empIterator(theEmployees);
  while (empIterator.isExhausted() == LFALSE ) {
    Employee* emp = empIterator.selection();
    emp->display();
    empIterator.advance();
  }
}
```

These ideas are captured in Program 6.3 (see Appendix F). Here we create an instance of class `Company` then hire a number of `Employees`. The `Company` object is then requested to present its name and its total salary bill. If we run this program with the data set:

```
Barclay 2500
Beddie 3000
Savage 2200
Kennedy 2400
ZZZ 0
```

then the resulting input and output is:

```
Enter staff list:
Barclay 2500
Beddie 3000
Savage 2200
Kennedy 2400
ZZZ 0
Staff bill for Napier is 10100
```

Notice how in the `Employee` class there is one function introduced to support the use of the `POrderedCollection` container. The function `lessThan` compares two `Employee` objects by comparing the name of the first with the name of the second. The container provides, for illustration, the operation `isMember` which determines if the argument object is a member of the collection. This operation obviously involves object comparisons (here, `Employee` objects) and is expressed with the `lessThan` function.

Where some kind of non-indexable collection such as `PSet` is used a second function is required in the object class (here, `Employee`). The storage mechanism employed by the non-indexed `PSet` container requires that each object must supply a random value to determine where, in the internal storage structure used, the object is positioned. The `hashValue` function delivers some random value from an `Employee` object and might, for example, use the `hashValue` function on the Employee's name (a CString data member), already defined for the class CString (see Appendix D).

```
int Employee::hashValue(void) const
{
  return theName.hashValue();
}
```

6.10 Two-way traversal

Associations can involve a two-way traversal of the relationship between the objects involved. For example, in Figure 6.4 an employee object may be interrogated for the name of its employer object. In addition to the employer sending each employee the message name?, we might have an employee object sending the employer object the name? message. To achieve this each Employee object will require a LINK to the Company object acting as that person's employer. From Chapter 3, we know that pairs of matching LINKs must be properly maintained, and this we express with the INVERSE OF clause.

```
CLASS Employee
WITH
PUBLIC INTERFACE
  setCompanyLink(aCompany :Company LINK)
  // ...
  ASSOCIATIONS
  theEmployer :Company LINK INVERSE OF theEmployees
  // ...

ENDCLASS Employer


CLASS Company
WITH
PUBLIC INTERFACE
  hire(anEmployee :Employee LINK INOUT)
  // ...
ASSOCIATIONS
  theEmployees :POrderedCollection[Employee LINK]
    INVERSE OF theEmployer
DEFINITIONS
  METHOD hire(anEmployee :Employee LINK INOUT) AS
    SEND anEmployee THE MESSAGE setCompanyLink(me)
    SEND theEmployees THE MESSAGE add(anEmployee)
  ENDMETHOD hire
  // ...

ENDCLASS Company
```

Observe how we ensure the integrity of the LINKs by linking the employee and the organisation at effectively one and the same time. Both LINKs are established by the `hire` method of the `Company` class. Inverses must be set in this way, otherwise separating the operations across, say, functions in the classes `Company` and `Employee` invites the possibility that one may be forgotten, with disastrous consequences.

The C++ code for all of this is:

```
class Employee {
public:  // PUBLIC INTERFACE
  void setCompanyLink(Company* aCompany);
  // ...
private:  // ASSOCIATION
  Company* theEmployer;
};


class Company {
public:  // PUBLIC INTERFACE
  void hire(Employee* anEmployee);
  // ...
private:  // ASSOCIATION
  POrderedCollection<Employee*> theEmployees;
};


  void Company::hire(Employee* anEmployee)
  {
  anEmployee->setCompanyLink(this);
  theEmployees.add(anEmployee);
  }
```

Note the first statement in the `hire` function:

```
anEmployee->setCompanyLink(this);
```

Since the argument `anEmployee` is an `Employee` pointer we send it one of its messages with the notation `anEmployee->`. The message we send is `setCompanyLink` which requires a pointer to the company object to which this employee object connects. When we execute the `hire` method it will, of course, be associated with some `Company` object. In C++ the keyword `this` refers to the recipient of the message. Hence the LOOM object me is translated into the C++ member function `this`.

6.11 **Recursive associations**

We noted in Chapter 2 that we may have recursive associations where the relationship is between objects of the same class. This arrangement is shown in Figure 6.5.

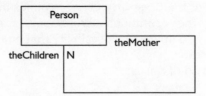

Figure 6.5 *Recursive association*

It is important to note here the role names. Unique names are used to identify which Person object is under consideration. The role names also indicate that two entries will appear in our LOOM ASSOCIATION clause. The first will be a single LINK to the Person object acting as the mother. The second is a collection of such LINKs for the children of the Person object.

```
CLASS Person
WITH
PUBLIC INTERFACE
  NONE
PRIVATE IMPLEMENTATION
  REPRESENTATION
    theName :String
  AGGREGATIONS NONE
  ASSOCIATIONS
    theMother :Person LINK INVERSE OF theChildren
    theChildren :POrderedCollection[Person LINK]
      INVERSE OF theMother
  DEFINITIONS NONE

ENDCLASS Person
```

From this specification the resulting C++ follows familiar lines:

```
class Person {
public:
  // ...
private:
  CString theName;
  Person* theMother;
  POrderedCollection<Person*> theChildren;
};
```

6.12 **Many-to-many associations**

The associations we have discussed so far have had a multiplicity of either one-to-one or one-to-many. For example, one person owns one car and one Company employs many Employees. However, we frequently encounter many-to-many associations in applications. For example, many Tutors teach many Students.

Two strategies for implementing such a relation are considered. The first is

Figure 6.6 *Many-to-many association*

to embed LINKs at both ends of the association, and the second is to model the relation as an object.

Assuming a two-way traversal of the association, we should embed a collection of LINKs on each side of the relation. For a one-way traversal the problem simplifies to embedding a collection of LINKs on the appropriate side of the relation. We can ignore this case as we have already discussed it with one-to-many associations.

Consider the Tutor–Student example described by Figure 6.6. Let us propose that each Student and each Tutor has a name property. A Tutor should respond to a request to display the names of the students he teaches, and a Student should respond to a request to display the tutors he is taught by. Partial LOOM scripts are:

```
CLASS Tutor
WITH
PUBLIC INTERFACE
  name? -> String
  displayStudents?
  // ...
PRIVATE IMPLEMENTATION
  REPRESENTATION
    theName : String
  AGGREGATIONS NONE
  ASSOCIATIONS
    theStudents : POrderedCollection [Student LINK]
      INVERSE OF theTutors
  DEFINITIONS
    // ...
    METHOD displayStudents?
    AS
      FOREACH student : Student LINK IN theStudents DO
        SEND theScreen THE MESSAGE
          insert (SEND student THE MESSAGE name?)
      ENDFOREACH
    ENDMETHOD displayStudents?

ENDCLASS Tutor


CLASS Student
WITH
PUBLIC INTERFACE
  name? -> String
  displayTutors?
```

```
// ...
PRIVATE IMPLEMENTATION
 REPRESENTATION
  theName :String
 AGGREGATIONS NONE
 ASSOCIATIONS
  theTutors :POrderedCollection[Tutor LINK]
   INVERSE OF theStudents
 DEFINITIONS
  // ...
  METHOD displayTutors?
  AS
   FOREACH tutor :Tutor LINK IN theTutors DO
    SEND theScreen THE MESSAGE
     insert(SEND tutor THE MESSAGE name?)
   ENDFOREACH
  ENDMETHOD displayTutors?

ENDCLASS Student
```

The C++ code that follows from these discussions should now not surprise us.
Following the earlier studies, the C++ is derived by application of the mappings
provided.

Commonly with these many-to-many associations we have properties that
don't rightly belong to either class at the ends of the association. Consider the
model in Figure 6.7 in which a Company employs a number of Employees, and
an individual may work for more than one organisation or perhaps have two jobs
with the same company. If a person has two employers or two jobs with the same
company, then he will have two distinct job titles and salaries. In that case the
job title and salary properties belong with the employment relation rather than,
say, with the Employee.

Figure 6.7   Company—Employee *many-to-many association*

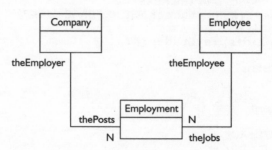

Figure 6.8   *Partitioning a many-to-many association*

In effect, the job title and salary properties belong with the association. When there are several properties as we have here, it is common to create a new class for this purpose. The new model is given in Figure 6.8. Observe how the many-to-many association has been resolved into two simpler many-to-one associations.

An Application class to run such a system is given below and listed under Program 6.4 (see Appendix F). The LOOM specification and the program's output is:

```
CLASS Application
WITH
PUBLIC INTERFACE
  run
PRIVATE IMPLEMENTATION
  REPRESENTATION NONE
  AGGREGATIONS NONE
  ASSOCIATIONS NONE
  DEFINITIONS
   METHOD run
   AS
     //
     // First, create some employing organisation.
     //
     INSTANCE napier : Company LINK("Napier")


     //
     // Then establish some people who might work for
     //   the company
     //
     INSTANCE john : Employee LINK("John Savage")
     INSTANCE ken : Employee LINK("Ken Barclay")
     INSTANCE jessie : Employee LINK("Jessie Kennedy")


     //
     // Now give john and ken a job with Napier.
     //
     INSTANCE johnsJob :
       Employment LINK("Lecturer", 1000, napier, john)
     INSTANCE kensJob :
       Employment LINK("Systems Manager", 800, napier, ken)
     SEND napier THE MESSAGE addEmployment(johnsJob)
     SEND john THE MESSAGE addEmployment(johnsJob)
     SEND napier THE MESSAGE addEmployment(kensJob)
     SEND ken THE MESSAGE addEmployment(kensJob)


     //
     // And see the effect.
     //
     SEND napier THE MESSAGE displayEmployees?
```

```
//
// Give jessie two jobs with napier.
//
INSTANCE jessiesFirstJob :
  Employment LINK ("Part Time Lecturer",
    500, napier, jessie)
INSTANCE jessiesSecondJob :
  Employment LINK ("Part Time Research Assistant",
    300, napier, jessie)
SEND napier THE MESSAGE
  addEmployment (jessiesFirstJob)
SEND napier THE MESSAGE
  addEmployment (jessiesSecondJob)
SEND jessie THE MESSAGE
  addEmployment (jessiesFirstJob)
SEND jessie THE MESSAGE
  addEmployment (jessiesSecondJob)

SEND napier THE MESSAGE displayEmployees?
ENDMETHOD run

ENDCLASS Application
```

Program's output:

```
Napier
----------
John Savage: Lecturer, 1000
Ken Barclay: Systems Manager, 800


Napier
----------
John Savage: Lecturer, 1000
Ken Barclay: Systems Manager, 800
Jessie Kennedy: Part Time Lecturer, 500
Jessie Kennedy: Part Time Research Assistant, 300
```

6.13 Argument passing revisited

We briefly outlined function argument passing in Section 6.2.2. Here we shall revisit argument-passing schemes in more detail. Consider the definition:

```
int x = 27;
```

Our understanding of such a definition is that an area of memory is set aside sufficient to accommodate an integer value. This area of memory is referenced in the program by the identifier x. At the machine level, this memory area has an address (say, 5678). The area of memory is initialised with the binary pattern representing decimal 27. Pictorially we have Figure 6.9.

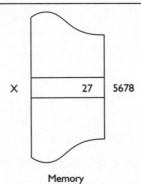

Memory

Figure 6.9 *Memory allocation and variable definition*

Alternatively, following the notation of Barclay (1994), we may show this relationship as in Figure 6.10. A program variable possesses an internal memory address and is depicted in the diagram by a line from the variable identifier to the address (represented by a hexagonal box). The relation 'to refer' relates the address to the value at that address. This is shown by an arrow to the memory cell containing the value of the variable. The relation 'to refer' is strictly between two *internal objects*, namely, the memory address and the value. The internals are 'possessed' by an *external object* – the program identifier. The internal address (sometimes known as its *name*) we shall discover is an object of another related type which we can also manipulate in our programs.

A *reference* is an alternative name, or *alias*, for an object which is currently in scope. One principal use for a reference type is as an argument or return type of a function, particularly when employed with user-defined class types. Consider the definition:

```
int& b = k;
```

The result of the declarations is that the two identifiers b and k both refer to the same integer object. Assigning to b or to k has the same result; different identifiers but the same value. In some programming languages this phenomenon is known as *equivalencing*.

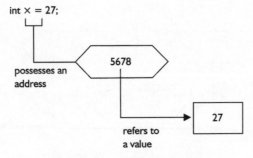

Figure 6.10 *Addresses and values*

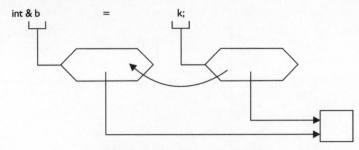

Figure 6.11   *Effect of referencing*

Figure 6.11 describes the effect of the above definition. In particular, note how the initialising value must be another variable to effect the equivalence.

The `const` qualifier may also prepend a reference type to emphasise that the object may not be changed through the reference. For example, in:

```
int k = 5;
const int& b = k;
k = 10;          // ok, k is variable
b = 12;          // error, b is constant
```

no value may be assigned through b because of the constancy associated with it.

Figure 6.12 presents a pictorial representation for the initialised definition:

```
int* pVar = &var;
```

As usual, the variable pVar possesses an address. The difference, however, is that the value to which the address refers is itself an address (the address of var). The value of the expression pVar is the address to which it refers, while the value of the expression *pVar is the object to which pVar points.

When a function is called with expressions for arguments, the value of each actual expression is calculated. The computed values are then matched with the corresponding formal arguments. The formal arguments within the function body behave as initialised local variables (initialised to the value of the actual

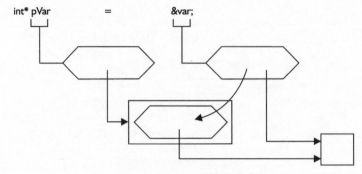

Figure 6.12   *Pointer variables*

arguments). Thereafter, they may be treated as local variables and have their local copies modified. Only the local copy is changed. The changes do not alter the actual arguments. The argument-passing strategy is referred to as *pass by value*. This is demonstrated in the following code:

```
class Employee {
public:
  Employee(CString aName);
  void changeName(CString aName);
  // ...
};

Employee el("John Savage");
CString s2("Kenneth Barclay");
el.changeName(s2);
```

To fully appreciate this argument-passing mechanism we remind ourselves of variable definitions as described by Figure 6.10. The above listing calls the function changeName, passing the value of the variables s2. This is represented by Figure 6.13. The code for the function changeName is depicted by a circle into which the value of the actual argument is delivered.

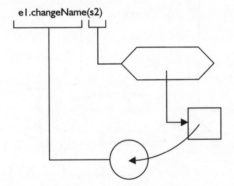

el.changeName(s2)

Figure 6.13 *Pass by value*

The supply of the actual argument to the C++ function changeName is through the pass by value mechanism. Our understanding is that the formal argument is treated as an initialised local variable for the called function. The formal argument is initialised with the value of the actual argument expression. Figure 6.14 illustrates how this is achieved for the argument to the function changeName. The formal argument aName is initialised with the actual argument. Thereafter, the formal argument operates as a variable local to changeName and any changes made to aName apply to the copy and not to the actual argument.

Consider now the declaration for the Employee class, modified to use reference argument passing:

```
class Employee {
public:
  Employee(CString& aName);
  void changeName(CString& aName);
  // ...
};

Employee  e1("John Savage");
CString   s2("Kenneth Barclay");
e1.changeName(s2);
```

Figure 6.15 gives the meaning of the call to the function `changeName`. In particular, the handling of the actual argument is shown. Observe how, as described above, the variable `s2` is made available to the function by aliasing it with the formal argument `aName`. This function may then access the value at that reference, or place a computed value at that reference thus implementing a change in the actual argument.

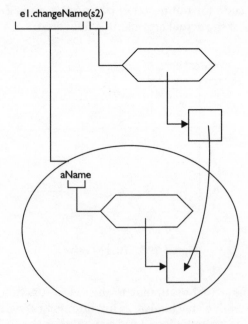

Figure 6.14   *Pass by value implementation*

Since the formal argument is aliased with the actual argument, a new value may be given to the actual argument through the formal argument name. To protect against this, yet still enjoy the efficiency of pass by reference, we specify the formal argument as a `const` reference:

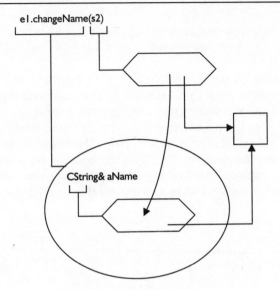

Figure 6.15   *Pass by reference*

```
class Employee {
public:
  Employee (const CString& aName) ;
  void changeName (const CString& aName) ;
  // ...
};
```

To allow a called function access to the value of a variable in the calling function, the latter may supply the *address* of one of its automatic (local) variables. If the called function then has the address of a variable in the calling function, it can arrange to assign a new value at that address.

Consider the classes:

```
class Company;  // forward reference

class Employee {
public:
  void  hiredBy (Company* aCompany) ;
  // ...
};

class Company {
public
  void  hire (Employee* anEmployee) ;
  // ...
};
void  Company::hire (Employee* anEmployee)
{
  anEmployee->hiredBy (this) ;
  // ...
```

```
}
Company* cl = new Company ("Napier");
Employee* e2 = new Employee ("John Savage");
cl->hire(e2);
```

Observe the coding for the hire function. The argument anEmployee is sent the message hiredBy such that it is made to associate with the Company object through the Company pointer this, acting as its employer.

Figure 6.16 gives the meaning of the call to the function hire. In particular, the handling of the actual argument is shown. Observe how, as described above, the address of the Employee object referenced by the variable e2 is made available to the function. This function may then place a computed value at that address, effectively implementing a change in the actual argument.

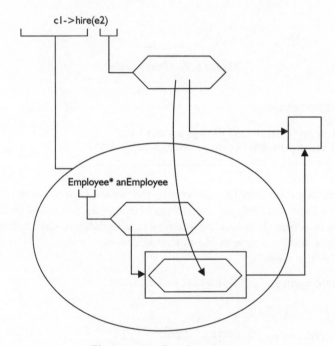

Figure 6.16 *Pass by pointer*

6.14 Summary

1. A single LOOM class specification yields two C++ program files: a header file containing the class declaration and a program unit having the code for the class function members.

2. A C++ class declaration has a public section containing (primarily) the

member functions of the class corresponding to LOOM operations, and a private section for the data members (properties and architectural elements).

3. A C++ class declaration introduces the function members with prototype declarations which name the function, specify its return type and specify the type of the formal arguments. Formal arguments also document the argument-passing strategy. C++ has three argument-passing schemes: pass by value, pass by reference and pass by pointer.

4. Method bodies are given as function definitions in C++ program units. All member function definitions include the scope resolution operator, specifying the class to which they belong.

5. Aggregations and associations are realised as C++ pointers. A one-to-many aggregation or a one-to-many association uses a container of pointers such as a POrderedCollection. The latter is a template class in which the actual pointer type is specified in the application by instantiating a particular version.

6.15 Exercises

1. Identify the two C++ program files required for each LOOM class specification. Briefly outline the content of each.
2. A LOOM specification includes a PUBLIC INTERFACE and a private REPRESEN-TATION. Respectively they document *operation signatures* and class *properties*. What are the corresponding C++ elements called in a class declaration and how are they presented?
3. Consider the following C++ class declaration in a header file book.h in which the data members are class types CString and CDate:

```
class Book {
public:
 // ...
private:
  CString theAuthor;
  CString theTitle;
  CDate thePublication;
};
```

What additional information is required by this header file and how is it obtained? What language features do we use to achieve this?

4. The following LOOM fragment gives rise to the corresponding C++ class declaration:

```
CLASS Employee WITH          class Employee {
PUBLIC INTERFACE             public:
  name? -> String              CString  name(void) const;
  changeName(aName:String)     void  changeName(CString
                                         aName);
  // ...
ENDCLASS Employee            };
```

Present a mapping scheme to convert LOOM operation signatures into C++ function prototypes.

Identify which LOOM operation and corresponding C++ function member requires special treatment under this scheme.

5. Carefully distinguish the argument-passing strategies of C++: pass by value, pass by reference and pass by pointer. Identify, by example, their appropriate usage.

6. Message sending in C++ is achieved by either of the following two constructs:

```
recipient.message(actual-arguments)
recipient->message(actual-arguments)
```

Carefully distinguish these two forms, identifying the nature and type of the `recipient` object.

7. LOOM method bodies give rise to C++ function definitions. Each function name is prefixed with its class name in a construct of the form:

```
CString Employee::name(void) const
{
  // ...
}
```

Explain the need for the class name prefix. What benefits do we get from this? What do we call the :: symbol?

8. A C++ function body as shown in the preceding exercise presents the executing logic through one or more C++ statements. Identify and discuss the additional syntax unique to C++ constructor function definitions.

9. Consider the following C++ class declaration in a header file `employee.h`:

```
#include "ccstring.h"

class Company;  // forward reference

class Employee {
public:
  // ...
private:
  CString    theName;
  Company*   theEmployer;
};
```

Explain the need for the `#include "ccstring.h"` preprocessor directive. Discuss the need for the `class Company` forward reference, explaining why this, rather than `#include "company.h"`, is sufficient.

10. Investigate the `POrderedCollection` class provided in the LOOM library. The two files are called `pordcol.h` and `xpordcol.h`. The former introduces the class declaration while the latter gives the function definitions.

Observe how the function definitions are also in a header file and how the file `pordcol.h` uses a `#include "xpordcol.h"`. Refer to a C++ language reference text (see bibliography) to see why this is so.

In the file `xpordcol.h` carefully note the form of the *template function* definitions. Some are also prefixed with the C++ keyword `inline`. Again, refer to a language reference text to find their meaning and usage.

11. Present classes `Car`, `Student` and `House` from exercises 2, 3 and 4 respectively of Chapter 3 in C++. For each class, produce an accompanying `Application` class with a `run` method which creates instances and sends appropriate messages.

12. For the classes `Point`, `Line` and `Rectangle` of exercises 5, 6 and 7 of Chapter 3 prepare an `Application` class which properly exercises the method behaviours. Convert these classes into C++ and execute the resulting program.

13. Present the `Store` class of exercise 8 from Chapter 3 as C++. Develop an application which creates two `Store` instances and copies the value of the first into the second.

    Extend the `Store` class with operations up and down which respectively increment and decrement the stored value. Test these with a suitable application.

14. Implement the `Country–City` scenario given in exercise 2 of Chapter 2.

15. Using the LOOM script from exercise 9 of Chapter 3, develop an executable program to test a `Beetle` object.

    Enhance your program to include the classes `Player` and `Game` and produce a working program. Use a `DOrderedCollection` to hold `Player` objects.

    Note that you require access to a random number generator. This is easily accomplished by using the function `rand()` in the standard library C library. It delivers a pseudo random number in the range 1 to 99. All you need do is to replace the LOOM sentence

    ```
    SEND theRandomNumberGenerator THE MESSAGE
        randomise(theDie)
    ```

    with

    ```
    theDie = ( rand() % 6) + 1;
    ```

    and #include the file <stdlib.h>.

16. Carefully follow the specification of the library in the case study from Chapter 4 and then prepare the corresponding C++ for the second version. Produce an executable program.

Chapter 7

Specialisation

In Chapter 2 we examined the association and aggregation relationships that can exist between classes. There is another relationship, referred to as *specialisation*, that is also used extensively in an OOAD. Consider the class diagram of Figure 7.1.

The corresponding LOOM script for the Employee class defines its public interface and private implementation.

Figure 7.1 *Class diagram*

```
CLASS Employee
WITH
PUBLIC INTERFACE
  Employee(aName :String, aDateOfBirth :Date,
    aSalary :Integer, aReferenceNumber :Integer)
  name? -> String
  age? -> Integer
  changeName(aName :String)
  display?
  companyName? -> String
  salary? -> Integer
  referenceNumber? -> Integer
  hiredBy(anEmployer :Company LINK)
  fired
PRIVATE IMPLEMENTATION
  REPRESENTATION
    theName :String
    theDateOfBirth :Date
    theSalary :Integer
    theReferenceNumber :Integer
  AGGREGATIONS NONE
  ASSOCIATIONS
    theEmployer :Company LINK INVERSE OF
```

```
        theEmployees
   DEFINITIONS
     //Suitable method definitions ...
```

ENDCLASS Employee

However, after careful examination of this LOOM script, it is clear that the operations that are special to Employees, rather than just people in general, are:

```
companyName?
referenceNumber?
salary?
hiredBy
```

and

fired

Similarly, the properties

theReferenceNumber

and

theSalary

used for the representation, are special to Employees. The other operations and properties describe a person and have no direct relevance to employment.

Given that an association is application dependent, it is not surprising to find that theEmployer is special to this architecture. We anticipate that in a different architecture it might not be present. These considerations lead us to set up a relationship between a Person class and an *Employee* class as shown in Figure 7.2.

It shows that the Employee class is related to the Person class by specialisation. It is implicit in this relationship that the Employee class has the same public interface as the Person class. However, there may be extra operations added to the public interface of the Employee class. It is important to note that none may be deleted. The class Person is usually referred to as the *parent* (superclass) class and the class Employee as the *descendent* (subclass or child class).

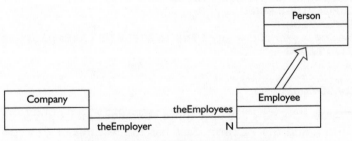

Figure 7.2 *A specialisation relationship*

It follows that an object of class Employee can respond to the same messages as an object of class Person. In other words an Employee object *isA* Person object. However, the reverse is not true. A Person object is not an Employee object.

With the introduction of the LOOM reserved words SPECIALISATION OF we are able to capture the specialisation relationship as follows:

```
CLASS Person
WITH
PUBLIC INTERFACE
  Person(aName :String, aDateOfBirth :Date)
  name? -> String
  age? -> Integer
  changeName(aName :String)
  display?
PRIVATE IMPLEMENTATION
  REPRESENTATION
    theName :String
    theDateOfBirth :Date
  AGGREGATIONS NONE
  ASSOCIATIONS NONE
  DEFINITIONS
  // ...

ENDCLASS Person

CLASS Employee
  SPECIALISATION OF Person
WITH
PUBLIC INTERFACE
  Employee(aName :String, aDateOfBirth :Date,
    aSalary :Integer, aReferenceNumber :Integer)
  companyName? -> String
  salary? -> Integer
  referenceNumber? -> Integer
  hiredBy(anEmployer :Company LINK)
  fired
PRIVATE IMPLEMENTATION
  REPRESENTATION
    theSalary :Integer
    theReferenceNumber :Integer
  AGGREGATIONS NONE
  ASSOCIATIONS
    theEmployer :Company LINK INVERSE OF theEmployees
  DEFINITIONS
  // ...

ENDCLASS Employee
```

The Employee class now has only those operations on its public interface that are special to it and the Person class has the features of Person objects in general. This makes the LOOM scripts much easier to construct and understand.

It is also important to realise that the class Person may be reused in other applications by specialising it in a different manner. For example, a class Student as defined below could be used as part of a student records system.

```
CLASS Student
  SPECIALISATION OF Person
WITH
PUBLIC INTERFACE
  Student (aName :String, aDateOfBirth :Date,
    aMatriculationNumber :Integer,
    aYearOfStudy :Integer, aCourse :String)
  matriculationNumber? -> Integer
  yearOfStudy? -> Integer
  course? -> String
  taughtAt (aUniversity :University LINK)
PRIVATE IMPLEMENTATION
  REPRESENTATION
    theMatriculationNumber :Integer
    theYearOfStudy :Integer
    theCourse :String
AGGREGATIONS NONE
ASSOCIATIONS
  theUniversity :University LINK
DEFINITIONS
  // Suitable definitions of methods.

ENDCLASS Student
```

7.1 Inherited methods

So far, we have not considered the methods that define the behaviour of each operation. In LOOM unless it is otherwise stated, an operation method, defined in the parent class, is inherited by the descendent class. In other words they are *invariant over specialisation*. This means that the specification **and** the implementation of an operation is inherited from a parent class by a descendent class. Note that the methods defined in the parent class are still private to it and cannot be accessed by any other class, including a descendent class (this rule also applies to the representation). Only the methods for the additional operations available in the descendent class are defined in the descendent class. Outline LOOM scripts for the Person and Employee classes clarify the situation.

```
CLASS Person
WITH
PUBLIC INTERFACE
  Person (aName :String, aDateOfBirth :Date)
  name? -> String
  age? -> Integer
```

```
      changeName(aName :String)
      display?
    PRIVATE IMPLEMENTATION
      REPRESENTATION
        theName :String
        theDateOfBirth :Date
      AGGREGATIONS NONE
      ASSOCIATIONS NONE
      DEFINITIONS
        METHOD Person(aName :String, aDateOfBirth :Date)
        AS
          // Detailed logic.
        ENDMETHOD Person

        METHOD name? -> String
        AS
          // Detailed logic.
        ENDMETHOD name?

        METHOD age? -> Integer
        AS
          // Detailed logic.
        ENDMETHOD age?

        METHOD changeName(aName :String)
        AS
          // Detailed logic.
        ENDMETHOD changeName

        METHOD display?
        AS
          // Detailed logic.
        ENDMETHOD display?

    ENDCLASS Person


    CLASS Employee
      SPECIALISATION OF Person
    WITH
    PUBLIC INTERFACE
      Employee(aName :String, aDateOfBirth :Date,
      aSalary :Integer, aReferenceNumber :Integer)
      companyName? -> String
      salary? -> Integer
      referenceNumber? -> Integer
      hiredBy(anEmployer :Company LINK)
      fired
    PRIVATE IMPLEMENTATION
      REPRESENTATION
        theSalary :Integer
        theReferenceNumber :Integer
      AGGREGATIONS NONE
```

```
      ASSOCIATIONS
        theEmployer : Company LINK INVERSE OF theEmployees
      DEFINITIONS
        // No method definitions for name?, age?,
        // changeName and display? are
        // required; they are all defined in the parent
        // class Person.

      METHOD Employee (aName : String, aDateOfBirth
        : Date,
          aSalary : Integer, aReferenceNumber : Integer)
      AS
        // Detailed logic.
      ENDMETHOD Employee

      METHOD companyName? -> String
      AS
        // Detailed logic.
      ENDMETHOD companyName?

      METHOD salary? -> Integer
      AS
        // Detailed logic.
      ENDMETHOD salary?

      METHOD referenceNumber? -> Integer
      AS
        // Detailed logic.
      ENDMETHOD referenceNumber?

      METHOD hiredBy (anEmployer : Company LINK)
      AS
        // Detailed logic.
      ENDMETHOD hiredBy

      METHOD fired
      AS
        // Detailed logic.
      ENDMETHOD fired

    ENDCLASS Employee
```

Typical instantiations and messages are:

```
    INSTANCE thePerson : Person ("Ken",
      Date (12,5,1948))
    INSTANCE theEmployee : Employee ("John",
      Date (19,2,1949), 14500, 6701)

    SEND thePerson THE MESSAGE age?

      // An Employee object is a special kind of Person object
      // so this operation is inherited from the class Person.
```

```
SEND theEmployee THE MESSAGE age?

// This operation is defined for Employee
// objects only.
SEND theEmployee THE MESSAGE salary?
```

The message:

```
SEND thePerson THE MESSAGE salary?
```

is not allowed as a `Person` object is not a special kind of `Employee` object.

Before we leave this section we should consider the construction of an instance of a descendent class. One would expect that as the `Employee` class is a specialisation of the `Person` class we should be able to make use of the constructor for a `Person` when we construct an `Employee`. This is in fact the case. So if the method for a `Person` constructor is:

```
METHOD Person(aName : String, aDateOfBirth : Date)
AS
  SEND theName THE MESSAGE initialise(aName)
  SEND theDateOfBirth THE MESSAGE
    initialise(aDateOfBirth)
ENDMETHOD Person
```

then the constructor for an `Employee` is:

```
METHOD Employee(aName : String, aDateOfBirth : Date,
  aSalary : Integer,
  aReferenceNumber : Integer)
AS
  SEND SUPERCLASS Person THE MESSAGE
    initialise(aName, aDateOfBirth)
  SEND theSalary THE MESSAGE
    initialise(aSalary)
  SEND theReferenceNumber THE MESSAGE
    initialise(aReferenceNumber)
ENDMETHOD Employee
```

Note the use of the syntax:

```
SEND SUPERCLASS Person THE MESSAGE
  initialise(aName, aDateOfBirth)
```

to clarify the situation that initialisation of an `Employee` object involves the initialisation of, effectively, the `Person` subobject.

7.2 Redefined methods

Although the inheritance of an operation and its corresponding method is the default, it is sometimes necessary to redefine the method for an inherited operation in a descendent class. For example, the method for the operation display? in the Employee class must be able to display information about a Person object. However, it must also be able to display information about an Employee object. Clearly, two different behaviours are required for the class Person and the class Employee. In other words the operation display? is not invariant over specialisation, but is changed in a descendent class. A Person object will execute the method for display? defined in its class, but an Employee object will execute the display? method defined in the Employee class. An obvious strategy is to make use of the method for the display? operation inherited from the Person class in the Employee class, but to augment it with additional logic as part of its redefinition. LOOM uses an operation qualifier REDEFINED to register the fact that an inherited method is changed in a descendent class.

```
CLASS Employee
  SPECIALISATION OF Person
WITH
PUBLIC INTERFACE
  Employee (aName :String, aDateOfBirth :Date,
    aSalary :Integer, aReferenceNumber :Integer)
  companyName? -> String
  salary? -> Integer
  referenceNumber? -> Integer
  hiredBy (anEmployer :Company LINK)
  fired
  display?  REDEFINED
PRIVATE IMPLEMENTATION
  REPRESENTATION
    theSalary :Integer
    theReferenceNumber :Integer
  AGGREGATIONS NONE
  ASSOCIATIONS
    theEmployer :Company LINK INVERSE OF
      theEmployees
  DEFINITIONS
    // As previously defined

  METHOD display?
  AS
    SEND me THE MESSAGE display? FROM Person
    SEND theScreen THE MESSAGE
      insert (theReferenceNumber)
    SEND theScreen THE MESSAGE insert (theSalary)
  ENDMETHOD display?

ENDCLASS Employee
```

It shows that the method for the operation display?, originally defined in the class Person, has the logic for the method defined in the parent class along with extra logic specific to the Employee class. Note that a redefined method must have an identical signature to the original. The message:

```
SEND me THE MESSAGE display? FROM Person
```

is the mechanism by which LOOM requests the execution of the operation `display?` defined in the parent class. The object me identifies the object that is sending the message and is implicitly defined for all LOOM classes (see Section 3.8).

7.3 The protected interface

It is clear that a descendent class and its parent are very closely related. In fact, in some situations they are the same. This is the nature of the specialisation relationship. For this reason, it is common in object-oriented systems for a descendent class to be given unlimited access to the private implementation of its parent. In other words, it does not need to use its parent's interface but may interrogate or change its representation directly. We do not permit this in LOOM as it violates the fundamental rule that an object is intended to encapsulate its representation. Private information is private and should not be directly accessible by any other object, even of a descendent class.

Note that since an `Employee` *isA* `Person` we expect that the redefinition of the operation `display?` should behave like a `Person` but should have additional behaviour associated with being an `Employee`. This means that we normally expect to see a message of the form:

```
SEND me THE MESSAGE
  operationName(arguments) FROM Parent
```

in the redefined `operationName` of the descendent class.

However, it is likely that a descendent class will require privileged access to its parent that a normal associate would not be given. In order to make this possible LOOM provides a PROTECTED INTERFACE as well as a PUBLIC INTERFACE section. Descendants have access to both but associates can access only the public interface.

For example, the public interface of the class `Person` does not allow access to the date of birth property of a `Person` object. However, by supplying an accessor operation as part of a protected interface we can permit access by the class `Employee`, or any other descendent classes. Similarly, a transformer operation `changeDateOfBirth` is part of the protected interface to allow descendent classes to request a change to the private property `theDateOf-Birth` to be made.

```
CLASS Person
WITH
PUBLIC INTERFACE
  Person(aName :String, aDateOfBirth :Date)
  name? -> String
  age? -> Integer
  changeName(aName :String)
  display?  POLYMORPHIC
PROTECTED INTERFACE
```

```
  dateOfBirth? -> Date
  changeDateOfBirth(aDate :Date)
PRIVATE IMPLEMENTATION
 REPRESENTATION
   theName :String
   theDateOfBirth :Date
 AGGREGATIONS NONE
 ASSOCIATIONS NONE
 DEFINITIONS
   // ...

 METHOD dateOfBirth? -> Date
 AS
   RETURN theDateOfBirth
 ENDMETHOD dateOfBirth?

 METHOD changeDateOfBirth(aDate :Date)
 AS
   SEND theDateOfBirth THE MESSAGE assign(aDate)
 ENDMETHOD changeDateOfBirth

ENDCLASS Person
```

7.4 **Polymorphism**

The *polymorphic* effect in object oriented systems is extremely useful and is a distinguishing characteristic of these systems. It allows a message to be received by an object of a particular class as usual but also allows the message to be received by an object of a descendent class. This style of programming may seem strange at first but when used properly can lead to implementations that are apparently simple but actually have complex execution behaviours. It is unique to object orientation.

In order to illustrate its use, consider Employees as salespersons who have managers, responsible for several salespersons, as shown in Figure 7.3.

The class diagram shows that the class SalesPerson is a specialisation of the class Person, and the class Manager in turn is a specialisation of the class SalesPerson. It also shows that the Company class has an association relationship with both the SalesPerson class and the Manager class. This indicates that messages can be sent from a Company object to a SalesPerson object and a Manager object. However, it places a burden on the developer to maintain two container objects in the Company class to hold the necessary LINK values. For example:

```
theEmployees :POrderedCollection[SalesPerson LINK]
```

and

```
theManagers :POrderedCollection[Manager LINK]
```

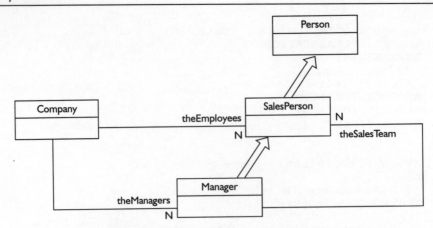

Figure 7.3   *Class diagram with specialisation*

This approach can prove clumsy especially when more classes and identical messages are sent to objects of each class.

The use of the polymorphic effect is an alternative approach. Before we put it into practice we must understand two fundamental points. The first is that since a descendent class must have at least the same interface as its parent, an object of a descendent class can be used in place of an object of a parent class. In other words a child can be substituted for its parent. In our example, it follows that a container of `SalesPerson LINK` values may also hold `Manager LINK` values, as the class `Manager` is a descendant of the class `SalesPerson`.

The second point is that the binding of a message to a corresponding method may occur before the system starts to execute or it may occur when it is actually running. The former is usually referred to as *static binding* or *early binding*, the latter as *dynamic binding*, *late binding* or *virtual binding*. Early binding is the default in LOOM.

If we combine descendent class substitution with late binding then we have the polymorphic effect. A message sent from a `Company` object, through a `LINK` value to a `SalesPerson` object, can now be received by a `SalesPerson` object **or** by a `Manager` object. Note that the polymorphic effect only works with messages sent through a `LINK`. This simplifies the situation as shown in Figure 7.4.

We no longer need an explicit association relationship between the `Company` and `Manager` classes. An association with its parent is sufficient. Now we need only one container for `SalesPerson LINK`s instead of two and there is no need for the duplication of messages to `SalesPerson` and `Manager` objects in the `Company` class methods.

To illustrate the point further, if we assume that the `SalesPerson` and `Manager` classes have operations `salary?` and `display?`, and:

```
theEmployees:POrderedCollection[SalesPerson LINK]
```

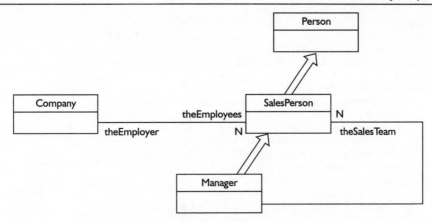

Figure 7.4 *Improved class diagram with specialisation*

is part of the ASSOCIATION clause in the Company class, a Company object could do as follows:

```
FOREACH anEmployee : SalesPerson LINK IN
  theEmployees DO
  SEND theScreen THE MESSAGE
    insert (SEND anEmployee THE MESSAGE salary?)
  SEND anEmployee THE MESSAGE display?
ENDFOREACH
```

The messages sent to anEmployee could now be received by Sales Person or Manager objects depending on the values of the LINKs in the container theEmployees. Clearly, this is a very effective way of constructing software.

Before we examine the LOOM scripts for these classes in more detail, we need to extend their descriptions as follows:

- In addition to the features previously described for Employee objects (see Section 7.1), each SalesPerson object has an individual sales figure that records the value of sales made for a particular time period.
- Manager objects are special in that they have an association with a sales team made up of several SalesPerson objects. The combined sales of a sales team, as well as a Manager object's individual sales figure, make up the overall sales figure for a Manager object.

The class Person is summarized by:

```
CLASS Person
WITH
PUBLIC INTERFACE
  display? POLYMORPHIC
  name? -> String
  // ...
ENDCLASS Person
```

The class `SalesPerson` is described in LOOM as:

```
CLASS SalesPerson
  SPECIALISATION OF Person
WITH
PUBLIC INTERFACE
  SalesPerson(aName :String, aDateOfBirth
   :Date,
   aSalary :Integer,
     aReferenceNumber :Integer,
   aSalesFigure :Integer)
  companyName? -> String
  salary? -> Integer
  referenceNumber? -> Integer
  hiredBy(anEmployer :Company LINK)
  fired
  display?  REDEFINED
  salesFigure? -> Integer
PROTECTED INTERFACE
  NONE
PRIVATE IMPLEMENTATION
  REPRESENTATION
    theSalary :Integer
    theReferenceNumber :Integer
    theSalesFigure :Integer
  AGGREGATIONS NONE
  ASSOCIATIONS
    theEmployer :Company LINK INVERSE OF
      theEmployees
  DEFINITIONS
    // Other methods for operations specified in
    // the interface.
  METHOD display?
  AS
    SEND me THE MESSAGE display? FROM Person
    SEND theScreen THE MESSAGE insert(theSalesFigure)
  ENDMETHOD display?

  METHOD salesFigure? -> Integer
  AS
    RETURN theSalesFigure
  ENDMETHOD salesFigure?
  // ...

ENDCLASS SalesPerson
```

All the operations on the public interface of the class `SalesPerson` are particular to that class. The one exception is the operation `display?` which is given both in this class and in the superclass `Person`. The method `display?` in the superclass `Person` is specified as POLYMORPHIC, meaning that it may engage in this polymorphic activity. In the subclass `SalesPerson` the operation `display?` is reintroduced with a new definition, hence the qualifier

REDEFINED. The POLYMORPHIC qualification introduced in the superclass continues to operate.

Observe how the redefinition of the display? method for the class SalesPerson is qualified as a REDEFINED version of a POLYMORPHIC superclass operation, yet its implementation involves a statically bound execution of the display? operation from the superclass, using the sentence:

SEND me THE MESSAGE display? FROM Person

The operation qualifier POLYMORPHIC is used to register the fact that an operation may execute its method as a result of a message sent to an object of a descendent class. It must be clearly understood that the binding of the method to its class will be made automatically during the execution of the system. In other words the operation qualifier POLYMORPHIC forces late binding of a method to an operation request.

Simply put, the rule is that an operation qualified as POLYMORPHIC may then be REDEFINED in subclasses. We should not expect to see a redefinition without the REDEFINED qualifier. If we were to do so then we would be mixing static and dynamic binding of the same operation with very misleading behaviours (see Section 7.11).

Similarly the class Manager redefines the method for the POLYMORPHIC operation display?. Its LOOM script is as follows:

```
CLASS Manager
  SPECIALISATION OF SalesPerson
WITH
PUBLIC INTERFACE
  Manager(aName :String, aDateOfBirth :Date,
    aSalary :Integer,
    aReferenceNumber :Integer,
    aSalesFigure :Integer,
    aSalesTarget :Integer)
    display?  REDEFINED
PROTECTED INTERFACE
  NONE
PRIVATE IMPLEMENTATION
  REPRESENTATION
    theSalesTarget :Integer
  AGGREGATIONS NONE
  ASSOCIATIONS
    theSalesTeam :
      POrderedCollection[SalesPerson LINK]
  DEFINITIONS
  // ...

  METHOD display?
  AS
    // Re-implementation, showing sales figures,
    // sales targets, etc.
  ENDMETHOD display?

ENDCLASS Manager
```

Note that the POLYMORPHIC qualifier for an operation does not affect the inheritance of its method or its redefinition in a child class. It only imposes late binding of the method to the operation requested.

7.5   Abstract base classes

It is often useful to be able to define a class that acts as a basis for establishing other classes. There is no intention to make an instance of this class but only to use it as a base for other classes. It is a way of guaranteeing that all descendants will share a common set of operations on their public interface. This kind of class is referred to as an *abstract base class* (ABC).

For example, we may decide that there will never be an instance of the class Employee. Perhaps it is just too general a description. Employees will always be SalesPersons or Managers but never just Employees. However, we must be sure that all Employees share common operations such as company-Name?, referenceNumber? and salary?. In other words, the class Employee should be an ABC. A LOOM script for the class Employee follows. The language word ABSTRACT signals the fact that it is an ABC.

```
ABSTRACT CLASS Employee
  SPECIALISATION OF Person
WITH
PUBLIC INTERFACE
  Employee(aName :String, aDateOfBirth :Date,
    aSalary :Integer, aReferenceNumber :Integer)
  companyName? -> String
  salary? -> Integer // See later.
  referenceNumber? -> Integer
  hiredBy(anEmployer :Company LINK)
  fired
  display?  REDEFINED
PROTECTED INTERFACE
  NONE
PRIVATE IMPLEMENTATION
  REPRESENTATION
    theReferenceNumber :Integer
  AGGREGATIONS NONE
  ASSOCIATIONS
    theEmployer :Company LINK INVERSE OF theEmployees
  DEFINITIONS
    // As previously defined.

ENDCLASS Employee
```

The fact that the class Employee is an ABC imposes the restriction that the instantiation:

```
anEmployee :Employee
```

is illegal. However, anticipating the use of the polymorphic effect:

    anEmployee : Employee LINK

or perhaps:

    theEmployees : POrderedCollection [Employee LINK]

is allowed as no instance is made but only a LINK. Specialisation of the class and qualification of its operations as POLYMORPHIC or REDEFINED are unaffected.

Clearly, the operation salary? in the abstract base class Employee registers the fact that a client needs to be able to access the salary of all Employees. However, it is obvious that we cannot define a method for this operation in the class Employee as it depends on the nature of the descendent class. In recognition of the fact that there is no method for the operation salary?, the reserved word DEFERRED is used to qualify it.

    ABSTRACT CLASS Employee
      SPECIALISATION OF Person
    WITH
    PUBLIC INTERFACE
      // As before ...

      salary? -> Integer DEFERRED
      // ...

    ENDCLASS Employee

Each of the concrete descendent classes SalesPerson and Manager must define a method for the inherited operation salary? as appropriate. Once again, it will be qualified as a REDEFINED operation. By definition, a class that has a method qualified as DEFERRED is an ABC. We indicate that a class is abstract by using dotted lines in a class diagram as shown in Figure 7.5.

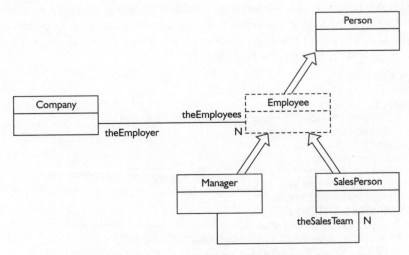

Figure 7.5 *Class diagram with an abstract base class*

Qualifying the `salary?` operation as `DEFERRED` in the ABC `Employee` class implies that it is also `POLYMORPHIC`. That way, dynamic binding will be employed, and any such message sent through an `Employee` `LINK` will be bound to the particular implementation for that method according to whether the particular instance receiving the message is a `Manager` object or a `SalesPerson` object.

Observe also how the operation `referenceNumber?` introduced in the ABC `Employee` may be defined for this class, returning a copy of the property `theReferenceNumber`. Here we see that ABCs can still employ static binding for operations that may be inherited, without change, by the subclasses.

7.6 **Public and protected properties**

So far we have assumed that only operations defined in a class are available to associates or descendants. Sometimes, there are situations where this may be too severe a restriction. For example, a person's age will almost certainly change and so it is reasonable that an operation `age?` should be available. However, it is certain that a person's blood group will not change under any circumstances and so there is no good reason why a client should not be given direct access to it.

To solve this problem, LOOM allows the possibility of making a selected property directly accessible through the public or protected interface of a class. However, there is a restriction imposed on it by LOOM. It is that its value cannot be changed by clients or by the instance to which it belongs. In addition, it must be given its value when the instance, of which it is part, is created. In other words it must have a constant value established when the object of which it is a property is instantiated.

LOOM captures the decision to make a property directly available by extending the ? naming convention for accessor operations to properties. A sample LOOM script showing a public property is shown below. A protected property is treated in a similar fashion.

```
CLASS Person
WITH
PUBLIC INTERFACE
  Person(aName :String, aDateOfBirth :Date,
    aBloodGroup :String)
  name? -> String
  age? -> Integer
  theBloodGroup? :String  // Note: public property.
  changeName(aName :String)
  display? POLYMORPHIC
PROTECTED INTERFACE
  dateOfBirth? -> Date
  changeDateOfBirth(aDateOfBirth :Date)
PRIVATE IMPLEMENTATION
  REPRESENTATION
```

```
      theName :String
      theDateOfBirth :Date
       // Note that the public property,
       // theBloodGroup?, is actually part
       // of the representation but is declared on
       // the interface.

  // As previously defined

  ENDCLASS Person
```

Typical uses are:

```
  INSTANCE p1 :Person("Ken", Date(21,8,1972), "ABNeg")

  SEND theScreen THE MESSAGE
    insert(SEND p1 THE MESSAGE theBloodGroup?)
```

Another possible use we might envisage for public properties is to make available the class name to which an instance belongs. However, because of the issues raised in Section 7.11, LOOM chooses to provide an implicit POLYMORPHIC accessor operation className?. For example:

```
  CLASS Person
  WITH
  PUBLIC INTERFACE
    Person(aName :String, aDateOfBirth :Date,
      aBloodGroup :String)
    className? -> String    POLYMORPHIC
      // Public property, implicitly defined for all classes
    name? -> String
    age? -> Integer
    theBloodGroup? :String
    // Public property.
    changeName(aName :String)
    display?    POLYMORPHIC
  PROTECTED INTERFACE
    dateOfBirth? -> Date
    changeDateOfBirth(aDateOfBirth :Date)
  PRIVATE IMPLEMENTATION
  REPRESENTATION
    theName :String
    theDateOfBirth :Date

    METHOD className? -> String AS
      RETURN "Person"
    ENDMETHOD className?
    // ...

  ENDCLASS Person
```

7.7 Private operations

The examples we have chosen so far are relatively simple and result in method definitions that consist of only a few LOOM sentences. However, this is not always the case and to help reduce the complexity of LOOM scripts we may designate an operation for the private implementation of a class. As such it is not available to associates or descendants.

As an illustration, consider the method `display?` previously described for the class `Manager`. It displays the details of the recipient `Manager` object as well as the details of the sales team for which it is responsible. For this example we impose a further requirement that the sales team details should be displayed in the ascending order of their sales figures.

To simplify the LOOM script, a private operation `displaySalesTeam?` is introduced. It establishes a local instance that is a sorted collection of `SalesPerson` LINKs before displaying it. Note that the method makes use of the private operation by sending a message to itself. This is similar to making use of an operation defined in a parent class when redefining a method in a descendent class.

```
CLASS Manager
  SPECIALISATION OF Employee
WITH
PUBLIC INTERFACE
  Manager (aName : String, aDateOfBirth : Date,
    aReferenceNumber : Integer,
    aSalary : Integer)
  display?  REDEFINED
  // As previously defined.
PROTECTED INTERFACE
  NONE
PRIVATE IMPLEMENTATION
  REPRESENTATION
    // As previously defined.

  displaySalesTeam?  // Private operation
AGGREGATIONS NONE
ASSOCIATIONS
  theSalesTeam : POrderedCollection [SalesPerson
LINK]

DEFINITIONS
// Methods for other operations.

METHOD displaySalesTeam?
AS
  INSTANCE salesForce :
    Integer (SEND theSalesTeam THE MESSAGE cardinality?)
  INSTANCE theSortedSalesTeam :
    PSortedList [SalesPerson LINK]
      (salesForce, UNMANAGED)
```

```
        // Add the salespersons in the order of their
        // sales figures.
   FOREACH theTeamMember : SalesPerson LINK IN
      theSalesTeam DO
      SEND theSortedSalesTeam THE MESSAGE
         add(theTeamMember)
   ENDFOREACH

     // Display the salespersons in the order of their
     // sales figures.
   FOREACH aTeamMember : SalesPerson LINK IN
     theSortedSalesTeam DO
     SEND aTeamMember THE MESSAGE display?
   ENDFOREACH

   ENDMETHOD displaySalesTeam?

   METHOD display?
   AS
     // A manager's basic properties are displayed.
     SEND me THE MESSAGE display? FROM Employee

     // A Manager object's sales
     // target.
   SEND theScreen THE MESSAGE
     insert(theSalesTarget)

     // Basic properties, sales figures and sales
     // targets for the
     // team of salespersons as a private operation.
   SEND me THE MESSAGE displaySalesTeam?

   ENDMETHOD display?

   ENDCLASS Manager
```

7.8 Inheritance for implementation

There is a growing recognition among practitioners of object oriented technologies that the use of inheritance should be controlled. In the hands of an implementor who understands why it is being used it is a powerful and effective tool. Unfortunately, it is all too easy to misuse inheritance and produce inferior systems. In this discussion we distinguish between the terms specialisation and inheritance in which the former is realised by using the latter as the mechanism.

A parallel can be drawn between the use of inheritance in object oriented systems development and the use of the goto in traditional structured programming. The goto is clearly an implementation concern that should not be part of an analysis or design. Experience has shown that its undisciplined use invariably leads to 'spaghetti' code. For this reason it has been almost exclusively replaced by explicit control constructs for sequence, selection and iteration.

Similarly, inheritance can be considered as an implementation concern and so it should not feature in an object oriented analysis and design. Clearly, higher-level constructs need to be identified that may be implemented by the mechanism of inheritance.

A LOOM script captures the specialisation (or *isA*) relationship between a descendent class and its parent with the reserved words SPECIALISATION OF. Although it is not strictly necessary, there is the implicit assumption that it will actually be implemented by the inheritance mechanism. In this way the operations and properties advertised on the public and protected parent class interfaces are available to the descendent class. In keeping with the fact that it is the *isA* relation that is modelled, an instance of the descendent class can be substituted for an instance of the parent. This makes the use of the polymorphic effect possible.

For example, we modelled the relationship between the Person and Employee classes as one of specialisation and so made an unequivocal statement that an Employee *isA* Person object. However, we have assumed that if a class requires another class (or classes) for its implementation then aggregation or association relationships are the only possibilities available. In either case, the using class has access to the public operations and properties of the associate or aggregate component.

For the very large majority of cases, association and aggregation are sufficient for the implementation of classes. However, there are some situations where a class requires another class for its implementation and in addition it must use inheritance. There is no *isA* relation implied. For example, the class used for implementation may be ABSTRACT. Alternatively access to its PROTECTED INTERFACE may be necessary but there is no implication of the *isA* relation between the classes. In other words inheritance is used exclusively for implementation purposes.

Consider a situation where we have identified a class Consultant in the example from Section 7.5. After some thought we might reach the decision that although an instance of this class has many similarities to an instance of the class Employee we do not want there to be an *isA* relationship between them. Essentially we want Employees and Consultants to be treated differently but, given that they have many similarities, it is clearly unwise not to make use of the work done in defining the Employee class. A solution is to use inheritance for implementation.

LOOM records the need for the use of inheritance for implementation by the reserved words INHERITS FROM in the PRIVATE IMPLEMENTATION part of a LOOM script. For example, a class Consultant could be described by:

```
CLASS Consultant
WITH
PUBLIC INTERFACE
  Consultant (aName :String, aDateOfBirth :Date,
```

```
    aFee : Integer)
  name? -> String
  companyName? -> String
  fee? -> Integer
  hiredBy(anEmployer : Company LINK)
PROTECTED INTERFACE
  NONE
PRIVATE IMPLEMENTATION
  INHERITS FROM Employee
  REPRESENTATION
    theFee : Integer
  AGGREGATIONS NONE
  ASSOCIATIONS
    theEmployer : Company LINK
  DEFINITIONS
    METHOD name? -> String AS
      RETURN SEND me THE MESSAGE name? FROM Employee
    ENDMETHOD name?
// Other suitable definitions.
```

  ENDCLASS Consultant

A Consultant class can then make use of the operations and properties of the Employee class in just the same way as with specialisation.

However, the *isA* relation does not hold between the Consultant and Employee classes. A Consultant object is not an Employee object so the polymorphic effect cannot be used. In addition, the operations defined for the Employee class are not automatically available for export by the Consultant class. In the example above the name of an Employee object is available to a client by the design. Operations inherited from the Employee class are actually private. Diagrammatically the implementation inheritance relationship is shown as a dashed arrow as in Figure 7.6.

Clearly, this use of inheritance for implementation purposes must not be confused with the use of inheritance to model the *isA* relation. For this reason, LOOM prohibits the use of any features unique to specialisation when inheritance is used for implementation only. In other words there can be no use of the polymorphic effect and no automatic export of the parent class interface in the descendent class.

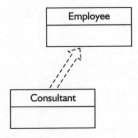

Figure 7.6 *Inheritance for implementation*

It must be stressed that the use of inheritance for implementation should be avoided wherever possible. Unless it is well documented and justified it can lead to confusion.

7.9 Disinheritance

Sometimes when modelling the *isA* relationship a developer feels the need to disinherit some of the operations of a parent class. In order to illustrate the difficulties associated with disinheriting operations the example of a Penguin class inheriting from a Bird class is often cited. As shown in Figure 7.7 the class Penguin is a specialisation of the class Bird.

The difficulty is that in real life a Bird can fly but a Penguin cannot. If a Penguin cannot respond to the operation fly then we cannot substitute a Penguin object for a Bird object. This goes against the rule that a child must be able to be substituted for a parent if the *isA* relation is to hold. Even though it is an unusual circumstance it presents us with a problem that must be solved.

Although the Bird–Penguin example is intended to be humorous it contains the essential elements of a possible software disaster. The hard fact of the matter is that if a designer models the relationship between the class Penguin and the class Bird as one of specialisation then a Penguin *isA* Bird. There can be no disinheritance and that must be the end of the matter. Any compromise with the meaning of specialisation is forbidden.

The question we have to answer is how to establish a relationship between the classes Bird and Penguin that is not one of specialisation. Let us consider a few possibilities:

- Establish a new relation KIND OF that allows disinheritance.

- Model the relation as an association.

- Model the relation as one of specialisation as normal but redefine the operation fly.

- Use inheritance for implementation.

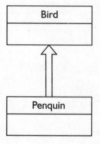

Figure 7.7   *The class* Penguin *as a specialisation of the class* Bird

- Establish a class for flying and non-flying `Birds` specialised from the class `Bird` and then specialise from the class `NonFlyingBird` for the class `Penguin`.

We can easily discard the first candidate which establishes a new KIND OF relation as it is not necessary and can only lead to confusion. It also has the fundamental difficulty of knowing when to stop disinheriting. For example, is a `Penguin` a kind of `Brick` except that it has none of the operations of a `Brick`? (Armstrong and Mitchell, 1994)

The second possibility, that we model the relation as an association between the class `Penguin` and the class `Bird` is a very weak candidate. Our intention is that messages sent to a `Penguin` object are in fact relayed to its `Bird` associate. Clearly we would not put the operation fly on the `Penguin` class interface so the problem of disinheritance would not arise. However, it is not in the spirit of the object oriented paradigm, does not permit the use of the polymorphic effect and is really a misuse of association.

The third possibility should be discarded on the grounds that if an operation fly is on a `Penguin`'s public interface then the designer is specifying that it can fly. The fact that it actually does nothing or, worse, does something else, such as swimming, is just too confusing. Although this course of action is initially attractive and apparently harmless it should not be used. In fact it is far from harmless and is a clear sign that a design is flawed. Recall from Section 7.2 that redefinition of a method should normally involve the use of the parent's method.

The fourth possibility, that we use inheritance for implementation, is a reasonable candidate as it allows the `Penguin` class to export selected inherited parts of the interface of the `Bird` class as described in the following partial LOOM scripts. However, it does not allow the polymorphic effect to be used and it seems contrary to common sense that we are stating that a `Penguin` is not a `Bird` when we know that it is.

```
CLASS Bird
WITH
PUBLIC INTERFACE
  fly
  hop
  peck
  // ...
PROTECTED INTERFACE
  // ...
PRIVATE IMPLEMENTATION
  // ...
DEFINITIONS
// Suitable definitions of the operations that implement
// the behaviour of a Bird.

ENDCLASS Bird

CLASS Penguin
```

```
WITH
PUBLIC INTERFACE
  hop
  peck
  // ...
PROTECTED INTERFACE
  // ...
PRIVATE IMPLEMENTATION
  INHERITS FROM Bird
  // ...
  DEFINITIONS
    METHOD hop
    AS
      SEND me THE MESSAGE hop FROM Bird
    ENDMETHOD hop

    METHOD peck
    AS
      SEND me THE MESSAGE peck FROM Bird
    ENDMETHOD peck
  // ...
```

ENDCLASS Penguin

The last possibility is that we establish different class hierarchies for flying and non-flying birds as shown in Figure 7.8. It is a strong candidate as it is a clear statement that flying and non-flying birds are different and so instances of them cannot be substituted for each other. While the former has an operation fly defined the latter does not. Clearly the Penguin class is a specialisation of the class NonFlyingBird. Although it is a good solution to the problem of disinheritance, if taken to an extreme there is a danger that the designer may have to invent classes that are unreasonable or just too numerous. For example, if we want to disinherit another operation then we would have to establish another two independent class hierarchies.

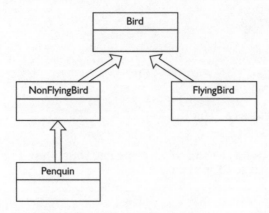

Figure 7.8   *Different class hierarchies for flying and non-flying birds*

On balance the best solution is to adopt the last candidate to solve the problem of disinheritance of an operation and define the class hierarchy so that there is a class for flying and non-flying birds. However, in different circumstances the fourth candidate which uses inheritance for implementation could also be adopted. As a last resort the third candidate which redefines the operation fly might also be used with suitably commented methods to alert a developer to what was being done.

7.10 Multiple inheritance

So far we have considered single inheritance for modelling the *isA* relation. In every case, a descendent class has only one parent. However, it is sometimes necessary to model situations where a descendent class has some of the features of two or more parents. A frequently quoted example is shown in Figure 7.9.

An amphibious vehicle has features of a land and a water vehicle and so it makes sense to model it as a specialisation of both the LandVehicle and WaterVehicle classes. The LOOM script for the class Amphibious Vehicle records this fact by specialising the classes LandVehicle and WaterVehicle.

```
CLASS AmphibiousVehicle
  SPECIALISATION OF LandVehicle, WaterVehicle
WITH
  // As normal.
ENDCLASS  AmphibiousVehicle
```

Clearly this is not the simple *isA* relation as we have defined it, as an amphibious vehicle is not just an example of a land vehicle or a water vehicle but a mixture of both. Although there is nothing intrinsically wrong with multiple inheritance and it can be clearly expressed with LOOM, it is an advanced feature of object orientation that is beyond the scope of this book.

However, before we leave this topic we should note that an alternative to the use of multiple inheritance is to specify an *isA* relation (specialisation) with one of the parents (the parent that most closely resembles the child) and inheritance for implementation with the other, as shown in Figure 7.10.

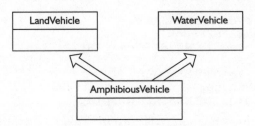

Figure 7.9 *Multiple inheritance*

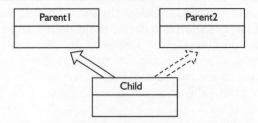

Figure 7.10 *Single inheritance and inheritance for implementation*

For example, in the amphibious water vehicle case we can remove multiple inheritance for specialisation if we decide that an amphibious vehicle is really a specialisation of a land vehicle with just a few extra features implemented by a water vehicle.

7.11 Method redefinition

It is generally acknowledged that it is good practice only to redefine the method for an inherited operation that is qualified as POLYMORPHIC in the parent (Meyers, 1992). The reason for this advice is best explained by an example. Using the definitions of the SalesPerson and Manager classes from Section 7.4, if we have the instantiations:

```
// Create initialised LINK
INSTANCE theEmployee :SalesPerson LINK
INSTANCE theSalesPerson :SalesPerson LINK( ... )
INSTANCE theManager :Manager LINK( ... )
```

then the messages:

```
SEND theSalesPerson THE MESSAGE display?
```

and

```
SEND theManager THE MESSAGE display?
```

would have the expected behaviour as the binding of the appropriate method to the operation display? would normally occur before the program starts to execute, i.e. it is statically bound. Similarly, if we have the messages:

```
SEND theEmployee THE MESSAGE
  assign(theSalesPerson)
SEND theEmployee THE MESSAGE display?

SEND theEmployee THE MESSAGE
  assign(theManager)
SEND theEmployee THE MESSAGE display?
```

then the correct interpretation will result. This is because the operation display? is qualified as POLYMORPHIC in the class SalesPerson and so its method is bound dynamically when the system is executing. First it is bound to the method for a SalesPerson object, then to the method for a Manager object.

However, a different behaviour results if the method display? in the SalesPerson class is not qualified as POLYMORPHIC. The messages:

SEND theSalesPerson THE MESSAGE display?

and

SEND theManager THE MESSAGE display?

execute correctly, as before. The problem lies with the example where the display? message is sent through theEmployee. Even though the message:

SEND theEmployee THE MESSAGE display?

is received by theSalesPerson and theManager as before, they both execute the method for the operation display? defined for an object of class SalesPerson. The reason is that dynamic binding does not occur when POLYMORPHIC is not introduced on the operation signature, and the object theEmployee can only reference the methods defined for the class Sales-Person and not for the classes SalesPerson **and** Manager as we intend. Clearly this is a serious problem and the rule that we should never redefine the method for an operation that is not qualified as POLYMORPHIC should be followed.

7.12 Summary

1. A class is a specialisation of a parent class if it can be considered as an example of the parent. The descendent class normally has additional behaviours not present in the parent but must respond to the same messages as the parent.

2. A descendent class has privileged access to its parent through a protected interface.

3. The polymorphic effect permits a message sent through a LINK to an object of a parent class to be received and interpreted by an object of a descendent class.

4. An abstract base class can have no instances but acts only to define the interface of its descendants.

5. A property of a class may be public provided it is designated as a constant.

6. An operation may be private to a class.

7. Inheritance may be used for the purpose of implementation and not for specialisation if there is no *isA* relation between a parent and descendent class.

8. Disinheritance by a descendent class of an operation advertised by a parent class is not allowed.

9. Multiple inheritance should not be used unless it is really necessary.

10. Only methods that are polymorphic should be redefined if schizophrenic behaviour is to be avoided.

7.13 Exercises

1. Animals that populate the earth can be categorized according to the outline class diagram in Figure 7.11.
   (a) Extend this diagram to encompass other animals, e.g. apes, snakes, birds and dogs.
   (b) Consider which classes should be designated as ABSTRACT.
   (c) Consider an operation move advertised on the PUBLIC INTERFACE of the class Animal, e.g. it could be POLYMORPHIC, DEFERRED or REDEFINED.

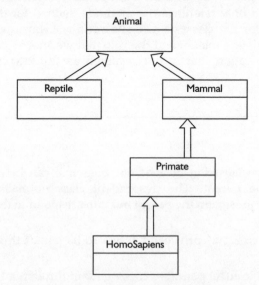

Figure 7.11   *An outline class diagram for animals*

2. A university has a records system to store and retrieve information about its staff and students. Typically records are added and viewed. Staff have a name, address, employee number and department while students have a name, address, matriculation number and course name.
   (a) Construct a class diagram for the records system.
   (b) Develop LOOM scripts for each class and a suitable Application class to exercise them.
   (c) Extend the details held on staff and students.

3. A bank offers two kinds of account to its customers that they can make withdrawals from, deposit funds into and enquire as to the current balance. The first is an ordinary account and the second a current account. Both have an account number and hold the current balance. However, the current account has an overdraft limit that is normally agreed with the bank manager when the account is created. Withdrawals can be made up to the overdraft limit. There is no overdraft limit available for ordinary accounts. Clearly there is no limit on deposits that can be made in either case.
    (a) Construct a class diagram for the bank accounts.
    (b) Develop LOOM scripts to define each class.
    (c) Construct the LOOM script for an `Application` object to exercise the system.
4. Academic staff in a University are designated as either a lecturer or a senior lecturer. Both teach students but a lecturer does a small amount of research while a senior lecturer does a lot of research.
    (a) Construct a class diagram for academic staff.
    (b) Define outline LOOM scripts for each class assuming the polymorphic effect is to be used to its full extent. Method bodies should consist of simple insert messages to the screen such as:

    ```
    SEND theScreen THE MESSAGE
      insert ("Doing some teaching"),

    SEND theScreen THE MESSAGE
      insert ("Doing a little research")
    ```

    and

    ```
    SEND theScreen THE MESSAGE
      insert ("Doing extra research")
    ```

    (c) What changes would be necessary if senior lecturers carry out administrative tasks but lecturers do no administration?
5. A class diagram consists of several symbols. They may be either a class symbol or a relation symbol. With the former the symbol may describe a concrete or abstract class. With the latter the symbol may describe an association, aggregation or specialisation relation. A relation symbol always connects two class symbols but a class symbol may have zero or more relation symbols connected to it.
    (a) Construct a class diagram to describe a class diagram.
    (b) Develop outline LOOM scripts for each class. In particular focus on an operation `draw` that draws a complete class diagram on a computer screen.
6. Object oriented software is commonly developed as successive versions. The first version might be quite rudimentary and later versions increasingly sophisticated. Although this approach is very useful it does pose the problem of version control. We must always be sure that a later version can be used in place of an earlier one. In other words a new version must be compatible with earlier ones. Assume that the versions are numbered as 1.1, 1.2, 1.3, . . . then 2.1, 2.2, 2.3 and so on. Version 1 objects should have the same interface, as should version 2 objects.
    (a) Construct a class diagram and corresponding LOOM scripts that ensures that the `Application` object for each version complies with this requirement.
    (b) Develop an `Application` object to implement a simple version controller.
7. If we return to exercise 4 we find that University staff consist of not just lecturers and senior lecturers but readers and professors as well. They all teach students to the same extent but in addition:

- a lecturer does a small amount of research
- a senior lecturer does a moderate amount of research and some administration
- a reader does a lot of research but no administration
- a professor does a lot of research and some administration.

(a) Construct a class diagram for academic staff.

(b) Define outline LOOM scripts for each class.

8. Sometimes an aggregate component is composed of another aggregate component. We refer to it as a *composite* object. For example, we might have a picture object that is composed of some text, lines, rectangles and another picture. Clearly a picture that is embedded in a picture may have some text, lines, rectangles or another picture. In other words a component of a composite object can be just a single component (a leaf) such as a piece of text, a line or a rectangle or it may have another composite such as another picture.

When constructing a composite object it is important that we develop a simple way of treating a leaf and a composite in the same way. The class diagram of Figure 7.12 solves the problem.

The class Component acts as a common interface for a Leaf or Composite object. Clients refer to LINKs to Components and by using the polymorphic effect we can implement operations advertised by it in the Leaf and Composite classes as appropriate. Typical operations allow clients to add, remove and display? Components. The first two allow a suitable architecture to be constructed and the last allow its inspection. A Leaf object would normally implement operations fully while a Composite object would iterate over its components sending messages to each as appropriate.

(a) Construct an instance diagram showing a Component composed of several Leaf and Composite objects.

(b) Develop scenarios to show how a Component object might implement the operations add and display?.

As this is a rather complex situation that occurs quite frequently we can capture it as a *design pattern* (Gamm et al., 1995) which we can name as *the composite design pattern*. To accomplish this we specialise the Leaf class into Text, Line and Rectangle classes and the Composite class into the Picture class. They have responsibility for implementing operations such as display? that are unique to them. Operations that are not specific are implemented by the classes Component, Leaf and Composite as appropriate.

(c) Develop a LOOM specification for the Composite design pattern.

(d) Show how it might be used with the picture example.

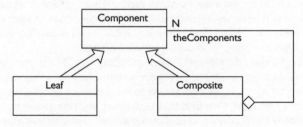

Figure 7.12   *Class diagram for a composite object*

Chapter 8

Case study:
library system revisited

This case study uses the same problem domain as that of Chapter 4 but is intended to highlight the more advanced elements of an object-oriented analysis and design. As before, a simplified system is developed but interested readers can modify it in a variety of ways as indicated in the exercises at the chapter end. As in Chapter 4 the User class is introduced into the design so that a fully working model can be developed.

8.1 System specification

In the case study of Chapter 4 the library held only books. In this case study other items, namely maps and periodicals, are also held. A specification for the system is:

> A library has a name and holds a collection of publications that may be
> periodicals, books or maps. All publications have a title, publication date,
> publisher and reference number. However, periodicals also have an editor
> and a list of articles each with a title and an author. Books have an author
> and edition number. Maps have a series name and sheet number associated
> with them.

There are several users of the library but each has a unique name and address. A user may:

- request a display of the current list of library publications available for loan
- borrow a periodical, book or map from the library by supplying its reference number
- return a periodical, book or map to the library.

The library may:

- ask each user for a display of the publications currently out on loan.

The publications held by the library are ordered by their reference number. Publications held by users are held in the order in which they are borrowed with the least recent one last and the most recent first. For simplicity, the last

publication held is always returned by a user. However, users may make a request
to the library to borrow a publication with a specified reference number.

8.2   Strategy

In the previous case study we adopted a waterfall life cycle consisting of an
analysis, followed by an architectural design, followed by a main design and
finally a detailed design. In this case study we use a modified form of the waterfall
life cycle in which we construct the complete system through a series of *versions*.
Successive versions are a better approximation to the final system. However, we
anticipate that we will revise some of the decisions taken during the construction
of previous versions. This incremental approach to software development has the
advantages of the discipline imposed by the waterfall life cycle but still allows us
some flexibility to experiment and gain confidence in our decisions.

However, we must emphasise that care must be taken with this strategy as
it can encourage an undisciplined approach to software development. It can
quickly get out of control and degenerate to *hacking*. For this reason we insist that
each version must have a clearly specified purpose.

8.3   Version 1

This version has two major aims. The first is to make sure that the initial object
model developed is a good reflection of the problem domain. Clearly, if the object
model is not correct then the rest of the development effort is severely
jeopardised. The second aim is more concerned with the implementation of the
final system and is intended to minimise the risk that it will not execute as we
intend. The second aim will demonstrate that we can use the polymorphic effect
successfully.

8.3.1   *Analysis*

From the system specification it is clear that a user must be able to borrow, return
and display a periodical, book or map from the library. Using our everyday
experience we can readily identify user and library objects. The nomination of
the classes User and Library follow. However, we must decide whether a
periodical, book and map are sufficiently distinct to merit the designation of an
object. The alternative is that they are just a property of another class such as a
publication. This decision is crucial to the analysis, and determines the fundamental structure of the final system. It is not a decision that should be taken lightly.

Clearly periodicals, maps and books have some similarities in that they are a
kind of publication. However, they are also quite different in some important
respects. For example:

- a periodical has an editor and several independent articles,
- a book has an author and appears in different editions,
- a map has a series name and a sheet number,
- users of the library perceive periodicals, books and maps to be conceptually and physically different.

The conclusion is that their differences are sufficient to merit their designation as objects. Therefore, we can identify the classes `Periodical`, `Book` and `Map` of which they are instances. Partial LOOM scripts for the classes identified are:

```
CLASS Library
WITH
  // To be done.
ENDCLASS Libary
```

```
CLASS User
WITH
  // To be done.
ENDCLASS User
```

```
CLASS Periodical
WITH
  // To be done.
ENDCLASS Periodical
```

```
CLASS Book
WITH
  // To be done.
ENDCLASS Book
```

```
CLASS Map
WITH
  // To be done.
ENDCLASS Map
```

8.3.2 *Architectural design*

It is important to understand that two distinct hierarchies are developed in this part of the design. The first is based on specialisations and gives information about the relationships between a class and its ancestors. The second is based on associations or aggregations and gives information about the scope and visibility of classes. Usually both hierarchies are combined in the same class architecture diagram.

If we consider the first hierarchy, then given that we intend using the polymorphic effect, it is reasonable to decide that `Periodical` objects, `Book` objects and `Map` objects are examples of a more general class, `Publication`. Our intention is to send messages to `Publication` objects through a `LINK` but to anticipate that the message will be actually received, and interpreted at run time, by a `Periodical`, `Book` or `Map` object. Clearly, this is a very important decision.

Figure 8.1 describes this hierarchy. Note that the class `Publication` is abstract and so no instance of it can be made. However, we can still have a `LINK` to a `Publication` object (see Section 7.5).

If we consider the second hierarchy, it is clear that there is an association between many `User` objects, which act as the borrowers, and one `Library` object, which acts as the lender. So that the association can be traversed there is a private property `theBorrowers` in the class `Library` which is a container of `User` `LINK`s and a private property `theLender` in the class `User` which is a `LINK` to a `Library` object. In this case study `Users` are held in the container `theBorrowers`, sorted by name, and so a `PSortedCollection` is appropriate (see Appendix B).

It is also clear that each `User` and `Library` object has many `Publication` objects as aggregate components. However, we have a choice of the kind of container that we can use. We can use either a container of complete `Publication` objects or a container of `Publication` `LINK`s. The first implies local memory allocation and the second dynamic memory allocation (see Section 4.9). As we intend using the polymorphic effect, which relies on sending a message through a `LINK`, there is in fact no choice and we must use the second kind of container, i.e. a container of `Publication` `LINK`s.

As the `Publications` borrowed by a `User` are held in the order in which they are borrowed, a `POrderedCollection` is appropriate for the `Users`. Similarly, as we intend holding the `Publications` in the `Library` sorted by their reference number, a `PSortedCollection` is appropriate for the `Library` (see Appendix B).

Figures 8.2(a) and 8.2(b) summarise the position so far. Note that there is no need to use different names for the collection of `Publication` `LINK`s in each class as they are private to the classes concerned.

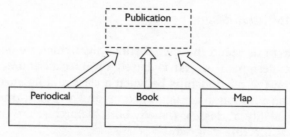

Figure 8.1   *Specialisation heirarchy*

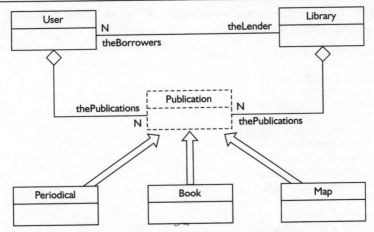

Figure 8.2(a) *Initial architecture class diagram*

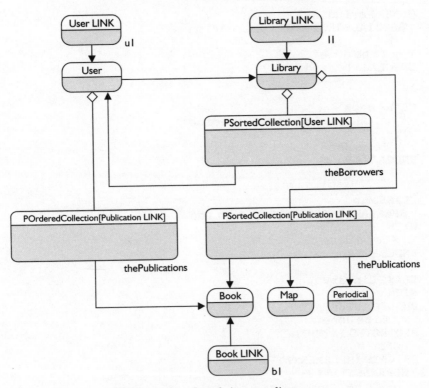

Figure 8.2(b) *Sample instance diagram*

As with the case study of Chapter 4 we should note at this stage that we must supply a lessThan? operation for the classes User and Publication later in the development of the system. This is because objects of these classes are held in containers that use the operation lessThan? to make comparisons. Corresponding LOOM scripts are:

```
ABSTRACT CLASS Publication
WITH
PUBLIC INTERFACE
  // To be done.
PROTECTED INTERFACE
  // To be done.
PRIVATE IMPLEMENTATION
  REPRESENTATION
    // To be done.
  AGGREGATIONS NONE
  ASSOCIATIONS NONE
  DEFINITIONS
    // To be done.
ENDCLASS Publication


CLASS Periodical
  SPECIALISATION OF Publication
WITH
  // To be done.
ENDCLASS Periodical


CLASS Book
  SPECIALISATION OF Publication
WITH
  // To be done.
ENDCLASS Book


CLASS Map
  SPECIALISATION OF Publication
WITH
  // To be done.
ENDCLASS Map

CLASS Library
WITH
PUBLIC INTERFACE
  // To be done.
PROTECTED INTERFACE
  NONE
PRIVATE IMPLEMENTATION
  REPRESENTATION
    // To be done.
  AGGREGATIONS
    thePublications :
      PSortedCollection [Publication LINK]
  ASSOCIATIONS
    theBorrowers : PSortedCollection [User LINK]
      INVERSE OF theLender
```

```
    DEFINITIONS
      // To be done.
    ENDCLASS Library


    CLASS User
    WITH
    PUBLIC INTERFACE
      // To be done.
    PROTECTED INTERFACE
      NONE
    PRIVATE IMPLEMENTATION
      REPRESENTATION
        // To be done.
      AGGREGATIONS NONE
      ASSOCIATIONS
        theLender : Library LINK INVERSE OF theBorrowers
        thePublications :
          POrderedCollection[Publication LINK]
    DEFINITIONS
      // To be done.
    ENDCLASS User
```

Note that an entry of NONE in the PROTECTED INTERFACE section of a class implies that it has no descendent classes. Similarly, an entry of NONE in the AGGREGATIONS or ASSOCIATIONS section means that it has no aggregate components or associates. Clearly, if a class has an associate in the architecture then it should have a PUBLIC INTERFACE entry. If it has a descendent class in the architecture then it would normally have a PROTECTED INTERFACE entry.

8.3.3 *Design*

This part of the development is relatively straightforward as we can use the work done in the first part of the case study of Chapter 4. However, there is one major difference in this case study in that instead of referring to complete copies of Books, the Users and Library refer to LINKs to Publications. This brings with it the potential problems of a dangling reference or memory leakage (see Section 4.9). These are serious problems and it is best to take steps to avoid them as early in the design of the system as possible and not to leave them as implementation concerns. If not properly addressed they could catastrophically damage the integrity of the system. Therefore, it is entirely appropriate that they should be an important element of the design.

At least four courses of action to minimise the risk associated with LINKs are open to us:

• Ensure that the container thePublications in the Library is the sole manager of Publication objects. This means that although another object, e.g. an `Application` object, can create a `Publication` object only a `Library` object, is capable of destroying a `Publication` object.

- Ensure that any other object that refers to a `Publication` object, e.g. a `User`, has at least the same lifetime (or shorter) as the `Library`. This means that the `Publication` it refers to cannot be destroyed as a consequence of the `Library` being destroyed.

- Have tight control over the borrowing, adding and returning of `Publications` from and to the `Library` as well as the borrowing and returning of `Publications` by `Users`. Although we could have a class of `Publications` that are available for borrowing and a class that cannot be borrowed this seems too sophisticated for the current situation. A simpler alternative is to have a `Boolean` property such as `onLoan` associated with the class `Publication`. It is a precondition that before a `User` can borrow a `Publication` from the `Library` the property `onLoan` should be `FALSE` and a postcondition that it is set to `TRUE`. Similarly it is a postcondition that when a `Publication` has been returned or added to the `Library`, the property `onLoan` is set to `FALSE`.

- Make use of the reserved word `NIL` in methods to check that a `LINK` actually refers to a `Publication` before a message is sent through the `LINK` or before a `LINK` is added to a container.

All four courses of action are adopted in this case study.

The detailed design of the `User` and `Library` classes is essentially the same as in the previous case study but the class `Book` has been modified to be a specialisation of a `Publication` class and the class `Map` added.

The class `Publication` is intended to capture all the features of its descendants that are pertinent to a `Library`. As no instances of it are required, it is designated as `ABSTRACT`. A default and a parameterised constructor are supplied on its public interface as well as a `DEFERRED` operation `display?`. The reason it is designated as `DEFERRED` rather than the alternative of `POLYMORPHIC` is so that we can illustrate the use of the `PROTECTED` operation `displayPublicationPart?`. Note that a `DEFERRED` operation is implicitly `POLYMORPHIC` (see Section 7.5). The operations `isOnLoan?` and `setOnLoan` support our strategy for borrowing and returning `Publications`. The operations `lessThan?` and `referenceNumber?` support the use of ordered containers. The private properties of the class `Publication` are those that are common to all `Publications`.

The concrete class `Book` behaves just like a `Publication`. However, it has some additional private properties and a default and a parameterised constructor as well as a method for the operation `display?`. Note the use of the `PROTECTED` operation `displayPublicationPart?` in its method. The class `Map` is essentially the same as the class `Book`.

Corresponding LOOM scripts for the `Publication`, `Book`, `Map` and `Library` classes are detailed in Appendix E.

8.3.4 *Construction of the* `Application` *class*

As this is a first version we do not need to construct the full system. The first aim that we demonstrate is that the object model is a good reflection of the problem domain and this has largely been met in the analysis. The second aim, that we use the polymorphic effect successfully, can be met if we demonstrate the addition of `Publications` to the `Library` and then display them. For the moment we will consider `Publications` as `Books` or `Maps`. `Periodicals` and the rest of the system behaviour can be left to later versions. In general, the aim of a version should be met in as simple a manner as possible. Detail can always be added later.

As with the case study of Chapter 4, the control logic is so straightforward that a dynamic model for the `Application` class is not required. All we need to do to satisfy the aims of the version is to:

- create a `Library` object
- create `Book` and `Map` objects
- add the `Book` and `Map` objects to the `Library`
- display the contents of the `Library`.

Note that the use of object oriented concepts, particularly polymorphism, often simplifies or even eliminates the control logic necessary to construct our software. This is a major advantage whose value should not be underestimated. It has an impact on just about every aspect of the software life cycle from its original development to its long-term maintenance.

Full listings are given in Appendix E but an outline LOOM script for the `run` method of the `Application` class is:

```
// Application class.
METHOD run
AS
  // Create a Library.
  INSTANCE theLibrary : Library LINK ("Dunning Library")

// Create some Book and Map objects with dynamic duration.
INSTANCE b1 :
  Book LINK ("C++ Problem Solving and Programming",
    "Prentice Hall", Date(1,1,1994), "AA1",
    "Barclay",1)
  // ...
INSTANCE m1 :
  Map LINK ("Burgundy", "Michelin", Date(5,5,1994),
    "EE5", "Michelin", 5)

// Add LINKs to Books and Maps to the Library.
SEND theLibrary THE MESSAGE
  addOnePublication(b1)
```

```
// ...
SEND theLibrary THE MESSAGE
  addOnePublication(m1)

// Now see what is in stock.
SEND theLibrary THE MESSAGE
  displayLoanStock?
ENDMETHOD run
```

Note that the Books and Maps are created dynamically by the Application class and then added to the Library which manages them for the rest of the duration of the system.

8.4 Version 2

Now that we have completed the first version we can consider refining it. It seems sensible to focus on the Library class, so that its functionality can be extended to include the borrowing and returning of Publications by Users. Therefore, the aim of this version is to refine the Library class to support the adding, borrowing and returning of Publications by Users.

8.4.1 *Analysis*

The life cycle we have adopted insists that we reconsider our previous analysis as part of the development of the current version. Although in this case there is no additional analysis to be done, it is important to realise that this is not a trivial decision. It is in no sense a waste of effort as it avoids the ever present danger that we construct a version without a proper analysis. Undisciplined hacking is to be avoided at all costs. It is also good to check that all is well and that previous decisions do not need to be changed.

8.4.2 *Architectural design*

As with the analysis, there is no additional architectural design to be done for this version but for the same reasons it is important to register this decision explicitly.

8.4.3 *Design*

As with the design of the previous version, we can draw on the experiences of the case study of Chapter 4 to accelerate its development. No changes are required for the classes Book and Map. Similarly, there are no changes to the classes

Library and User except that we refer to LINKs to Publications rather than Books as previously discussed. Full listings are given in Appendix E.

8.4.4 *Construction of the* Application *class*

A danger with this kind of incremental development is that a change can have an unforeseen effect. Clearly, it is best to discover any problems as soon as possible so that they can be rectified. One way to accomplish this is to make sure that the previous version has not been invalidated by changes introduced in the current version. Therefore a good strategy for the execution of the second version is to append the necessary LOOM sentences to the run method of the previous Application class. Unfortunately the run method can become unacceptably large and complex. A solution is to make use of PRIVATE operations (see exercise 6 of Section 7.13 for a more sophisticated treatment).

Although exhaustive testing is normally inappropriate, the most important test cases should be considered for each version. In this manner final system testing effort can be minimised or even eliminated.

For this version, changes to classes must not affect the first version and in addition we should be able to:

- add Users to the architecture
- instruct a User to borrow a Book or Map from the Library
- instruct a User to return a Book or Map to the Library.

This forms the basis for the design of the LOOM script for the run method of the Application object for the second version. Full listings are given in Appendix E.

```
// Application class.
METHOD run
AS
  // Create a Library with dynamic duration.
  INSTANCE theLibrary :
    Library LINK ("Dunning Library")

  // Initialise the Library using a private
  // operation.
  SEND me THE MESSAGE
  initialiseLibrary(theLibrary)

  // Create and initialise two Users with dynamic
  // duration.
  INSTANCE u1 :User LINK ("Ken", "21 High Street")
  INSTANCE u2 :User LINK ("John", "42 Croft Square")

  // Configure the architecture.
  SEND theLibrary THE MESSAGE addUser (u1)
  SEND theLibrary THE MESSAGE addUser (u2)
```

```
        SEND u1 THE MESSAGE addLibrary(theLibrary)
        SEND u2 THE MESSAGE addLibrary(theLibrary)

        // Display the Users.
        SEND theLibrary THE MESSAGE displayUsers?

        // Borrow some Publications.
        SEND theLibrary THE MESSAGE displayLoanStock?
        SEND u1 THE MESSAGE borrowOnePublication("AA1")
        // ...

        // Display the results.
        SEND theLibrary THE MESSAGE displayLoanStock?
        SEND theLibrary THE MESSAGE
          displayBorrowedStock?

        // Return some Publications.
        SEND u1 THE MESSAGE returnOnePublication
        SEND u2 THE MESSAGE returnOnePublication

        // Display the results.
        SEND theLibrary THE MESSAGE displayLoanStock?
        SEND theLibrary THE MESSAGE
          displayBorrowedStock?
     ENDMETHOD run

     METHOD initialiseLibrary(aLibrary :Library
       INOUT)
     AS
       // Create some Book and Map objects with dynamic
       // duration.
       INSTANCE b1 :
         Book LINK("C++ Problem Solving and Programming",
         "Prentice Hall", Date(1, 1, 1994), "AA1",
           "Barclay", 1)
       // ...
       INSTANCE m1 :
         Map LINK("Burgundy", "Michelin", Date(5,5,1994), "EE5",
           "Michelin", 5)

       // Add LINKs to Books and Maps to the Library.
       SEND aLibrary THE MESSAGE
         addOnePublication(b1)
       // ...
       SEND aLibrary THE MESSAGE addOnePublication(m1)

     ENDMETHOD initialiseLibrary
```

Note the use of the PRIVATE operation initialiseLibrary to simplify the run method. It is also important to realise that our strategy for borrowing and returning Publications means that the container thepublications held by each User must be designated as UNMANAGED. This means that when a Publication LINK is removed on returning a Book or Map the storage associated with the Book or Map is not destroyed. In a sense the Books and Maps never leave the Library. Only a LINK is passed to Users.

8.5 Version 3

8.5.1 Analysis

It is common with this style of systems development that we need to carry out less and less work to develop new versions. In our case all we need do is to introduce the class Periodical. The User, Library, Publication, Book and Map classes require no modifications.

8.5.2 Architectural design

If we reconsider the original system specification it is clear that a Periodical has aggregate components that are Articles. As ever there is the alternative of designating an Article as a property. The class diagram for Figure 8.3(a) and the instance diagram of Figure 8.3(b) describe, respectively, the relationships between the classes and the objects.

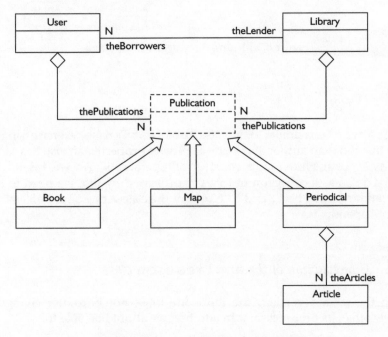

Figure 8.3(a) *Class diagram for version 3*

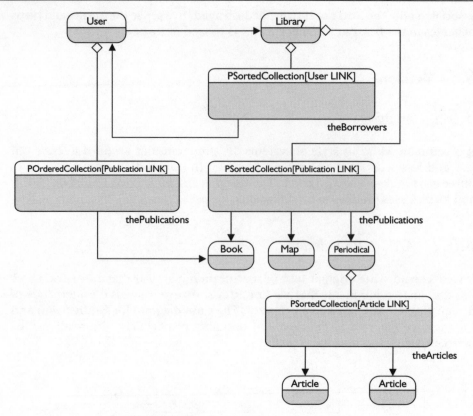

Figure 8.3(b)   *Instance diagram for version 3*

8.5.3 *Design*

The class `Article` is similar to the class `Publication` (see exercise 6 in Section 8.10) in that it has an author and a title as private properties. It also has the usual `display?`, `lessThan?` and constructor operations. As we intend that a `Periodical` has a collection of `Articles` sorted by title we need to supply the operations `lessThan?` and `title?` for the class `Article`. Full listings are given in Appendix E.

8.5.4 *Construction of the* `Application` *class*

As with the second version, the third one must not introduce changes that adversely affect its predecessors. In addition we should be able to:

● add `Periodicals` to the architecture.

This forms the basis for the design of the LOOM script for the `initialise-Library` method of the `Application` object for the third version. Full listings are given in Appendix E.

```
// Application class.
METHOD initialiseLibrary(aLibrary :Library
  INOUT)
AS
  // ...
  // Create some Periodical objects with dynamic
     duration.
  INSTANCE per1 :
    Periodical LINK ("Journal of Object Oriented Programming",
    "SIGS Publications Inc.", Date(1,3,1994),
    "FF6", "R Weiner")
  //...

  // Create some articles with dynamic duration.
  INSTANCE a1 :
    Article LINK ("Guide to OO Training and Mentoring Services",
    "H Newling")
  // ...

  // Add some Articles to the Periodicals.
  SEND per1 THE MESSAGE addOneArticle(a1)
  // ...

  // Add the Periodicals to the Library.
  SEND aLibrary THE MESSAGE
    addOnePublication(per1)
  //...
ENDMETHOD initialiseLibrary
```

Note that the construction and initialisation of the `Periodical` class is treated in exactly the same way as for the `Library` class. This makes sense as they have the same form and it is best to aim for consistency in approach unless there is a very good reason for doing things differently.

8.6 **Consideration of the polymorphic effect**

During the development of the third version we showed how the hierarchy based on the `Publication` class could be widened to include the `Periodical` class. In a similar manner we can also deepen the hierarchy to include new classes that are specialisations of other classes. For example, as part of an analysis we might decide that the `Book` class should be abstract and the classes `Fiction` and `NonFiction` are specialisations of it. Figure 8.4 shows the modified class hierarchy.

Note that for this illustration we have decided that Books that are fiction or non-fiction are sufficiently distinct that they should belong to separate classes. An alternative is to decide they are not really distinct and that the class Book

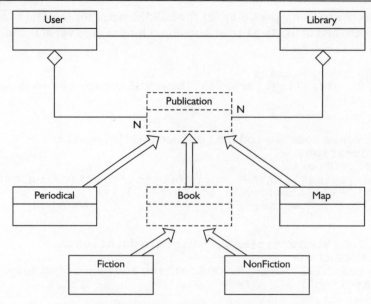

Figure 8.4 *Modified class hierarchy*

should have a property such as theClassification, with a value fiction or non-fiction. The actual decision made depends entirely on the designer and the nature of the problem at hand. To take the first course of action might result in too many somewhat artificial classes and be a bad decision. To take the second might lead to a class with too many properties and a blurring of important distinctions that actually exist in the problem domain. As ever the design process is about making decisions based on experience and human intelligence.

Assuming we adopt the architecture of Figure 8.4, it would have only a slight impact on the rest of the system. Messages could still be sent to Publication objects as before but received by Periodical, Fiction, NonFiction or Map objects to interpret as required. This is a major advantage of using polymorphism.

However, we must be careful that when we add a class to a hierarchy it rightfully belongs to it. For example, the Library could change its stock to include recorded music. We might be tempted to consider recordings as Publication objects and extend the hierarchy as before. However, this would be a mistake. They are recordings, not publications, and should have their own class. To treat them as Publication objects leads to an artificial hierarchy that defeats the primary goal of modelling the problem at hand.

As frequently happens when designing a system, having made this decision we have another one to make. We could have one hierarchy of general Items held in the Library. They could be Publications or Recordings or anything else for that matter. Figure 8.5 describes this architecture.

Clearly the polymorphic effect can be used to its full effect. The cost of this decision is that we must edit all of the LOOM scripts to have Item LINKs instead

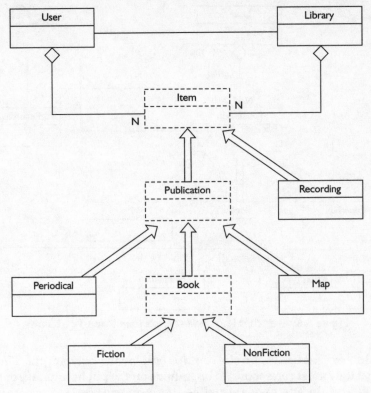

Figure 8.5 Recordings *in the hierarchy*

of Publication LINKs and make the classes Publication and Recording specialisations of the class Item. This is a significant change to make and is really an admission that something has gone wrong with the analysis and design of the earlier version.

Alternatively, we can have a hierarchy of Publications and an independent hierarchy of Recordings held in the library. Figure 8.6 describes this architecture.

Although the polymorphic effect is slightly limited, the impact on the rest of the system is minimised. In addition we can easily distinguish between Recordings and Publications if necessary and have operations such as displayRecordings. The cost of this decision is that we must update the Library and User classes so that they have a container of Recordings as well as Publications.

Before we leave this section we should address a situation that occurs frequently when using the polymorphic effect. If we consider the architecture of Figure 8.2, then as designers we are making the explicit statement that the Library and Users have an aggregation relationship with Publication objects that can be Periodicals, Books or Maps. The point is that the messages

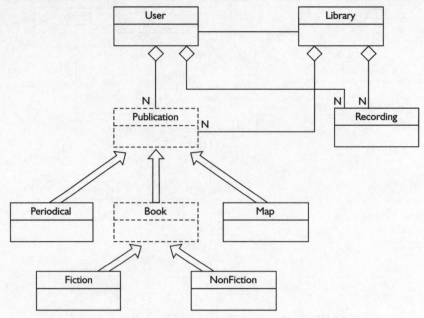

Figure 8.6   Recordings *held separate from* Publications

we send to Periodicals, Books or Maps employ the polymorphic effect. This means that they must correspond to operations on the public interface of the class Publication. In effect we are stating that Periodicals, Books and Maps are all the same in so far as they are Publications.

This leaves us with a problem if we need to distinguish between them. For example, we may need to have operations such as displayPeriodicals?, displayBooks? and displayMaps? available on the public interface of the Library. The solution is straightforward if somewhat clumsy. We iterate over the collection of Publication LINKs and decide if the LINK refers to a Periodical, Book or Map object (see exercise 5 of Section 8.10 for an alternative). The implicit accessor operation className? is defined for every class by LOOM. Its signature is:

    className? -> String POLYMORPHIC

and it returns the name of the class to which some object instance belongs as a String. A LOOM script for the definition of the method for the proposed operation displayBooks? for the class Library follows. The others can be defined in a similar manner.

```
// Class Library.
  METHOD displayBooks?
    AS
      FOREACH aPublication :
      Publication LINK IN thePublications DO
        IF SEND aPublication THE MESSAGE
```

```
         className? == "Book" THEN
         SEND aPublication THE MESSAGE display?
       ENDIF
     ENDFOREACH
   ENDMETHOD displayBooks?
```

8.7 Illegal data entry

Although exception handling is beyond the scope of this book we should consider the possibility of illegal data entry. We do not want to end up in a situation where an object cannot respond in a sensible way to a legal message. An obvious potential problem is when a User attempts to borrow a Publication with a specified reference number. The assumption is that the Publication actually exists in the Library. This may not be true and so a useful strategy to minimise the risk of a run-time error occurring is to check that the Publication is in the Library before sending a message to borrow it.

To implement this strategy we need an operation:

```
exists?(aReferenceNumber :Integer) -> Boolean
```

as part of the public interface of the Library class. Any client wishing to borrow a Publication from the Library would first use this operation to check that it exists. The following LOOM fragments for the Library and User classes clarify the situation.

```
CLASS Libary
WITH
PUBLIC INTERFACE
  exists?(aReferenceNumber :String) -> Boolean
  // ...

DEFINITIONS
  METHOD exists?(aReferenceNumber :String) -> Boolean
  AS
    FOREACH aPublication :Publication LINK IN
         thePublications DO
      IF (SEND aPublication THE MESSAGE
        referenceNumber?) ==
        aReferenceNumber THEN
        RETURN TRUE
      ENDIF
    ENDFOREACH
    RETURN FALSE
ENDMETHOD exists?

ENDCLASS Library
CLASS User
WITH
PUBLIC INTERFACE
```

```
borrowOnePublication(aReferenceNumber :String)
// ...

DEFINITIONS
 METHOD borrowOnePublication(aReferenceNumber :String)
 AS
   IF SEND theLender THE MESSAGE
     exists?(aReferenceNumber) THEN
   SEND thePublications THE MESSAGE
     addFirst(SEND theLender THE MESSAGE
       borrowOnePublication(aReferenceNumber))
   ENDIF
 ENDMETHOD borrowOnePublication

ENDCLASS User
```

An alternative is to make use of the value NIL that is defined for all LINKs to objects, knowing that there is a check before adding NIL to a container. This is the strategy we have adopted in the LOOM scripts detailed in Appendix E.

```
// CLASS Library
METHOD borrowOnePublication?
 (aReferenceNumber :String) ->Publication LINK
AS
 // Deliver a Publication with a specified
 // reference number to a client.

 FOREACH aPublication :
   Publication LINK IN
   thePublications DO
   IF (SEND aPublication THE MESSAGE
     referenceNumber?) == aReferenceNumber AND
     (SEND aPublication THE MESSAGE isOnLoan?) ==
       FALSE THEN
     SEND aPublication THE MESSAGE setOnLoan(TRUE)
     RETURN aPublication
   ENDIF
 ENDFOREACH

 RETURN NIL
ENDMETHOD borrowOnePublication?
```

8.8 Copying an object

In Section 4.9 we discussed the difference between a full copy of an object and a LINK to it. For simplicity we implied that the process of making a full copy of an object involved copying each part of its REPRESENTATION clause. For example, if a Book has the REPRESENTATION

```
theAuthor :String
```

```
theTitle :String
theReferenceNumber :Integer
```

and b1 and b2 are Book objects then the LOOM sentence

```
SEND b2 THE MESSAGE assign(b1)
```

copies the values of the properties theAuthor, theTitle and theReferenceNumber held by b1 to the corresponding properties of b2.

However, the situation is not so clear-cut as it seems. For example, if we introduce a property theLibrarian into the Book class, representing the Library staff member who has subject responsibility for the material covered by that Book:

```
// Class Book.
theLibrarian :Librarian LINK(" ... ")
```

then the situation changes completely. A copy of the kind we have described will result in the LINK value being copied and not the object to which it is LINKed. In other words b1 and b2 will share a LINK to a single Librarian object as shown in Figure 8.7. Perhaps what we really want is a copy of the object to which theLibrarian is LINKed to be made as shown in Figure 8.8. The first is often referred to as a *shallow copy* while the second is a *deep copy*. Clearly they are fundamentally different and each has advantages and disadvantages. For example, a shallow copy has the danger of a dangling reference occurring and a deep copy uses more memory.

A similar situation occurs if we decide that the process of copying an object should copy the AGGREGATIONS and ASSOCIATIONS clauses as well. Unfortunately, a full discussion of the problems that can arise is beyond the scope

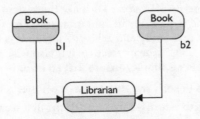

Figure 8.7   *Shallow copy*

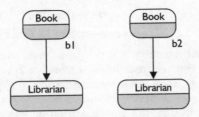

Figure 8.8   *Deep copy*

of this book. However, it is our experience that it is best to avoid deep copying wherever possible and so we have assumed that all copies are shallow.

8.9 Summary

1.   An incremental approach to software development can be used with an OOAD.
2.   Use of the polymorphic effect can often simplify control logic.
3.   The use of LINK values should be treated with great care and every precaution taken as early in the design as possible.
4.   It is relatively easy to add a new class to the bottom of a hierarchy but it can be costly in terms of redevelopment effort to add one to the top.
5.   An object can identify which class it belongs to by use of the implicit operation className?.
6.   Shallow copying of objects is the default.

8.10 Exercises

It is intended that these exercises develop version 3 of the case study detailed in Appendix E. You should start with exercise 1 and work through to the last exercise. As with previous exercises we recommend the use of the modelling environment detailed in Chapter 10. Do not try to do everything at once.

1.   Design a dynamic model for the system following the guidelines in Chapter 5 and the discussions in the exercises of Chapter 4 to make the system menu-driven. You should create a Library and two Users in the run method for the Application object as in version 3 of this case study and achieve more or less the same functionality.

     As the system is going to be interactive, it is also wise to take this opportunity to make it more robust. For example, ensure that an error is reported if:

●   a User attempts to borrow a Publication that is not in the Library
●   a User attempts to return a Publication that was not borrowed
●   a User attempts to return a Publication when he has none out on loan
●   a User attempts to borrow from the Library when it has no Publications available
●   there is an attempt to connect a non-existent User to the Library
●   there is an attempt to connect a non-existent Library to a User.

It is very important that you strive to make your design as consistent as possible. For this reason make sure that you treat the same situation in your software in exactly the same way. For example, error reporting, connection of objects to other objects and the addition of aggregate components should be uniform in all respects across all of the design. This will diminish the risk of an omission or a misunderstanding occurring.

Discussion

It is clear that we should have a Menu object available for the use of the run method
in the Application object. Apart from a default constructor, the only public
operation we require is display?. The items offered by the menu will determine
the functionality of the system.

Consider the following LOOM script for a Menu class:

```
CLASS Menu
WITH
PUBLIC INTERFACE
  Menu
  display?
PROTECTED INTERFACE
  NONE
PRIVATE IMPLEMENTATION
  REPRESENTATION NONE
  AGGREGATIONS NONE
  ASSOCIATIONS NONE
  DEFINITIONS
    METHOD Menu
    AS
      // Nothing to do but an explicit default
      // constructor is good practice
    ENDMETHOD Menu


    METHOD display?
    AS
    SEND theScreen THE MESSAGE
      insert("\n\t\tMENU\n")
    SEND theScreen THE MESSAGE
      insert("\t\t=====\n")

    SEND theScreen THE MESSAGE
      insert("\n\t1:\tadd a Book")
    SEND theScreen THE MESSAGE
      insert("\n\t2:\tadd a Map")
    SEND theScreen THE MESSAGE
      insert("\n\t3:\tadd a Periodical")
    SEND theScreen THE MESSAGE
      insert("\n\t4:\tdisplay items available for loan")
    SEND theScreen THE MESSAGE
      insert("\n\t5:\tdisplay items out on loan")
    SEND theScreen THE MESSAGE
      insert("\n\t6:\tdisplay details of users")
    SEND theScreen THE MESSAGE
      insert("\n\t7:\tborrow an item from the library")
    SEND theScreen THE MESSAGE
      insert("\n\t8:\treturn an item to the library")
    SEND theScreen THE MESSAGE
      insert("\n\t99:\tterminate the system\n")
    SEND theScreen THE MESSAGE
      insert("\n\t\tKey in your choice >>> ")
```

```
ENDMETHOD display?
```

```
ENDCLASS Menu
```

Our error handling is very simple as it merely consists of a message inserted on the screen to inform a system user that a problem has occurred. A typical piece of LOOM taken from the class `Library` that deals with an error condition is:

```
METHOD returnOnePublication(aReferenceNumber
  :String)
AS
  FOREACH aPublication :Publication LINK IN
    thePublications DO

IF (SEND aPublication THE MESSAGE
  referenceNumber?) == aReferenceNumber
    AND (SEND aPublication THE MESSAGE onLoan?) ==
      TRUE
THEN
  SEND aPublication THE MESSAGE setOnLoan(FALSE)
  RETURN
ENDIF

  ENDFOREACH

// Only reached if the Publication was not loaned
// to a User.
SEND theScreen THE MESSAGE
insert("\n\nError detected in
  Library:\npublication to be returned was not
  on loan\n\n")
ENDMETHOD returnOnePublication
```

The `run` method for the `Application` object requires considerable effort to reflect the new system behaviour. In particular, it must be able to extract a choice made and then respond to it in the appropriate manner. This implies an extensive selection sentence with rather tedious keyboard and screen interactions. We can minimise the latter by using `PRIVATE` operations but for the moment at least (see exercise 3) we are faced with the prospect of constructing a rather extensive `run` method. Consider the following partial LOOM script for the `run` method:

```
METHOD run
AS
  // Create top-level objects with dynamic duration.
  INSTANCE theLibrary :Library LINK("Dunning Library")
  INSTANCE u1 :User LINK("Ken", "21 High Street")
  INSTANCE u2 :User LINK("John", "42 Croft Square")
  INSTANCE theMenu :Menu

  // Configure the architecture.
  SEND theLibrary THE MESSAGE addUser(u1)
  SEND theLibrary THE MESSAGE addUser(u2)
  SEND u1 THE MESSAGE addLibrary(theLibrary)
  SEND u2 THE MESSAGE addLibrary(theLibrary)
```

```
// Objects required for interaction with the
// keyboard.
// Publications.
INSTANCE theTitle : String("")
INSTANCE thePublisher : String("")
INSTANCE theDate : Date
INSTANCE theReferenceNumber : String("")

// Books.
INSTANCE theAuthor : String("")
INSTANCE theEdition : Integer(1)

// Maps.
INSTANCE theSeriesName : String("")
INSTANCE theSheetNumber : Integer(1)

// Periodicals.
INSTANCE theEditor : String("")

// Substitute for a user identity.
INSTANCE theUserId : Integer(0)
INSTANCE theResponse : String("")

SEND theScreen THE MESSAGE
  insert("\tSTART OF PROGRAM EXECUTION\n")
SEND theScreen THE MESSAGE
  insert("\t=============================\n")

// Start of the user interaction loop.
  WHILE theResponse != "99" DO

  SEND theScreen THE MESSAGE
    insert("\n\tPress enter to continue\t >>> ")
  SEND theKeyboard THE MESSAGE
    extractLine(theResponse)

  SEND theMenu THE MESSAGE display?
  SEND theKeyboard THE MESSAGE
    extractLine(theResponse )

  // Start of the event handling.

  // Add a Book.
  IF theResponse == "1" THEN

    SEND me THE MESSAGE
      getBookDetail(theTitle, thePublisher, theDate,
      theReferenceNumber, theAuthor, theEdition)

    INSTANCE theBook :
      Book LINK(theTitle, thePublisher, theDate,
      theReferenceNumber, theAuthor, theEdition)
    SEND theLibrary THE MESSAGE
      addOnePublication(theBook)
```

```
                    // Add a Map.
                    ELSEIF theResponse == "2" THEN

                       SEND me THE MESSAGE
                         getMapDetail(theTitle, thePublisher, theDate,
                         theReferenceNumber, theSeriesName,
                          theSheetNumber)

                       INSTANCE theMap :
                         Map LINK(theTitle, thePublisher, theDate,
                         theReferenceNumber,
                         theSeriesName, theSheetNumber)
                       SEND theLibrary THE MESSAGE
                         addOnePublication(theMap)

                    // Add a Periodical.
                    ELSEIF theResponse == "3" THEN

                       SEND me THE MESSAGE
                       getPeriodicalDetail(theTitle, thePublisher,
                         theDate,
                         theReferenceNumber, theEditor)

                       INSTANCE thePeriodical :
                         Periodical LINK(theTitle, thePublisher, theDate,
                         theReferenceNumber, theEditor)

                       SEND theScreen THE MESSAGE
                         insert("\n\t\tadd an article?(YES/NO) >>> ")
                       SEND theKeyboard THE MESSAGE extract(theResponse )
                       SEND theResponse THE MESSAGE toUpper
                       // convert all characters to uppercase

                       // Add Articles as required.
                       WHILE theResponse == "YES" DO

                       SEND me THE MESSAGE
                         getArticleDetail(theTitle, theAuthor)

                       INSTANCE theArticle :
                         Article LINK(theTitle, theAuthor)
                       SEND thePeriodical THE MESSAGE
                         addOneArticle(theArticle)

                       SEND theScreen THE MESSAGE
                         insert("\n\t\tadd another article?(YES/NO) >>> ")
                       SEND theKeyboard THE MESSAGE extract(theResponse)
                       SEND theResponse THE MESSAGE toUpper

                       ENDWHILE

                       SEND theLibrary THE MESSAGE
                         addOnePublication(thePeriodical)
```

```
// Display Publications in the Library available for
// loan.
ELSEIF theResponse == "4" THEN
  SEND theLibrary THE MESSAGE displayLoanStock?

// Display the Publications in the Library out on
// loan.
ELSEIF theResponse == "5" THEN
  SEND theLibrary THE MESSAGE displayBorrowedStock?

// Display the User details.
ELSEIF theResponse == "6" THEN
  SEND theLibrary THE MESSAGE displayUsers?

// Direct a User to borrow a Publication.
ELSEIF theResponse == "7" THEN
  SEND me THE MESSAGE getUserId(theUserId)
  SEND me THE MESSAGE
    getReferenceNumber(theReferenceNumber)
  IF theUserId == 1 THEN
    SEND u1 THE MESSAGE
      borrowOnePublication(theReferenceNumber)
  ELSE
    SEND u2 THE MESSAGE
      borrowOnePublication(theReferenceNumber)
  ENDIF

// Direct a User to return a Publication.
ELSEIF theResponse == "8" THEN
  SEND me THE MESSAGE getUserId(theUserId)

  IF theUserId == 1 THEN
    SEND u1 THE MESSAGE returnOnePublication
  ELSE
    SEND u2 THE MESSAGE returnOnePublication
  ENDIF

// Terminate the system run.
ELSEIF theResponse == "99" THEN
  SEND theScreen THE MESSAGE
    insert("\n\n\t\tSYSTEM TERMINATING\n")

// Report error.
ELSE
  SEND theScreen THE MESSAGE
    insert("\n\nError detected in Application
    :\n\tchoice not recognised\n\n")

ENDIF

ENDWHILE

ENDMETHOD run
```

A typical PRIVATE operation to carry out interactions with the system User is:

```
METHOD getBookDetail(aTitle :String OUT,
  aPublisher :String OUT, aDate :Date OUT,
    aReferenceNumber :String OUT,
      anAuthor :String OUT,
      anEdition :Integer OUT)
AS
  SEND me THE MESSAGE
    getPublicationDetail(aTitle, aPublisher,
    aDate, aReferenceNumber)

  SEND theScreen THE MESSAGE
    insert("\n\tAuthor\t\t\t >>> ")
  SEND theKeyboard THE MESSAGE
    extractLine(anAuthor)

  SEND theScreen THE MESSAGE
    insert("\n\tEdition\t\t\t >>> ")
  SEND theKeyboard THE MESSAGE extract(anEdition)
ENDMETHOD getBookDetail
```

2. Modify the system so that Users of the Library can be created and deleted interactively.

Discussion

So far in this chapter we have effectively *hard-wired* the number of the Users of the Library. However, this does not reflect what we might actually require of the system in practice. An alternative is to create Users interactively, configure them into the architecture and then send messages to them as appropriate.

Following on from the discussions of heap-based storage in Section 8.3.2 it is clear that we should have a MANAGED container for User LINKs. Rather than give the responsibility for looking after this container to the Library or the Application we have chosen to designate a specific object of the class UserManager for this purpose. Its LOOM specification is:

```
CLASS UserManager
  WITH
  PUBLIC INTERFACE
    UserManager
    addUser(aUser :User LINK )
    deleteUser(aName :String)
    targetUser?(aName :String) -> User LINK
PROTECTED INTERFACE
  NONE
PRIVATE IMPLEMENTATION
  REPRESENTATION NONE
  AGGREGATIONS NONE
  ASSOCIATIONS
    theUsers :POrderedCollection[User LINK]
  DEFINITIONS
    METHOD UserManager
    AS
      SEND theUsers THE MESSAGE
```

```
            initialise(DEFAULTSIZE, MANAGED)
      ENDMETHOD UserManager

      METHOD addUser(aUser : User LINK )
      AS
        IF aUser != NIL THEN
          SEND theUsers THE MESSAGE add(aUser)

        ELSE
          SEND theScreen THE MESSAGE
            insert("\n\nError detected in User
              Manager:\n\tattempt to add an illegal
              User\n\n")
        ENDIF
ENDMETHOD addUser

METHOD deleteUser(aName : String)
AS
  FOREACH aUser : User LINK IN theUsers DO

    IF (SEND aUser THE MESSAGE name?) == aName THEN

    WHILE (SEND aUser THE MESSAGE
      numberOfPublications?) > 0 DO
      SEND aUser THE MESSAGE returnOnePublication
    ENDWHILE
    SEND theUsers THE MESSAGE remove(aUser)

    RETURN

ENDIF

ENDFOREACH

// Only reached if no User is found.
SEND theScreen THE MESSAGE
  insert("\n\nError detected in User
    Manager:\n\tattempt to delete a non-existent
    User\n\n")

ENDMETHOD deleteUser

METHOD targetUser?(aName : String) -> User LINK
AS
  FOREACH aUser : User LINK IN theUsers DO

  IF (SEND aUser THE MESSAGE name?) == aName THEN
    RETURN aUser
  ENDIF

  ENDFOREACH

  // Only reached if no user with aName is found.
  RETURN NIL
```

```
    ENDMETHOD targetUser?

  ENDCLASS UserManager
```

Note how the operation deleteUser (aName :String) makes sure that a User has returned all of his Publications to the Library before he is deleted from the system. Also note how the operation targetUser? (aName :String) -> User LINK delivers a LINK to a designated User so that a message can be sent to it in the normal way.

The Menu class requires slight adjustments so that we can add and delete a User as well as direct a User to borrow and return a Publication.

The run method in the Application class is now:

```
METHOD run
AS
  // Create top-level objects with dynamic duration.
  INSTANCE theLibrary :Library LINK ("University")
  INSTANCE theMenu :Menu
  INSTANCE theUserManager :
    UserManager LINK ("Manager")

  //...

  // Start of main execution loop.
  WHILE theResponse != "99" DO

    //...

    // Add a new user to the system.
  IF theResponse == "1" THEN
    SEND me THE MESSAGE
      getUserDetail (theName, theAddress)
    INSTANCE theNewUser :User LINK (theName,
      theAddress)

  SEND theLibrary THE MESSAGE addUser (theNewUser)
  SEND theNewUser THE MESSAGE addLibrary (theLibrary)
  SEND theUserManager THE MESSAGE
    addUser (theNewUser)

  // Direct a user to borrow a publication.
  ELSEIF theResponse == "8" THEN
    SEND me THE MESSAGE getUserName (theName)
    SEND theUser THE MESSAGE
      assign (SEND theUserManager THE MESSAGE
        targetUser? (theName))
    IF theUser != NIL THEN
      SEND me THE MESSAGE
        getReferenceNumber (theReferenceNumber)
      SEND theUser THE MESSAGE
        borrowOnePublication (theReferenceNumber)
    ELSE
      SEND theScreen THE MESSAGE
        insert ("\n\nError detected in
```

```
                  Application:\n\tattempt to send a message to a
                  non-existent user\n\n")
        ENDIF

     // Direct a user to return a publication.
     ELSEIF theResponse == "9" THEN
        SEND me THE MESSAGE getUserName(theName)
        SEND theUser THE MESSAGE
          assign(SEND theUserManager THE MESSAGE
            targetUser?(theName))

        IF theUser != NIL THEN
        SEND theUser THE MESSAGE returnOnePublication
        ELSE
          SEND theScreen THE MESSAGE insert("\n\nError
            detected in Application:\n\tattempt to send a
            message to a non-existent user\n\n")
        ENDIF

     // Delete a user from the system.
     ELSEIF theResponse == "10" THEN
        SEND me THE MESSAGE getUserName(theName)
        SEND theLibrary THE MESSAGE deleteUser(theName)
        SEND theUserManager THE MESSAGE
          deleteUser(theName)

     // ...

     ENDIF

     ENDWHILE

     ENDMETHOD run
```

3. Clearly, the `run` method in the `Application` object of exercise 2 is uncomfortably large. With object-oriented systems we expect methods to be rather small but it is clear that as the system is enhanced the problem can only get worse. The conclusion is that it is important that we propose a solution then implement it with LOOM.

Discussion

The reason that the run method of the `Application` object is too large is that it has too much *work* to do. It has to act as an event recogniser as well as an event handler. A good object oriented solution is to delegate responsibility to another object.

We can leave the `Application` object with the responsibility for recognising events but propose a new object of class `Controller` that acts as the event handler. In effect it controls the overall behaviour of the system. All we need do is to make sure that the top-level objects of the previous exercise are aggregate components of the `Controller` object and we have a workable solution.

Figure 8.9 describes the essence of new system architecture.

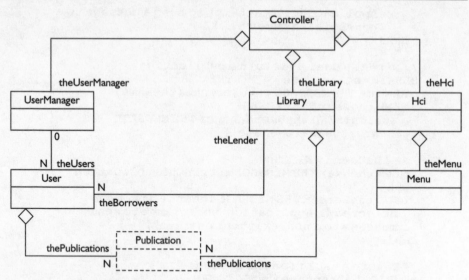

Figure 8.9 *The new system architecture with a* `Controller` *object*

The LOOM script of the `run` method of the `Application` object is now much simplified:

```
METHOD run
AS
// Create top-level object with local duration.
INSTANCE theController :Controller

INSTANCE theResponse :String("")

SEND theScreen THE MESSAGE
  insert("\tSTART OF PROGRAM EXECUTION\n")
SEND theScreen THE MESSAGE
  insert("\t=============================\n")

// Main execution loop (actually an event
   recogniser).
WHILE theResponse != "99" DO

  SEND theScreen THE MESSAGE
    insert("\nPress Enter to continue\t >>> ")
  SEND theKeyboard THE MESSAGE
    extractLine(theResponse)
  SEND theResponse THE MESSAGE toUpper

  SEND theController THE MESSAGE displayMenu?
  SEND theKeyboard THE MESSAGE extract(theResponse)

  // Add a new user to the system.
  IF theResponse == "1" THEN
    SEND theController THE MESSAGE addUser

  // Add a new Book to the system.
```

```
        ELSEIF theResponse == "2" THEN
          SEND theController THE MESSAGE addBook

        // Add a new Map to the system.
        ELSEIF theResponse == "3" THEN
          SEND theController THE MESSAGE addMap

        // Add a new Periodical to the system.
        ELSEIF theResponse == "4" THEN
          SEND theController THE MESSAGE addPeriodical

        // Display the library stock available for loan to users.
        ELSEIF theResponse == "5" THEN
          SEND theController THE MESSAGE displayLoanStock?

        // Display the library stock out on loan to users.
        ELSEIF theResponse == "6" THEN
          SEND theController THE MESSAGE
            displayBorrowedStock?

        // Display details of the users of the library.
        ELSEIF theResponse == "7" THEN
          SEND theController THE MESSAGE displayUsers?

        // Direct a user to borrow a publication.
        ELSEIF theResponse == "8" THEN
          SEND theController THE MESSAGE
            borrowOnePublication

        // Direct a user to return a publication.
        ELSEIF theResponse == "9" THEN
          SEND theController THE MESSAGE
            returnOnePublication

        // Delete a user from the system.
        ELSEIF theResponse == "10" THEN
          SEND theController THE MESSAGE deleteUser

        // Finish the session.
        ELSEIF theResponse == "99" THEN
          SEND theScreen THE MESSAGE
            insert("\n\n\t\tSYSTEM TERMINATING\n")

        ELSE
          SEND theScreen THE MESSAGE insert("\n\nError
            detected in Application :\n\tchoice not
            recognised\n\n")

        ENDIF

    ENDWHILE

ENDMETHOD run
```

The LOOM script for the Controller class is:

```
CLASS Controller
WITH
PUBLIC INTERFACE
  Controller
  addUser
  deleteUser
  addBook
  addMap
  addPeriodical
  borrowOnePublication
  returnOnePublication
  displayLoanStock?
  displayBorrowedStock?
  displayUsers?
  displayMenu?
PROTECTED INTERFACE
  NONE
PRIVATE IMPLEMENTATION
  REPRESENTATION
    theTitle :String
    thePublisher :String
    theDate :Date
    theReferenceNumber :String
    theAuthor :String
    theEdition :Integer
    theSeriesName :String
    theSheetNumber :Integer
    theEditor :String
    theName :String
    theAddress :String
    theResponse :String
    theUser :User LINK
  AGGREGATIONS
    theHci :Hci
    theLibrary :Library LINK
    theUserManager :UserManager LINK
  ASSOCIATIONS NONE
  DEFINITIONS
    METHOD Controller
    AS
      // Nothing to do but the use of an explicit default
      // contructor is wise.
    ENDMETHOD Controller

METHOD addUser
AS
  SEND theHci THE MESSAGE
    getUserDetail(theName, theAddress)
  INSTANCE theNewUser :
    User LINK(theName, theAddress)

  SEND theLibrary THE MESSAGE addUser(theNewUser)
```

```
      SEND theNewUser THE MESSAGE addLibrary(theLibrary)

      SEND theUserManager THE MESSAGE
        addUser(theNewUser)
   ENDMETHOD addUser

   METHOD deleteUser
   AS
     SEND theHci THE MESSAGE getUserName(theName)

       SEND theLibrary THE MESSAGE deleteUser(theName)

       SEND theUserManager THE MESSAGE
         deleteUser(theName)
   ENDMETHOD deleteUser

   METHOD addBook
   AS
     SEND theHci THE MESSAGE
       getBookDetail(theTitle, thePublisher, theDate,
       theReferenceNumber, theAuthor, theEdition)
     INSTANCE theBook :
       Book LINK(theTitle, thePublisher, theDate,
         theReferenceNumber, theAuthor, theEdition)

   SEND theLibrary THE MESSAGE
     addOnePublication(theBook)

   ENDMETHOD addBook

   METHOD addMap
   AS
     SEND theHci THE MESSAGE
       getMapDetail(theTitle, thePublisher, theDate,
       theReferenceNumber, theSeriesName,
         theSheetNumber)
     INSTANCE theMap :
       Map LINK(theTitle, thePublisher, theDate,
         theReferenceNumber,
         theSeriesName, theSheetNumber)

     SEND theLibrary THE MESSAGE
       addOnePublication(theMap)
   ENDMETHOD addMap

   METHOD addPeriodical
   AS
     SEND theHci THE MESSAGE
       getPeriodicalDetail(theTitle, thePublisher, theDate,
         theReferenceNumber, theEditor)
     INSTANCE thePeriodical :
       Periodical LINK(theTitle, thePublisher, theDate,
         theReferenceNumber, theEditor)
```

```
        SEND theScreen THE MESSAGE
          insert("\n\t\tadd an article?(YES/NO) >>> ")
        SEND theKeyboard THE MESSAGE extract(theResponse )
        SEND theResponse THE MESSAGE toUpper

        WHILE theResponse == "YES" DO
          SEND theHci THE MESSAGE
            getArticleDetail(theTitle, theAuthor)
          INSTANCE theArticle :Article LINK(theTitle, theAuthor)

          SEND thePeriodical THE MESSAGE
            addOneArticle(theArticle)

          SEND theScreen THE MESSAGE
            insert("\n\t\tadd another article?(YES/NO)
              >>> ")
          SEND theKeyboard THE MESSAGE extract(theResponse)
          SEND theResponse THE MESSAGE toUpper
          ENDWHILE
        ENDMETHOD addPeriodical

        METHOD displayLoanStock?
        AS
          SEND theLibrary THE MESSAGE displayLoanStock?
        ENDMETHOD displayLoanStock?

        METHOD displayBorrowedStock?
        AS
          SEND theLibrary THE MESSAGE displayBorrowedStock?
        ENDMETHOD displayBorrowedStock?

        METHOD displayUsers?
        AS
          SEND theLibrary THE MESSAGE displayUsers?
        ENDMETHOD displayUsers?

        METHOD displayMenu?
        AS
          SEND theHci THE MESSAGE displayMenu?
        ENDMETHOD displayMenu?

        ENDCLASS Controller
```

The rest of the system is of course unchanged.

4. Clearly, as the number of Publications held by the Library increases it is inevitable that there will be a requirement to save and initialise the state of the Library using a file. Modify the model from the previous exercise accordingly. You can assume that only Publications not out on loan are saved.

5. As the Publications in the Library grow in number it becomes more and more difficult to justify one container of Publications. Consider having a container for each kind of Publication and reconstruct the system accordingly (see Section 8.6).

6. Redesign the class diagram for the system so that an Article is a specialisation of a Publication (see Section 8.6). Reconstruct the system accordingly.

7. Using the version control strategy described in exercise 6 of Section 7.13, develop three versions of the class `Library`. The first should support adding and displaying `Publications`. The second should also support `Users` borrowing and returning `Publications`. Finally, the third version should support loading and saving `Publications` stored in a file.

   The second version must be able to be used in place of the first. The third must also be able to be used in place of the second and first.

   Construct a suitable `Application` class to test your version control.

Chapter 9

Inheritance

The previous chapters introduced the SPECIALISATION OF clause into a LOOM class specification. Such a class, referred to as the subclass, inherits all the PUBLIC and PROTECTED features of its superclass introduced by this clause. Additionally, of course, the subclass may introduce new features which are particular to this subclass. An instance of the subclass may be sent any of the messages that could be received by an instance of the superclass. An instance of the subclass may also be sent any new messages defined for that class. A subclass may redefine the behaviour of any of its inherited methods. The superclass may qualify some of its operations as POLYMORPHIC to obtain the effect of dynamic binding. Finally, the superclass may be marked as ABSTRACT with DEFERRED operations which the concrete specialisations define. We shall now consider these design features and their realisation in C++.

9.1 Specialisation

In C++ a subclass is referred to as the *derived class*, and the superclass is known as the *base class*. While we should normally consider the terms as synonyms, here we shall deliberately retain the distinction to separate our design concerns from the implementation issues. Consider the Person class of Chapter 7 of which the Employee class is a specialisation. The Person class might appear in C++ as:

```
class Person {
public:
 Person(const CString& aName, const CDate& aDOB);

 CString name(void) const;
 int age(void) const;

 private:
 CString theName;
 CDate theDateOfBirth;
};
```

in which the properties are represented by the data members `theName` and
`theDateOfBirth`. The operations supported by this class are the interrogatives
`name?` and `age?` realised by the two C++ member functions `name` and `age` as
described in Chapter 6.

Suppose we now wish to introduce the new class `Employee`. An `Employee`
is also a person, distinguished by having a job title and salary associated with
being an employee of some organisation. Class inheritance allows some of the
members of the base class to be used as if they are the members of the derived
class. The class `Employee` can be introduced inheriting all the `public` and
`protected` members of the base class `Person`. This means that all operations
that can be performed on a `Person` can also be performed on an instance of class
`Employee`. Thus we may have:

```
Employee e1( ... ); // constructor
cout << e1.name(); // print name
```

An employee also has the properties `theJobTitle` and `theSalary` noted
above which distinguish it from an ordinary person. We can, therefore, extend
the inherited features by providing in the subclass additional properties and
operations particular to that category of object.

Class derivation is denoted by including in the C++ class header a
`derivation list` of the classes from which to inherit members. The named
classes in the derivation list are the base classes. The header for class `Employee`
would appear as:

```
class Employee : public Person { ... };
```

The keyword `public` denotes that `Employee` is a publicly derived class of
the base class `Person`. This means that the public members of the base class
are also public members of the derived class. This is, of course, our
interpretation from the LOOM `SPECIALISATION OF` clause:

```
CLASS Employee
  SPECIALISATION OF Person
WITH
  // ...
ENDCLASS Employee
```

Because of the derivation list, there is no need to repeat the inherited services
of the base classes. They are automatically part of the derived class services. The
definition for `Employee` is:

```
class Employee : public Person {
public:
  Employee(const CString& aName,
  const CDate& aDOB,
  const CString& aTitle, int aSalary);

CString  jobTitle(void) const;
int      salary(void) const;
```

```
private:
  CString theJobTitle;
  int     theSalary;
};
```

As we have already noted, a derived class incorporates some additional features not present in the base class. Here, class Employee includes two data members representing the title of the job and its associated salary. Two member functions provide access to these data values. Hence we may write:

```
Employee e2("John Savage", CDate(1, 1, 1973), "Lecturer",
20000);

cout << e2.jobTitle();  // Lecturer
cout << e2.name();      // John Savage
```

Note how the last statement permits us to send e2, an instance of class Employee, the message name, an operation defined in the base class Person and inherited by the derived class Employee without further definition. Significantly, only the differences between the two classes need be implemented.

Not all members of the base class are inherited by the derived class. Constructors, destructors and the overloaded assignment operator only apply to the base class and are not automatically inherited. This is not unreasonable since, as we have seen, a derived class may include additional data members which will require appropriate treatment under, for example, initialisation. The constructor for the derived class will be responsible for initialising both its own and its inherited data members. When we create an instance of the class Person, we initialise its data members by a constructor call. By the same token, the constructor for the derived class Employee achieves proper initialisation of its inherited data members through its base class constructor. This we denote by a base class constructor call in the member initialisation list of the derived class constructor:

```
Employee::Employee(const CString& aName,
  const CDate& aDOB, const CString& aTitle,
  int aSalary)
: Person(aName, aDOB),      // base constructor
  theJobTitle(aTitle),
  theSalary(aSalary)
{}
```

This is, of course, a direct mapping of the LOOM method:

```
CLASS Employee
  SPECIALISATION OF Person
WITH
  // ...
    METHOD Employee(aName : String, aDOB : Date,
      aTitle : String, aSalary : Integer)
    AS
      SEND SUPERCLASS PersonTHE MESSAGE
        initialise(aName, aDOB)
```

```
        SEND theJobTitleTHE MESSAGE
          initialise(aTitle)
        SEND theSalaryTHE MESSAGE
          initialise(aSalary)
      ENDMETHOD Employee

      ENDCLASS Employee
```

A derived class may consider redefining some of the service functions of the base class. For example, a company employing a number of employees may require a precise age value for each of its `Employee` objects. Here then we shall wish to redefine the service function `age` inherited from the base class `Person`. The name and signature for the redefined function appearing in the derived class must match exactly the function prototype in the base class:

```
      class Employee : public Person {
      public:
      int age(void) const; // redefinition
      };
```

The implementation of function `age` from the derived class `Employee` will involve a more complex date-handling algorithm than that used by the base class, but will of course involve today's date and the person's date of birth:

```
      intEmployee::age(void) const
      {
        CDate  today;
        int    todayYear(today.year());
        int    dobYear(theDateOfBirth.year());
                       // reference to inherited member
                       // ... but see discussion below
        // ... remainder of new algorithm
        return ...
```

The problem with this implementation is that the derived class member function `age` needs to reference a data member of the base class, i.e. `theDateOfBirth`. The base class `Person` has rightly placed its data member `theDateOfBirth` in a private section. The principle of information hiding would be violated if it were made a public member. To resolve this conflict, a class, that is to be the subject of inheritance for which some of its data members will be referenced in a function of the derived class needs some way to respect the principle of information hiding yet make accessible its otherwise hidden members. This we achieve with an additional access level called `protected` class members. Protected class members under normal circumstances behave as private members inaccessible to clients using the class. However, under inheritance a protected class member operates as a public member to the derived class:

```
      class Person {
      public:
        // ...
```

```
protected:
  CDate          dob(void) const;              // for use by
                                               // subclasses
private:
  CString        theName;
  CDate          theDateOfBirth;
};
```

The implementation for the derived class version of function age now gains access to the data member theDateOfBirth through the function dob which is not otherwise accessible to clients of the Person class:

```
int Employee::age(void) const
{
  CDate    today;
  int      todayYear(today.year());
  int      dobYear(dob().year());               // note syntax
  // ... remainder of new algorithm
  return ...
}
```

Pay particular attention to the syntax of the expression dob().year(). The sub expression dob() invokes the inherited (protected) member function and delivers a copy of the CDate object representing the person's date of birth. To this CDate object we now apply the query operation year() to obtain the year component of that date value. Strictly, this compact C++ code has come from the two LOOM sentences:

```
INSTANCE myDOB :Date(SEND me THE MESSAGE dob?)
INSTANCE dobYear :Integer(SEND myDOB THE
  MESSAGE year?)
```

and we see that the function call dob() is a permissible abbreviation for this->dob().

It is appropriate to consider how objects of the base and derived classes find the code for some function applied to it. Consider, for example, the code:

```
Person     p1( ... );      // constructor
int p1sAge = p1.age();     // member function
```

Here the Person object p1 executes the code for the member function age defined in class Person. This we show in Figure 9.1 with objects represented as soft rectangular figures and function execution as arrowed lines.

Equally, when we execute the fragment:

```
Employee e1( ... );        // constructor
int e1sAge = e1.age();     // member function
```

the code for the member function age of class Employee is executed since class Employee redefines this function (see Figure 9.2).

However, when we execute the fragment:

```
Employee e2( ... ); // constructor
CString e2sName = e2.name(); // member function
```

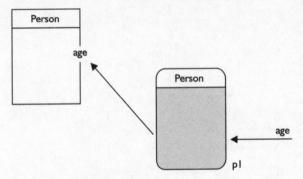

Figure 9.1   *Method lookup*

the compiler will have first looked in the class `Employee` for the definition for the function name. If it is not defined there then it looks for it in the immediate superclass, and so on up the class hierarchy. Here, since function name is defined in the base class `Person`, the effect is as shown in Figure 9.3. Had no such function existed of course, a compile-time error would have occurred.

For an object to respond to a member function call it must look up and execute the body of the function. In a conventional programming language this association of the function name to the function body is performed by the compiler and the process is known as binding. In OOP languages, when the binding is done at compile time we refer to it as static binding. This is the model

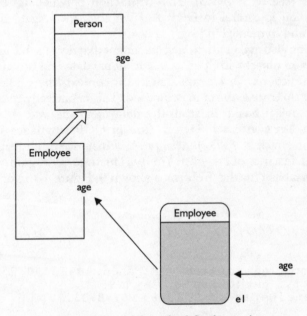

Figure 9.2   *Lookup of redefined operation*

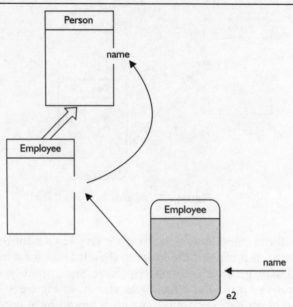

Figure 9.3   *Lookup of inherited operation*

for Figures 9.1, 9.2 and 9.3. In the code associated with Figure 9.3 the compiler statically binds the call to member function name to the code defined in class Person. When the binding is performed at execution time we refer to it as *dynamic binding* (see Section 9.3). This distinction between function call and function execution is central to OOP and we shall investigate the difference between static and dynamic binding.

Specialisation also makes an explicit statement that reveals that an Employee object *isA* Person object with, perhaps, additional data and function members, and redefined functions. This means that in any context where a Person object is required an Employee object may be used. This is perfectly reasonable since an Employee object has at least all the data members and supports all the services of the Person class. This feature of OOP languages is sometimes described as the *principle of substitutability*. Any instance of an Employee may substitute for an instance of Person. This we illustrate in Program 9.1. The class hierarchy we establish for the problem is shown in Figure 9.4(a) on page 246.

Program 9.1

```
//////////////////////////////////////////////////////////
//
//              main
// ROME Copyright (c) Richard McMahon. 1993, 1994.
// ROME Copyright (c) Ken Barclay 1995.
// Generated On January 3, 1996 At 6:38:33.51 pm
//
//////////////////////////////////////////////////////////
```

```
#include "ccstring.h"
#include "application.h"

int main()
{
  Application     app;
  app.run();

  return 0;
}

//-- End Implementation -----------------------
```

```
/////////////////////////////////////////////////////
//
//              application.h
// ROME Copyright (c) Richard McMahon. 1993, 1994.
// ROME Copyright (c) Ken Barclay 1995.
// Generated On January 3, 1996 At 6:38:33.51 pm
//
/////////////////////////////////////////////////////

#ifndef APPLICATION
  #define APPLICATION
  #include "loom.h"
  #include "ccstring.h"


  class Application {
  public:  // PUBLIC INTERFACE
    Application(void);
    void  run(void);

  };

#endif

//-- End Specification ------------------------------------
```

```
/////////////////////////////////////////////////////
//
//           application.cpp
// ROME Copyright (c) Richard McMahon. 1993, 1994.
// ROME Copyright (c) Ken Barclay 1995.
// Generated On January 3, 1996 At 6:38:33.51 pm
//
/////////////////////////////////////////////////////

#include "Employee.h"
#include "Manager.h"
#include "Application.h"
```

```
Application::Application(void)
{
}

void
Application::run(void)
{
  //
  // Demonstrate the effect of static binding.
  //
  Employee* e1 = new Employee("Ken Barclay",
    CDate(2, 2, 1974), "Systems Manager", 1000);
  Manager* m1 = new Manager("John Savage",
    CDate(1, 1, 1973), "Lecturer", 1200, 1000);
  Manager* m2 = new Manager("Jessie Kennedy",
    CDate(3, 3, 1975), "Senior Lecturer", 1600, 1500);
  Employee* e2 = m2;
  cout << e1->name();
  cout << ":";
  cout << e1->jobTitle();
  cout << "\n";
  cout << m1->name();
  cout << ":";
  cout << m1->budget();
  cout << "\n";
  cout << e2->name();
  cout << ":";
  cout << e2->jobTitle();
  cout << "\n";
}



//-- End Implementation -----------------------------------




//////////////////////////////////////////////////////////
//
//                person.h
// ROME Copyright (c) Richard McMahon. 1993, 1994.
// ROME Copyright (c) Ken Barclay 1995.
// Generated On January 3, 1996 At 6:38:33.51 pm
//
//////////////////////////////////////////////////////////

#ifndef PERSON
  #define PERSON

  #include "loom.h"
  #include "ccstring.h"
  #include "ccdate.h"
```

```
//
// The Person class acts as the superclass for real classes
//   such as Employee, Student, ClubMember etc. The class
//   Person holds a name and a date of birth as its primary
//   properties.
//
//

class Person {
public:          // PUBLIC INTERFACE
        Person(const CString& aName,
          const CDate& aDateOfBirth);
  CString    name(void) const;
  Integer    age(void) const;

private:         // REPRESENTATION
  CString    theName;
  CDate      theDateOfBirth;

};

#endif

//-- End Specification -----------------------------------


/////////////////////////////////////////////////////
//
//              person.cpp
// ROME Copyright (c) Richard McMahon. 1993, 1994.
// ROME Copyright (c) Ken Barclay 1995.
// Generated On January 3, 1996 At 6:38:33.51 pm
//
/////////////////////////////////////////////////////

#include "Person.h"

//
//   The Person class acts as the superclass for real classes
//     such as Employee, Student, ClubMember etc. The class
//     Person holds a name and a date of birth as its primary
//     properties.
//
//


Person::Person(const CString& aName,
  const CDate& aDateOfBirth)
  : theName(aName),
    theDateOfBirth(aDateOfBirth)
{

}
```

```
CString
Person::name(void) const
{
  return theName;
}
Integer
Person::age(void) const
{
  //
  //  Simplistic algorithm, taking no account of months
  //     or days within the month.
  //
  CDate today;
  Integer todayYear = today.year();
  Integer dobYear = theDateOfBirth.year();
  return todayYear − dobYear;
}
```

```
//-- End Implementation --------------------------------
```

```
///////////////////////////////////////////////////////
//
//              employee.h
// ROME Copyright (c) Richard McMahon. 1993, 1994.
// ROME Copyright (c) Ken Barclay 1995.
// Generated On January 3, 1996 At 6:38:33.51 pm
//
///////////////////////////////////////////////////////

#ifndef EMPLOYEE
  #define EMPLOYEE

  #include "loom.h"
  #include "Person.h"
  #include "ccstring.h"
  #include "ccdate.h"


  //
  // An Employee is a specialised kind of Person with a job
  //    title and a job salary as its additional properties.
  //
  //

  class Employee : public Person {
  public:        //PUBLIC INTERFACE
    Employee(const CString& aName,
      const CDate& aDateOfBirth,
          const CString& aJobTitle,
            const Integer& aSalary);
    CString    jobTitle(void) const;
```

```
    Integer    salary(void) const;

  private:    // REPRESENTATION
    CString    theJobTitle;
    Integer    theSalary;

  };

#endif
```

//-- End Specification -------------------------------------

```
///////////////////////////////////////////////////
//
//              employee.cpp
// ROME Copyright (c) Richard McMahon. 1993, 1994.
// ROME Copyright (c) Ken Barclay 1995.
// Generated On January 3, 1996 At 6:38:33.51 pm
//
///////////////////////////////////////////////////

#include "Employee.h"

//
//   An Employee is a specialised kind of Person with a job
//     title and a job salary as its additional properties.
//
//

Employee::Employee(const CString& aName,
  const CDate& aDateOfBirth, const CString& aJobTitle,
  const Integer& aSalary)
  : Person(aName, aDateOfBirth),
    theJobTitle(aJobTitle),
    theSalary(aSalary)
{

}

CString
Employee::jobTitle(void) const
{
  return theJobTitle;
}

Integer
Employee::salary(void) const
{
  return theSalary;
}
```

//-- End Implementation -------------------------------------

```
////////////////////////////////////////////////////////
//
//              manager.h
// ROME Copyright (c) Richard McMahon. 1993, 1994.
// ROME Copyright (c) Ken Barclay 1995.
// Generated On January 3, 1996 At 6:38:33.51 pm
//
////////////////////////////////////////////////////////

#ifndef MANAGER
  #define MANAGER

  #include "loom.h"
  #include "Employee.h"
  #include "ccstring.h"
  #include "ccdate.h"


  //
  //   A Manager is an Employee who, additionally, has
  //     a budget assigned to him/her.
  //
  //

  class Manager : public Employee {
  public:            // PUBLIC INTERFACE
    Manager (const CString& aName, const CDate& aDateOfBirth,
      const CString& aJobTitle,
      const Integer& aSalary,
      const Integer& aBudget);
    Integer    budget(void) const;

  private:          // REPRESENTATION
    Integer    theBudget;

  };

#endif

//-- End Specification --------------------------------


////////////////////////////////////////////////////////
//
//              manager.cpp
// ROME Copyright (c) Richard McMahon. 1993, 1994.
// ROME Copyright (c) Ken Barclay 1995.
// Generated On January 3, 1996 At 6:38:33.51 pm
//
////////////////////////////////////////////////////////

#include "Manager.h"

//
//   A Manager is an Employee who, additionally, has
//     a budget assigned to him/her.
```

```
//
//

Manager::Manager(const CString& aName,
  const CDate& aDateOfBirth, const CString& aJobTitle,
  const Integer& aSalary, const Integer& aBudget)
  : Employee(aName, aDateOfBirth, aJobTitle,
  aSalary), theBudget(aBudget)
{

}

Integer
Manager::budget(void) const
{
  return theBudget;
}
```

```
//-- End Implementation --------------------------------
```

The classes involved in this illustration are Person, Employee and Manager. Person is the superclass of Employee while Manager is the subclass of Employee. In the run function of the Application class the Employee object e1 and the Manager object m1 are defined in the usual way. The Employee object e1 is then sent messages to obtain its name and jobTitle. Similarly, m1 is sent messages to determine its name and budget. The name message applied to both e1 and m1 is statically bound to the function definition in the Person superclass. The budget message is, of course, bound to the definition in the Manager class.

The final declaration introduces a pointer to an Employee object e2 which is assigned the address of a Manager object. This is in keeping with the rule on substitutability. A Manager object may substitute for an Employee and hence, implicitly, a Manager pointer may be assigned to an Employee pointer and a Manager reference may be given to an Employee reference. The same holds true between Employee and Person. The *isA* relationship is transitive across any number of levels of specialisation and, hence, we may also use a Manager where a Person is expected.

When the messages name and jobTitle are sent to the object pointed to by Employee pointer e2, the compiler will have determined the type of e2 as an Employee*. The message jobTitle is statically bound to the method defined in the Employee class to which the pointer e2 belongs. The name message is bound to that defined in the Person superclass. The program output is given below:

```
Ken Barclay: System Manager
John Savage: 1000
Jessie Kennedy: Senior Lecturer
```

Program 9.2 exploits this *isA* relationship between the Manager class and the Employee class. The model realised by this program is given in Figure 9.4(a). Here, a single Company object maintains a container of LINKs to Employee objects. Since a Manager object may substitute for an occurrence of an Employee object this container can legally contain a mixture of LINKs to Employee instances and LINKs to Manager instances as shown in the instance diagram of Figure 9.4(b).

The substitutability is, of course, constrained by the class inheritance hierarchy. A Date object or a Person object may not be part of this container of LINKs to Employee objects. The Date class has no *isA* relation with the Employee class and Person is the superclass to Employee and not a subclass. The listing for this program and subsequent programs from this chapter is given in Appendix F.

In the listings, observe how the Company class maintains a collection of Employee pointers representing the employees of the organisation. The class member function hire puts the Employee* parameter into this collection. In function run of the Application class either an Employee object or a Manager object is created according to the input data, and the address of either is passed to the hire operation with the underlying POrderedCollection container prepared to accept either pointer.

Note also that since we are using a POrderedCollection collection of Employee objects, we are required to supply the function lessThan in the Employee class which is used to compare one Employee object with another.

The Company operation salaryBill determines the total salary expenses for the organisation. This is achieved by iterating over the collection of employees and sending each the salary message. Irrespective of whether the object is an Employee instance or a Manager instance, the message salary is bound to the definition in the Employee class.

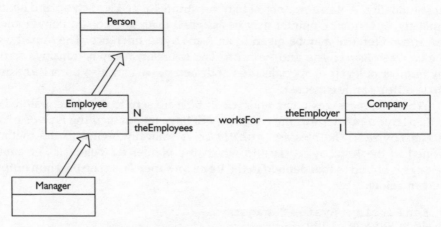

Figure 9.4(a)   *Class diagram for program 9.2*

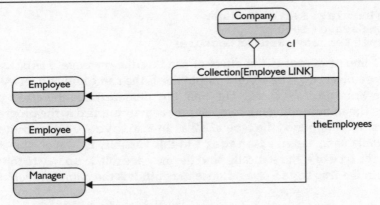

Figure 9.4(b) *Possible instance diagram for Program 9.2*

```
Integer  Company::salaryBill(void) const
{
  Integer totalSalary(0);
  PIterator< Employee* > empIterator(theEmployees);
  while( empIterator.isExhausted() == LFALSE ) {
    Employee* emp = empIterator.selection();
    Integer empSalary(emp->salary());
    totalSalary = totalSalary+empSalary;
    empIterator.advance();
  }
    return totalSalary;
}
```

9.2 Operation redefinition

Program 9.3 demonstrates the effect of redefining a function in a derived class. The class `Employee` provides an implementation of the `display` function which displays the name and job title of that employee. The subclass `Manager` modifies the behaviour of its redefined version for `display` so that it prints the manager's name and assigned budget. In LOOM this is explicitly recorded with the `REDEFINED` qualifier:

```
CLASS Manager
  SPECIALISATION OF Employee
WITH
PUBLIC INTERFACE
  // ...
  display?  REDEFINED

ENDCLASS Manager
```

The program output is given below:

```
Ken Barclay: System Manager
John Savage: 1000
Jessie Kennedy: Senior Lecturer
```

The first line of output is the effect of sending the message display to the Employee object e1. The second output line is the name and budget associated with the Manager object m1. The final line demonstrates the effect of static binding. The static binding is a compile-time activity applied to the program. The compiler has determined the type of e2 as an Employee*. The substitutability rule permits us to assign a Manager* to this variable. However, the compiler will use the type of e2 to statically bind the message call display to the version defined in the Employee class. Hence the output is the name and job title.

9.3 Dynamic binding

Program 9.3 demonstrates the effect of static binding on the object e2. The compile-time definition for this object is that it is a pointer to an Employee. At run time it is set to point to a Manager object dynamically created on the heap. When, however, we send that object instance the display message it executes the version of that function in the class Employee to which the pointer e2 associates. To have the display function of the class of the object to which e2 refers (a Manager object) requires some mechanism other than static binding.

Inheritance also gives rise to the notions of *polymorphism* and *dynamic binding*. Polymorphism is defined as having several forms. In an object-oriented programming language this means that some object refers to instances of various classes during run time. Polymorphism is the means by which the principle of substitutability is fully realised.

In C++ static or compile-time checking is employed and, by definition, is incompatible with the notion of full polymorphism. This contention is resolved by the inheritance mechanism constraining the extent of the permitted polymorphism as demonstrated in the previous sections. Polymorphism gives a measure of controlled relaxation of the type system imposed by C++. This has the effect of offering the programmer a degree of flexibility not otherwise achievable with strongly typed programming languages.

If in Program 9.3 we would like the proper display function to be determined by the actual run-time object type and not by the compile-time type then we must employ dynamic binding. Here, the compiler issues code so that when the display message is received by the recipient object then, in effect, the object asks itself 'to which type do I belong?' and executes the corresponding method. In LOOM we obtain this effect by employing the qualifiers POLYMORPHIC and REDEFINED:

```
CLASS Employee
  SPECIALISATION OF Person
WITH
PUBLIC INTERFACE
```

```
// ...
display?  POLYMORPHIC

ENDCLASS Employee

CLASS Manager
  SPECIALISATION OF Employee
WITH
PUBLIC INTERFACE
  // ...
  display?  REDEFINED

ENDCLASS Manager
```

This is demonstrated in Program 9.4. To obtain the polymorphic effect of dynamic binding the `display` function in the `Employee` class is prefixed with the keyword `virtual`. In the base class `Employee` the effect of this function is to print the employee's name and job title. The redefined version for this function in the derived class `Manager` prints the name of the manager and associated budget. The program's output is then:

```
Ken Barclay: System Manager
John Savage: 1000
Jessie Kennedy: 1500
```

in which the `Manager` object referred to by the `Employee*` object e2 obeys its version of the `display` function, i.e. the one in the `Manager` class.

```
class Employee : public Person {
public:       // PUBLIC INTERFACE
  // ...
  virtual void   display(void) const;
                                        // POLYMORPHIC

};


class Manager : public Employee {
public:  // PUBLIC INTERFACE
  // ...
  virtual void   display(void) const;
                                        // REDEFINED
};
```

In C++ a member function qualified as `virtual` retains that property across derived class boundaries. Hence it would not have been necessary to specify function `display` in class `Manager` in this way. It is often considered good practice to do so, however, since it clearly documents this and would prove useful if we were considering deriving a new class using `Manager` as the base class. The `virtual` keyword only appears on the function signature in the class declaration. It is not used in the function definition.

The dynamic binding effect is put to good use in the following problem.

A sales organisation employs both sales staff and sales managers. A `Sales-employee` is a specialised kind of `Person` with additional properties for the job title, the job salary and the sales achieved by a salesperson. A `SalesManager` is a specialised kind of `SalesEmployee` having a sales target set against his managerial duties. The model is depicted in Figures 9.5(a) and 9.5(b). The program listing is given as Program 9.5 in Appendix F.

The company is required to produce a sales report detailing the sales results of each employee. This report is produced by sending a `Company` instance the message `salesReport`. The effect of this operation is to send each employee the message `displaySales`. For a `SalesEmployee` this results in a print of the name and the achieved sales for that employee. For a `SalesManager` the effect is to display the name, the sales achieved and the sales target. To obtain a different effect according to the differing kinds of employee in the organisation the `displaySales` function in the `SalesEmployee` class is marked as `virtual`.

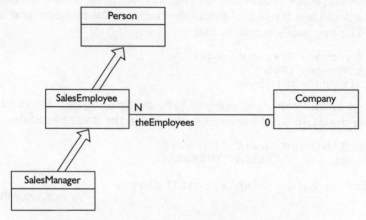

Figure 9.5(a)   *Class diagram for a selling organisation*

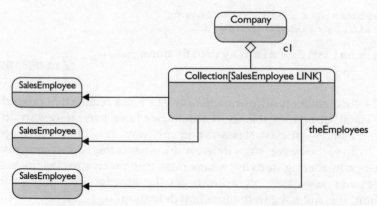

Figure 9.5(b)   *Instance diagram for selling organisation*

Observe how the code for the salesReport function is relatively simple. There is no complexity associated with determining the kind of each employee and then sending, perhaps, differing messages to achieve the required printouts. Further, the code is implicitly extendible without the need for any change. A further derivation can be added to the class hierarchy for SalesEmployee types without having to modify the salesReport function of the Company class or any other similar function.

Note how the classes are each given a member function className which returns the actual class name. The need for this function was introduced in Section 8.6 when considering the polymorphic effect. In the context of this illustration, a Company object could select from its collection of employees those that are SalesEmployees and those that are SalesManagers.

In this example, the Company class object has a container, referred to as theEmployees, holding a collection of pointers to SalesEmployee objects. These objects, which can be either SalesEmployee or SalesManager objects as suggested by Figure 9.5(b), are created dynamically in the run method of the Application class, then managed by the Company object collection. When the Company object goes out of scope its destructor is invoked. Since none is defined a default destructor is assumed which invokes the destructor for the underlying container. Since this container was created as a MANAGED collection, it applies the destructor to the elements which it holds.

The problem is that the container holds both SalesEmployee and SalesManager objects and we need the correct destructor applied to the correct object. The problem is, of course, exactly the problem we have solved by dynamic binding and virtual functions. Here what we require is virtual destructors as shown by:

```
class SalesEmployee : public Person {
public:
  virtual ~SalesEmployee(void);
                                  // define as empty body
  // ...
};

class SalesManager : public SalesEmployee {
  virtual ~SalesManager(void);
                                  // define as empty body
  // ...
};
```

9.4 Abstract base classes

The sales employees illustrated in the last example consisted of the class SalesEmployee at the root of the sales staff class hierarchy (ultimately rooted in the Person class). SalesEmployee defines the data and function members common to all sales staff. Derivations from SalesEmployee define what is unique to a specific class of such employees. Subsequent derivations may refine this still further.

Classes derived from `SalesEmployee` either inherit unchanged the member functions defined there or redefine them as a specialisation. In a class hierarchy a `virtual` function introduced in a base class is usually redefined in the derived class to obtain the effect of dynamic binding. Sometimes it is useful to include in the base class an operation for which there is no meaningful definition. The expectation is that such an operation can only be given meaning in a derived class. The operation is incorporated into the class hierarchy by its presence in the base class but its behaviour is *deferred* until a derived class defines it. Such a base class is referred to as an *abstract base class*.

Much of the power of C++ comes from arranging its classes into hierarchies. Classes higher in the hierarchy represent more general characteristics, while classes lower in the hierarchy represent more specific characteristics. In a class hierarchy we often develop a generic solution using abstract base classes, and then develop more application-specific solutions in the derived classes.

In C++ a deferred function is known as a *pure virtual function*. This is indicated with the initialiser `"=0"` as a suffix to the function prototype. For the base class in which a pure virtual function is introduced, no function definition is provided. An abstract base class specifies an interface at a general level providing a *form* or *protocol* upon which other derived classes can be established. An abstract class is never used to declare object instances. One may not declare a variable whose type is given by an abstract base class. We can, however, declare polymorphic items of this type.

We exploit abstract base classes in the following problem. An organisation employs two kinds of staff: sales staff and managers. A `Sales` employee is a specialisation of the general notion of an `Employee`. The latter, in turn, is a specialisation of the `Person` class with job title and salary as additional properties. The `Sales` class introduces a record of the sales achieved by that staff member. The `Manager` class is also a specialisation of the general `Employee` class. A `Manager` is set a sales target against which the team of sales staff he oversees is assessed. A `Manager` is not involved in any direct selling and hence is not a specialisation of the `Sales` class.

An organisation is required to produce a sales report for each of its employees. For a `Sales` employee we need to tabulate that employee's name, job title and achieved sales. For a `Manager` we wish a printout of the manager's name, job title, the sales target set for the manager, and the total sales achieved by the sales team for which the manager has responsibility. The reports are obtained by sending each `Employee` a `displaySales` message. It is not meaningful to define this operation in the `Employee` class since this represents the general notion of a staff member. Here we introduce a deferred version of the `displaySales` operation, making the `Employee` class abstract.

The model for the problem is described in Figures 9.6(a) and 9.6(b). A Company employs any number of employees who are either `Sales` or `Manager` types. A `Manager`, in turn, has responsibility for a number of `Sales` staff. The

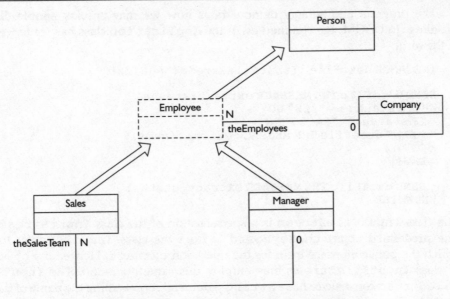

Figure 9.6(a) `Sales` *and* `Manager` *employees*

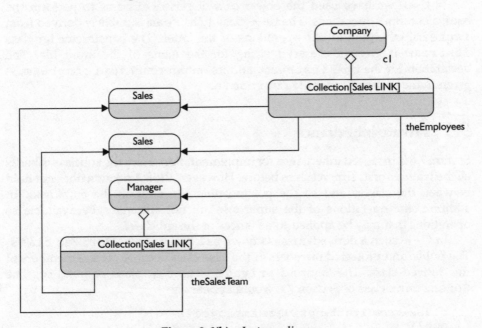

Figure 9.6(b) *Instance diagram*

`Sales` and `Manager` classes are both derived from the abstract `Employee` class shown in the diagram with a dotted border. The problem solution is given as Program 9.6 in Appendix F.

The program additionally demonstrates how we may employ simple file handling. In LOOM, the run method of the `Application` class has sentences of the form:

```
INSTANCE dataFile : InputFileStream("p06.dat")

SEND dataFile THE MESSAGE extract(status)
WHILE status != "ZZZ" DO
  IF status == "SAL" THEN
    SEND dataFile THE MESSAGE extract(name)
    // ...
  ENDIF

  SEND dataFile THE MESSAGE extract(status)
ENDWHILE
```

The class `InputFileStream` is a specialisation of the class `InputStream`. The predefined object `theKeyboard` is from the class `InputStream`, for which the public interface includes the operation `extract`. Hence, any object of class `InputFileStream` may employ this same operation. The `Input-FileStream` constructor has a `String` parameter representing the name of the file to be opened for input.

In C++ we have used the object `cin` of class `istream` to perform the equivalent input operations. The C++ class `ifstream` is publicly derived from `istream`, inheriting all the operations of the latter. The constructor for class `ifstream` is given a character string for the name of the input file. The declaration for the class `ifstream`, and its output counterpart `ofstream`, is given in the system header file `fstream.h`.

9.5 **Private inheritance**

Section 7.8 introduced inheritance for implementation. Here the subclass inherits all the features of its superclass as before. However, the *isA* relation does not hold between the classes and so the polymorphic effect cannot be employed. In addition, the operations of the superclass are not automatically available as operations that may be applied to instances of the subclass.

In C++ such a derived class is known as a `privately derived class`. The public and protected members of the base class become private members of the derived class. The keyword `private` is used in place of `public`. The `Consultant` class of Section 7.8 would appear as:

```
class Consultant : private Employee {
public:
  Consultant(const CString& aName,
    const CDate& aDateOfBirth, Integer aFee);
  CString    name(void) const;
  CString    companyName(void) const;
  Integer    fee(void) const;
  void       hiredBy(Company* anEmployer);
```

```
// ...
};
```

Instances of the derived class can be sent any of the messages appearing on its interface. Hence the following is valid:

```
Consultant cl ("John Savage", CDate(2, 2, 1971), 1000);
cout << cl.fee();
```

However, functions appearing on the public interface of its base class Employee are not implicitly part of Company's interface. Hence we cannot use:

```
cout << cl.salary();
```

In effect, the public functions of the base class have become private functions of the derived class, and clients of the derived class have no access rights to them. However, as private member functions of the derived class they may be used in the implementation of that class's public functions. For example, since Company INHERITS FROM Employee and the Employee class is a SPECIALISATION OF Person for which the public operation name? is available, we may implement the name? operation in the Consultant class with:

```
CLASS Consultant
WITH
  // ...
PRIVATE IMPLEMENTATION
  INHERITS FROM Employee
  REPRESENTATION
    // ...
  DEFINITIONS
    // ...
    METHOD name? -> String
      RETURN (SEND me THE MESSAGE name? FROM Person)
    ENDMETHOD name?

ENDCLASS Consultant
```

The subclause FROM Person identifies the class in which the name? message is defined, otherwise it will be assumed that the message is from the Consultant class and the method will recursively call itself. In C++ the corresponding function is:

```
String  Company::name(void) const
{
  return this->Person::name();
}
```

with the scope resolution operator replacing the FROM clause.

9.6 **Summary**

1. Specialisation is supported in C++ through public inheritance, and inheritance of implementation with private inheritance. In C++ the

superclass is referred to as the base class and the subclass by the term derived class.

2. An inherited class is introduced with a derivation list in the header for a class declaration. The class declaration may include function prototypes qualified with the keyword virtual when introducing polymorphic operations. A virtual function with the suffix '=0' is a pure virtual function and describes in C++ a deferred operation. Such a function in a class declaration denotes that class as abstract.

3. A derived class constructor uses the base class constructor to initialise the inherited data members. A derived class has no special rights of access to the private data members of the base class. The C++ solution is to provide access members in the protected section of the base class for specific use by the derived class.

9.7 Exercises

1. Show by example how class specialisation is denoted in C++. What extension to the basic class declaration is employed? What terms does C++ use for, respectively, the terms superclass and subclass?

2. How is the LOOM message initialise used with the keyword SUPERCLASS realised as C++?

3. Explain what is meant by the principle of substitutability. What constraints apply to limit the amount of permissible substitution?

4. C++ supports both static and dynamic binding. How are the two distinguished in a class declaration?

5. Dynamic binding is presented in C++ by prefixing the function prototype with the keyword virtual. Is this keyword required in a redefined version of the function in a derived class? If not, explain.

6. How is an abstract base class introduced in C++?

7. An abstract base class AAA introduces the pure virtual function fff. Class BBB, publicly derived from class AAA, presents a definition for the function fff. Is class BBB abstract or concrete? Explain.

      Class CCC, publicly derived from class AAA, presents a definition for the function ggg. Is class CCC abstract or concrete? Provide an explanation.

8. Implement the LOOM scripts developed for the university records system in exercises 2(a) and 2(b) of Chapter 7.

9. Implement the LOOM scripts developed for the bank described in exercise 3 of Chapter 7.

10. Implement the LOOM scripts developed for the university lecturers in exercise 4(a) and 4(b) of Chapter 7.

11. Implement the LOOM script developed for the Picture class developed in the discussion of the composite design pattern in exercise 8 of Chapter 7.

Chapter 10

Tool support

Many software engineers develop systems with the assistance of computer aided software engineering (CASE) tools. These range from very sophisticated and expensive upper CASE tools to simpler lower CASE tools. The upper CASE tools have a range of powerful subsystems supporting most of the software development life cycle. We present with this book a simple lower case tool to support and automate the method described in this book.

10.1 ROME

ROME is an object modelling environment built to support the materials in this book. It is a graphical design tool in which object models can be presented and LOOM scripts developed. ROME is equipped with a number of language bindings from which C++ and other program code can be automatically generated. The usual edit–compile–run cycle of program development is replaced with a design–compile–run cycle. The editing phase of a source program is replaced with a phase involving editing an object-oriented design. At no time is the user expected to interact directly with the C++ sources. If at execution time the running program produces an error result, the development cycle recommences with a reconsideration of the model. The ROME tool will then re-create new program code from the revised model.

The ROME tool is a graphical development environment operating under Microsoft Windows version 3.1. The program has been developed using Borland's Object Windows Library, OWL. Upon completion of an early prototype, the design element of the tool was used to document the development of much of the remainder of the software in a manner not unlike that described in Chapter 8.

10.2 User interface

ROME has the look and feel of any standard Microsoft Windows application. Upon start-up, a ROME session appears as shown in Figure 10.1.

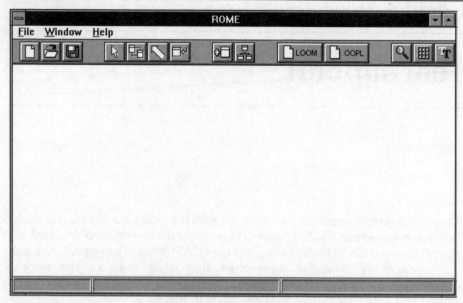

Figure 10.1 *ROME start-up*

The principal elements of a ROME window are typical of those found in most Windows products. The window has a caption bar across the top bearing the title ROME. In the upper left of the window is the usual control menu box. In the top right are the minimise and maximise buttons. Below the caption is the menu bar with, initially, the three commands File, Window and Help. When we select a menu option we choose a command from the list to carry out some action. The File menu offers the choice shown in Figure 10.2.

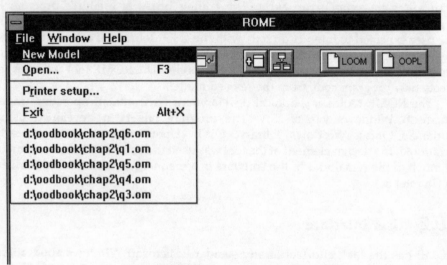

Figure 10.2 File *menu*

Below the menu bar is a toolbar, sometimes also known as a speedbar. The toolbar presents a list of iconic buttons providing fast and convenient access to the more common operations supported by ROME. For example, we may start a new design by selecting the command New Model from the File menu, or by simply clicking the leftmost button on the toolbar.

At the foot of the window is a status bar by which ROME advises the user of its activities. For example, when we compile a model into its C++ sources, the status bar contains a message to this effect. In the centre of the window is the workarea in which models will be developed.

10.3 **Preparing models**

To describe the stages involved and the use of the ROME tool, we shall reconsider the first model shown in Chapter 3. The model was that of an organisation, its many employees and the departments within the company. The model is shown in Figure 10.3.

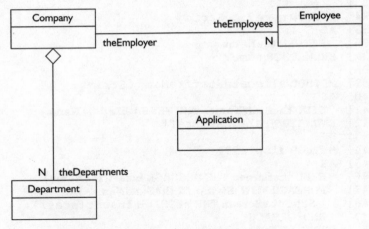

Figure 10.3 *Completed model*

We noted early in Chapter 3 that a conscious design decision made concerning LOOM was that it would be verbose. The aim here was to avoid ambiguity and document clearly any design decisions. For example, the LOOM script for the Department class resulting from the model of Figure 10.3 is listed below. In particular, those items which the user must supply to ROME are shown emboldened. We see from the listing that much of the bulk of LOOM is produced automatically by ROME, reducing the overall burden on the user.

```
[0010] CLASS Department
[0011] WITH
[0012] PUBLIC INTERFACE
```

```
[0013]  Department(aName :String)
[0014]  name? -> String
[0015]  allocateStaff(aName :String)
[0016]  display?
[0017]  Department
[0018]  lessThan?(aDepartment :Department) -> Boolean
[0019] PROTECTED INTERFACE
[0020]  NONE
[0021] PRIVATE IMPLEMENTATION
[0022]  REPRESENTATION
[0023]    theName :String
[0024]    theStaffNames :DSortedList[String]
[0025] AGGREGATIONS NONE
[0026] ASSOCIATIONS NONE
[0027] DEFINITIONS
[0028]  METHOD Department (aName :String)
[0029]  AS
[0030]   SEND theName THE MESSAGE initialise(aName)
[0031]   SEND theStaffNames THE MESSAGE
          initialise(DEFAULTSIZE, "")
[0032]  ENDMETHOD Department
[0033]
[0034]  METHOD name? -> String
[0035]  AS
[0036]    RETURN theName
[0037]  ENDMETHOD name?
[0038]
[0039]  METHOD allocateStaff (aName :String)
[0040]  AS
[0041]   SEND theStaffNames THE MESSAGE add(aName)
[0042]  ENDMETHOD allocateStaff
[0043]
[0044]  METHOD display?
[0045]  AS
[0046]   SEND theScreen THE MESSAGE insert(theName)
[0047]   FOREACH staff :String IN theStaffNames DO
[0048]     SEND theScreen THE MESSAGE insert (staff)
[0049]   ENDFOREACH
[0050]  ENDMETHOD display?
[0051]
[0052]  METHOD Department
[0053]  AS
[0054]   SEND theName THE MESSAGE initialise("")
[0055]   SEND theStaffNames THE MESSAGE
          initialise(DEFAULTSIZE, "")
[0056]  ENDMETHOD Department
[0057]
[0058]  METHOD lessThan? (aDepartment :Department)
        -> Boolean
[0059]  AS
[0060]   INSTANCE departmentName :
                  String(SEND aDepartment THE MESSAGE name?)
[0061]   IF theName < departmentName THEN
[0062]   RETURN TRUE
```

```
[0063]     ELSE
[0064]     RETURN FALSE
[0065]     ENDIF
[0066]  ENDMETHOD lessThan?
[0067]
[0068] ENDCLASS Department
```

Listing 10.1   *LOOM script for the* Department *class*

To illustrate aspects of ROME we will consider how we produce the design shown in Figure 10.3 from the starting point given by Figure 10.4. Here, the Department class and the aggregation between it and the Company class have been removed. From the interaction diagrams we shall use, we will also see how the features for the Department class are entered into the model.

To complete the model we must first reintroduce the Department class into the figure. In ROME we can do this in a variety of ways. With the mouse positioned over the active model window we simply press the 'Insert' key of the keyboard. A new class box figure appears in the model at the position of the mouse cursor. Alternatively, if we click the right mouse button, a floating menu appears and if we select the first option A̲dd Class, then once again we get an empty class box. Again, the same can be achieved by using the command A̲dd Class under the menu bar item M̲odel. The final way we can include a class box is to press the toolbar button shown circled in Figure 10.5. Note that when we position the mouse cursor above this toolbar button the status bar reminds us that this button is for adding a class to the model. When we click the toolbar button with the left mouse button a class box appears in the upper left of the model as shown in Figure 10.5.

From Figure 10.5 we see that the newly entered class is obscuring an existing class box. If we position the mouse cursor over this new box and then press and hold down the left mouse button, a rectangular outline for the selected class appears. While still holding the left mouse button we may drag the selected box to the desired location. When we are satisfied with the new position for the box we simply release the left mouse button.

We should regularly save our work to disk. The third button on the toolbar has an icon for a (floppy) disk and represents a save to disk operation. Press the

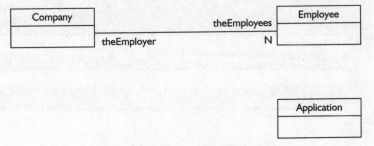

Figure 10.4   *Incomplete object model*

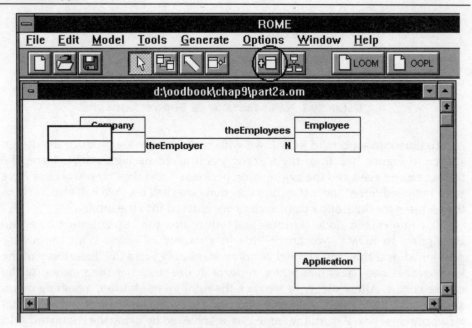

Figure 10.5   *The effect of adding a new class*

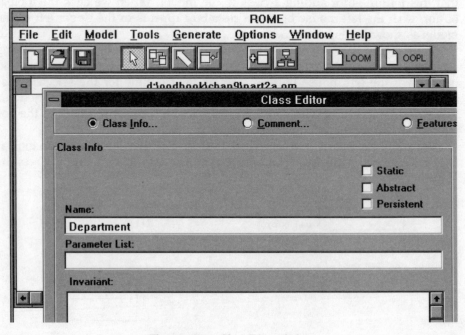

Figure 10.6   *Class Editor dialog*

button once to have the updated design saved. The file name for the model is given in the caption.

We now name this new class `Department`. This we do with the `Class Editor` dialog shown in Figure 10.6. The dialog appears by first positioning the mouse cursor above the unnamed class, clicking the right mouse button and selecting `Edit Class...` from the floating menu. The primary information we give through this dialog is the class name. This is entered into the edit control labelled `Name:`. Other aspects of the class can also be set by this dialog. For example, an abstract class is established by clicking the `Abstract` check box. Further, commentary associated with the class can be given by clicking the `Comment...` button.

We need now to establish the aggregation relationship between the `Company` and `Department` classes. This we do using the aggregate button on the toolbar shown in Figure 10.7. Select this tool (the status bar indicates that this tool is 'For part–whole relationships') then move the mouse cursor to the class representing the part in the whole–part relationship (here, the class `Department`). Note that ROME has changed the mouse cursor to reflect the kind of operation that is under way. Press down the left mouse button at this class and drag the mouse to the class acting as the whole in the whole–part relationship (`Company`). Releasing the mouse results in ROME drawing the aggregation relation between these classes. Restore the selection mouse cursor by pressing the appropriate toolbar button.

To complete this aggregation we must label it, attach the multiplicities and choose the appropriate implementation. This we enter with the `Aggregation Editor` dialog shown in Figure 10.8. The role name for this end of the aggregation is entered into the edit control labelled `Component Role`. The multiplicity is chosen from the list under `Multiplicity`, and the choice of implementation (here a `DSortedList`) from the list under the `Strategy...` button. The dialog is obtained by carefully positioning the tip of the mouse cursor over the aggregation line, clicking the right mouse button and selecting the `Edit PartOf Link...` option from the floating menu.

When we click on the aggregation line, it is highlighted by colouring. If we select the aggregation this way then by pressing and holding down the left mouse button we may drag the line either left or right. When we release the button the effect may be as shown in Figure 10.9. Note how ROME continues to retain the relationship between the two classes by extending the line in an appropriate manner.

Now we shall enter the properties and operations into the `Department` class. From the LOOM script shown earlier, we know that the two properties are `theName` and `theStaffNames`, respectively, the name for the department and the list of staff working for that department. To enter these details we invoke the `Class Editor` dialog we saw in Figure 10.6 and repeated in Figure 10.10. This time, however, we activate the dialog by positioning the mouse cursor above the `Department` class, clicking the right mouse button, and selecting `Properties...` from the floating menu. Note this time the central list box in which we record and list the class properties and the `Insert Feature...`

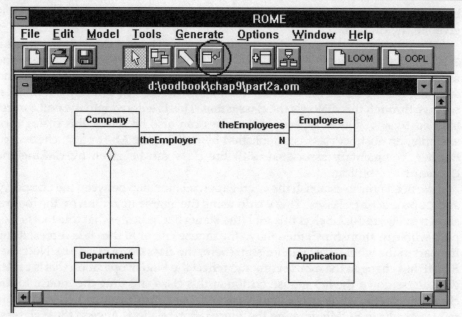

Figure 10.7 *Adding an aggregation relation*

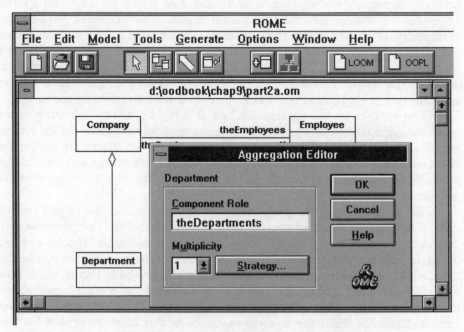

Figure 10.8 Aggregation Editor *dialog*

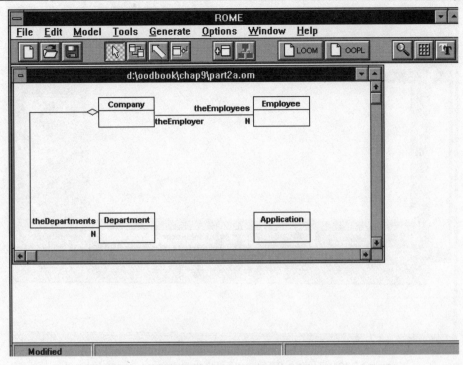

Figure 10.9 *Moving and stretching the aggregation relation*

button at the lower left of the dialog. Initially, of course, the list is empty. The button is used to obtain a second dialog into which we enter theName property.

Press the Insert Feature... button on the Class Editor dialog. This pops up the Signature Editor dialog shown in Figure 10.11. Into the Signature edit control we enter the property theName and its type as theName :String. Since this property is part of the private representation for the class, we also select the Private Access radio button. We repeat this exercise and submit theStaffNames property.

Having entered both representational properties, the Class Editor dialog now appears as shown in Figure 10.12. The 'p' prefix attached to each entry reminds us that it is a property ('o' indicates operation), and the '−' symbol indicates that the property is private (a '+' means public and an '=' means protected).

Figure 10.12 also shows the two active filters at the lower right of the dialog. They are labelled All Interfaces and Properties. All Interfaces specifies that public, protected and private entries are being shown. Similarly, Properties informs us that only class properties are being displayed. If we select Operations from this drop-down list, the features list box once again empties since we have no operations as yet. We enter the first of the operations by again pressing the Insert Feature... button and completing the

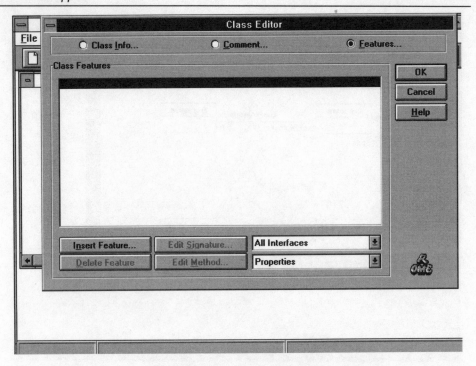

Figure 10.10   Class Editor *dialog with empty property list and*
Insert Feature...*button*

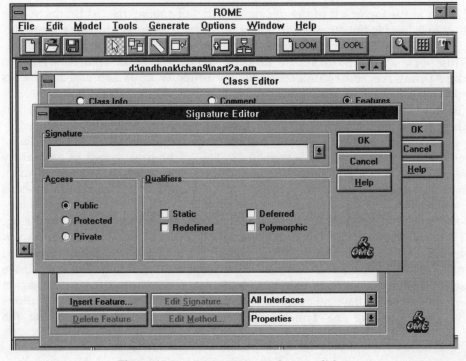

Figure 10.11   Signature Editor *dialog*

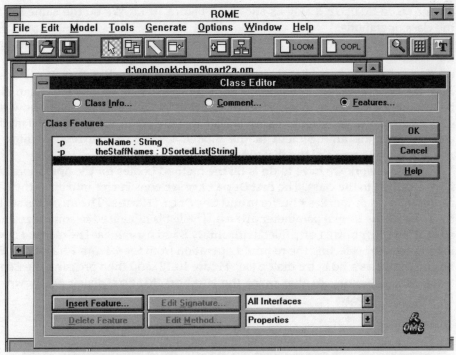

Figure 10.12 Class Editor *dialog and property list*

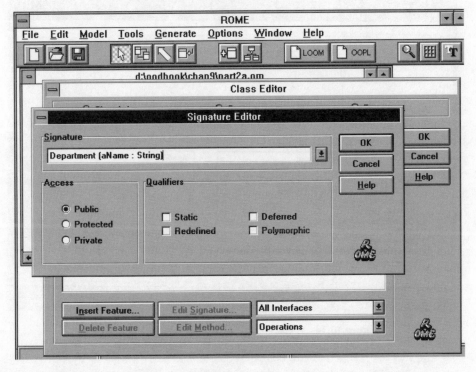

Figure 10.13 Signature Editor *dialog and an operation signature*

Signature Editor dialog as shown in Figure 10.13. We do the same for all the class operations.

We can always see what features are associated with a class by requesting the class to show these details on the model. Place the mouse cursor over the Department class, click the right mouse button and select ShowFeatures from the floating menu. The effect is shown in Figure 10.14. The effect can also be undone by choosing Hide Features from the same menu. Note how the effect is done on a per-class basis. Note also how the expanded box fills the model and disrupts the arrangement of the model. Usually, some repositioning is needed to make sense of the diagram.

The final work we have to do is fill the method bodies for the operations we have attached to the class. The first Department constructor initialises the two representation properties theName and theStaffNames. The former is set by the value of the formal parameter aName. The list is initialised to some size and, since it is a DSortedList, filled with empty String values. The method body is completed by selecting the required operation from the Class Features list box on the Class Editor dialog (see Figure 10.12) and then pressing the Edit Method... button. At that point the Method Editor dialog as shown in Figure 10.15 appears.

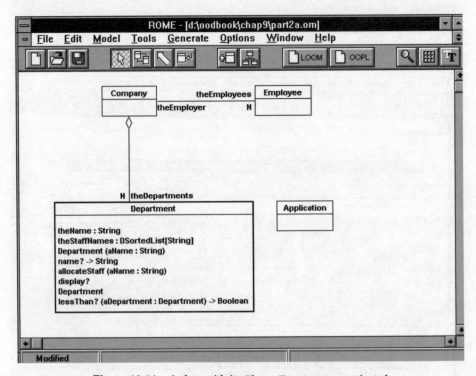

Figure 10.14 *A class with its* Show Features *activated*

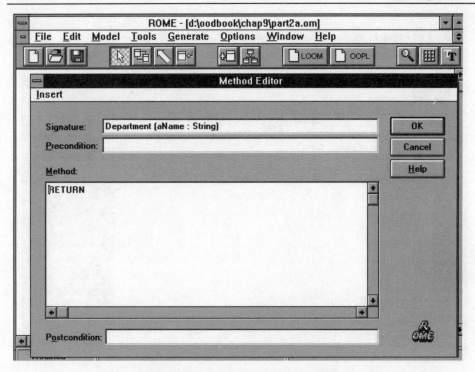

Figure 10.15 Method Editor *dialog*

The Method Editor dialog repeats the operation signature in a noneditable field at the top of the dialog. The cursor is positioned in an edit field alongside the LOOM keyword RETURN. ROME anticipates that the method body will require one of these statements. We have no need for one here so we first delete it. We then enter the method body as shown at the beginning of this chapter (see Listing 10.1) and press the OK button when complete. We then repeat this action for the other operations.

Note the Insert menu at the top of the dialog, producing the list shown in Figure 10.16. Selecting, for example, the fourth entry in the list will place into the Method Editor the skeleton of a SEND . . . THE MESSAGE . . . sentence. The cursor is located after the keyword SEND, awaiting the user entering the recipient object name. By pressing the End on the keyboard we can skip to the end of the statement and supply the message name and its parameters. This same effect can be achieved by using the underlined accessor keys. In this case they are Alt-IS.

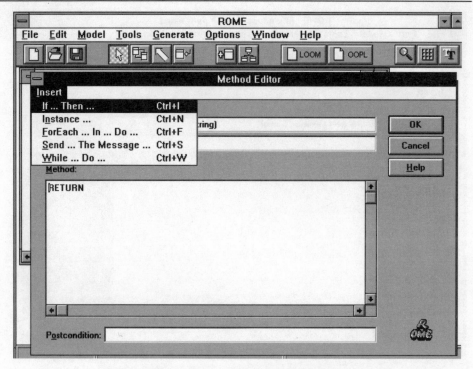

Figure 10.16   Method Editor *accelerator keys*

10.4 Code generation

When we have completed the model, ROME offers us two code generation facilities. We can have ROME produce the full LOOM script or we can have the target programming language generated. The two buttons on the toolbar labelled LOOM and OOPL activate these services. Both involve producing one or more text files and we need to nominate the directory in which they will be placed. Before we use these buttons we must first set the directory to the current working directory with the Preferences... command of the Options menu. The result is the Preferences dialog shown in Figure 10.17.

The important fields on this dialog are the Output Directory, Default Viewer and the OOPL Code Generator. The Output Directory specifies where all files are placed. We set this as the same directory in which the model resides (here the directory is d:\oodbook \chap9). We may edit this field directly, or use the Browse... button to select the desired directory. When we use the LOOM button on the toolbar it asks if we wish to see the outcome. The editor tool named in Default Viewer is used to display the LOOM script. Here, the Microsoft Notepad program is being used and is located in the windows subdirectory of the C drive. The OOPL Code Generator nominates

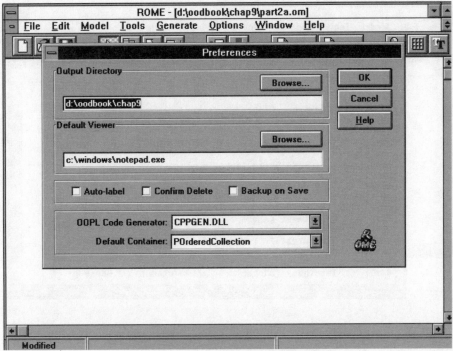

Figure 10.17 Preferences *dialog*

which target programming language is required, and here CPPGEN (C++ generator) is the desired entry.

Having set and checked these entries we now press the LOOM button on the toolbar. If we choose to view the output file then the result is as shown in Figure 10.18. The LOOM script is placed in a file with the same filename prefix as the model and with the suffix .oom. Note how the LOOM script is prefixed by line numbers by which fragments can be readily located.

If we press the OOPL button on the toolbar, ROME creates C++ header and code files for each class in the model. Thus we would have the files department.h, department.cpp etc. ROME also produces a C++ code file called main.cpp containing the C++ main function which creates an Application object and sends it the run method.

When we operate the OOPL button on the toolbar two actions are invoked. The first action re-creates the LOOM file. This is necessary because changes to the model may have occurred since the last use of the LOOM button. From this file the LOOM script is translated into the target programming language. ROME checks the LOOM script during this phase and reports any errors. For example, if we had mistyped theName property of the Department class as (see Figure 10.12):

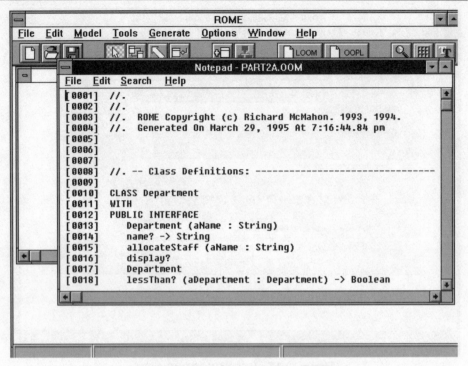

Figure 10.18   *Viewing the LOOM script*

```
theName : Strung
```

then the OOPL button produces the diagnostic shown in Figure 10.19. The error indicates that on line 23 of the LOOM script in the specification of the Department class the type name Strung has not been recognised.

10.5   Further developments

The version of ROME delivered with this book has a number of placeholders for further developments. For example, if we revisit the Preferences dialog in Figure 10.17 we note that other code generators have been installed. Most are simply the C++ code generator renamed. The ADA9X generator is an experimental version targeting the object-oriented Ada 95. It is anticipated that other generators will be developed in the future.

LOOM classes can be tagged as STATIC or PERSISTENT (see Figure 10.6). Presently, neither is processed by the generators. With PERSISTENT classes it is anticipated that they may be hooked into an object oriented database so that the instances may persist across program runs.

Some work is ongoing to incorporate contractual information (Meyer, 1988)

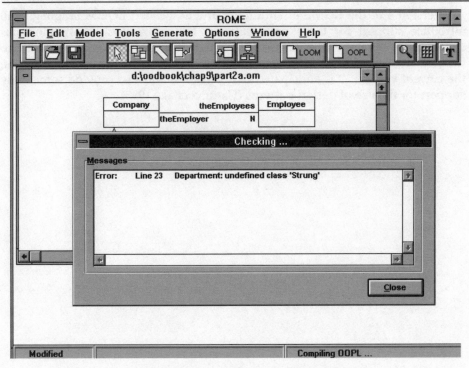

Figure 10.19 OOPL *error messages*

into the specification of classes. Contracts can be used to make the software more robust. Contracts are established as class invariants (see Figure 10.6) and as method pre- and post-conditions (see Figure 10.16). Again, the current version of ROME simply ignores these entries if they are given.

An associated tool is a browser called NAPLES. NAPLES permits us to build one or more libraries of LOOM classes. The browser allows us to view the classes in a library, to see their inheritance relationships, their list of properties and operations, and the method bodies. Classes can be dragged from ROME and dropped into NAPLES and added to the library. Equally, classes can be copied from NAPLES into a ROME model. Thus usable classes can be developed for one application, stored in the NAPLES repository, and reused in further applications.

Some further work is being done to instrument the LOOM code. Here, an interpreter will execute the LOOM code directly without the need to generate and compile the target programming code. Instances created during this interpretation will be presented as icons on a separate window. As the code is stepped through, the instances may be interrogated to view their property values.

Version 4 of the ROME environment and associated LOOM language will introduce support for these new features. The contractual information has already been developed for release 302g of ROME and will be incorporated into the present release ROME 302x. Work on the animator is already under way using the current version. It is anticipated that version 4 will also provide some early support for the use of design patterns (Gamma et al., 1995).

Bibliography

Armstrong, J. and Mitchell, R. (1994) 'Users and abuses of inheritance', *Software Engineering Journal*, January

Barclay, K. (1994) *C++ Problem Solving and Programming*, Prentice Hall

Beck, K. and Cunningham, W. (1989) 'A laboratory for object-oriented thinking', OOPLSA Conference

Booch, G. (1991) *Object-Oriented Design with Applications*, Benjamin Cummings

Cattell, R.G.G. (1994) *The Object Database Standard ODMG-93*, Morgan Kaufmann

Coad, P. and Yourdon, E. (1990) *Object Oriented Analysis*, Prentice Hall

Gamma, E., Helm, R., Johnson, R. and Vlissides, J. (1995) *Design Patterns*, Addison-Wesley

Jacobson, I., Christerson, M., Jonsson, P. and Overgaard, G. (1992) *Object-Oriented Software Engineering: A Use Case Driven Approach*, Addison-Wesley

Lippman, S. (1991) *C++ Primer*, Addison-Wesley

Martin, J. and Odell, J. (1992) *Object-Oriented Analysis and Design*, Prentice Hall

Meyer, B. (1988) *Object Oriented Software Construction*, Prentice Hall

Meyers, S. (1992) *Effective C++*, Addison-Wesley

Rumbaugh, J., Blaha, M., Premerlani, W., Eddy, F. and Lorensen, W. (1991) *Object Oriented Modelling and Design*, Prentice Hall

Shlaer, S. and Mellor, S. (1992) *Object Lifecycles: Modelling the World in States*, Yourdon Press

Stroustrup, B. (1991) *The C++ Programming Language*, Addison-Wesley

Yourdon, E. (1994) *Object-Oriented System Design: An Integrated Approach*, Prentice Hall

Appendix A

LOOM grammar

The following grammar defines the core language revision 3.02x. LOOM and its associated design tool ROME are issued as major revisions and minor releases. The present revision is revision 3 with 3.02x the current operational release.

A.1 Metasymbols

The grammar is described by employing a number of metasyntactic symbols. These are:

'x'	literally the symbol x
XXX	the token described by XXX
a ‖ b ‖ …	the terms a or b or …
[[a]]	none or one occurrence of the term a
{{ b }}	zero or more repetitions of the term b

Hence the grammar rule:

class_tail : ENDCLASS NAME

specifies that the tail to a class specification consists of the keyword ENDCLASS followed immediately by an identifier NAME. The rule:

operation_qualifier : DEFERRED ‖ POLYMORPHIC ‖ REDEFINED ‖ STATIC

suggests one of the language keywords is expected. Finally, the grammar rule:

formal_parameter_list : formal_parameter {{ ',' formal_parameter }}

defines a list of one or more formal parameters separated by comma symbols.

A.2 Class specification

Syntax

class_specification

276

: class_head [[specialisation_clause]] WITH class_body class_tail

class_head
  : [[ABSTRACT ‖ STATIC ‖ PERSISTENT ‖
    PERSISTENT ABSTRACT ‖ ABSTRACT PERSISTENT]]
      CLASS NAME [['[' template_parameter_name_list ']']]

template_parameter_name_list
  : NAME {{ ',' NAME }}

class_tail
  : ENDCLASS NAME

Synopsis

A class specification is a single syntactic unit presenting all the definitions associated with the named class. The class name, introduced in the class header, must be matched by the ENDCLASS terminator. The template parameter names, if present, document the class as a generic class, for example a set of items. If the keyword STATIC is present, then the class represents an abstract state machine in which all the operations and data members are static, and for which there are no associations or aggregations. An abstract state machine is not expected to provide a constructor operation. The keyword ABSTRACT documents that the class is abstract with one or more deferred operation members. The keyword PERSISTENT permits the structure to reside on a file store.

Examples

```
CLASS Employee
WITH
 // ... permissible comment form ...
 //> ... raw target language comment ...
ENDCLASS Employee

CLASS Set[TYPE]  // generic container
WITH
 // ...
ENDCLASS Set

ABSTRACT CLASS Person  // expects some deferred operations
WITH
 // ...
ENDCLASS Person

STATIC CLASS Lexical  // all members are static
```

```
WITH
 // ...
ENDCLASS Lexical
```

Note

STATIC and PERSISTENT are not implemented.

A.3   Specialisation clause

Syntax

```
specialisation_clause
 : SPECIALISATION OF property_type_list
```

Synopsis

The superclasses named in the specialisation clause specify the classes from which the defined class will inherit its features. The specialisation clause documents *isA* substitutability between objects of the subclass and objects of the superclass.

Examples

```
CLASS Employee     // conventional isA
  SPECIALISATION OF Person
WITH
 // ...
ENDCLASS Employee

CLASS SalesManager     // multiple inheritance
  SPECIALISATION OF SalesPerson, Manager
WITH
 // ...
ENDCLASS SalesManager

CLASS DSortedCollection [TYPE]     // generic subclass
  SPECIALISATION OF
   DSequentialCollection [TYPE]
WITH
 // ...
ENDCLASS DSortedCollection
```

A.4 Class body

Syntax

class_body
  : public_interface_clause protected_interface_clause
    private_implementation_clause

Synopsis

The class body consists of three major clauses: the public part available to any
client; the protected part available to the class and to its subclasses; the private
part relevant only to the class implementation. The public and protected parts are
a list of property and operation signatures. The private part specifies the data and
operations of the implementation, the architectural details (e.g. aggregations) and
the method definitions for all the operations.

Examples

```
CLASS Person
WITH
PUBLIC INTERFACE
  Person(aName :String, aDateOfBirth :Date)
  changeName(aName :String)
  name? -> String
  age? -> Integer
PROTECTED INTERFACE
  NONE
PRIVATE IMPLEMENTATION
  REPRESENTATION
    theName  :String
    theDateOfBirth  :Date
AGGREGATIONS NONE
ASSOCIATIONS NONE
DEFINITIONS
  METHOD Person(aName :String, aDateOfBirth :Date)
  AS
    SEND theName THE MESSAGE initialise(aName)
    SEND theDateOfBirth THE MESSAGE
      initialise(aDateOfBirth)
  ENDMETHOD Person
  METHOD changeName(aName :String)
  AS
    SEND theName THE MESSAGE assign(aName)
  ENDMETHOD changeName
```

```
METHOD name? -> String
AS
  RETURN theName
ENDMETHOD name?
METHOD age? -> Integer
AS
  INSTANCE today :Date
  INSTANCE todayYear :
    Integer(SEND today THE MESSAGE year?)
  INSTANCE dobYear :
    Integer(SEND theDateOfBirth THE MESSAGE year?)
  RETURN todayYear - dobYear
ENDMETHOD age?

ENDCLASS Person
```

A.5 **Public interface clause**

Syntax

public_interface_clause
: PUBLIC INTERFACE signature {{ signature }}
‖ PUBLIC INTERFACE NONE

signature
: property_signature ‖ operation_signature

property_signature
: NAME ':' property_type [[INVERSE OF NAME]]

operation_signature
: NAME [['(' formal_parameter_list ')']] [['->' simple_type]]
   [[DEFERRED ‖ POLYMORPHIC ‖ REDEFINED ‖ STATIC]]

formal_parameter_list
: formal_parameter {{ ',' formal_parameter }}

formal_parameter
: NAME ':' property_type [[IN ‖ OUT ‖ INOUT]]

Synopsis

The public interface documents the set of services available to clients of the class. This includes either operations or property items. The latter are always understood to represent constant data items initialised by the class constructor. The optional operation qualifiers are only applicable to operation signatures and must not appear elsewhere. Equally, the optional INVERSE OF subclause may only be used in conjunction with data members.

An operation signature presents the signature for an operation, including any formal parameters and any result type. Both components may be omitted in which case the operation represents some procedural action. The formal parameters are presented as a list of names and types enclosed in parentheses. The parameters may also be qualified with their access mode. If no mode is given then IN is assumed.

Examples

```
PUBLIC INTERFACE
  changeName(aName :String)
                  // transformer operation
  age?    -> Integer
                  // query operator
  bloodGroup?  :String
                  // constant data member
  displaySales?  REDEFINED
                  // qualified operation without
                  //arguments
```

A.6 Protected interface clause

Syntax

```
protected_interface_clause
  : PROTECTED INTERFACE signature {{ signature }}
  || PROTECTED INTERFACE NONE
```

Synopsis

The protected interface documents the set of services available to subclasses. This includes either operations or data items. The latter are always understood to represent constant data items initialised by the class constructor.

Examples

```
PROTECTED INTERFACE
  dob? -> Date  // accessor operation
```

A.7 **Property type**

Syntax

    property_type
      : NAME [['[' property_type_list ']']] [[LINK]]

    property_type_list
      : property_type {{ ',' property_type }}

Synopsis

A property type is represented by a type name, or a type name followed by the keyword LINK, or an instantiated type. The latter instantiates a particular version of a generic type.

Examples

```
theDateOfBirth        :Date
                      // simple data type
theEmployer           :Company LINK
                      // reference to some other object
theEmployees          :PSet[Employee LINK]
                      // instantiated type
age?                  -> Integer
                      // operation with result
changeName            (aName :String)
                      // operation with parameter
displaySales?
                      // procedural operation
```

A.8 **Private implementation clause**

Syntax

    private_implementation_clause
      : PRIVATE IMPLEMENTATION [[inherits_clause]] representation_ clause
        aggregation_clause association_clause
        [[invariant_clause]] definition_clause

Synopsis

The PRIVATE IMPLEMENTATION documents the representation of the class, any architectural relations with other class types and the definition for the methods.

Examples

```
PRIVATE IMPLEMENTATION
  INHERITS FROM Person
  REPRESENTATION
    theJobTitle        :String
    theSalary          :Integer
  AGGREGATION NONE
  ASSOCIATION
    theEmployer        :Company LINK
```

A.9 **Inherits clause**

Syntax

```
inherits_clause
  : INHERITS FROM property_type_list
```

Synopsis

An inherits clause introduces subclassing for the purpose of implementation. The subclass does not share an *isA* relationship with its superclass.

Examples

```
CLASS DStack [TYPE]                        // generic container
WITH
PUBLIC INTERFACE
  // ...
PROTECTED INTERFACE
  NONE
PRIVATE IMPLEMENTATION
  INHERITS FROM DVector [TYPE]
    // implementation
    // ...
ENDCLASS DStack
```

A.10 **Representation clause**

Syntax

```
representation_clause
  : REPRESENTATION signature {{ signature }}
  || REPRESENTATION NONE
```

Synopsis

The properties of a class represent the basic data items. They are non-constant, non-static members accessible only to the class operations. The implementation may also specify support operations inaccessible to clients.

Examples

```
REPRESENTATION
  theName          :String
  theDateOfBirth   :Date
```

A.11 Aggregation clause

Syntax

```
aggregation_clause
  : AGGREGATIONS aggregation {{ aggregation }}
  ‖ AGGREGATIONS NONE
aggregation
  : NAME ':' property_type
```

Synopsis

The aggregations are used to introduce whole–part relationships. Aggregations have a semantically strong relationship between the whole and its parts. For example, when the whole is removed then so too are the parts. The leading keyword can be either singular or plural, irrespective of the number presented.

Examples

```
AGGREGATION
  theDepartments   :PSet[Department LINK]
```

A.12 Association clause

Syntax

```
association_clause
  : ASSOCIATIONS association {{ association }}
```

```
|| ASSOCIATIONS NONE
association
   : NAME ':' property_type [[ INVERSE OF NAME ]]
```

Synopsis

An association is a relation between two independently existing objects. The relationship is looser than that of aggregation. The expectation is that a LINK type will be used. The leading keyword can be either singular or plural, irrespective of the number presented. The INVERSE OF subclause documents where the integrity of LINKs must be properly maintained.

Examples

```
ASSOCIATION
   theEmployer   : Company LINK INVERSE OF theEmployees
```

A.13 **Invariant clause**

Syntax

```
invariant_clause
   : INVARIANT logical_expression
```

Synopsis

The INVARIANT specifies the state of objects of the given class which will be respected by all class methods. The INVARIANT is not yet implemented, but may be present in a class specification.

Examples

```
INVARIANT theName != ""   // the name field is never blank
```

Notes

In the present release, ROME and LOOM accept and parse such a clause, but otherwise disregard it.

A.14 **Definition clause**

Syntax

```
definition_clause
  : DEFINITIONS definition {{ definition }}
  || DEFINITIONS NONE
definition
  : METHOD operation_signature
    [[ precondition ]]
    [[ postcondition ]]
  AS
    paragraph
  ENDMETHOD NAME
```

Synopsis

The definitions clause supplies the method bodies for each operation. Pre- and post-conditions may be defined as well as handling exceptional behaviour. The method body is expressed as a paragraph consisting of a number of sentences. The PRECONDITION and POSTCONDITION clauses are not yet implemented.

Examples

```
METHOD changeName(aName :String)
AS
  SEND theName THE MESSAGE assign(aName)
ENDMETHOD changeName
```

Notes

In the present release, ROME and LOOM accept and parse the PRECONDITION and POSTCONDITION clauses, but otherwise disregard them.

A.15 **Precondition**

Syntax

```
precondition
  : PRECONDITION logical_expression
```

Synopsis

A PRECONDITION makes a statement about the conditions that must prevail upon entry to the method. It acts as a contract to the client, stating that if the precondition holds, then correct behaviour can be assured by the method.

Examples

```
PRECONDITION
  SEND theEmployees THE MESSAGE isMember?(me) == TRUE
```

A.16 Postcondition

Syntax

```
postcondition
  : POSTCONDITION logical_expression
```

Synopsis

A POSTCONDITION specifies the conditions which will apply following execution of the method. The statement guarantees the condition.

Examples

```
POSTCONDITION
  theName != " "
```

A.17 Paragraph

Syntax

```
paragraph
  : {{ sentence }}

sentence
  : instance_sentence
  || let_sentence
  || if_sentence
  || while_sentence
```

|| foreach_sentence
|| return_sentence
|| message_sentence

Synopsis

A paragraph is a series of none or more sentences. Each sentence has a unique leading keyword permitting ready recognition. That way, punctuation separators need not be employed. When no sentences are given for a paragraph, this permits a placeholder to be used for, say, a method body. Equally, the method body may simply comment some standard algorithm.

A paragraph is consistent with the normal structured programming concepts, supporting sequence, selection and iteration. Further, block structure and scoping rules are present.

Examples

```
INSTANCE today : Date
INSTANCE todayYear :
  Integer ( SEND today THE MESSAGE year?)
INSTANCE dobYear :
  Integer ( SEND theDateOfBirth THE MESSAGE year?)
RETURN todayYear - dobYear
```

The INSTANCEs today, todayYear and dobYear are within the scope of the enclosing paragraph in which they are introduced.

A.18 Instance sentence

Syntax

instance_sentence
: INSTANCE NAME ':' simple_type [['(' logical_expression_list ')']]

Synopsis

An instance sentence introduces a new object into the current scope. The expression list is passed to the type constructor to properly initialise the object. If no expression list is present then the default constructor is assumed.

Examples

```
   // Local duration objects
INSTANCE today : Date  // use default constructor
INSTANCE total : Integer(0)
INSTANCE name : String("Ken Barclay")
INSTANCE p1 : Person("John Savage", Date(1, 1, 1972))

   // Dynamic duration objects
INSTANCE xmas : Date LINK(25, 12, 1995)
   // using parameterised constructor
INSTANCE dp : Date LINK Date
   // using default constructor
```

A.19 **If sentence**

Syntax

```
if_sentence
  : IF logical_expression THEN paragraph
    {{ ELSEIF logical_expression THEN paragraph }}
    [[ ELSE paragraph ]]
  ENDIF
```

Synopsis

An IF statement is the principal selection statement. The ELSEIF clause may be repeated any number of times including zero. The ELSE clause is optional. The IF sentence provides the usual selection mechanism and is reserved primarily for this purpose. The statement should be considered alongside the use of polymorphic-style behaviour where the compiler provides the necessary selection code.

Examples

```
IF aName != "" THEN
  SEND theName THE MESSAGE assign(aName)
ENDIF
```

A.20 **While sentence**

Syntax

```
while_sentence
```

```
: WHILE logical_expression DO
    paragraph
  ENDWHILE
```

Synopsis

The WHILE statement is the conventional iteration statement. The loop termination is determined by the logical expression.

Examples

```
INSTANCE theCount : Integer (0)
WHILE theCount < theLimit DO
  // ...
  SEND theCount THE MESSAGE assign (1 + theCount)
ENDWHILE
```

A.21 Foreach sentence

Syntax

```
foreach_sentence
  : FOREACH NAME ':' property_type IN NAME DO
    paragraph
  ENDFOREACH
```

Synopsis

The FOREACH clause is the iteration mechanism for visiting all the members of a container. The first NAME introduced in this statement contains the next item from the container upon each iteration. The NAME following the keyword IN identifies the container over which we intend to iterate.

Examples

```
FOREACH emp : Employee LINK IN theEmployees DO
  INSTANCE empName : String (SEND emp THE MESSAGE name?)
  IF empName == aName THEN
    RETURN TRUE
  ENDIF
ENDFOREACH
RETURN FALSE
```

A.22 **Return sentence**

Syntax

return_sentence
    : RETURN [[logical_expression]]

Synopsis

Return control from some method to the method sender with/without a value.

Examples

```
RETURN          // plain return
RETURN theName  // returned value
```

A.23 **Message sentence**

Syntax

message_sentence
    : message

message
    : SEND NAME THE MESSAGE
        NAME [['(' logical_expression_list ')']] [[FROM NAME]]

Synopsis

A message sentence is the only message-passing mechanism. The first NAME is the label for the receiving object. The second NAME with/without the associated expression list identifies the message. The expression list is the actual parameters passed along with the message. The name introduced in the FROM subclause uniquely identifies the class of the required message.

Examples

```
SEND p1 THE MESSAGE age?
SEND p1 THE MESSAGE changeName("Dr John Savage")
SEND me THE MESSAGE displaySales FROM SalesEmployee
```

A.24 **Let sentence**

Syntax

> let_sentence
>   : LET NAME ':=' logical_expression

Synopsis

A let sentence is a simple assignment mechanism. The NAME is the label for the receiving object. The expression to the right is evaluated and assigned to the variable on the left. Effectively the LET is realised as an assign message.

Examples

```
SEND theName THE MESSAGE assign(aName)
LET theName := aName  // equivalent
```

A.25 **Expressions**

Syntax

> logical_expression_list
>   : logical_expression {{ ',' logical_expression }}

> logical_expression
>   ¦ NOT logical_implies_expression
>   ‖ logical_implies_expression

> logical_implies_expression
>   : logical_or_expression {{ IMPLIES logical_implies_expression }}

> logical_or_expression
>   : logical_and_expression {{ OR logical_or_expression }}

> logical_and_expression
>   : relational_expression {{ AND logical_and_expression }}

> relational_expression
> : add_expression {{ < ‖ <= ‖ > ‖ >= ‖ == ‖ != relational_expression }}

add_expression
  : mult_expression {{ + || − add_expression }}

mult_expression
: primary_expression {{ * || / || % mult_expression }}

primary_expression
  : [['-']] factor
factor
  : NIL
  || NAME
  || INTEGER
  || DECIMAL
  || STRING
  || message
  || NAME '(' logical_expression_list ')'
  || NAME '[' logical_expression ']'
  || '(' logical_expression ')'
  || FORALL NAME ':' simple_type IN NAME
     SUCHTHAT logical_expression
  || THEREEXISTS NAME ':' simple_type IN NAME
     SUCHTHAT logical_expression

Synopsis

Keyword NIL represents a nullified LINK type.

Examples

```
NIL  // NULL pointer
theEmployer  // simple name
123  // simple integer
123.456  // simple decimal
"Ken Barclay"  // simple string constant
SEND theEmployer THE MESSAGE name?  // a message
theEmployees[k]  // SEND theEmployees THE MESSAGE at?(k)
theAge < = 21  // relational expression
theAge < = 21 AND theAge >70  // logical expression
theAge +20  // add_expression
theAge *20  // multi_expression
```

Appendix B

LOOM base types

LOOM specifications can be constructed from both user-defined class types and pre-specified class types. The latter are the base types provided by LOOM. These predefined class types are partitioned into two categories, namely, the fundamental classes and the container classes.

The fundamental classes are `Boolean`, `Integer`, `Decimal`, `String`, `Date` and `Time`. The final three are true classes in so far as we can give them LOOM specifications from which we may derive their corresponding implementation. For example, a partial LOOM specification for the `String` class is:

```
CLASS String
WITH
PUBLIC INTERFACE
  String(aText :String)
  length? -> Integer
  lessThan?(aText :String) -> Boolean
  hashValue? -> Integer
  // ...
ENDCLASS String
```

Correspondingly, the resulting C++ class is (see Appendix D):

```
class CString {
public:
  CString (char* aText = "");
  int  length(void) const;
  Logical  lessThan(const CString& aText) const;
  int  hashValue(void) const;
  // ...
};
```

The fundamental types `Boolean`, `Integer` and `Decimal` are, strictly, not class types. They mimic their respective counterparts in the target implementation language. They are, of course, expected to support the usual logical, arithmetic and relational operators.

The `String`, `Date` and `Time` types are represented by class specifications. Their outline is given by:

```
CLASS String
WITH
PUBLIC INTERFACE
  String(aValue :String)
  hashValue? -> Integer
  lessThan?(aString :String) -> Boolean
  String
  append(aValue :String)
  insert(aValue :String, index :Integer)
  isSubstring?(aValue :String) -> Integer
  length? -> Integer
  prepend(aValue :String)
  remove (position :Integer, length :Integer)
  toLower
  toUpper
  value? -> String   // strictly, char* in C++
PROTECTED INTERFACE
  NONE
PRIVATE IMPLEMENTATION
  REPRESENTATION NONE
  AGGREGATIONS NONE
  ASSOCIATIONS NONE
  DEFINITIONS
    // ...
ENDCLASS String
```

and:

```
CLASS Date
WITH
PUBLIC INTERFACE
  Date
  Date(aDay :Integer, aMonth :Integer, aYear :Integer)
  day? -> Integer
  month? -> Integer
  year? -> Integer
  hashValue? -> Integer
  lessThan?(aDate :Date) -> Boolean
  dayOfWeek? -> Integer
  daysInMonth? -> Integer
  daysInYear? -> Integer
  dayOfYear? -> Integer
  dayName? -> String
  abbreviatedDayName? -> String
  monthName? -> String
  abbreviatedMonthName? -> String
PROTECTED INTERFACE
  NONE
PRIVATE IMPLEMENTATION
  REPRESENTATION NONE
  AGGREGATIONS NONE
  ASSOCIATIONS NONE
  DEFINITIONS
```

```
    // ...
ENDCLASS Date
```

and:

```
CLASS Time
WITH
PUBLIC INTERFACE
  Time(anHour :Integer, aMinute :Integer,
    aSecond :Integer)
  hours? -> Integer
  minutes? -> Integer
  seconds? -> Integer
  hashValue? -> Integer
  lessThan?(aTime :Time) -> Boolean
  Time
PROTECTED INTERFACE
  NONE
PRIVATE IMPLEMENTATION
  REPRESENTATION NONE
  AGGREGATIONS NONE
  ASSOCIATIONS NONE
  DEFINITIONS
    // ...
ENDCLASS Time
```

The container classes are partitioned into two subgroups: the direct and the indirect containers. The direct containers hold full copies of the objects they manage, while the indirect containers manage LINK values. Otherwise, both sets of classes are mirrors of each other.

A part of the container class hierarchy is given in Figure B.1.

The usable concrete classes are DSet, DBag, DSortedList, DOrdered-List, DSortedCollection and DOrderedCollection. They are generic classes which are instantiated with a particular type, for example:

```
theNames :DSortedCollection[String]
theStaff :DSet[Employee]
```

All have methods that involve comparing the items they manage and, therefore, require that the actual type supplies the comparison operator lessThan?. For example:

```
CLASS Employee
WITH
PUBLIC INTERFACE
  lessThan?(anEmployee :Employee) -> Boolean
  // ...
ENDCLASS Employee
```

Further, those classes derived from DNonIndexedCollection employ a simple hashing strategy to distribute the items across the underlying implementation structure. As such, these containers also require the operation hashValue? from the instantiated type, e.g.:

```
CLASS Employee
WITH
PUBLIC INTERFACE
  lessThan?(anEmployee:Employee) -> Boolean
  hashValue? -> Integer
  // ...
REPRESENTATION
  theName        :String
  // ...
DEFINITIONS
  METHOD hashValue? -> Integer
  AS
    RETURN SEND theName THE MESSAGE hashValue?
  ENDMETHOD hashValue?
  // ...
ENDCLASS Employee
```

Note the implementation for the method. We simply return the value obtained by hashing the employee's name. The operation `hashValue?` is defined for the fundamental types `String`, `Date` and `Time`.

The constructor for the containers specialised from `DNonIndexed-Collection` require two arguments: a size argument and a distinguishing item. The size argument is the initial capacity for the container. They do, of course, grow dynamically as items are added when the structure is full. They can also be reconfigured with the `reSize` method. The second constructor argument is some unique value of the instantiated type used to distinguish unfilled entries in the container from true entries. This value is required because of the hashing

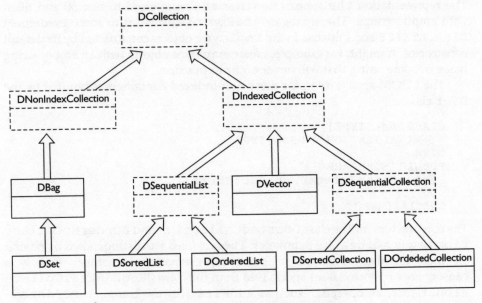

Figure B.1 *Direct container class hierarchy*

scheme used by these containers. Initially, the collections are filled with these unique values. As entries are added to the container, they overwrite these unfilled markers. The absent markers should be chosen so that they can be distinguished from any actual entry. For example, given the class Company:

```
CLASS Company
WITH
PUBLIC INTERFACE
  Company(aName :String)
  // ...
PRIVATE IMPLEMENTATION
  REPRESENTATION
    theName   :String
    theDepartmentNames  :DSet[ String ]
AGGREGATIONS
    theEmployees  :DSet[ Employee ]
    // ...
ENDCLASS Company
```

then an implementation for the Company constructor might be:

```
METHOD Company(aName :String)
AS
  SEND theName THE MESSAGE initialise(aName)
  SEND theDepartmentNames THE MESSAGE
    initialise(30, "")
  SEND theEmployees THE MESSAGE
    initialise(DEFAULTSIZE, Employee())
ENDMETHOD Company
```

The representation theDepartmentNames is initialised to size 30 and filled with empty strings. The aggregate theEmployees is set to some predefined DEFAULTSIZE and initialised with Employee objects constructed by its default constructor. It might, for example, create employee objects with an empty string name or some string that will never occur in practice.

The LOOM specification for these non-indexed containers is typified by the DSet class:

```
CLASS DSet[TYPE]
  SPECIALISATION OF DBag[TYPE]
WITH
PUBLIC INTERFACE
  Set(aSize :Integer, absent :TYPE)
  // ...
ENDCLASS DSet
```

The constructors for the class DSortedCollection and DOrderedCollection simply require a size parameter. These classes are distinguished by having all their members adjacent in some representation structure. This is a consequence of both classes specialised from the class DSequentialCollection. Hence, an operation such as addFirst for the container DOrderedCollection injects the incoming item into the first position and displaces the existing elements one place. A similar arrangement applies with removal operations.

The two concrete classes DSortedCollection and DOrderedCollection obtain the majority of their functionality from the superclass DSequentialCollection. It is worthwhile, then, investigating the realisation of this class. The implementation is a DVector item and an Integer value. The former holds the objects at index positions 0, 1, 2, ..., while the integer records a count of how many items are present.

```
ABSTRACT CLASS DSequentialCollection[TYPE]
  SPECIALISATION OF DIndexedCollection[TYPE]
WITH
PUBLIC INTERFACE
  DSequentialCollection(aSize : Integer)
  cardinality? -> Integer
  isMember?(anItem : TYPE) -> Boolean
  removeFirst
  // ...
PROTECTED INTERFACE
  theCardinality : Integer
  theCollection : DVector[TYPE]
PRIVATE IMPLEMENTATION
  REPRESENTATION NONE
  AGGREGATIONS NONE
  ASSOCIATIONS NONE
  DEFINITIONS
    METHOD DSequentialCollection(aSize : Integer)
    AS
  //
  // Create a sequential collection structure as given by the
  // size argument. The collection is represented by an
  // underlying DVector type.
  //
  SEND theCollection THE MESSAGE initialise(aSize)
  SEND theCardinality THE MESSAGE initialise(0)
ENDMETHOD DSequentialCollection

METHOD cardinality? -> Integer
AS
  RETURN theCardinality
ENDMETHOD cardinality?

METHOD isMember?(anItem : TYPE) -> Boolean
AS
  //
  // Determine if the argument value is present in
  // the collection.
  //
  INSTANCE index : Integer(0)
  WHILE index < theCardinality DO
    IF anItem == SEND theCollection THE MESSAGE
      at(index) THEN
      RETURN TRUE
```

```
      ENDIF
      SEND index THE MESSAGE assign(1 + index)
    ENDWHILE
    RETURN FALSE
  ENDMETHOD isMember?

  METHOD removeFirst
  AS
    //
    // Take first item off the front of the collection. If the
    // collection is empty, then do nothing.
    //
    INSTANCE index : Integer(1)
    WHILE index < theCardinality DO
      INSTANCE copy : ITEM(SEND theCollection THE
        MESSAGE at(index))
      SEND theCollection THE MESSAGE atPut(index - 1, copy)
      SEND index THE MESSAGE assign(1 + index)
    ENDWHILE
    SEND theCardinality THE MESSAGE
      assign(theCardinality - 1)
  ENDMETHOD removeFirst

// ...
ENDCLASS DSequentialCollection
```

The classes `DSortedList` and `DOrderedList` use a linked list structure for their implementation. Otherwise, they offer similar functionality to, respectively, `DSortedCollection` and `DOrderedCollection`. The `DOrderedList` constructor requires a unique data item in the manner of class `DSet`, while `DSortedList` requires a size value too:

```
CLASS DOrderedList[TYPE]
  SPECIALISATION OF DSequentialList[TYPE]
WITH
PUBLIC INTERFACE
  DOrderedList(absent : TYPE)
  // ...
ENDCLASS DOrderedList

CLASS DSortedList[TYPE]
  SPECIALISATION OF DSequentialList[TYPE]
WITH
PUBLIC INTERFACE
  DSortedList(depth : Integer, absent : TYPE)
  // ...
ENDCLASS DSortedList
```

For class `DSortedList` the first constructor argument is the `Integer` value `depth`. This value determines the maximum possible capacity for the structure, and is determined by the formula 2^{depth}. For example, a value of 6 would set the maximum at 64 items.

The indirect containers parallel their equivalents in the direct category. The indirect containers hold LINKs to the objects and not full copies, for example:

```
theEmployees  :PSet[Employee LINK]
```

Apart from the constructors, all the services are as in the direct container classes. All PCollection class constructors require two Integer values: a size value (or depth for class PSortedList), and a management scheme indicator. The latter informs the container whether it has responsibility for the objects (MANAGED) or whether responsibility resides with the client using the container (UNMANAGED). MANAGED is deployed where the client creates the objects but then adds them to the container, relinquishing control of the object to that container. UNMANAGED is used when the client retains control of the objects and uses the container as a storage medium. UNMANAGED may also be employed where two containers wish to refer to the same (shared) objects, with one container acting as the manager and the other as the slave.

B.1 The direct containers

This section gives a summary of the direct container class hierarchy. It shows the interface and implementation for some of the classes. The listing is intended to outline the implementation, identify the class interfaces, and show some complete LOOM scripts. As indicated above, the indirect containers have a similar arrangement:

```
//
// A DCollection is the abstract class at the root of the
// DIRECT container hierarchy. A direct container is one in
// which full copies of the values are maintained (cf.
// INDIRECT containers). All working containers are
// derived from this root. The concrete classes in this
// hierarchy are generic and must be instantiated with a
// particular type, e.g.:
//
//  theEmployees  :DSortedCollection[ Employee ]
//
// The actual type parameter must comply with the following
// mandatory profile. All actual types must supply a
// lessThan? method as:
//
//  CLASS SomeType
//  WITH
//  PUBLIC INTERFACE
//    lessThan?(anItem :SomeType) -> Boolean
//    // ...
//  ENDCLASS SomeType
//
// This method is used by the comparison operations of the
// container classes, such as the operation isMember?.
//
```

```
// The concrete classes derived from
// DNonIndexedCollection must also include the
// hashValue? method:
//
// CLASS SomeType
// WITH
// PUBLIC INTERFACE
// lessThan?(anItem :SomeType) -> Boolean
// hashValue? -> Integer
// // ...
// ENDCLASS SomeType
//
// This operation is used by the randomising process
// employed by these types of containers.
//
ABSTRACT CLASS DCollection
WITH
PUBLIC INTERFACE
  capacity? -> Integer                              DEFERRED
  reSize(anIncrement :Integer)                      DEFERRED
PROTECTED INTERFACE
  NONE
PRIVATE IMPLEMENTATION
  REPRESENTATION NONE
  AGGREGATIONS NONE
  ASSOCIATIONS NONE
  DEFINITIONS NONE
ENDCLASS DCollection


//
// A DIndexedCollection extends the DCollection Protocol
// by providing an indexing operation by which an item at
// some given integer index may be accessed.
//
ABSTRACT CLASS DIndexedCollection[TYPE]
  SPECIALISATION OF DCollection
WITH
PUBLIC INTERFACE
  at(anIndex :Integer) -> TYPE                      DEFERRED
PROTECTED INTERFACE
  NONE
PRIVATE IMPLEMENTATION
  REPRESENTATION NONE
  AGGREGATIONS NONE
  ASSOCIATIONS NONE
  DEFINITIONS NONE
ENDCLASS DIndexedCollection


//
// A DSequentialCollection is a specialised index
// collection in which all the elements are held
// sequentially from the base index position zero
// without any absent members. All additions and
```

```
// deletions are achieved through various add...
// and remove... operations. No direct (indexed)
// access update operation is available to destroy
// the integrity of the container.
//
// A DSequentialCollection class and its derived classes
// use a DVector for its underlying storage structure. At
// times when this structure becomes full it will be
// necessary to reSize itself to accommodate further items.
//
ABSTRACT CLASS DSequentialCollection [TYPE]
  SPECIALISATION OF DIndexedCollection [TYPE]
WITH
PUBLIC INTERFACE
  DSequentialCollection (aSize : Integer)
  capacity? -> Integer  REDEFINED
  reSize (anIncrement : Integer)  REDEFINED
  at (anIndex : Integer) -> TYPE  REDEFINED
  isEmpty? -> Boolean
  cardinality? -> Integer
  isMember? (anItem : TYPE) -> Boolean
  occurrencesOf? (anItem : TYPE) -> Integer
  first? -> TYPE
  last? -> TYPE
  remove (anItem : TYPE)
  removeFirst
  removeLast
  removeAt (anIndex : Integer)
  add (anItem : TYPE)  DEFERRED
PROTECTED INTERFACE
  theCardinality : Integer
  theCollection : DVector [TYPE]
PRIVATE IMPLEMENTATION
  REPRESENTATION NONE
  AGGREGATIONS NONE
  ASSOCIATIONS NONE
  DEFINITIONS
    METHOD DSequentialCollection (aSize : Integer)
    AS
      //
      // Create a sequential collection structure as given
      // by the size argument. The collection is
      // represented by an underlying DVector type.
      //
      SEND theCollection THE MESSAGE initialise (aSize)
      SEND theCardinality THE MESSAGE initialise (0)
    ENDMETHOD DSequentialCollection

METHOD capacity? -> Integer
AS
  //
  // Obtain the overall working capacity of the
  // collection.
  //
```

```
            RETURN (SEND theCollection THE MESSAGE capacity?)
        ENDMETHOD capacity?

        METHOD reSize(anIncrement : Integer)
        AS
            //
            // Increase the overall working capacity of the container.
            //
            SEND theCollection THE MESSAGE reSize(anIncrement)
        ENDMETHOD reSize

        METHOD at(anIndex : Integer) -> TYPE
        AS
            //
            // Fetch the item from the collection at the given index
            // position.
            //
            RETURN (SEND theCollection THE MESSAGE at(anIndex))
        ENDMETHOD at

        METHOD isEmpty? -> Boolean
        AS
            IF theCardinality == 0 THEN
                RETURN TRUE
            ELSE
                RETURN FALSE
            ENDIF
        ENDMETHOD isEmpty?

        METHOD cardinality? -> Integer
        AS
            RETURN theCardinality
        ENDMETHOD cardinality?

        METHOD isMember?(anItem : TYPE) -> Boolean
        AS
            //
            // Determine if the argument value is present in
            // the collection.
            //
            INSTANCE index : Integer(0)
            WHILE index < theCardinality DO
                IF anItem == SEND theCollection THE MESSAGE
                    at(index) THEN
                    RETURN TRUE
                ENDIF
                SEND index THE MESSAGE assign(1 + index)
            ENDWHILE
            RETURN FALSE
        ENDMETHOD isMember?

        METHOD occurrencesOf?(anItem : TYPE) -> Integer
        AS
            //
```

```
// Find how many copies of the argument value are
// present in the container.
//
INSTANCE index : Integer(0)
INSTANCE count : Integer(0)
WHILE index < theCardinality DO
  IF anItem == SEND theCollection THE MESSAGE
    at(index) THEN
    SEND count THE MESSAGE assign(1 + count)
  ENDIF
  SEND index THE MESSAGE assign(1 + index)
ENDWHILE
RETURN count
ENDMETHOD occurrencesOf?


METHOD first? -> TYPE
AS
 //
 // Fetch the first item in the set.
 //
 RETURN (SEND theCollection THE MESSAGE at(0))
ENDMETHOD first?


METHOD last? -> TYPE
AS
 //
 // Fetch the final item in the collection.
 //
 RETURN (SEND theCollection THE MESSAGE
   at(theCardinality - 1))
ENDMETHOD last?


METHOD remove(anItem : TYPE)
AS
 //
 // Locate the first occurrence of the argument value in the
 // collection and remove it. Reposition all subsequent
 // values to retain the required container semantics.
 // If no such item is present, then do nothing.
 //
 INSTANCE index : Integer(0)
 WHILE index < theCardinality DO
   IF anItem == SEND theCollection THE MESSAGE
     at(index) THEN
     INSTANCE position : Integer(1 + index)
     WHILE position < theCardinality DO
       INSTANCE copy :
         TYPE(SEND theCollection THE MESSAGE at(position))
       SEND theCollection THE MESSAGE
         atPut(position - 1, copy)
       SEND position THE MESSAGE assign(1 + position)
     ENDWHILE
     SEND theCardinality THE MESSAGE
       assign(theCardinality - 1)
```

```
            RETURN
         ENDIF
         SEND index THE MESSAGE assign (1 + index)
      ENDWHILE
   ENDMETHOD remove

   METHOD removeFirst
   AS
      //
      // Take first item off the front of the collection.
      // If the collection is empty, then do nothing.
      //
      INSTANCE index : Integer (1)
      WHILE index < theCardinality DO
         INSTANCE copy :
            ITEM (SEND theCollection THE MESSAGE at (index))
         SEND theCollection THE MESSAGE atPut (index - 1, copy)
         SEND index THE MESSAGE assign (1 + index)
      ENDWHILE
      SEND theCardinality THE MESSAGE
         assign (theCardinality - 1)
   ENDMETHOD removeFirst

   METHOD removeLast
   AS
      //
      // Take the final element off the collection. If
      // empty, then do nothing.
      //
      SEND theCardinality THE MESSAGE
         assign (theCardinality - 1)
   ENDMETHOD removeLast

   METHOD removeAt (anIndex : Integer)
   AS
      //
      // Remove the item from the collection at the given index
      // position. If the position does not refer to a valid
      // location, then do nothing.
      //
      INSTANCE position : Integer (1 + anIndex)
      WHILE position < theCardinality DO
         INSTANCE copy : TYPE (SEND theCollection THE
            MESSAGE at (position))
         SEND theCollection THE MESSAGE atPut (position
            - 1, copy)
         SEND position THE MESSAGE assign (1 + position)
      ENDWHILE
      SEND theCardinality THE MESSAGE
         assign (theCardinality - 1)
      RETURN
   ENDMETHOD removeAt

ENDCLASS DSequentialCollection
```

```
//
// A DOrderedCollection behaves as a
// DSequentialCollection with additional add
// operations. In all cases, these add operations
// double the size of the container if it is already
// full. The DOrderedCollection is a concrete
// class for which instances can be created:
//
// theEmployees  :DOrderedCollection[Employee]
//
CLASS DOrderedCollection[TYPE]
  SPECIALISATION OF DSequentialCollection[TYPE]
WITH
PUBLIC INTERFACE
  DOrderedCollection(aSize :Integer)
  add(anItem :TYPE)  REDEFINED
  addAt(anIndex :Integer, anItem :TYPE)
  addFirst(anItem :TYPE)
  addLast(anItem :TYPE)
PROTECTED INTERFACE
  NONE
PRIVATE IMPLEMENTATION
  REPRESENTATION NONE
  AGGREGATIONS NONE
  ASSOCIATIONS NONE
  DEFINITIONS
    METHOD DOrderedCollection(aSize :Integer)
    AS
      //
      // Construct a container of the initial given size
      //
      SEND DSequentialCollection THE MESSAGE
        initialise(aSize)
    ENDMETHOD DOrderedCollection


METHOD add(anItem :TYPE)
AS
  //
  // Add the new item in the final position
  //
  SEND me THE MESSAGE addLast(anItem)
ENDMETHOD add


METHOD addAt(anIndex :Integer, anItem :TYPE)
AS
  //
  // Place incoming item in the given index position. Move
  // all subsequent elements one place in the collection.
  //
  IF theCardinality == SEND theCollection THE
    MESSAGE capacity? THEN
    INSTANCE increment :
      Integer(SEND theCollection THE MESSAGE capacity?)
```

```
    SEND theCollection THE MESSAGE
      reSize(increment)
  ENDIF

INSTANCE index :Integer(theCardinality - 1)
WHILE index >= anIndex DO
  INSTANCE copy :
   TYPE(SEND theCollection THE MESSAGE at(index))
   SEND theCollection THE MESSAGE atPut(index + 1, copy)
   SEND index THE MESSAGE assign(index - 1)
ENDWHILE

  SEND theCollection THE MESSAGE atPut(anIndex, anItem)
  SEND theCardinality THE MESSAGE
    assign(1 + theCardinality)
ENDMETHOD addAt

METHOD addFirst(anItem :TYPE)
AS
  //
  // Force the incoming item into the first position. Move
  // existing items into next location. If the underlying
  // vector is full then increase its size.
  //
  IF theCardinality == SEND theCollection THE
   MESSAGE capacity? THEN
   INSTANCE increment :
    Integer(SEND theCollection THE MESSAGE capacity?)
   SEND theCollection THE MESSAGE
     reSize(increment)
  ENDIF

INSTANCE index :Integer(theCardinality - 1)
WHILE index >= 0 DO
  INSTANCE copy :
   TYPE(SEND theCollection THE MESSAGE at(index))
   SEND theCollection THE MESSAGE atPut(index + 1, copy)
   SEND index THE MESSAGE assign(index - 1)
ENDWHILE

  SEND theCollection THE MESSAGE atPut(0, anItem)
  SEND theCardinality THE MESSAGE
    assign(1 + theCardinality)
ENDMETHOD addFirst

METHOD addLast(anItem :TYPE)
AS
  //
  // Place incoming item on the end of the
  // container.
  //
  IF theCardinality == SEND theCollection THE
   MESSAGE capacity? THEN
```

```
      INSTANCE increment :
        Integer(SEND theCollection THE MESSAGE capacity?)
      SEND theCollection THE MESSAGE reSize(increment)
      ENDIF

    SEND theCollection THE MESSAGE
      atPut(theCardinality, anItem)
    SEND theCardinality THE MESSAGE
      assign(1 + theCardinality)
  ENDMETHOD addLast

  ENDCLASS DOrderedCollection


//
// A DSortedCollection maintains its items according to the
// sort order of the element type. When elements are added or
// removed, the ordering is maintained.
//
CLASS DSortedCollection[TYPE]
  SPECIALISATION OF DSequentialCollection[TYPE]
WITH
PUBLIC INTERFACE
  DSortedCollection(aSize : Integer)
  add(anItem : TYPE)          REDEFINED
PROTECTED INTERFACE
  NONE
PRIVATE IMPLEMENTATION
  REPRESENTATION NONE
  AGGREGATIONS NONE
  ASSOCIATIONS NONE
  DEFINITIONS
    METHOD DSortedCollection(aSize : Integer)
    AS
    //
    // Build a collection of the given size.
    //
    SEND theCollection THE MESSAGE initialise(aSize)
    SEND theCardinality THE MESSAGE initialise(0)
    ENDMETHOD DSortedCollection

    METHOD add(anItem : TYPE)
    AS
      //
      // Insert the new item into the collection, retaining the
      // sort order among the elements.
      //
      IF theCardinality == SEND theCollection THE
        MESSAGE capacity? THEN
        INSTANCE increment : Integer(SEND theCollection THE MESSAGE
        capacity?) SEND theCollection THE MESSAGE
        reSize(increment)
      ENDIF
```

```
INSTANCE index : Integer (0)
WHILE index < theCardinality DO
  INSTANCE copy :
   TYPE (SEND theCollection THE MESSAGE at (index))
  IF SEND anItem THE MESSAGE lessThan (copy) THEN
   INSTANCE position :
    Integer (theCardinality -1)
   WHILE position >= index DO
    INSTANCE posCopy :
     TYPE (SEND theCollection THE MESSAGE at (position))
    SEND theCollection THE MESSAGE
    atPut (1 + position, posCopy)
    SEND position THE MESSAGE
     assign (position -1)
   ENDWHILE
   SEND theCollection THE MESSAGE
    atPut (index, anItem)
   SEND theCardinality THE MESSAGE
    assign (1 + theCardinality)
   RETURN
  ENDIF
  SEND index THE MESSAGE assign (1 + index)
ENDWHILE

  SEND theCollection THE MESSAGE
   atPut (theCardinality, anItem)
  SEND theCardinality THE MESSAGE
   assign (1 + theCardinality)
ENDMETHOD add

ENDCLASS DSortedCollection


//
// A DSequentialList is a specialised DIndexedCollection
// in which all the elements are held sequentially from the
// base index position zero, without any absent members. All
// additions and deletions are achieved through various
// add... and remove... operations. No direct (indexed)
// access update operation is available to destroy the
// integrity of the container.
//
// DSequentialLists, and its derived classes, use
// linked-list storage structures for their
// representation. Storage for each new item is created on
// demand, hence unlike DSequentialCollections there is no
// need to reSize themselves at regular intervals.
//
ABSTRACT CLASS DSequentialList [TYPE]
  SPECIALISATION OF DIndexedCollection [TYPE]
WITH
PUBLIC INTERFACE
  DSequentialList (depth : Integer, absent : TYPE)
```

```
  capacity? -> Integer                                   REDEFINED
  reSize(aSize : Integer)                                REDEFINED
  at(anIndex : Integer) -> TYPE                          REDEFINED
  isEmpty? -> Boolean
  cardinality? -> Integer
  isMember?(anItem : TYPE) -> Boolean
                                                         POLYMORPHIC
  occurrencesOf?(anItem : TYPE) -> Integer
                                                         POLYMORPHIC
  first? -> TYPE
  last? -> TYPE
  removeFirst
  removeLast
  removeAt(anIndex : Integer)
  add(anItem : TYPE)                                     DEFERRED
  remove(anItem : TYPE)                                  DEFERRED
PROTECTED INTERFACE
  // ...
PRIVATE IMPLEMENTATION
  REPRESENTATION NONE
  AGGREGATIONS NONE
  ASSOCIATIONS NONE
  DEFINITIONS
    // ...
ENDCLASS DSequentialList


CLASS DOrderedList [TYPE]
  SPECIALISATION OF DSequentialList [TYPE]
WITH
PUBLIC INTERFACE
  DOrderedList(absent : TYPE)
  add(anItem : TYPE)                                     REDEFINED
  addFirst(anItem : TYPE)
  addLast(anItem : TYPE)
  remove(anItem : TYPE)                                  REDEFINED
  removeAt(anIndex : Integer)
  isMember?(anItem : TYPE) -> Boolean                    REDEFINED
  occurrencesOf?(anItem : TYPE) -> Integer
                                                         REDEFINED
PROTECTED INTERFACE
  NONE
PRIVATE IMPLEMENTATION
  REPRESENTATION NONE
  AGGREGATIONS NONE
  ASSOCIATIONS NONE
  DEFINITIONS
    // ...
ENDCLASS DOrderedList


CLASS DSortedList [TYPE]
  SPECIALISATION OF DSequentialList [TYPE]
WITH
PUBLIC INTERFACE
```

```
      DSortedList(depth :Integer, absent :TYPE)
      add(anItem :TYPE)                                    REDEFINED
      remove(anItem :TYPE)                                 REDEFINED
      isMember?(anItem :TYPE) -> Boolean                   REDEFINED
      remove(anItem :TYPE)                                 REDEFINED
    PROTECTED INTERFACE
      NONE
    PRIVATE IMPLEMENTATION
      REPRESENTATION NONE
      AGGREGATIONS NONE
      ASSOCIATIONS NONE
      DEFINITIONS
      // ...
    ENDCLASS DSortedList


    //
    // A DNonIndexed collection represents an abstract base
    // class for which there is no notion of ordering among the
    // elements. Typically we have DBag and DSet as concrete
    // examples.
    //
    // Such classes employ a hashing algorithm to distribute the
    // items randomly through the underlying vector. As noted in
    // the DCollection class, the actual element types must
    // support the hashValue method to perform this randomizing
    // process.
    //
    // The class constructors have, in addition to the usual size
    // argument, a second argument which is some element value
    // different from those which will be stored in these
    // containers. This value is distributed across the vector
    // to denote the fact that the cell is unused.
    //
    ABSTRACT CLASS DNonIndexedCollection[TYPE]
      SPECIALISATION OF DCollection
    WITH
    PUBLIC INTERFACE
      DNonIndexedCollection(aSize :Integer,
        absent :TYPE)
      capacity? -> Integer                                 REDEFINED
      reSize(anIncrement :Integer)                         REDEFINED
      isEmpty? -> Boolean
      cardinality? -> Integer
      isMember?(anItem :TYPE) -> Boolean
      occurrencesOf?(anItem :TYPE) -> Integer
      remove(anItem :TYPE)
      add(anItem :TYPE)                                    DEFERRED
    PROTECTED INTERFACE
      theCollection :DVector [TYPE]
      theCardinality :Integer
      theAbsent :TYPE
    PRIVATE IMPLEMENTATION
      REPRESENTATION NONE
```

```
AGGREGATIONS NONE
ASSOCIATIONS NONE
DEFINITIONS
  METHOD DNonIndexedCollection(aSize :Integer,
    absent :TYPE)
  AS
    //
    // Create a vector of the required size, then fill it.
    //
    SEND theCollection THE MESSAGE
      initialise(aSize)
    SEND theCardinality THE MESSAGE
      initialise(0)
    SEND theAbsent THE MESSAGE
      initialise(absent)

  INSTANCE index :Integer(0)
  WHILE index < theCardinality DO
    SEND theCollection THE MESSAGE
      atPut(index, theAbsent)
    SEND index THE MESSAGE assign(1 + index)
  ENDWHILE
ENDMETHOD DNonIndexedCollection

METHOD capacity? -> Integer
AS
  //
  // Obtain the overall working storage.
  //
  RETURN (SEND theCollection THE MESSAGE capacity?)
ENDMETHOD capacity?

METHOD reSize(anIncrement :Integer)
AS
  //
  // Increase the size of the underlying vector by the
  // amount given, redistributing the existing elements
  // through this new structure.
  //
ENDMETHOD reSize

METHOD isEmpty? -> Boolean
AS
  IF theCardinality == 0 THEN
    RETURN TRUE
  ELSE
    RETURN FALSE
  ENDIF
ENDMETHOD isEmpty?

METHOD cardinality? -> Integer
AS
  RETURN theCardinality
ENDMETHOD cardinality?
```

```
METHOD isMember?(anItem :TYPE) -> Boolean
AS
  //
  // Determine if the given value is present in the
  // collection. Search the container using a simple open
  // hash strategy.
  //
  INSTANCE maxSize :
    Integer(SEND theCollection THE MESSAGE capacity?)

INSTANCE hash :
  Integer(SEND anItem THE MESSAGE hashValue?)
INSTANCE position :Integer(hash % maxSize)
INSTANCE element :
  TYPE(SEND theCollection THE MESSAGE at(position))
WHILE element != theAbsent DO
  IF anItem == element THEN
    RETURN TRUE
  ENDIF
  SEND position THE MESSAGE assign(1 + position)
  SEND element THE MESSAGE
  assign(SEND theCollection THE MESSAGE
    at(position))
ENDWHILE

  RETURN FALSE
ENDMETHOD isMember?

METHOD occurrencesOf?(anItem :TYPE) -> Integer
AS
  //
  // Determine if the given value is present in the
  // collection and by how many times. Search the
  // container using a simple open hash strategy.
  //
INSTANCE count :
  Integer(0)
INSTANCE maxSize :Integer(SEND theCollection
  THE MESSAGE capacity?)

INSTANCE hash :
  Integer(SEND anItem THE MESSAGE hashValue?)
INSTANCE position :Integer(hash % maxSize)
INSTANCE element :
  TYPE(SEND theCollection THE MESSAGE at(position))
WHILE element != theAbsent DO
  IF anItem == element THEN
    SEND count THE MESSAGE assign(1 + count)
  ENDIF
  SEND position THE MESSAGE assign(1 + position)
  SEND element THE MESSAGE
    assign(SEND theCollection THE MESSAGE
      at(position))
ENDWHILE
```

```
RETURN count
ENDMETHOD occurrencesOf?

METHOD remove(anItem :TYPE)
AS
  //
  // Remove the given item from the collection. Ensure that
  // the open hash structures are not invalidated.
  //
ENDMETHOD remove

ENDCLASS DNonIndexedCollection



//
// A DBag is an unordered collection of items in which
// duplicates are permitted.
//
CLASS DBag[TYPE]
  SPECIALISATION OF DNonIndexedCollection[TYPE]
WITH
PUBLIC INTERFACE
  DBag(aSize :Integer, absent :TYPE)
  add(anItem :TYPE)   REDEFINED
PROTECTED INTERFACE
  NONE
PRIVATE IMPLEMENTATION
  REPRESENTATION NONE
  AGGREGATIONS NONE
  ASSOCIATIONS NONE
  DEFINITIONS
    METHOD DBag(aSize :Integer, absent :TYPE)
    AS
      //
      // Create a structure of the required size.
      //
      SEND DNonIndexedCollection THE MESSAGE
        initialise(aSize, absent)
    ENDMETHOD DBag

METHOD add(anItem :TYPE)
AS
  //
  // Add a new item to the collection. Apply the simple open
  // hash algorithm to structure the deployment of the
  // elements.
  //
  INSTANCE maxSize :
    Integer(SEND theCollection THE MESSAGE capacity?)
  IF theCardinality >= (3 * maxSize / 4) THEN
    SEND me THE MESSAGE reSize(maxSize)
    SEND maxSize THE MESSAGE assign(maxSize + maxSize)
  ENDIF
```

```
      INSTANCE hash :
        Integer(SEND anItem THE MESSAGE hashValue?)
      INSTANCE position :Integer(hash % maxSize)
      INSTANCE element :
        TYPE(SEND theCollection THE MESSAGE at(position))
      WHILE element != theAbsent DO
        SEND position THE MESSAGE assign(1 + position)
        SEND element THE MESSAGE
          assign(SEND theCollection THE MESSAGE
           at(position))
      ENDWHILE

        SEND theCollection THE MESSAGE atPut(position, anItem)
        SEND theCardinality THE MESSAGE
          assign(1 + theCardinality)
      ENDMETHOD add

      ENDCLASS DBag


      CLASS DSet[TYPE]
        SPECIALISATION OF DBag[TYPE]
      WITH
      PUBLIC INTERFACE
        DSet(aSize :Integer, absent :TYPE)
        add(anItem :TYPE)   REDEFINED
      PROTECTED INTERFACE
        NONE
      PRIVATE IMPLEMENTATION
        REPRESENTATION NONE
        AGGREGATIONS NONE
        ASSOCIATIONS NONE
        DEFINITIONS
          METHOD DSet(aSize :Integer, absent :TYPE)
          AS
            //
            // Create a container of the appropriate size.
            //
            SEND DBag THE MESSAGE initialise(aSize, absent)
      ENDMETHOD DSet

      METHOD add(anItem :TYPE)
      AS
        //
        // Add a new item to the collection without duplication.
        // Apply the simple open hash algorithm to structure the
        // deployment of the elements.
        //
        INSTANCE maxSize :
          Integer(SEND theCollection THE MESSAGE capacity?)
        IF theCardinality >= (3 * maxSize / 4) THEN
          SEND me THE MESSAGE reSize(maxSize)
          SEND maxSize THE MESSAGE assign(maxSize + maxSize)
        ENDIF
```

```
INSTANCE hash : Integer (SEND anItem THE MESSAGE
  hashValue?)
INSTANCE position : Integer (hash % maxSize)
INSTANCE element :
  TYPE (SEND theCollection THE MESSAGE at (position))
WHILE element != theAbsent DO
  IF anItem == element THEN
    RETURN
  ENDIF
    SEND position THE MESSAGE assign (1 + position)
    SEND element THE MESSAGE
      assign (SEND theCollection THE MESSAGE at (position))
ENDWHILE

  SEND theCollection THE MESSAGE atPut (position, anItem)
  SEND theCardinality THE MESSAGE
    assign (1 + theCardinality)
ENDMETHOD add

ENDCLASS DSet
```

Appendix C

C++ classes

This appendix presents a brief summary of classes in the C++ programming language. We do not present a detailed description, rather we identify and describe the major highlights which have been the focus of this book. The bibliography identifies a number of key publications which detail the language.

C.1 Class essentials

The C++ programming language supports an aggregate type known as the *class*. It is a composite of components which are distinct. The components of a class can be *data members* or *function members*. These class members are given access levels which specify which components are restricted and which are available to users of the class. The access levels are introduced by the keywords public:, protected: and private:. Typically, the data members appear in the private section and the function members in the public section. This is not a requirement from the language. It is perfectly reasonable to have, say, a function member in the private section which provides some support role to the class, but which does not need to be available to clients. Here is a class to represent bank accounts:

```
class Account {
public:
  Account(const CString& anAccountNumber,
    int initialBalance);

  CString            accountNumber(void) const;
  int                balance(void) const;

  void               credit(int money);
  void               debit(int money);

private:
  CString            theAccountNumber;
  int                theBalance;
};
```

The class name is given by the *tag-name* `Account`. The class is represented by an account number and the present balance of the account. These values are given by the private data members `theAccountNumber` and `theBalance`. They are manipulated by users of the class through the public member functions `balance`, `credit`, `debit` and `accountNumber`. For example, function `balance` is an interrogative function requesting to know the present balance of the account. Function `credit` updates the account's balance by the monetary amount given by its argument.

Instances of this `Account` class are introduced by the definition:

```
Account          myAccount("ABC123", 100);
```

Here the program variable `myAccount` is declared and initialised by the string value `"ABC123"` and the integer value `100`. The initialisation sets the otherwise private data members to, respectively, these two values. This initialisation is performed by the *constructor member function* which is that function in the class declaration bearing the same name as the class name.

The presence of such a constructor means that the example shown is the only valid way in which an `Account` object may be defined. Two actual arguments must be given, the first being a string value and the second an int.

The members of a class are referenced by the *class member access operator* (.). Since we have only placed member functions into the public section of the `Account` class, these are the only accessible members with this selection operator. The construction we use is:

```
object-name.member-function-name
  (actual-arguments)
```

If there are no arguments required by the member function then we have the arrangement (). We might credit `myAccount` with 10 monetary units with the statement:

```
myAccount.credit(10);
```

or we might determine the present balance in the account with:

```
if(myAccount.balance() > 1000) ...
```

The definition for the member functions determines their behaviour when applied to some instance of the `Account` class. For example, the first statement above presumably adds the actual argument 10 to the present balance in the account which, through the earlier initialising constructor, is currently 100 monetary units. A function's behaviour is specified in the *member function's definition*. A function definition is a mixture of program statements which describe the actions performed together with any number of temporary data items required by the function when executing its tasks. The definition for member function `credit` might appear as:

```
void        Account::credit(int monetary)
{
```

```
        theBalance += monetary;
    }
```

Here, the function definition consists of a *function header* and a *function body*. The function body contains the statements and data definitions. In this example, the function body is the single statement `theBalance += monetary` which increments the value of the data member `theBalance` by the value of the argument `monetary`.

The function header introduces the name of the function, the function arguments and their types (if any), and the return type of the function. The function name is `credit`. This is the `credit` function for the `Account` class, and since C++ permits this function name to be introduced in other classes we qualify the function name with the *scope resolution operator* (::) which is prefixed with the class name. Here, function `credit` returns no value as indicated by the language word `void`, and expects to be supplied with a single actual argument which is captured by the corresponding formal `int` argument `monetary`.

When the member function is invoked as in the statement `myAccount.-credit(10)` the actual argument 10 is used to initialise the value of the formal argument `monetary`. This process is referred to as argument passing and C++ supports three distinct argument-passing strategies. For member function `credit`, the *pass by value* scheme is being used. In this arrangement the value of the actual argument is determined and is then used to initialise the value of the formal argument `monetary`. Thereafter, the body of the function operates with this pre-initialised formal argument.

The constructor function of a class has a special role. It is used to properly initialise every object instance of the class type, and as such it is not documented with some return type since no value is returned. When an object of class `Account` is defined as shown earlier, the constructor function is called. For this class we expect the constructor to initialise the values of the data members with the values of the actual arguments. The constructor for the `Account` class might be shown by:

```
Account::Account(const CString& anAccountNumber,
    int initialBalance)
{
    theAccountNumber = anAccountNumber;
    theBalance = initialBalance;
}
```

Here we see simple assignment of the arguments to the data members used to perform the initialisation.

Strictly, a C++ constructor has two phases called the *initialisation phase* and the *assignment phase*. The assignment phase is associated with the constructor function body and is used in the above example to set the values into the data members. The initialisation phase precedes the assignment phase and is presented in a *member initialisation list*, unique to constructor functions. A member initialisation list is a comma-separated list of data members and the initial values they are to be given. This is shown with the data member and its initial value expression enclosed in parentheses. The list is set off from the function header by a colon (:) as shown below:

```
Account::Account(const CString& anAccountNumber,
  int initialBalance)
  : theAccountNumber(anAccountNumber),
    theBalance(initialBalance)
{
}
```

Here, of course, there is nothing for this constructor to do during its assignment phase and the function body is left blank. It is perfectly permissible to employ a mixture of these as in:

```
Account::Account(const CString& anAccountNumber,
  int initialBalance)
  : theAccountNumber(anAccountNumber)
{
  theBalance = initialBalance;
}
```

For the data member `theBalance` any of the schemes shown above is correct. However, for the string data member `theAccountNumber` it is more appropriate to use the initialisation phase. The data member `theAccount-Number` is of type `CString` which is itself a user-defined class much like the `Account` class. When the `Account` object is being created, the two sub-objects which are the data members are created. Since `CString` is a user-defined class, presumably a `CString` constructor is executed to perform the initialisation. This applies even if no initialisation phase is given for our `Account` class constructor. This means that the `CString` class needs to have some way of initialising the `CString` sub-object `theAccountNumber` and implies that a suitable construc-tor exists in the `CString` class. When this is done we enter the function body to perform the assignment phase of the `Account` class constructor and we immediately overwrite the default value given to `theAccountNumber`. Better, we have this achieved in one step through the member initialisation scheme as described above.

When the `Account` class constructor is called to initialise the object `myAccount` as in:

```
Account myAccount("ABC123", 100);
```

the actual string `"ABC123"` is used to initialise the formal argument `anAccountNumber`. Potentially this might be a very long string requiring a large amount of data to be copied from the actual argument into the corresponding formal argument, were we to employ pass by value semantics. C++ also supports *pass by reference* argument passing. In this scheme, a reference formal argument is made to act as an alias for the actual argument. No copying of the actual argument is performed, rather the formal argument is made to act as another name for the actual argument.

A reference formal argument is shown as above. The type name `CString` is followed by the ampersand symbol "&". Since the formal argument is now a reference to the actual argument, any changes made within the body of the function to the formal argument will be reflected back into the actual argument, resulting in the actual argument being changed. In this example we simply wish to deploy reference argument passing because of its efficiencies, but would not wish to permit changes to the formal and hence to the actual argument. This we achieve by prefixing the type with the qualifier keyword const. This ensures that in the function body we cannot make any changes to the formal argument anAccountNumber.

We have already noted above that the same function name may appear in one or more classes. This is referred to as *function overloading*. The same holds true within a class provided the functions either have different numbers of arguments or they are of different types. This is necessary so that the C++compiler can distinguish between them. This overloading equally well applies to constructors and is commonly used to give users different ways to initialise objects. In particular, we often find a *default constructor* along with other conventional constructors. The default constructor is one with no arguments:

```
class Account {
public :
  Account(const CString& anAccountNumber,
    int initialBalance);
  Account(void);
  // ...
};
```

As before, we expect the constructor to properly initialise its data members. This time, of course, we have no formal arguments to utilise. In that case we must define sensible semantics for the behaviour of the default constructor. Perhaps in this example we might set the account number to the empty string and the balance to zero:

```
Account::Account(void)
  : theAccountNumber(""),
    theBalance(0)
{
}
```

The keyword const also figures in the description of the interrogative functions accountNumber and balance. Here the keyword documents the fact that the function's behaviour is guaranteed not to modify the data members of the object to which it is applied. Further, if when we define these functions we inadvertently write program statements which conflict with this, the C++ compiler will generate error messages advising us of this situation.

```
CString  Account::accountNumber(void) const
{
  return theAccountNumber;
}
```

C.2 Class derivation

Rather than develop a class from new we can introduce our new class as a derivation of an existing class. The existing class is referred to as the *base class* and the new class is called the *derived* class. Derivation permits the members of the base class to be used as if they were members of the derived class without the need to redefine them. For example, the class `SavingsAccount` may be introduced as a derivation of the `Account` class. Since the `Account` class supports a member function `credit`, we may apply this function to a `SavingsAccount` object:

```
SavingsAccount mySavings("XYX789", 10000);
mySavings.credit(1000);
```

All the operations that can be performed on an `Account` object can also be performed on a `SavingsAccount` object. We can, if necessary, extend the list of data members and function members inherited from the base class. We can also replace one or more of the inherited functions of the base class by a process referred to as *redefined function definitions*.

To denote class derivation, a class declaration includes a *derivation list* of classes from which to inherit members. The classes named in this derivation list are the base classes. The class declaration for `SavingsAccount` would appear as:

```
class SavingsAccount : public Account {
public:
  // ...
};
```

The derivation list is set off from the class name by a colon symbol. The keyword `public` indicates that class `SavingsAccount` is a publicly derived class of the base class `Account`. Any public members of the base class are also public members of the derived class. Because of the derivation list, there is no need to repeat the inherited services of the base class. Commonly, the derived class incorporates additional data and function members. For example, our `Savings-Account` class might hold the value of the interest rate pertaining to the account. Two functions, `interestRate` and `setInterestRate`, allow a user to determine and reset the interest level.

```
class SavingsAccount : public Account {
public:
  // ...
  int  interestRate(void) const;
  void setInterestRate(int rate);

private:
  int  theInterestRate;
};
```

Hence the following is perfectly legal:

```
SavingsAccount mySavings( ... );     // see below
mySavings.credit(1000);              // inherited function
mySavings.setInterestRate(4);        // additional
  functions
int presentRate = mySavings.interestRate();
```

Constructor member functions are not automatically inherited by the derived class. This is not unreasonable since, as we have shown, the derived class SavingsAccount has an additional data member which the constructor of the base class does not initialise. Hence we require:

```
class SavingsAccount : public Account {
public:
  SavingsAccount(const CString& anAccountNumber,
    int initialBalance,
    int initialRate);
  // ...

private:
  int theInterestRate;
};
```

The derived class constructor initialises the base class data members through the base class constructor, presented in a member initialisation list. We cannot initialise these members directly in the derived class constructor since they are in the private section of the base class. Private always means private even under derivation. Anyway, we have already established that the correct way to initialise the members of a class is through a constructor.

```
SavingsAccount::SavingsAccount(const CString&
  anAccountNumber, int initialBalance,
  int initialRate)
  : Account(anAccountNumber, initialBalance),
    theInterestRate(initialRate)
{
}
```

It is appropriate to consider redefining some of the inherited functions of the base class. For example, the function balance might consider both the amount presently in the account and the interest accruing on that sum. Let us imagine that the function balance in the derived class adds the present balance and the simple interest for that amount as the delivered value. Two things must happen. First we must explicitly present the function in the derived class and we must provide a definition for it.

```
class SavingsAccount : public Account {
public:
  int balance(void) const;  // introduce
                            // redefined function
  // ...
```

```
private:
  int  theInterestRate;
};

int  SavingsAccount::balance(void) const
{
  int interestDue = theBalance * theInterestRate / 100;
   // BUT see below
  return theBalance + interestDue;
}
```

For this function to act as a redefined function it must match exactly that which appears in the base class. Our difficulty is that the function definition for this redefined version refers to the data member `theBalance` from the base class. As we have already observed, this member is in the private section of the base class and is, therefore, inaccessible. The principle of information hiding would be violated if we were to move the member into the public section. Users of the class would then have direct access to this member. To resolve this conflict we use the public operation `balance` from the base class:

```
int  SavingsAccount::balance(void) const
{
  int interestDue = Account::balance() *
    theInterestRate / 100;      // BUT see below
  return theBalance + interestDue;
}
```

The syntax:

```
class Derived : private Base { ... };
```

introduces the `Derived` class as privately derived from the `Base` class. The public members of the `Base` class are private members of the `Derived` class and therefore cannot be used by users of the `Derived` class. Private derivation is used where the internal representation of the `Derived` class is provided by the data type defined by the `Base` class. Consider the class `Vector` which imitates a one-dimensional array of integers.

```
class Vector {
public:
  Vector(int initialSize);

  void  atPut(int index, int anItem);  // place new entry
  int  at(int index) const;  // access particular position
  // ...
};
```

A `Stack` is a collection of integers which operate a strict last-in-first-out storage regime. We might consider deriving `Stack` from `Vector` for its representation. Typically this would be used where some member of the `Vector` class is on its protected interface and is required in the derived `Stack` class.

```
class Stack : private Vector {
public:
```

```
Stack(int initialSize);

void  push(int anItem);
void  pop(void);
int  top(void) const;

private:
  int  theStackTop;  // indexing the vector
};

void  Stack::push(int anItem)
{
  theStackTop++;
  atPut(theStackTop, anItem);
}
```

Inheritance is a mechanism in which one class is formed as a development of an existing class. This proves to be a particularly important concept which supports re-usability of existing code. Inheritance also gives rise to the notions of *polymorphism* and *dynamic binding*. These new concepts provide support by which software systems may be adapted to accommodate change in specification.

Polymorphism is defined as 'having several forms'. In an object oriented programming language this means that some object refers to instances of various classes during run time. For example, the class definition for `SavingsAccount` declares the explicit inheritance from class `Account` and reveals that a savings account *isA* an account with, perhaps, additional data and function members and redefined functions. This introduces the notion of substitution. Any instance of a derived class object (or reference, or pointer) may substitute for an instance of a base class object (or reference or pointer). Hence we may have:

```
SavingsAccount  mySavings("XYZ789", 10000, 4);
Account& accReference  = mySavings;
Account* accPointer  = &mySavings;  // care!
```

When `mySavings` executes the function `balance` as in `mySavings.balance()` then since `mySavings` is an object of the `SavingsAccount` class, the redefined version for that function is executed. When `accReference` or `accPointer` applies the same function:

```
accReference.balance()
accPointer->balance()
```

then since the object references are specified by the types `Account&` and `Account*` respectively they both obey the function definition in the `Account` class. This is referred to as *static binding* and is similar to procedure calls in conventional programming languages. The language compiler knows the type to which the object references belong and associates the function calls accordingly.

Consider a `Bank` class which holds a table of accounts. In this table we would expect there to be both `Account` and `SavingsAccount` objects. We readily realise this by representing the table as an array of `Account` class pointers. These pointers may, of course, refer to Account and to SavingsAccount objects because of the substitution rule. The Bank class might appear as:

```
class Bank {
public:
  int  bankBalance(void) const;
  // ...
private:
  Account*  theAccounts[MAXACCOUNTS];
                          // table of accounts
  int  theAccountsSize;   // number in use
};
```

Now if a Bank object wishes to determine the balance of every account, we might expect that by sending the function balance to every account in the table we obtain the desired effect:

```
int  Bank::bankBalance(void) const
{
  int  totalBalance = 0;
  for(int k = 0; k < theAccountsSize; k++)
    totalBalance += theAccounts[k]->balance();
  return totalBalance;
}
```

While the programmed solution is correct, the effect we obtain is not the desired one. The problem is the compiler's use of static binding. The table theAccounts is an array of Account pointers. Static binding means that we shall execute the function balance defined in the Account class for all items in this table irrespective of whether they are Account objects or SavingsAccount objects.

The solution we desire is obtained by employing *dynamic binding*. When we send the balance message to every object in the table theAccounts, we wish the recipient object to recognise the type to which it belongs and bind at runtime to the appropriate version of the balance function. This polymorphic effect is obtained by tagging the function balance in the Account class as virtual. This keyword indicates that we wish to exploit the effect of dynamic binding. A function tagged as virtual in a base class is also, by default, virtual in any redefinition appearing in derived classes. The keyword is optional in derived classes but often appears as useful documentation:

```
class Account {
public :
  virtual int  balance(void) const;
  // ...
};

class SavingsAccount : public Account {
public:
  virtual int  balance(void) const;
    // redefinition
  // ...
  };
```

Class `Account` and `SavingsAccount` are both *concrete* classes in-so-far as we may create instances of either type. Often a class hierarchy is a mixture of concrete and *abstract* classes. No instances of an abstract class may be created. Their usefulness, however, lies in the structuring of the class hierarchy. An abstract class may hold properties and services common to all derived classes. Further, abstract classes can introduce functions which cannot be defined for the abstract class but for which implementations must be given in any derived concrete class. Such a function's implementation is deferred for the concrete class, but its introduction into the abstract base class means that it must be included at the concrete class level. A function deferred in this way is called a *pure virtual function*. The appearance of a pure virtual function in a class declaration makes that class an abstract base class. A derived class must define an implementation for that function to be concrete, otherwise it too is abstract because of the inheritance of that member function.

Consider once again our `Account` class. This time we may have two derived classes `SavingsAccount` and `CurrentAccount`. To ensure that both derived classes present a definition for a `balance` function we may introduce a deferred version into the `Account` class. In this new class hierarchy structure, definitions for the `balance` function may only be appropriate at the derived classes. No such definition may be plausible at the level of the general `Account` class. To ensure both derived classes present definitions we introduce the function balance as pure virtual:

```
class Account {
public:
  virtual int  balance(void) const =0;
   // note notation "=0" for pure virtual
  // ...
};

class SavingsAccount : public Account {
public:
  virtual int  balance(void) const;
  // defined for this class
   // ...
};

class CurrentAccount : public Account {
public:
  virtual int  balance(void) const;
  // defined for this class
 // ...
};
```

C.3 Template classes

The `Stack` class of the previous section stored ints in a `Vector` implementation. Here it was assumed that the `Vector` class also stored `int` types. Clearly, a

Stack of doubles or a Stack of SavingsAccounts would be programmed similarly. C++ supports a *template class* mechanism in which a family of stack types can be produced from a single definition.

```
template <class TYPE>
class Vector {
public:
  Vector(int initialSize);

  void  atPut(int index, const TYPE& anItem);
   //place new entry
  TYPE  at(int index) const;
   // access particular position
  // ...
};

template <class TYPE>
class Stack : private Vector<TYPE> {
public:
  Stack(int initialSize);

void  push(const TYPE& anItem);
void  pop(void);
TYPE  top(void) const;

private:
  int  theStackTop;     // indexing the vector
};

template <class TYPE>
void  Stack<TYPE>::push(const TYPE& anItem)
{
  theStackTop++;
  atPut(theStackTop, anItem);
}
```

The prefix template <class TYPE> to the Stack class declaration introduces a generic class of some arbitrary type denoted by the user-defined name TYPE. This type name TYPE has the class declaration as its scope. Hence within the declaration the push function expects an argument of this type. Note how the function members are defined. They too are *function templates*. The additional notation includes the same prefix, with the scope resolution specified as Stack<TYPE> indicating to which class the function belongs.

This naming device is also used to *instantiate* specific instances. Replacing the type parameter name TYPE with, say, SavingsAccount:

```
Stack<SavingsAccount> myStack;
  // instantiated
```

defines an object myStack of some class Stack<SavingsAccount>.

Appendix D

C++ class reference

The fundamental LOOM types such as `Integer` and `String` and the container types such as `POrderedCollection` have all been realised as C++ code. The simple types `Integer` and `Decimal` have been aliased with their corresponding C++ types with `typedef` statements:

```
typedef int         Integer;
typedef double      Decimal;
```

These two statements appear in the class library header file `loomlib.h`. This file is automatically included by any ROME-produced code. The header file also contains an enumeration declaration for the `Logical` type used to imitate the LOOM type `Boolean`:

```
enum Logical { LFALSE, LTRUE };
```

The remaining types in LOOM are presented as C++ classes. For example, the LOOM type `String` is implemented as a C++ class type `CString` defined in the header file `ccstring.h`. The header files and corresponding code files should be consulted for details. Below is the documentation presented for the common classes used throughout the book.

D.1 CString

Synopsis   Class `CString` offers a flexible and convenient facility for manipulating `CStrings`. A `CString` is a variable length data structure of character values. `CStrings` may be assigned, compared, modified and interrogated for a range of properties.

```
#include "ccstring.h"
```

Constructor   `CString(char* cs = "");`

Standard constructor for the conversion of a null-terminated C-style character string. The string argument `cs` is copied into the `CString` object. If no actual argument is given, a null string with zero characters is used.

Constructor `CString(char c, int rep = 1);`

Standard constructor to create a `CString` object initialised with a character string effectively composed of a number of copies of the single argument character `c`. The number of repetitions of `c` is given by the `rep` argument.

Constructor `CString(const CString& str);`

Standard copy constructor. Copies the `CString` object represented by the argument `str` into instance being created.

Destructor `~CString(void);`

Destroys an instance of class `CString`, removing any space allocated from the memory heap.

Assignment `CString& operator= (const CString& str);`

Copies the source `CString` object represented by the argument `str` into an existing destination `CString` variable denoted by that on the left of the operator. Any existing space used by the `CString` variable is released to the heap manager, and new space is allocated according to the size of the source `CString`.

Concatenation `CString operator+ (const CString& str1,`
operator   `const CString& str2);`

Returns a new `CString` object which is the concatenation of the two `CString` arguments `str1` and `str2`.

Input/Output `istream& operator>> (istream& is,`
operator   `CString& str);`
          `ostream& operator<< (ostream& os,`
                `const CString& str);`

Reads (writes) the `CString` value `str` from (to) an input (output) stream.

Logical `Logical operator< (const CString& str1,`
operators   `const CString& str2);`
      `Logical operator<= (const CString& str1,`
              `const CString& str2);`
      `Logical operator> (const CString& str1,`
              `const CString& str2);`
      `Logical operator>= (const CString& str1,`
              `const CString& str2);`
      `Logical operator== (const CString& str1,`
              `const CString& str2);`
      `Logical operator!= (const CString& str1,`
              `const CString& str2);`

Perform a lexicographic comparison of the two CString arguments str1 and str2.

Subscript operator

```
char    operator[] (int index) const;
```

Returns that character from the CString object according to the index position. The index value must be between zero and the string length less 1, inclusive.

Substring operator

```
CString    operator() (int pos, int len) const;
```

Extracts the substring of length len from the CString object starting from position pos. If the index position pos is not a valid position, then the empty string is returned.

append

```
void    append(char ch);
void    append(const CString& str);
```

Appends the given character (or CString) argument to the CString object.

hashValue

```
Int    hashValue(void) const;
```

Returns the randomized hash value for the CString object.

insert

```
void    insert(char ch, int index);
void    insert(const CString& str, Int index);
```

Inserts a character ch (or CString, str) into the recipient CString object at the given index position. Characters in the original CString are displaced toward the string end to accommodate the incoming symbol(s).

isSubstring

```
int    isSubstring(const CString& str) const;
```

Determines if the CString argument str is a substring of the CString object.

length

```
int    length(void) const;
```

Returns the number of characters in a CString object.

prepend

```
void    prepend(char ch);
void    prepend(const CString& str);
```

Prepends the given character (or CString) argument to the CString object.

remove

```
void    remove(int pos, int len);
```

Removes the substring of length len starting from the index position pos. If the position index pos is outwith the string bounds, then no action is performed.

toLower	`void    toLower(void);`
toUpper	`void    toUpper(void);`

Converts all alphabetic symbols in the `CString` object to, respectively, lower case or upper case.

value   `const char*  value(void) const;`

Direct access to the underlying representation used in the `CString` class. Notice that the null-terminated string delivered is tagged as `const`, expecting no direct changes.

Class declaration

```
class CString {

friend ostream&  operator<< (ostream&, const CString&);
friend istream&  operator>> (istream&, CString&);
  // Overloading the standard input/output operators to
  // enable the manipulation of input from and to a nominated
  // stream using this CString class.

friend CString  operator+ (const CString&, const CString&);
  // Overloading the addition operator to enable the
  // concatenation of two CStrings to give the one
  // longer one.

friend Logical  operator< (const CString&,
                const CString&);
friend Logical  operator<= (const CString&,
                const CString&);
friend Logical  operator== (const CString&,
                const CString&);
friend Logical  operator!= (const CString&,
                const CString&);
friend Logical  operator> (const CString&,
                const CString&);
friend Logical  operator>= (const CString&,
                const CString&);
  // The above all return either LRUE or LFALSE upon
  // completion of the relational operators.
  // i.e. if CString1 = "Hello", and CString2 =
  // "there" CString1 > CString2 == FALSE, but
  // CString1 !=CString2 == TRUE
```

```
public:
  CString(char* = "");
  // Standard Constructor from C-style string

CString(char, int = 1);
  // Standard Constructor of a duplicated character

CString(const CString&);
  // Copy Constructor

~CString(void);
  // Destructor

CString& operator= (const CString&);
  // Overloading the assignment operator to allow one CString
  // to be assigned to another.

int length(void) const;
  // Number of characters in string

const char* value(void) const;
  // Direct access to the representation
char operator[] (int index) const;
  // Subscript access to individual character;
  // error if beyond the length of the string

void insert(char, int);
void insert(const CString&, int);
  // Insert character (string) at given index position, moving
  // the character and all following characters at that position
  // to the right; if the index is outwith the string length then
  // no action is performed.

void remove(int, int);
  // Remove the substring of length len (second argument)
  // starting at position pos (first argument); if pos is
  // outwith the string then no action is performed.

void prepend(const CString&);
void append(const CString&);
void prepend(char);
void append(char);
  // Prepend (append) the given string (char) to the string
  // object itself.

CString operator() (int, int) const;
  // Extract the substring of length len (second argument)
  // starting at position pos (first argument); if pos is
  // outwith the string then the empty string is returned.

int isSubstring(const CString&) const;
  // Is the string argument part of the object
  // itself?
```

```
void  toLower(void);
void  toUpper(void);
 //Convert all letters in the string to lowercase
 //(uppercase) leaving all other characters
 //unchanged.

Int  hashValue(void) const;
 //Returns the hash value of the CString in question.

Logical  lessThan(const CString&) const;
 //Same as operator<

private:
 //The representation of the CString

};
```

D.2 CDate

Synopsis   Class CDate represents a date, stored as a Julian day number.

#include "ccdate.h"

Constructor   CDate(void);

Default constructor to establish a CDate object with the values from the system clock.

Constructor   CDate(int day, int month, int year);

Standard constructor to create a CDate object initialised with the international date values given. The third argument is expected to be the full year value, e.g. 1995.

Constructor   CDate(int jul);

Standard constructor to create a CDate object initialised with the Julian day number as given by the argument jul.

Constructor   CDate(const CDate& date);

Standard copy constructor. Copies the CDate object represented by the argument date into the instance being created.

Assignment   CDate& operator= (const CDate& date);

Copies the source CDate object represented by the argument date into an existing destination CDate variable denoted by that on the left of the operator.

Addition operator	`CDate operator+ (const CDate& date, int days);`
	Returns a new `CDate` object which is the sum of the `CDate` argument `date` and the number of `days`.
Subtraction operator	`CDate operator- (const CDate& date, int days);`
	Returns a new `CDate` object which is the difference of the `CDate` argument `date` and the number of days.
Subtraction operator	`int operator- (const CDate& date1,` `    const CDate& date2);`
	Determines the number of days between two `CDate` objects.
Output operator	`ostream& operator<< (ostream& os,` `        const CDate& date);`
	Writes the `CDate` value date to an output stream.

Logical operators	`Logical  operator< (const CDate& date1,`
	`        const CDate& date2);`
	`Logical  operator<= (const CDate& date1,`
	`        const CDate& date2);`
	`Logical  operator> (const CDate& date1,`
	`        const CDate& date2);`
	`Logical  operator>= (const CDate& date1,`
	`        const CDate& date2);`
	`Logical  operator== (const CDate& date1,`
	`        const CDate& date2);`
	`Logical  operator!= (const CDate& date1,`
	`        const CDate& date2);`

	Perform a comparison of the two `CDate` arguments `date1` and `date2`.

day
month
year
	`int day(void) const;`
	`int month(void) const;`
	`int year(void) const;`

	Selector functions which obtain, respectively, the day, month and year components of a `CDate` object.

dayOfWeek
daysInMonth
daysInYear
dayOfYear
	`int dayOfWeek(void) const;`
	`int daysInMonth(void) const;`
	`int daysInYear(void) const;`
	`int dayOfYear(void) const;`

	Interrogative functions to determine a range of self-explanatory properties of a `CDate` object.

dayName   `const CString& dayName(void)`
                       `const;`

abbreviatedDayName `const CString&`
                        `abbreviatedDayName (void) const;`

monthName   `const CString& monthName(void)`
                       `const;`

abbreviatedMonthName `const CString&`
                         `abbreviatedMonthName(void) const;`

Interrogative functions to determine a range of name properties of a `CDate` object.

hashValue   `int hashValue(void) const;`

Returns the randomized hash value for a `CDate` object.

Julian   `int julian(void) const;`

Returns the Julian day number for a `CDate` object.

Class declaration

```
class CDate{
  friend CDate  operator+ (const CDate&, int);
    // Returns a CDate, from CDate + "no of days"

  friend CDate  operator- (const CDate&, int);
    // Returns a CDate, from CDate - "no of days"

  friend long  operator- (const CDate&, const CDate&);
    // Returns an integer number of days, from
    // CDate - CDate

  friend Logical  operator< (const CDate&, const CDate&);
  friend Logical  operator<= (const CDate&, const CDate&);
  friend Logical  operator== (const CDate&, const CDate&);
  friend Logical  operator!= (const CDate&, const CDate&);
  friend Logical  operator> (const CDate&, const CDate&);
  friend Logical  operator>= (const CDate&, const CDate&);
  // The above all return either LTRUE or LFALSE upon completion
  // of the relational operators.
  // i.e. if CDate1 = 24/12/1993 and CDate2 =
  // 05/11/1993, CDate1 < CDate2 = LFALSE, but
  // CDate1 != CDate2 = LTRUE

  friend ostream&  operator<< (ostream&, const CDate&);
  // Overloading the standard output operator to enable
  // the manipulation of output to the screen using this
  // CDate class.
```

```
public:
CDate(void);
  //Default Constructor using system date

CDate(int, int, int);
  //Standard Constructor, i.e. DD/MM/YYYY

CDate(int);
  //Standard Constructor using the date from epoch

~CDate(void);
  //Destructor

int  day(void) const;
  //Day part, e.g. for 31/12/1992 day is 31

int  month(void) const;
  //Month part, e.g. for 31/12/1992 month is 12

int  year(void) const;
  //Year part, e.g. for 31/12/1992 year is 1992

int  julian(void) const;
  //Julian value for date

int  dayOfWeek(void) const;
  //Returns the day of the week e.g. mon = 1

int  daysInMonth(void) const;
  //e.g. for 31/12/1992 daysInMonth is 31
int  daysInYear(void) const;
  //e.g. for 31/12/1992 daysInYear is 365

int  dayOfYear(void) const;
  //e.g. for 1/2/1992 dayOfYear is 32

const CString& dayName(void) const;
  //e.g. for 28/11/1992 dayName is Saturday

const CString&  abbreviatedDayName(void) const;
  //e.g. for 28/11/1992 abbreviatedDayName is Sat

const CString&  monthName(void) const;
  //e.g. for 28/11/1992 monthName is November

const CString&  abbreviatedMonthName(void) const;
  //e.g. for 28/11/1992 monthName is Nov

Logical  isLeapYear(void) const;
  //Returns TRUE if the year in question is a leap
    year else FALSE

int  hashValue(void) const;
  //Returns the hash value of the date in question
```

```
Logical lessThan(const CDate&) const;
  // Same as operator<


private:
  // The representation of the CDate
};
```

D.3 POrderedCollection

PCollection

|

PIndexedCollection

|

PSequentialCollection

|

POrderedCollection

Synopsis   A POrderedCollection is a generic container of object pointers in which the items in the collection are positioned serially without any intervening gaps. The ordering of the items is governed by the sequence of add and remove operations applied to the collection. The collection is realised as a vector of pointers, allowing for more efficient traversing than through a linked list (see POrderedList), but results in slower insertions at the centre. A POrderedCollection is a dynamic data structure which will grow by doubling its existing size when no more space exists for an incoming item. A POrderedCollection can be specified to take responsibility for the items and to ensure proper clean-up and removal of these elements when the container is removed.

The POrderedCollection is derived immediately from the class PSequentialCollection from which it gets much of its behaviour. The class POrderedCollection is primarily concerned with the services to add items to the collection.

```
#include "pordcol.h"
```

Constructor
```
template <class TYPE>
POrderedCollection(int initialSize,
  int managementScheme);
```

Constructs a POrderedCollection of the given TYPE with some initialSize. The actual TYPE is expected to be a pointer, e.g. POrderedCollection<Employee*>. The symbolic name DEFAULTSIZE is available for specifying the initial capacity. The second argument determines if the container takes responsibility for the objects it collects. If this value is MANAGED, then the collection removes from memory all the objects when it itself is removed or goes out of scope. When an object is removed from the container its storage space is also removed under this regime. When the second argument is UNMANAGED, the container has no responsibility for the objects.

To use this collection class we must supply a member function lessThan in the class which represents the object types held by the container. If, for example, we instantiate a POrdered-Collection of Employee* objects then the Employee class must have the member function 'Logical lessThan-(const Employee&) const'. This function will compare one Employee object with another using, perhaps, their name fields for the actual comparison.

Constructor

```
template<class TYPE>
POrderedCollection(const
  POrderedCollection<TYPE>& coll);
```

Standard copy constructor to create a new instance of some POrderedCollection with the same pointers as in the coll argument. This is conventionally described as a shallow copying process. The newly created POrderedCollection object will have pointers to the same objects as found in the parameter coll, but the storage management scheme is set as UNMANAGED.

Destructor

```
template<class TYPE>
~POrderedCollection(void);
```

Removes the storage structures employed by the container. If the container was established with the second argument of its constructor set as MANAGED, then the objects referenced by the collection are also removed.

Assignment

```
template<class TYPE>
POrderedCollection& operator=
  (const POrderedCollection<TYPE>& coll);
```

Copies the source collection coll into the destination POrderedCollection object appearing to the left of the assignment operator. If the existing container was established as MANAGED then the object collection is removed before the storage structure is released. A new structure is then established and the objects referenced by the source collection coll are copied into the destination. The destination collection is set as UNMANAGED to effect a shallow copy.

Subscript
operator

```
template <class TYPE>
const TYPE operator[] (Int index) const;
```

Delivers a pointer to the element in the collection at the given index position.

add

```
template <class TYPE>
void add(const TYPE object);
```

Inserts the new object pointer at the end position in the container.

addAt

```
template <class TYPE>
void addAt(int index, const TYPE object);
```

Inserts the new object pointer into the container at the given index position. The existing objects are moved toward the end of the collection from that index position to accommodate the incoming element. If the index value is outwith the bounds of the collection then the operation fails.

addFirst

```
template <class TYPE>
void addFirst(const TYPE object);
```

Inserts the new object pointer into the first position in the container. All the existing objects are moved toward the end of the collection to accommodate the incoming element.

addLast

```
template <class TYPE>
void addLast(const TYPE object);
```

Inserts the new object pointer at the end position in the container.

at

```
template <class TYPE>
const TYPE at(int index) const;
```

Delivers a pointer to the element in the collection at the given index position.

cardinality

```
template <class TYPE>
int cardinality(void) const;
```

Returns a count of the number of items presently held by the collection.

capacity

```
template <class TYPE>
int capacity(void) const;
```

Obtains the present overall capacity of the collection.

first

```
template <class TYPE>
const TYPE first(void) const;
```

Delivers a pointer to the first item in the collection. This pointer to the object is shared with the collection. The constancy attached to the pointed object means that it cannot be modified.

isEmpty

```
template <class TYPE>
Logical    isEmpty(void) const;
```

Returns the Logical value LTRUE if the collection has no items, otherwise returns LFALSE.

isMember

```
template <class TYPE>
Logical    isMember(const TYPE object) const;
```

Determines if the given object is already present in the collection, returning the Logical value LTRUE if so. The function requires the instantiated TYPE to have a function lessThan by which the items may be compared.

last

```
template <class TYPE>
const TYPE    last(void) const;
```

Delivers a pointer to the last item in the collection. This pointer to the object is shared with the collection. The constancy attached to the pointed object means that it cannot be modified.

occurrencesOf

```
template <class TYPE>
int    occurrencesOf(const TYPE object) const;
```

Counts the number of times the given object is currently present in the collection.

remove

```
template <class TYPE>
void    remove(const TYPE object);
```

Removes from the collection the first occurrence of the given object. If no such item exists in the collection then the container is left unchanged. If the matching object is removed, then all other items in the collection following the removed element are moved forward. If the container is MANAGED then the removed object has its storage reclaimed.

removeAt

```
template <class TYPE>
void    removeAt(int index);
```

Removes from the collection the item at the given `index` position. All items in the collection following the removed element are moved forward. If the container is `MANAGED` then the removed object has its storage reclaimed.

removeFirst
```
template <class TYPE>
void    removeFirst(void);
```

Removes the first element from the container. All remaining items in the collection are moved forward. If the collection is `MANAGED` then the removed object has its storage reclaimed.

removeLast
```
template <class TYPE>
void    removeLast(void);
```

Removes the last element from the container. If the collection is `MANAGED` then the removed object has its storage reclaimed.

reSize
```
template <class TYPE>
void    reSize(int increment);
```

Increases the overall capacity by the given increment amount.

Class declaration

```
template <class TYPE>
class POrderedCollection : public
  PSequentialCollection<TYPE> {
public:
  POrderedCollection(Int size, Int manage);
  POrderedCollection(const
    POrderedCollection<TYPE>&);
  ~POrderedCollection(void);
  POrderedCollection<TYPE>& operator=
    (const POrderedCollection<TYPE>&
      anOrderedCollection);

// virtual const TYPE&    operator[] (int index) const;

  void    add(const TYPE object);
    // Include given item into the container; the exact
    // semantics for this operation is that for addLast

  void    addAt(int, const TYPE object);
    // Add the given item into the container at the given index
    // position; if the index position would destroy the
    // adjacency of the elements the operation fails; elements
    // in the container from the index position are moved
    // to the right to accommodate the new item
```

```
    void    addFirst(const TYPE object);
    // Insert the new element at index position zero,
    // moving all existing items one position rightward
    void    addLast(const TYPE object);
    // incorporate the new element immediately
    // following the present final item

    // virtual const TYPE     at(int index) const;
    // virtual int            capacity(void) const;
    // int                    cardinality(void) const;

    virtual const char*      className(void) const;
    virtual ClassType        classType(void) const;

    // const TYPE             first(void) const;
    // Logical                isEmpty(void) const;
    // Logical                isMember(const TYPE&
                              object) const;
    // const TYPE             last(void) const;
    // int                    occurrencesOf(const TYPE&
                              object) const;
    // virtual void           remove(const TYPE&object);
    // void                   removeAt(int index);
    // void                   removeFirst(void);
    // void                   removeLast(void);
    // virtual void           reSize(int increment);
    // virtual void           iteratorInitialize(void);
    // virtual Logical        iteratorIsExhausted(void)
                              const;
    // virtual const TYPE     iteratorSelection(void)
                              const;
    // virtual void           iteratorAdvance(void);

    };
```

D.4 PIterator

Synopsis   A PIterator is a generic iterator for accessing all the elements in a collection. Any container type derived from the base container class PCollection can be processed by this iterator.

```
#include "pcol.h"
```

Constructor   template <class TYPE>
              PIterator(const PCollection<TYPE>& coll);

Establishes an iterator object initialised to visit all the members of the container object coll.

advance
```
template <class TYPE>
void     advance(void);
```

Moves the iterator so that the next call to selection will reference the next available item.

isExhausted
```
template <class TYPE>
Logical    isExhausted(void) const;
```

If all the elements of the collection have been processed then returns the Logical value LTRUE, otherwise returns LFALSE.

selection
```
template <class TYPE>
const TYPE    selection(void) const;
```

Obtains a pointer to the next available element.

Class declaration

```
template <class TYPE>
class PIterator {
public:

PIterator(const PCollection<TYPE>& aCollection);

Logical        isExhausted(void) const;
const TYPE     selection(void) const;
void           advance(void);

private:
    // The representation of the PIterator
};
```

Appendix E

Case study LOOM scripts

The following listings are taken from models provided on the distribution disk. Readers are advised that a line number prefix indicates a single line of text.

E.1 Chapter 4, version 1 of the Library system

```
[0001]  //.
[0002]  //.
[0003]  //.  ROME Copyright (c) Richard McMahon. 1993, 1994.
[0004]  //.  Generated On January 5, 1996 At 5:58:08.17 pm
[0005]
[0006]
[0007]
[0008]  //. -- Class Definitions: ------------------
[0009]
[0010]  //
[0011]  //  CLASS User
[0012]  //
[0013]  //  REVISION HISTORY
[0014]  //
[0015]  //      VERSION NUMBER 1.0
[0016]  //
[0017]  //      DATE 1 September 1995
[0018]  //
[0019]  //      AUTHOR K Barclay / J Savage
[0020]  //
[0021]  //      PURPOSE First release.
[0022]  //
[0023]  //
[0024]  //      VERSION NUMBER 1.1
[0025]  //
[0026]  //      DATE 6 September 1995
[0027]  //
[0028]  //      AUTHOR K Barclay / J Savage
[0029]  //
[0030]  //      PURPOSE Addition of lessThan? and name?
                     to support containment.
[0031]  //
[0032]  //  DESCRIPTION
[0033]  //
[0034]  //      An instance of this class acts as a User
                     that can borrow and return
```

```
[0035]  //       Books to a Library. A User can also display books out
                  on loan.
[0036]  //
[0037]  //
[0038]  CLASS User
[0039]  WITH
[0040]  PUBLIC INTERFACE
[0041]    User
[0042]    User (aName : String, anAddress : String)
[0043]    displayBooks?
[0044]    borrowOneBook
[0045]    returnOneBook
[0046]    addLibrary (aLibrary : Library LINK)
[0047]    lessThan? (aUser : User) -> Boolean
[0048]    name? -> String
[0049]  PROTECTED INTERFACE
[0050]    NONE
[0051]  PRIVATE IMPLEMENTATION
[0052]    REPRESENTATION
[0053]      theName : String
[0054]      theAddress : String
[0055]    AGGREGATIONS
[0056]      theBooks : DOrderedCollection [Book]
[0057]    ASSOCIATIONS
[0058]      theLender : Library LINK INVERSE OF theBorrowers
[0059]    DEFINITIONS
[0060]      METHOD User
[0061]      AS
[0062]        // Default constructor.
[0063]
[0064]        // Set the representation entries to sensible values.
[0065]        SEND theName THE MESSAGE initialise ("")
[0066]        SEND theAddress THE MESSAGE initialise ("")
[0067]
[0068]        // Set the aggregate container theBooks and
[0069]        // the associate theLender to sensible values.
[0070]        SEND theBooks THE MESSAGE
                 initialise (DEFAULTSIZE)
[0071]        SEND theLender THE MESSAGE initialise (NIL)
[0072]      ENDMETHOD User
[0073]
[0074]      METHOD User (aName : String, anAddress : String)
[0075]      AS
[0076]        // Parameterized constructor.
[0077]
[0078]        // Set the representation entries to the
                 corresponding parameters of
[0079]        // the constructor.
[0080]        SEND theName THE MESSAGE initialise (aName)
[0081]        SEND theAddress THE MESSAGE initialise (anAddress)
[0082]
[0083]        // Set the aggregate container theBooks and
[0084]        // the associate theLender to sensible values.
[0085]        SEND theBooks THE MESSAGE initialise (DEFAULTSIZE)
```

```
[0086]        SEND theLender THE MESSAGE initialise(NIL)
[0087]      ENDMETHOD User
[0088]
[0089]      METHOD displayBooks?
[0090]      AS
[0091]        // Output to the screen the details of the Books on
                 loan to a User together
[0092]        // with his name and address.
[0093]
[0094]        SEND theScreen THE MESSAGE insert(theName)
[0095]        SEND theScreen THE MESSAGE insert(" [")
[0096]        SEND theScreen THE MESSAGE insert(theAddress)
[0097]        SEND theScreen THE MESSAGE insert("] Borrowed
                 books:\n")
[0098]
[0099]        // Note that aBook takes on the identity of each book
                 in turn.
[0100]        FOREACH aBook :Book IN theBooks DO
[0101]        SEND aBook THE MESSAGE display?
[0102]        ENDFOREACH
[0103]
[0104]        // If required the screen may be held with the
                 following sentences.
[0105]        // INSTANCE theResponse :String("")
[0106]        // SEND theScreen THE MESSAGE insert("\n\tType a
                 character to continue > ")
[0107]        // SEND theKeyboard THE MESSAGE
                 extract(theResponse)
[0108]        //
[0109]        // Similarly the screen may be held if these
                 sentences are embedded in the FOREACH
[0110]        // control sentence immediately after the message
                 display?
[0111]      ENDMETHOD displayBooks?
[0112]
[0113]      METHOD borrowOneBook
[0114]      AS
[0115]        // Take charge of a full copy of a Book from the
                 Library.
[0116]
[0117]        SEND theBooks THE MESSAGE addFirst
[0118]              (SEND theLender THE MESSAGE borrowOneBook?)
[0119]      ENDMETHOD borrowOneBook
[0120]
[0121]      METHOD returnOneBook
[0122]      AS
[0123]        // Deliver a full copy of a Book to the Library.
[0124]
[0125]        SEND theLender THE MESSAGE returnOneBook
[0126]                     (SEND theBooks THE MESSAGE last?)
[0127]        SEND theBooks THE MESSAGE removeLast
[0128]      ENDMETHOD returnOneBook
[0129]
[0130]      METHOD addLibrary(aLibrary :Library LINK)
```

```
[0131]    AS
[0132]       // Establish a LINK with the Library.
[0133]
[0134]       SEND theLender THE MESSAGE assign (aLibrary)
[0135]    ENDMETHOD addLibrary
[0136]
[0137]    METHOD lessThan? (aUser : User) -> Boolean
[0138]    AS
[0139]       // Compare two Users by name using the operator < for
                 comparing Strings.
[0140]
[0141]       IF theName < (SEND aUser THE MESSAGE name?) THEN
[0142]         RETURN TRUE
[0143]       ELSE
[0144]         RETURN FALSE
[0145]       ENDIF
[0146]    ENDMETHOD lessThan?
[0147]
[0148]    METHOD name? -> String
[0149]    AS
[0150]       // Deliver the private property theName to a
                 client.
[0151]
[0152]       RETURN theName
[0153]    ENDMETHOD name?
[0154]
[0155] ENDCLASS User
[0156]
[0157]
[0158] //
[0159] //   CLASS Book
[0160] //
[0161] //   REVISION HISTORY
[0162] //
[0163] //      VERSION NUMBER 1.0
[0164] //
[0165] //      DATE 1 September 1995
[0166] //
[0167] //      AUTHOR K Barclay / J Savage
[0168] //
[0169] //      PURPOSE First release.
[0170] //
[0171] //      VERSION NUMBER 1.1
[0172] //
[0173] //      DATE 6 September 1995
[0174] //
[0175] //      AUTHOR K Barclay / J Savage
[0176] //
[0177] //      PURPOSE Addition of lessThan? and title? public
                    operations
[0178] //             to support containment.
[0179] //
[0180] //   DESCRIPTION
[0181] //
```

```
[0182]  //      An instance of this class acts as a Book held by a
                 Library that
[0183]  //      can be borrowed or returned by a User. Details of
                 each Book
[0184]  //      can be displayed on request.
[0185]  //
[0186]  CLASS Book
[0187]  WITH
[0188]  PUBLIC INTERFACE
[0189]    Book
[0190]    Book(anAuthor : String, aTitle : String,
          aReferenceNumber : Integer)
[0191]    display?
[0192]    lessThan?(aBook : Book) -> Boolean
[0193]    title? -> String
[0194]  PROTECTED INTERFACE
[0195]    NONE
[0196]  PRIVATE IMPLEMENTATION
[0197]    REPRESENTATION
[0198]      theAuthor : String
[0199]      theTitle : String
[0200]      theReferenceNumber : Integer
[0201]    AGGREGATIONS NONE
[0202]    ASSOCIATIONS NONE
[0203]    DEFINITIONS
[0204]      METHOD Book
[0205]      AS
[0206]        //Default constructor
[0207]
[0208]        // Set the representation entries to sensible values.
[0209]        SEND theAuthor THE MESSAGE initialise("")
[0210]        SEND theTitle THE MESSAGE initialise("")
[0211]        SEND theReferenceNumber THE MESSAGE initialise(0)
[0212]      ENDMETHOD Book
[0213]
[0214]      METHOD Book(anAuthor : String, aTitle : String,
            aReferenceNumber : Integer)
[0215]      AS
[0216]        //Parameterized constructor.
[0217]
[0218]        // Set the representation entries to the
               corresponding parameters of
[0219]        // the constructor.
[0220]        SEND theAuthor THE MESSAGE initialise(anAuthor)
[0221]        SEND theTitle THE MESSAGE initialise(aTitle)
[0222]        SEND theReferenceNumber THE MESSAGE
              initialise(aReferenceNumber)
[0223]      ENDMETHOD Book
[0224]
[0225]      METHOD display?
[0226]      AS
[0227]        //Output Book details to the screen.
[0228]        // Note that "\n" takes a new line and "\t" moves to
               the next tab position.
```

```
[0229]
[0230]        SEND theScreen THE MESSAGE insert (theAuthor)
[0231]        SEND theScreen THE MESSAGE
              insert ("\n\t")
[0232]        SEND theScreen THE MESSAGE insert (theTitle)
[0233]        SEND theScreen THE MESSAGE
              insert (":\t")
[0234]        SEND theScreen THE MESSAGE
              insert (theReferenceNumber)
[0235]        SEND theScreen THE MESSAGE insert ("\n")
[0236]     ENDMETHOD display?
[0237]
[0238]     METHOD lessThan? (aBook : Book) -> Boolean
[0239]     AS
[0240]       // Compare two Books by title using the
                 operator < defined for Strings.
[0241]
[0242]       IF theTitle < (SEND aBook THE MESSAGE title?) THEN
[0243]         RETURN TRUE
[0244]       ELSE
[0245]         RETURN FALSE
[0246]       ENDIF
[0247]     ENDMETHOD lessThan?
[0248]
[0249]     METHOD title? -> String
[0250]     AS
[0251]       //Deliver the private property theTitle to a client.
[0252]
[0253]       RETURN theTitle
[0254]     ENDMETHOD title?
[0255]
[0256]  ENDCLASS Book
[0257]
[0258]
[0259]  //
[0260]  //   CLASS Library
[0261]  //
[0262]  //   REVISION HISTORY
[0263]  //
[0264]  //      VERSION NUMBER 1.0
[0265]  //
[0266]  //      DATE 1 September 1995
[0267]  //
[0268]  //      AUTHOR K Barclay / J Savage
[0269]  //
[0270]  //      PURPOSE First release
[0271]  //
[0272]  //   DESCRIPTION
[0273]  //
[0274]  //      An instance of this class acts as the Library object
              that holds
[0275]  //      Books that a User can request a display of, borrow or
              return.
[0276]  //
```

```
[0277]  CLASS Library
[0278]  WITH
[0279]  PUBLIC INTERFACE
[0280]    Library
[0281]    Library(aName : String)
[0282]    borrowOneBook? -> Book
[0283]    returnOneBook(aBook : Book)
[0284]    displayBooks?
[0285]    displayUserBooks?
[0286]    addUser(aUser : User LINK)
[0287]    addBook(aBook : Book)
[0288]  PROTECTED INTERFACE
[0289]    NONE
[0290]  PRIVATE IMPLEMENTATION
[0291]    REPRESENTATION
[0292]      theName : String
[0293]    AGGREGATIONS
[0294]      theBooks : DOrderedCollection[Book]
[0295]    ASSOCIATIONS
[0296]      theBorrowers : POrderedCollection[User LINK] INVERSE
             OF theLender
[0297]    DEFINITIONS
[0298]      METHOD Library
[0299]      AS
[0300]        // Default constructor.
[0301]
[0302]        //  Set the private property theName to an empty
                  String.
[0303]        SEND theName THE MESSAGE initialise("")
[0304]
[0305]        // Set the associates container theBorrowers and
[0306]        // the aggregate components container theBooks to
                  sensible values.
[0307]        SEND theBorrowers THE MESSAGE
              initialise(DEFAULTSIZE, UNMANAGED)
[0308]        SEND theBooks THE MESSAGE initialise(DEFAULTSIZE)
[0309]
[0310]      ENDMETHOD Library
[0311]
[0312]      METHOD Library(aName : String)
[0313]      AS
[0314]        // Parameterized constructor.
[0315]
[0316]        // Set the private property theName to the value of the
                  formal parameter.
[0317]        SEND theName THE MESSAGE initialise(aName)
[0318]
[0319]        // Set the associates container theBorrowers and
[0320]        // the aggregate components container theBooks to
                  sensible values.
[0321]        SEND theBorrowers THE MESSAGE
              initialise(DEFAULTSIZE, UNMANAGED)
[0322]        SEND theBooks THE MESSAGE initialise(DEFAULTSIZE)
[0323]      ENDMETHOD Library
```

```
[0324]
[0325]       METHOD borrowOneBook? -> Book
[0326]       AS
[0327]         // Deliver a full copy of a Book to a client.
[0328]
[0329]         INSTANCE borrowedBook : Book
[0330]
[0331]         SEND borrowedBook THE MESSAGE assign
[0332]                           (SEND theBooks THE MESSAGE last?)
[0333]         SEND theBooks THE MESSAGE removeLast
[0334]
[0335]         RETURN borrowedBook
[0336]       ENDMETHOD borrowOneBook?
[0337]
[0338]       METHOD returnOneBook (aBook : Book)
[0339]       AS
[0340]         // Take charge of a full copy of a Book returned by a
                  client.
[0341]
[0342]         SEND theBooks THE MESSAGE addFirst (aBook)
[0343]       ENDMETHOD returnOneBook
[0344]
[0345]       METHOD displayBooks?
[0346]       AS
[0347]         // Output to the screen details of all Books available
                  for loan.
[0348]         // Note that "\n" takes a new line and "\t" moves to the
                  next tab position.
[0349]
[0350]         SEND theScreen THE MESSAGE insert ("Current loan
                stock:\t")
[0351]         SEND theScreen THE MESSAGE insert (theName)
[0352]         SEND theScreen THE MESSAGE insert ("\n")
[0353]
[0354]         // Note that aBook takes on the identity of each book
                  in turn.
[0355]         FOREACH aBook : Book IN theBooks DO
[0356]           SEND aBook THE MESSAGE display?
[0357]         ENDFOREACH
[0358]
[0359]         // If required the screen may be held with the
                  following sentences.
[0360]         // INSTANCE theResponse : String("")
[0361]         // SEND theScreen THE MESSAGE insert ("\n\tType a
                  character to continue > ")
[0362]         // SEND theKeyboard THE MESSAGE extract (theResponse)
[0363]         //
[0364]         // Similarly the screen may be held if these sentences
                  are embedded in the FOREACH
[0365]         // control sentence immediately after the message
                  display?
[0366]       ENDMETHOD displayBooks?
[0367]
[0368]       METHOD displayUserBooks?
```

```
[0369]        AS
[0370]          // Output to the screen details of all Books out on loan
                   to Users.
[0371]          // Note that "\n" takes a new line and "\t" moves to the
                   next tab position.
[0372]
[0373]          SEND theScreen THE MESSAGE insert ("Current borrowed
                   stock:\t")
[0374]          SEND theScreen THE MESSAGE insert (theName)
[0375]          SEND theScreen THE MESSAGE insert ("\n")
[0376]
[0377]          // Note that aUser takes on the identity of each user
                   in turn.
[0378]          FOREACH aUser : User LINK IN theBorrowers DO
[0379]            SEND aUser THE MESSAGE displayBooks?
[0380]          ENDFOREACH
[0381]
[0382]          SEND theScreen THE MESSAGE insert ("\n")
[0383]
[0384]          // If required the screen may be held with the
                   following sentences.
[0385]          // INSTANCE theResponse : String ("")
[0386]          // SEND theScreen THE MESSAGE insert ("\n\tType a
                   character to continue > ")
[0387]          // SEND theKeyboard THE MESSAGE extract (theResponse)
[0388]        ENDMETHOD displayUserBooks?
[0389]
[0390]        METHOD addUser (aUser : User LINK)
[0391]        AS
[0392]          // Establish a LINK with a User.
[0393]
[0394]          SEND theBorrowers THE MESSAGE add (aUser)
[0395]        ENDMETHOD addUser
[0396]
[0397]        METHOD addBook (aBook : Book)
[0398]        AS
[0399]          // Add a full copy of a Book to the Library.
[0400]
[0401]          SEND theBooks THE MESSAGE add (aBook)
[0402]        ENDMETHOD addBook
[0403]
[0404] ENDCLASS Library
[0405]
[0406]
[0407] //
[0408] //   CLASS Application
[0409] //
[0410] //   REVISION HISTORY
[0411] //
[0412] //      VERSION NUMBER 1.0
[0413] //
[0414] //      DATE 1 September 1995
[0415] //
[0416] //      AUTHOR K Barclay / J Savage
```

```
[0417]  //
[0418]  //      PURPOSE First release.
[0419]  //
[0420]  //   DESCRIPTION
[0421]  //
[0422]  //      An instance of this class acts as the source of top-
                 level control.
[0423]  //      It also has the responsibility for the creation of
                 all objects in the
[0424]  //      system. Note that an object that is an associate,
                 i.e. a LINK to such
[0425]  //      an object is required, is created with dynamic
                 duration.
[0426]  //
[0427]  CLASS Application
[0428]  WITH
[0429]  PUBLIC INTERFACE
[0430]    Application
[0431]    run
[0432]  PROTECTED INTERFACE
[0433]    NONE
[0434]  PRIVATE IMPLEMENTATION
[0435]    REPRESENTATION NONE
[0436]    AGGREGATIONS NONE
[0437]    ASSOCIATIONS NONE
[0438]    DEFINITIONS
[0439]      METHOD Application
[0440]      AS
[0441]       // Default constructor.
[0442]
[0443]       // Although there is nothing to do, it is good practice
                  to provide an explicit
[0444]       // default constructor. The alternative is to assume
                  that the implementation
[0445]       // language will provide one.
[0446]
[0447]      ENDMETHOD Application
[0448]
[0449]      METHOD run
[0450]      AS
[0451]       // Top-level control messages for the system.
[0452]
[0453]       // Create a Library with dynamic duration.
[0454]       INSTANCE theLibrary : Library LINK ("Dunning
                 Library")
[0455]
[0456]       // Create two Users with dynamic duration.
[0457]       INSTANCE u1 : User LINK ("John", "21 High Street")
[0458]       INSTANCE u2 : User LINK ("Ken", "100 Black Road")
[0459]
[0460]       // Configure the object architecture.
[0461]       SEND theLibrary THE MESSAGE addUser (u1)
[0462]       SEND theLibrary THE MESSAGE addUser (u2)
[0463]       SEND u1 THE MESSAGE addLibrary (theLibrary)
```

```
[0464]        SEND u2 THE MESSAGE addLibrary(theLibrary)
[0465]
[0466]        // Add full copies of four different Books to the
              Library stock.
[0467]        SEND theLibrary THE MESSAGE addBook(Book("Barclay",
[0468]        "C++: Problem Solving and Programming", 1))
[0469]        SEND theLibrary THE MESSAGE
              addBook(Book("Rumbaugh",
[0470]        "Object Oriented Modelling and Design", 2))
[0471]        SEND theLibrary THE MESSAGE addBook(Book("Booch",
[0472]        "Object Oriented Design", 3))
[0473]        SEND theLibrary THE MESSAGE addBook(Book("Yourdon",
[0474]        "Object Oriented System Design", 4))
[0475]
[0476]        // User u1 borrows two Books.
[0477]        SEND u1 THE MESSAGE borrowOneBook
[0478]        SEND u1 THE MESSAGE borrowOneBook
[0479]
[0480]        // User u2 borrows one Book.
[0481]        SEND u2 THE MESSAGE borrowOneBook
[0482]
[0483]        // The Library displays Books held by its Users.
[0484]        SEND theLibrary THE MESSAGE displayUserBooks?
[0485]
[0486]        // User u1 returns a Book.
[0487]        SEND u1 THE MESSAGE returnOneBook
[0488]
[0489]        // Observe the effect on the Users and Library.
[0490]        SEND theLibrary THE MESSAGE displayUserBooks?
[0491]        SEND theLibrary THE MESSAGE displayBooks?
[0492]     ENDMETHOD run
[0493]
[0494]  ENDCLASS Application
[0495]
[0496]
[0497]
```

E.2 Chapter 4, version 2 of the Library system

```
[0001]  //.
[0002]  //.
[0003]  //. ROME Copyright (c) Richard McMahon. 1993, 1994.
[0004]  //. Generated On January 5, 1996 At 6:01:48.80 pm
[0005]
[0006]
[0007]
[0008]  //. -- Class Definitions: ----------------------------
[0009]
[0010]  //
[0011]  //  CLASS User
[0012]  //
[0013]  //  REVISION HISTORY
```

```
[0014]  //
[0015]  //      VERSION NUMBER 1.0
[0016]  //
[0017]  //      DATE 1 September 1995
[0018]  //
[0019]  //      AUTHOR K Barclay / J Savage
[0020]  //
[0021]  //      PURPOSE First release
[0022]  //
[0023]  //      VERSION NUMBER 1.1
[0024]  //
[0025]  //      DATE 6 September 1995
[0026]  //
[0027]  //      AUTHOR K Barclay / J Savage
[0028]  //
[0029]  //      PURPOSE addition of lessThan? and name? to support
                containment
[0030]  //
[0031]  //      VERSION NUMBER 2.
[0032]  //
[0033]  //      DATE 8 September 1995
[0034]  //
[0035]  //      AUTHOR K Barclay / J Savage
[0036]  //
[0037]  //      PURPOSE Demonstration of the use of LINKs to Books
[0038]  //
[0039]  //   DESCRIPTION
[0040]  //
[0041]  //      An instance of this class acts as a User that can
                borrow and return
[0042]  //      Books to a Library. A User can also display books out
                on loan.
[0043]  //
[0044]  //      In this demonstration LINKs to books are employed.
                However, it
[0045]  //      is intended to be for illustration only and has
                several major flaws.
[0046]  //
[0047]  //      See Chapter 8 for a more realistic approach.
[0048]  //
[0049]  //
[0050]  CLASS User
[0051]  WITH
[0052]  PUBLIC INTERFACE
[0053]    User
[0054]    User (aName : String, anAddress : String)
[0055]    displayBooks?
[0056]    borrowOneBook (aTitle : String)
[0057]    returnOneBook
[0058]    addLibrary (aLibrary : Library LINK)
[0059]    lessThan? (aUser : User) -> Boolean
[0060]    name? -> String
[0061]  PROTECTED INTERFACE
[0062]    NONE
```

```
[0063]  PRIVATE IMPLEMENTATION
[0064]    REPRESENTATION
[0065]      theName : String
[0066]      theAddress : String
[0067]    AGGREGATIONS
[0068]      theBooks : POrderedCollection [Book LINK]
[0069]    ASSOCIATIONS
[0070]      theLender : Library LINK INVERSE OF theBorrowers
[0071]    DEFINITIONS
[0072]      METHOD User
[0073]      AS
[0074]        // Default constructor.
[0075]
[0076]        // Set the representation entries to sensible values.
[0077]        SEND theName THE MESSAGE initialise("")
[0078]        SEND theAddress THE MESSAGE initialise("")
[0079]
[0080]        // Set the aggregate components container theBooks
[0081]        // and the associate theLender to sensible values.
[0082]        SEND theBooks THE MESSAGE initialise(DEFAULTSIZE,
               UNMANAGED)
[0083]        SEND theLender THE MESSAGE initialise(NIL)
[0084]      ENDMETHOD User
[0085]
[0086]      METHOD User(aName : String, anAddress : String)
[0087]      AS
[0088]        // Parameterised constructor.
[0089]
[0090]        // Set the representation entries to corresponding
[0091]        // parameters of the constructor.
[0092]        SEND theName THE MESSAGE initialise(aName)
[0093]        SEND theAddress THE MESSAGE initialise(anAddress)
[0094]
[0095]        // Set the aggregate components container theBooks
[0096]        // and the associate theLender to sensible values.
[0097]        SEND theBooks THE MESSAGE initialise(DEFAULTSIZE,
               UNMANAGED)
[0098]        SEND theLender THE MESSAGE initialise(NIL)
[0099]      ENDMETHOD User
[0100]
[0101]      METHOD displayBooks?
[0102]      AS
[0103]        // Output to the screen details of Books out on loan
[0104]        // together with the User's name and address.
[0105]
[0106]        SEND theScreen THE MESSAGE insert(theName)
[0107]        SEND theScreen THE MESSAGE insert(" [")
[0108]        SEND theScreen THE MESSAGE insert(theAddress)
[0109]        SEND theScreen THE MESSAGE insert("] Borrowed
               books:\n")
[0110]
[0111]        FOREACH aBook : Book LINK IN theBooks DO
[0112]        SEND aBook THE MESSAGE display?
[0113]        ENDFOREACH
```

```
[0114]
[0115]        // If required the screen may be held with the
                 following sentences.
[0116]        // INSTANCE theResponse : String("")
[0117]        // SEND theScreen THE MESSAGE insert ("\n\tType a
                 character to continue > ")
[0118]        // SEND theKeyboard THE MESSAGE extract (theResponse)
[0119]        //
[0120]        // Similarly the screen may be held if these sentences
                 are embedded in the FOREACH
[0121]        // control sentence immediately after the message
                 display?
[0122]        ENDMETHOD displayBooks?
[0123]
[0124]        METHOD borrowOneBook (aTitle : String)
[0125]        AS
[0126]          // Borrow a Book with a specified title from the
                   Library.
[0127]
[0128]          SEND theBooks THE MESSAGE addFirst
[0129]        (SEND theLender THE MESSAGE
              borrowOneBook? (aTitle))
[0130]        ENDMETHOD borrowOneBook
[0131]
[0132]        METHOD returnOneBook
[0133]        AS
[0134]          // Return a Book to the Library.
[0135]
[0136]          SEND theLender THE MESSAGE
                returnOneBook
[0137]                           (SEND theBooks THE MESSAGE last?)
[0138]          SEND theBooks THE MESSAGE removeLast
[0139]        ENDMETHOD returnOneBook
[0140]
[0141]        METHOD addLibrary (aLibrary : Library LINK)
[0142]        AS
[0143]          // Establish a LINK with a Library.
[0144]
[0145]          SEND theLender THE MESSAGE assign (aLibrary)
[0146]        ENDMETHOD addLibrary
[0147]
[0148]        METHOD lessThan? (aUser : User) -> Boolean
[0149]        AS
[0150]          // Compare two Users by name using the operator <
                   defined for Strings.
[0151]
[0152]          IF theName < (SEND aUser THE MESSAGE name?) THEN
[0153]          RETURN TRUE
[0154]          ELSE
[0155]          RETURN FALSE
[0156]          ENDIF
[0157]        ENDMETHOD lessThan?
[0158]
[0159]        METHOD name? -> String
```

```
[0160]      AS
[0161]         //Deliver the private property theName to a client.
[0162]
[0163]        RETURN theName
[0164]      ENDMETHOD name?
[0165]
[0166] ENDCLASS User
[0167]
[0168]
[0169] //
[0170] //  CLASS Book
[0171] //
[0172] //  REVISION HISTORY
[0173] //
[0174] //     VERSION NUMBER 1.0
[0175] //
[0176] //     DATE 1 September 1995
[0177] //
[0178] //     AUTHOR K Barclay /J Savage
[0179] //
[0180] //     PURPOSE First release.
[0181] //
[0182] //     VERSION NUMBER 1.1
[0183] //
[0184] //     DATE 6 September 1995
[0185] //
[0186] //     AUTHOR K Barclay / J Savage
[0187] //
[0188] //     PURPOSE Addition of lessThan? and title? to support
                    containment.
[0189] //
[0190] //
[0191] //  DESCRIPTION
[0192] //
[0193] //     An instance of this class acts as a Book held by a
[0194] //     Library that can be borrowed or returned by a User.
[0195] //     Details of each Book can be displayed.
[0196] //
[0197] CLASS Book
[0198] WITH
[0199] PUBLIC INTERFACE
[0200]   Book
[0201]   Book(anAuthor :String, aTitle :String,
[0202]   aReferenceNumber : Integer) display?
[0203]   lessThan? (aBook :Book) -> Boolean
[0204]   title? -> String
[0205] PROTECTED INTERFACE
[0206]   NONE
[0207] PRIVATE IMPLEMENTATION
[0208]   REPRESENTATION
[0209]     theAuthor :String
[0210]     theTitle :String
[0211]     theReferenceNumber : Integer
[0212]   AGGREGATIONS NONE
```

```
[0213]     ASSOCIATIONS NONE
[0214]     DEFINITIONS
[0215]       METHOD Book
[0216]       AS
[0217]         // Default constructor.
[0218]
[0219]         // Set the representation entries to sensible values.
[0220]         SEND theAuthor THE MESSAGE initialise("")
[0221]         SEND theTitle THE MESSAGE initialise("")
[0222]         SEND theReferenceNumber THE MESSAGE initialise(0)
[0223]       ENDMETHOD Book
[0224]
[0225]       METHOD Book(anAuthor : String, aTitle : String,
                  aReferenceNumber : Integer)
[0226]       AS
[0227]         // Parameterized constructor.
[0228]
[0229]         // Set the representation entries to corresponding
[0230]         // parameters of the constructor.
[0231]         SEND theAuthor THE MESSAGE initialise(anAuthor)
[0232]         SEND theTitle THE MESSAGE initialise(aTitle)
[0233]         SEND theReferenceNumber THE MESSAGE
                  initialise(aReferenceNumber)
[0234]       ENDMETHOD Book
[0235]
[0236]       METHOD display?
[0237]       AS
[0238]         // Output the representation to the screen.
[0239]         // Note that "\n" takes a new line and "\t" moves to the
                  next tab position.
[0240]
[0241]         SEND theScreen THE MESSAGE insert(theAuthor)
[0242]         SEND theScreen THE MESSAGE insert("\n\t")
[0243]         SEND theScreen THE MESSAGE insert(theTitle)
[0244]         SEND theScreen THE MESSAGE insert(":\t")
[0245]         SEND theScreen THE MESSAGE
                  insert(theReferenceNumber)
[0246]         SEND theScreen THE MESSAGE insert("\n")
[0247]       ENDMETHOD display?
[0248]
[0249]       METHOD lessThan?(aBook : Book) -> Boolean
[0250]       AS
[0251]         // Compare two Books by title using the operator <
                  defined for Strings.
[0252]
[0253]         IF theTitle < (SEND aBook THE MESSAGE title?) THEN
[0254]         RETURN TRUE
[0255]         ELSE
[0256]         RETURN FALSE
[0257]         ENDIF
[0258]       ENDMETHOD lessThan?
[0259]
[0260]       METHOD title? -> String
[0261]       AS
```

```
[0262]          //Deliver the private property theTitle to a client.
[0263]
[0264]          RETURN theTitle
[0265]        ENDMETHOD title?
[0266]
[0267] ENDCLASS Book
[0268]
[0269]
[0270] //
[0271] //   CLASS Library
[0272] //
[0273] //   REVISION HISTORY
[0274] //
[0275] //       VERSION NUMBER 1.0
[0276] //
[0277] //       DATE 1 September 1995
[0278] //
[0279] //       AUTHOR K Barclay / J Savage
[0280] //
[0281] //       PURPOSE First release
[0282] //
[0283] //
[0284] //       VERSION NUMBER 2.
[0285] //
[0286] //       DATE 8 September 1995
[0287] //
[0288] //       AUTHOR K Barclay / J Savage
[0289] //
[0290] //       PURPOSE Simple demonstration of LINKs to Books
[0291] //
[0292] //
[0293] //   DESCRIPTION
[0294] //
[0295] //       An instance of this class acts as the a library object
[0296] //       that holds books that a user can request a display
[0297] //       of, borrow or return.
[0298] //       For simplicity we assume that users can borrow a
[0299] //       book any number of times and that there is no record
[0300] //       of a book being borrowed or returned.
[0301] //
[0302] //       There are no error checks in place. In particular it
[0303] //       is assumed that a Book exists if a request to borrow
[0304] //       it is made and no consideration to removing a book
[0305] //       from the library is given.
[0306] //       See Chapter 8 for a more realistic approach.
[0307] //
[0308] CLASS Library
[0309] WITH
[0310] PUBLIC INTERFACE
[0311]   Library
[0312]   Library(aName : String)
[0313]   borrowOneBook?(aTitle : String) -> Book LINK
[0314]   returnOneBook(aBook : Book LINK)
[0315]   displayBooks?
```

```
[0316]    displayUserBooks?
[0317]    addUser (aUser : User LINK)
[0318]    addBook (aBook : Book LINK)
[0319] PROTECTED INTERFACE
[0320]    NONE
[0321] PRIVATE IMPLEMENTATION
[0322]    REPRESENTATION
[0323]      theName : String
[0324]    AGGREGATIONS
[0325]      theBooks : POrderedCollection [Book LINK]
[0326]    ASSOCIATIONS
[0327]      theBorrowers : POrderedCollection [User LINK] INVERSE
           OF theLender
[0328]    DEFINITIONS
[0329]      METHOD Library
[0330]      AS
[0331]        // Default constructor.
[0332]
[0333]        // Set the private property theName to an empty String.
[0334]        SEND theName THE MESSAGE initialise ("")
[0335]
[0336]        // Set the associates container theBorrowers and the
[0337]        // aggregate components container theBooks to
               sensible values.
[0338]        SEND theBorrowers THE MESSAGE
               initialise (DEFAULTSIZE, UNMANAGED)
[0339]        SEND theBooks THE MESSAGE initialise (DEFAULTSIZE,
               MANAGED)
[0340]      ENDMETHOD Library
[0341]
[0342]      METHOD Library (aName : String)
[0343]      AS
[0344]        // Parameterised constructor.
[0345]
[0346]        // Set the private property theName to the value of the
               formal parameter.
[0347]        SEND theName THE MESSAGE initialise (aName)
[0348]
[0349]        // Set the associates container theBorrowers and the
[0350]        // aggregate components container, theBooks to
               sensible values.
[0351]        SEND theBorrowers THE MESSAGE
               initialise (DEFAULTSIZE, UNMANAGED)
[0352]        SEND theBooks THE MESSAGE initialise (DEFAULTSIZE,
               MANAGED)
[0353]      ENDMETHOD Library
[0354]
[0355]      METHOD borrowOneBook? (aTitle : String) -> Book LINK
[0356]      AS
[0357]        // Deliver a LINK to a Book with a specified title to a
[0358]        // client. It is assumed that clients can borrow a Book
               any number of times.
[0359]
[0360]        FOREACH aBook : Book LINK IN theBooks DO
```

```
[0361]
[0362]            IF (SEND aBook THE MESSAGE title? ==aTitle) THEN
[0363]         RETURN aBook
[0364]           ENDIF
[0365]
[0366]        ENDFOREACH
[0367]
[0368]     ENDMETHOD borrowOneBook?
[0369]
[0370]     METHOD returnOneBook (aBook : Book LINK)
[0371]     AS
[0372]       // Accept a LINK to a Book from a client.
[0373]
[0374]       // No action is required but see Chapter 8.
[0375]     ENDMETHOD returnOneBook
[0376]
[0377]     METHOD displayBooks?
[0378]     AS
[0379]       // Output to the screen details of Books available for
[0380]       // loan. Note that "\n" takes a new line and "\t" moves
                 to the next tab position.
[0381]
[0382]        SEND theScreen THE MESSAGE insert ("Current loan
                 stock:\t")
[0383]        SEND theScreen THE MESSAGE insert (theName)
[0384]        SEND theScreen THE MESSAGE insert ("\n")
[0385]
[0386]        FOREACH aBook : Book LINK IN theBooks DO
[0387]          SEND aBook THE MESSAGE display?
[0388]        ENDFOREACH
[0389]
[0390]        // If required the screen may be held with the
                 following sentences.
[0391]        // INSTANCE theResponse : String ("")
[0392]        // SEND theScreen THE MESSAGE insert ("\n\tType a
                 character to continue > ")
[0393]        // SEND theKeyboard THE MESSAGE extract (theResponse)
[0394]        //
[0395]        // Similarly the screen may be held if these sentences
                 are embedded in the FOREACH
[0396]        // control sentence immediately after the message
                 display?
[0397]     ENDMETHOD displayBooks?
[0398]
[0399]     METHOD displayUserBooks?
[0400]     AS
[0401]       // Output to the screen details of Users and the Books
                 they have out on loan.
[0402]       // Note that "\n" takes a new line and "\t" moves to the
                 next tab position.
[0403]
[0404]        SEND theScreen THE MESSAGE insert ("Current borrowed
                 stock:\t")
[0405]        SEND theScreen THE MESSAGE insert (theName)
```

```
[0406]        SEND theScreen THE MESSAGE insert ("\n")
[0407]
[0408]        FOREACH aUser : User LINK IN theBorrowers DO
[0409]          SEND aUser THE MESSAGE displayBooks?
[0410]        ENDFOREACH
[0411]
[0412]        SEND theScreen THE MESSAGE insert ("\n")
[0413]
[0414]      // If required the screen may be held with the
                 following sentences.
[0415]      // INSTANCE theResponse : String ("")
[0416]      // SEND theScreen THE MESSAGE insert ("\n\tType a
                 character to continue > ")
[0417]      // SEND theKeyboard THE MESSAGE
                 extract (theResponse)
[0418]      ENDMETHOD displayUserBooks?
[0419]
[0420]      METHOD addUser (aUser : User LINK)
[0421]      AS
[0422]        // Add a User to the Library.
[0423]
[0424]        SEND theBorrowers THE MESSAGE add (aUser)
[0425]      ENDMETHOD addUser
[0426]
[0427]      METHOD addBook (aBook : Book LINK)
[0428]      AS
[0429]        // Add a Book to the Library.
[0430]
[0431]        SEND theBooks THE MESSAGE add (aBook)
[0432]      ENDMETHOD addBook
[0433]
[0434]  ENDCLASS Library
[0435]
[0436]
[0437]  //
[0438]  //    CLASS Application
[0439]  //
[0440]  //    REVISION HISTORY
[0441]  //
[0442]  //        VERSION NUMBER 1.0
[0443]  //
[0444]  //        DATE 1 September 1995
[0445]  //
[0446]  //        AUTHOR K Barclay / J Savage
[0447]  //
[0448]  //        PURPOSE First release
[0449]  //
[0450]  //
[0451]  //        VERSION NUMBER 2.0
[0452]  //
[0453]  //        DATE 6 September 1995
[0454]  //
[0455]  //        AUTHOR K Barclay / J Savage
[0456]  //
```

```
[0457] //      PURPOSE Use of LINKs to Book objects rather than
                full copies
[0458] //
[0459] //   DESCRIPTION
[0460] //
[0461] //      An instance of this class acts as the source of top-
[0462] //      level control. It also has the responsibility for
[0463] //      the creation of all objects in the system. Note that
[0464] //      an object that is an associate is created with
                dynamic duration.
[0465] //
[0466] //      This version is naive and is for illustration
                purposes only.
[0467] //
[0468] //      See Chapter 8 for a more realistic approach.
[0469] //
[0470] CLASS Application
[0471] WITH
[0472] PUBLIC INTERFACE
[0473]   Application
[0474]   run
[0475] PROTECTED INTERFACE
[0476]   NONE
[0477] PRIVATE IMPLEMENTATION
[0478]   REPRESENTATION NONE
[0479]   AGGREGATIONS NONE
[0480]   ASSOCIATIONS NONE
[0481]   DEFINITIONS
[0482]     METHOD Application
[0483]     AS
[0484]       //Default constructor.
[0485]
[0486]       //Although there is nothing to do, it is good practice
[0487]       //to have an explicit default constructor. The
                alternative is to assume that the implementation
[0488]       //language will supply one.
[0489]     ENDMETHOD Application
[0490]
[0491]     METHOD run
[0492]     AS
[0493]       //Top-level control of the system.
[0494]
[0495]       //Create a library with dynamic duration.
[0496]       INSTANCE theLibrary : Library LINK ("Dunning
                Library")
[0497]
[0498]       //Create two users with dynamic duration.
[0499]       INSTANCE u1 : User LINK ("John", "21 High Street")
[0500]       INSTANCE u2 : User LINK ("Ken", "100 Black Road")
[0501]
[0502]       //Configure the architecture.
[0503]       SEND theLibrary THE MESSAGE addUser (u1)
[0504]       SEND theLibrary THE MESSAGE addUser (u2)
[0505]       SEND u1 THE MESSAGE addLibrary (theLibrary)
```

```
[0506]          SEND u2 THE MESSAGE addLibrary (theLibrary)
[0507]
[0508]          // Create some book instances with dynamic duration.
[0509]          INSTANCE b1 : Book LINK ("Barclay",
[0510]          "C++: Problem Solving and Programming", 1)
[0511]          INSTANCE b2 : Book LINK ("Rumbaugh",
[0512]          "Object Oriented Modelling and Design", 2)
[0513]          INSTANCE b3 : Book LINK ("Booch",
[0514]          "Object Oriented Design", 3)
[0515]          INSTANCE b4 : Book LINK ("Yourdon",
[0516]          "Object Oriented System Design", 4)
[0517]
[0518]          // Pass book links to the library.
[0519]          SEND theLibrary THE MESSAGE addBook (b1)
[0520]          SEND theLibrary THE MESSAGE addBook (b2)
[0521]          SEND theLibrary THE MESSAGE addBook (b3)
[0522]          SEND theLibrary THE MESSAGE addBook (b4)
[0523]
[0524]          // The user u1 borrows two books.
[0525]          SEND u1 THE MESSAGE borrowOneBook ("Object Oriented
                System Design")
[0526]          SEND u1 THE MESSAGE borrowOneBook ("Object Oriented
                Modelling and Design")
[0527]
[0528]          // The user u2 borrows one book.
[0529]          SEND u2 THE MESSAGE borrowOneBook ("C++: Problem
                Solving and Programming")
[0530]
[0531]          // The library displays books held by its users.
[0532]          SEND theLibrary THE MESSAGE displayUserBooks?
[0533]
[0534]          // The user u1 returns a book then we see the effect on
                    the library.
[0535]          SEND u1 THE MESSAGE returnOneBook
[0536]          SEND theLibrary THE MESSAGE displayUserBooks?
[0537]
[0538]          // Display books currently held by the library.
[0539]          SEND theLibrary THE MESSAGE displayBooks?
[0540]
[0541]       ENDMETHOD run
[0542]
[0543]  ENDCLASS Application
[0544]
[0545]
[0546]
```

E.3 Chapter 8, version 1 of the Library system

```
[0001]  //.
[0002]  //.
[0003]  //. ROME Copyright (c) Richard McMahon. 1993, 1994.
[0004]  //. Generated On January 6, 1996 At 3:21:44.91 pm
```

```
[0005]
[0006]
[0007]
[0008] //.--Class Definitions: -----------------
[0009]
[0010] //
[0011] //  CLASS Publication
[0012] //
[0013] //  REVISION HISTORY
[0014] //
[0015] //     VERSION NUMBER 1.0
[0016] //
[0017] //     DATE 8 September 1995
[0018] //
[0019] //     AUTHOR K Barclay / J Savage
[0020] //
[0021] //     PURPOSE First release
[0022] //
[0023] //  DESCRIPTION
[0024] //
[0025] //     This class acts as a basis for the construction of
                all other Publications.
[0026] //     As such it guarantees a common interface.
[0027] //
[0028] ABSTRACT CLASS Publication
[0029] WITH
[0030] PUBLIC INTERFACE
[0031]   Publication
[0032]   Publication(aTitle :String, aPublisher :String,
            aPublicationDate :Date, aReferenceNumber :String)
[0033]   display?                                    DEFERRED
[0034]   referenceNumber? ->String
[0035]   lessThan?(aPublication :Publication) ->Boolean
[0036]   isOnLoan? ->Boolean
[0037]   setOnLoan(aValue :Boolean)
[0038] PROTECTED INTERFACE
[0039]   displayPublicationPart?
[0040] PRIVATE IMPLEMENTATION
[0041]   REPRESENTATION
[0042]     theTitle :String
[0043]     thePublisher :String
[0044]     thePublicationDate :Date
[0045]     theReferenceNumber :String
[0046]     onLoan :Boolean
[0047]   AGGREGATIONS NONE
[0048]   ASSOCIATIONS NONE
[0049]   DEFINITIONS
[0050]     METHOD Publication
[0051]     AS
[0052]       //Default constructor.
[0053]
[0054]       // Set representation entries to sensible values.
[0055]       SEND theTitle THE MESSAGE initialise("")
[0056]       SEND thePublisher THE MESSAGE initialise("")
```

```
[0057]      SEND thePublicationDate THE MESSAGE initialise
            (Date(1,1,1900))
[0058]      SEND theReferenceNumber THE MESSAGE
            initialise("000")
[0059]      SEND onLoan THE MESSAGE initialise(FALSE)
[0060]    ENDMETHOD Publication
[0061]
[0062]    METHOD Publication(aTitle :String, aPublisher
          :String, aPublicationDate :Date, aReferenceNumber
          :String)
[0063]    AS
[0064]      // Parameterised constructor.
[0065]
[0066]      // Set representation entries to corresponding
              parameters of
[0067]      // the constructor.
[0068]      SEND theTitle THE MESSAGE initialise(aTitle)
[0069]      SEND thePublisher THE MESSAGE
            initialise(aPublisher)
[0070]      SEND thePublicationDate THE MESSAGE
            initialise(aPublicationDate)
[0071]      SEND theReferenceNumber THE MESSAGE
            initialise(aReferenceNumber)
[0072]
[0073]      SEND onLoan THE MESSAGE initialise(FALSE)
[0074]    ENDMETHOD Publication
[0075]
[0076]    METHOD displayPublicationPart?
[0077]    AS
[0078]      // Output to the screen the relevant details of a
              Publication.
[0079]
[0080]      SEND theScreen THE MESSAGE insert(theTitle)
[0081]      SEND theScreen THE MESSAGE insert(", ")
[0082]      SEND theScreen THE MESSAGE
            insert(theReferenceNumber)
[0083]      SEND theScreen THE MESSAGE insert(", ")
[0084]    ENDMETHOD displayPublicationPart?
[0085]
[0086]    METHOD referenceNumber? ->String
[0087]    AS
[0088]      // Deliver the private property, theReferenceNumber
              to a client.
[0089]
[0090]      RETURN theReferenceNumber
[0091]    ENDMETHOD referenceNumber?
[0092]
[0093]    METHOD lessThan?(aPublication :Publication) -
          >Boolean
[0094]    AS
[0095]      // Compare two Publications by reference number using
              the operator <
[0096]      // defined for Strings.
[0097]
```

```
[0098]        IF theReferenceNumber < (SEND aPublication THE
              MESSAGE referenceNumber?) THEN
[0099]          RETURN TRUE
[0100]        ELSE
[0101]          RETURN FALSE
[0102]        ENDIF
[0103]      ENDMETHOD lessThan?
[0104]
[0105]      METHOD isOnLoan? ->Boolean
[0106]      AS
[0107]        //Deliver the private property onLoan to a client.
[0108]
[0109]        RETURN onLoan
[0110]      ENDMETHOD isOnLoan?
[0111]
[0112]      METHOD setOnLoan (aValue :Boolean)
[0113]      AS
[0114]        //Set the private property, onLoan to the parameter
               of the operation.
[0115]
[0116]        SEND onLoan THE MESSAGE assign (aValue)
[0117]      ENDMETHOD setOnLoan
[0118]
[0119] ENDCLASS Publication
[0120]
[0121]
[0122] //
[0123] //  CLASS Library
[0124] //
[0125] //  REVISION HISTORY
[0126] //
[0127] //      VERSION NUMBER 1.0
[0128] //
[0129] //      DATE 8 September 1995
[0130] //
[0131] //      AUTHOR K Barclay / J Savage
[0132] //
[0133] //      PURPOSE First release.
[0134] //
[0135] //  DESCRIPTION
[0136] //
[0137] //      An instance of this class acts as the Library object
               that holds
[0138] //      Publications that can be added or displayed.
[0139] //
[0140] CLASS Library
[0141] WITH
[0142] PUBLIC INTERFACE
[0143]   Library
[0144]   Library (aName :String)
[0145]   addOnePublication (aPublication :Publication LINK
         INOUT)
[0146]   displayLoanStock?
[0147] PROTECTED INTERFACE
[0148]   NONE
```

```
[0149]  PRIVATE IMPLEMENTATION
[0150]    REPRESENTATION
[0151]      theName : String
[0152]    AGGREGATIONS
[0153]      thePublications : POrderedCollection [Publication
          LINK]
[0154]    ASSOCIATIONS NONE
[0155]    DEFINITIONS
[0156]      METHOD Library
[0157]      AS
[0158]        // Default constructor.
[0159]
[0160]        // Set the private property theName to the value of an
              empty String.
[0161]        SEND theName THE MESSAGE initialise ("")
[0162]
[0163]        // Set the aggregate components container
              thePublications to
[0164]        // sensible values.
[0165]        SEND thePublications THE MESSAGE
              initialise (DEFAULTSIZE, MANAGED)
[0166]      ENDMETHOD Library
[0167]
[0168]      METHOD Library (aName : String)
[0169]      AS
[0170]        // Parameterized constructor.
[0171]
[0172]        // Set the private property theName to the value of the
              actual parameter.
[0173]        SEND theName THE MESSAGE initialise (aName)
[0174]
[0175]        // Set the aggregate components container
              thePublications to
[0176]        // sensible values.
[0177]        SEND thePublications THE MESSAGE
              initialise (DEFAULTSIZE, MANAGED)
[0178]      ENDMETHOD Library
[0179]
[0180]      METHOD addOnePublication (aPublication : Publication
          LINK INOUT)
[0181]      AS
[0182]        // Add a Publication to the Library.
[0183]
[0184]        IF aPublication ! = NIL THEN
[0185]          SEND aPublication THE MESSAGE setOnLoan (FALSE)
[0186]          SEND thePublications THE MESSAGE add (aPublication)
[0187]        ENDIF
[0188]      ENDMETHOD addOnePublication
[0189]
[0190]      METHOD displayLoanStock?
[0191]      AS
[0192]        // Output to the screen details of Publications
              available for loan.
[0193]
```

```
[0194]        SEND theScreen THE MESSAGE insert ("\nCurrent Loan
              Stock:\t")
[0195]        SEND theScreen THE MESSAGE insert (theName)
[0196]        SEND theScreen THE MESSAGE insert ("\n")
[0197]
[0198]        FOREACH aPublication : Publication LINK IN
              thePublications DO
[0199]          IF (SEND aPublication THE MESSAGE isOnLoan?) ==
              FALSE THEN
[0200]            SEND aPublication THE MESSAGE display?
[0201]          ENDIF
[0202]        ENDFOREACH
[0203]        SEND theScreen THE MESSAGE insert ("\n")
[0204]
[0205]        // If required the screen may be held with the
              following sentences.
[0206]        // INSTANCE theResponse : String("")
[0207]        // SEND theScreen THE MESSAGE insert ("\n\tType a
              character to continue > ")
[0208]        // SEND theKeyboard THE MESSAGE extract (theResponse)
[0209]        //
[0210]        // Similarly the screen may be held if these sentences
              are embedded in the FOREACH
[0211]        // control sentence immediately after the message
              display?
[0212]      ENDMETHOD displayLoanStock?
[0213]
[0214] ENDCLASS Library
[0215]
[0216]
[0217] //
[0218] //   CLASS Application
[0219] //
[0220] //   REVISION HISTORY
[0221] //
[0222] //      VERSION NUMBER 1.0
[0223] //
[0224] //      DATE 8 September 1995
[0225] //
[0226] //      AUTHOR J Savage / K Barclay
[0227] //
[0228] //      PURPOSE First release
[0229] //
[0230] //   DESCRIPTION
[0231] //
[0232] //      An instance of this class provides the top-level
              control of the system.
[0233] //
[0234] //      An object that uses the polymorphic effect such as a
              Book is created
[0235] //      with dynamic duration.
[0236] //
[0237] //
[0238] CLASS Application
```

```
[0239]  WITH
[0240]  PUBLIC INTERFACE
[0241]    Application
[0242]    run
[0243]  PROTECTED INTERFACE
[0244]    NONE
[0245]  PRIVATE IMPLEMENTATION
[0246]    REPRESENTATION NONE
[0247]    AGGREGATIONS NONE
[0248]    ASSOCIATIONS NONE
[0249]    DEFINITIONS
[0250]      METHOD Application
[0251]      AS
[0252]        // Default constructor.
[0253]
[0254]        // Although there is nothing to do it is good practice
                  to have an explicit
[0255]        // default constructor. The alternative is to assume
                  that the implementation
[0256]        // language will supply one.
[0257]      ENDMETHOD Application
[0258]
[0259]      METHOD run
[0260]      AS
[0261]        // Top-level control messages.
[0262]
[0263]        // Create a Library with local duration as it has no
                  associates in this version.
[0264]        INSTANCE theLibrary : Library ("Dunning Library")
[0265]
[0266]        // Create some Book and Map objects with dynamic
                  duration as we intend
[0267]        // using the polmorphic effect, i.e. they are treated
                  as Publications.
[0268]        INSTANCE b1 : Book LINK ("C++ Problem Solving and
               Programming",
[0269]                          "Prentice Hall", Date (1, 1, 1994),
                                        "AA1", "Barclay", 1)
[0270]        INSTANCE b2 : Book LINK ("Object Oriented Modelling
               and Design",
[0271]                          "Prentice Hall", Date (2, 2, 1994),
                                        "BB2", "Rumbaugh et al", 2)
[0272]        INSTANCE b3 : Book LINK ("Object Oriented Design",
[0273]                    "Benjamin Cummings", Date (3, 3, 1994),
                                        "CC3", "Booch", 1)
[0274]        INSTANCE b4 : Book LINK ("Object Oriented System
               Design",
[0275]                          "Prentice Hall", Date (4, 4, 1994),
                                        "DD4", "Yourdon", 1)
[0276]
[0277]        INSTANCE m1 : Map LINK ("Burgundy", "Michelin",
               Date (5, 5, 1994), "EE5",
[0278]                                        "Michelin", 5)
[0279]
```

```
[0280]         // Add LINKs to Books and Maps to the Library.
[0281]         SEND theLibrary THE MESSAGE addOnePublication(b1)
[0282]         SEND theLibrary THE MESSAGE addOnePublication(b2)
[0283]         SEND theLibrary THE MESSAGE addOnePublication(b3)
[0284]         SEND theLibrary THE MESSAGE addOnePublication(b4)
[0285]         SEND theLibrary THE MESSAGE addOnePublication(m1)
[0286]
[0287]         // Now see what is in the Library's stock.
[0288]         SEND theLibrary THE MESSAGE displayLoanStock?
[0289]       ENDMETHOD run
[0290]
[0291] ENDCLASS Application
[0292]
[0293]
[0294] //
[0295] //   CLASS Book
[0296] //
[0297] //   REVISION HISTORY
[0298] //
[0299] //       VERSION NUMBER 1.0
[0300] //
[0301] //       DATE 8 September 1995
[0302] //
[0303] //       AUTHOR K Barclay / J Savage
[0304] //
[0305] //       PURPOSE First release
[0306] //
[0307] //   DESCRIPTION
[0308] //
[0309] //       An instance of this class acts a Book that is held by
               a Library.
[0310] //
[0311] CLASS Book
[0312]   SPECIALISATION OF Publication
[0313] WITH
[0314] PUBLIC INTERFACE
[0315]   Book
[0316]   Book(aTitle : String, aPublisher : String, aDate : Date,
         aReferenceNumber : String, anAuthor : String, anEdition
         : Integer)
[0317]   display?                                    REDEFINED
[0318] PROTECTED INTERFACE
[0319]   NONE
[0320] PRIVATE IMPLEMENTATION
[0321]   REPRESENTATION
[0322]     theAuthor : String
[0323]     theEdition : Integer
[0324]   AGGREGATIONS NONE
[0325]   ASSOCIATIONS NONE
[0326]   DEFINITIONS
[0327]     METHOD Book
[0328]     AS
[0329]       // Default constructor.
[0330]
```

```
[0331]        // Initialise the Publication representation
                 entries.
[0332]        SEND SUPERCLASS Publication THE MESSAGE initialise
[0333]
[0334]        // Set the unique Book representation entries to
                 sensible values.
[0335]        SEND theAuthor THE MESSAGE initialise("")
[0336]        SEND theEdition THE MESSAGE initialise(1)
[0337]     ENDMETHOD Book
[0338]
[0339]     METHOD Book(aTitle : String, aPublisher : String, aDate
              : Date, aReferenceNumber : String, anAuthor : String,
              anEdition : Integer)
[0340]     AS
[0341]      // Parameterised constructor.
[0342]
[0343]      // Set the Publication representation entries to
                 corresponding parameters
[0344]      // of the constructor.
[0345]      SEND SUPERCLASS Publication THE MESSAGE initialise
[0346]                              (aTitle, aPublisher, aDate,
                                              aReferenceNumber)
[0347]
[0348]      // Set the unique Book representation parts to the
                 corresponding
[0349]      // parameters of the constructor.
[0350]      SEND theAuthor THE MESSAGE initialise(anAuthor)
[0351]      SEND theEdition THE MESSAGE initialise(anEdition)
[0352]     ENDMETHOD Book
[0353]
[0354]     METHOD display?
[0355]     AS
[0356]      // Output Book details to the screen.
[0357]
[0358]      SEND theScreen THE MESSAGE insert("Book[")
[0359]      SEND me THE MESSAGE displayPublicationPart?
[0360]      SEND theScreen THE MESSAGE insert(theAuthor)
[0361]      SEND theScreen THE MESSAGE insert(", ")
[0362]      SEND theScreen THE MESSAGE insert(theEdition)
[0363]      SEND theScreen THE MESSAGE insert("]\n")
[0364]     ENDMETHOD display?
[0365]
[0366] ENDCLASS Book
[0367]
[0368]
[0369] //
[0370] //   CLASS Map
[0371] //
[0372] //   REVISION HISTORY
[0373] //
[0374] //      VERSION NUMBER 1.0
[0375] //
[0376] //      DATE 8 September 1995
[0377] //
```

```
[0378]  //      AUTHOR K Barclay / J Savage
[0379]  //
[0380]  //      PURPOSE First release
[0381]  //
[0382]  //  DESCRIPTION
[0383]  //
[0384]  //      An instance of this class acts a Map that is held by
                a Library.
[0385]  //
[0386]  CLASS Map
[0387]    SPECIALISATION OF Publication
[0388]  WITH
[0389]  PUBLIC INTERFACE
[0390]    Map
[0391]    Map(aTitle : String, aPublisher : String, aDate : Date,
            aReferenceNumber : String, aSeriesName : String,
            aSheetNumber : Integer)
[0392]    display?                                      REDEFINED
[0393]  PROTECTED INTERFACE
[0394]    NONE
[0395]  PRIVATE IMPLEMENTATION
[0396]    REPRESENTATION
[0397]      theSeriesName : String
[0398]      theSheetNumber : Integer
[0399]    AGGREGATIONS NONE
[0400]    ASSOCIATIONS NONE
[0401]    DEFINITIONS
[0402]    METHOD Map
[0403]    AS
[0404]      // Default constructor.
[0405]
[0406]      // Initialise the Publication representation
              entries.
[0407]      SEND SUPERCLASS Publication THE MESSAGE initialise
[0408]
[0409]      // Set the unique Map representation entries to
              sensible values.
[0410]      SEND theSeriesName THE MESSAGE initialise("")
[0411]      SEND theSheetNumber THE MESSAGE initialise(0)
[0412]    ENDMETHOD Map
[0413]
[0414]    METHOD Map(aTitle : String, aPublisher : String, aDate
          : Date, aReferenceNumber : String, aSeriesName
          : String, aSheetNumber : Integer)
[0415]    AS
[0416]      // Parameterized constructor.
[0417]
[0418]      // Set the Publication representation entries to
              corresponding parameters
[0419]      // of the constructor.
[0420]
[0421]      SEND SUPERCLASS Publication THE MESSAGE
          initialise(aTitle, aPublisher,
[0422]                                 aDate, aReferenceNumber)
```

```
[0423]
[0424]        //Set the unique Map representation entries to
                 corresponding parameters
[0425]        //of the constructor.
[0426]        SEND theSeriesName THE MESSAGE
                 initialise(aSeriesName)
[0427]        SEND theSheetNumber THE MESSAGE
                 initialise(aSheetNumber)
[0428]     ENDMETHOD Map
[0429]
[0430]     METHOD display?
[0431]     AS
[0432]       //Output Map details to the screen.
[0433]
[0434]       SEND theScreen THE MESSAGE insert("Map[")
[0435]       SEND me THE MESSAGE displayPublicationPart?
[0436]       SEND theScreen THE MESSAGE insert(theSeriesName)
[0437]       SEND theScreen THE MESSAGE insert(", ")
[0438]       SEND theScreen THE MESSAGE insert(theSheetNumber)
[0439]       SEND theScreen THE MESSAGE insert("]\n")
[0440]     ENDMETHOD display?
[0441]
[0442] ENDCLASS Map
[0443]
[0444]
[0445]
```

E.4 Chapter 8, version 2 of the Library system

```
[0001] //.
[0002] //.
[0003] //. ROME Copyright (c) Richard McMahon. 1993, 1994.
[0004] //. Generated On January 6, 1996 At 3:29:07.83 pm
[0005]
[0006]
[0007]
[0008] //. --Class Definitions: -----------------
[0009]
[0010] //
[0011] // CLASS User
[0012] //
[0013] // REVISION HISTORY
[0014] //
[0015] //     VERSION NUMBER 1.0
[0016] //
[0017] //     DATE 8 September 1995
[0018] //
[0019] //     AUTHOR K Barclay / J Savage
[0020] //
[0021] //     PURPOSE First release
[0022] //
[0023] //
```

```
[0024]  //   DESCRIPTION
[0025]  //
[0026]  //        An instance of this class acts as a User that can
                  borrow and return
[0027]  //        Publications to a Library. A User can also display
                  Publications out
[0028]  //        on loan.
[0029]  //
[0030]  //
[0031]  CLASS User
[0032]  WITH
[0033]  PUBLIC INTERFACE
[0034]    User
[0035]    User (aName : String, anAddress : String)
[0036]    addLibrary (aLibrary : Library LINK)
[0037]    borrowOnePublication (aReferenceNumber : String)
[0038]    returnOnePublication
[0039]    name? ->String
[0040]    lessThan? (aUser : User) ->Boolean
[0041]    displayPublications?
[0042]  PROTECTED INTERFACE
[0043]    NONE
[0044]  PRIVATE IMPLEMENTATION
[0045]    REPRESENTATION
[0046]      theName : String
[0047]      theAddress : String
[0048]    AGGREGATIONS
[0049]      thePublications
                : POrderedCollection [Publication LINK]
[0050]    ASSOCIATIONS
[0051]      theLender : Library LINK INVERSE OF theBorrowers
[0052]    DEFINITIONS
[0053]      METHOD User
[0054]      AS
[0055]        //Default constructor.
[0056]
[0057]        //Set representation entries to sensible values.
[0058]        SEND theName THE MESSAGE initialise ("")
[0059]        SEND theAddress THE MESSAGE initialise ("")
[0060]
[0061]        //Set the associate theLender and the aggregate
                  components container
[0062]        //thePublications to sensible values.
[0063]        SEND theLender THE MESSAGE initialise (NIL)
[0064]        SEND thePublications THE MESSAGE
                initialise (DEFAULTSIZE, UNMANAGED)
[0065]      ENDMETHOD User
[0066]
[0067]      METHOD User (aName : String, anAddress : String)
[0068]      AS
[0069]        //Parameterised constructor.
[0070]
[0071]        //Set the representation entries to corresponding
[0072]        //parameters of the constructor.
```

```
[0073]        SEND theName THE MESSAGE initialise(aName)
[0074]        SEND theAddress THE MESSAGE initialise(anAddress)
[0075]
[0076]        // Set the associate theLender and the aggregate
                 components container
[0077]        // thePublications to sensible values.
[0078]        SEND theLender THE MESSAGE initialise(NIL)
[0079]        SEND thePublications THE MESSAGE
              initialise(DEFAULTSIZE, UNMANAGED)
[0080]     ENDMETHOD User
[0081]
[0082]     METHOD addLibrary(aLibrary : Library LINK)
[0083]     AS
[0084]       // Establish a LINK with a Library.
[0085]
[0086]       SEND theLender THE MESSAGE assign(aLibrary)
[0087]     ENDMETHOD addLibrary
[0088]
[0089]     METHOD borrowOnePublication
              (aReferenceNumber : String)
[0090]     AS
[0091]       // Borrow a Publication with a specified reference
                 number.
[0092]
[0093]       INSTANCE thePublication : Publication LINK(SEND
              theLender THE MESSAGE borrow
              OnePublication?(aReferenceNumber))
[0094]
[0095]       IF thePublication != NIL THEN
[0096]         SEND thePublications THE MESSAGE
                 addFirst(thePublication)
[0097]       ENDIF
[0098]     ENDMETHOD borrowOnePublication
[0099]
[0100]     METHOD returnOnePublication
[0101]     AS
[0102]       // Return a Publication to the Library.
[0103]
[0104]       INSTANCE thePublication : Publication LINK(SEND
              thePublications THE MESSAGE last?)
[0105]       SEND theLender THE MESSAGE
              returnOnePublication(SEND thePublication THE
              MESSAGE referenceNumber?)
[0106]       SEND thePublications THE MESSAGE removeFirst
[0107]     ENDMETHOD returnOnePublication
[0108]
[0109]     METHOD name? ->String
[0110]     AS
[0111]       // Deliver the private property theName to a client.
[0112]
[0113]       RETURN theName
[0114]     ENDMETHOD name?
[0115]
[0116]     METHOD lessThan?(aUser : User) ->Boolean
```

```
[0117]      AS
[0118]        // Compare two Users by name using the operator < for
              Strings.
[0119]
[0120]        IF (SEND aUser THE MESSAGE name?) < theName THEN
[0121]          RETURN TRUE
[0122]        ELSE
[0123]          RETURN FALSE
[0124]        ENDIF
[0125]      ENDMETHOD lessThan?
[0126]
[0127]      METHOD displayPublications?
[0128]      AS
[0129]        // Output to the screen details of Publications out on
              loan together with
[0130]        // the name of the User.
[0131]
[0132]        SEND theScreen THE MESSAGE insert ("\nPublications
              borrowed by ")
[0133]        SEND theScreen THE MESSAGE insert (theName)
[0134]        SEND theScreen THE MESSAGE insert ("\n")
[0135]
[0136]        IF (SEND thePublications THE MESSAGE isEmpty?) ==
              FALSE THEN
[0137]          FOREACH aPublication : Publication LINK IN
                thePublications DO
[0138]            SEND aPublication THE MESSAGE display?
[0139]          ENDFOREACH
[0140]        ELSE
[0141]          SEND theScreen THE MESSAGE insert ("\tNo
                publications on loan. \n")
[0142]        ENDIF
[0143]
[0144]        // If required the screen may be held with the
              following sentences.
[0145]        // INSTANCE theResponse : String("")
[0146]        // SEND theScreen THE MESSAGE insert ("\n\tType a
              character to continue > ")
[0147]        // SEND theKeyboard THE MESSAGE extract (theResponse)
[0148]        //
[0149]        // Similarly the screen may be held if these sentences
              are embedded in the FOREACH
[0150]        // control sentence immediately after the message
              display?
[0151]      ENDMETHOD displayPublications?
[0152]
[0153] ENDCLASS User
[0154]
[0155]
[0156] //
[0157] //   CLASS Publication
[0158] //
[0159] //   REVISION HISTORY
[0160] //
```

```
[0161]  //      VERSION NUMBER 1.0
[0162]  //
[0163]  //      DATE 8 September 1995
[0164]  //
[0165]  //      AUTHOR K Barclay / J Savage
[0166]  //
[0167]  //      PURPOSE First release
[0168]  //
[0169]  //  DESCRIPTION
[0170]  //
[0171]  //      This class acts as a basis for the construction of
                all other Publications.
[0172]  //      As such it guarantees a common interface.
[0173]  //
[0174]  ABSTRACT CLASS Publication
[0175]  WITH
[0176]  PUBLIC INTERFACE
[0177]    Publication
[0178]    Publication(aTitle:String, aPublisher:String,
              aPublicationDate:Date, aReferenceNumber:String)
[0179]    display?                                    DEFERRED
[0180]    referenceNumber?->String
[0181]    lessThan?(aPublication:Publication)->Boolean
[0182]    isOnLoan?->Boolean
[0183]    setOnLoan(aValue:Boolean)
[0184]  PROTECTED INTERFACE
[0185]    displayPublicationPart?
[0186]  PRIVATE IMPLEMENTATION
[0187]    REPRESENTATION
[0188]      theTitle:String
[0189]      thePublisher:String
[0190]      thePublicationDate:Date
[0191]      theReferenceNumber:String
[0192]      onLoan:Boolean
[0193]    AGGREGATIONS NONE
[0194]    ASSOCIATIONS NONE
[0195]    DEFINITIONS
[0196]      METHOD Publication
[0197]      AS
[0198]        //Default constructor.
[0199]
[0200]        //Set the representation entries to sensble values.
[0201]        SEND theTitle THE MESSAGE initialise("")
[0202]        SEND thePublisher THE MESSAGE initialise("")
[0203]        SEND thePublicationDate THE MESSAGE initialise(
                Date(1,1,1900))
[0204]        SEND theReferenceNumber THE MESSAGE
                initialise("000")
[0205]        SEND onLoan THE MESSAGE initialise(FALSE)
[0206]      ENDMETHOD Publication
[0207]
[0208]      METHOD Publication(aTitle:String, aPublisher
                :String, aPublicationDate:Date, aReferenceNumber
                :String)
```

```
[0209]        AS
[0210]          // Parameterized constructor.
[0211]
[0212]          // Set the representation entries to the
                    corresponding
[0213]          // parameters of the constructor.
[0214]          SEND theTitle THE MESSAGE initialise(aTitle)
[0215]          SEND thePublisher THE MESSAGE
                  initialise(aPublisher)
[0216]          SEND thePublicationDate THE MESSAGE
                  initialise(aPublicationDate)
[0217]          SEND theReferenceNumber THE MESSAGE
                  initialise(aReferenceNumber)
[0218]          SEND onLoan THE MESSAGE initialise(FALSE)
[0219]        ENDMETHOD Publication
[0220]
[0221]        METHOD displayPublicationPart?
[0222]        AS
[0223]          // Output to the screen the relevent details of a
                    Publication.
[0224]
[0225]          SEND theScreen THE MESSAGE insert(theTitle)
[0226]          SEND theScreen THE MESSAGE insert(", ")
[0227]          SEND theScreen THE MESSAGE
                  insert(theReferenceNumber)
[0228]          SEND theScreen THE MESSAGE insert(", ")
[0229]        ENDMETHOD displayPublicationPart?
[0230]
[0231]        METHOD referenceNumber? ->String
[0232]        AS
[0233]          // Deliver the private property theReferenceNumber
                    to a client.
[0234]
[0235]          RETURN theReferenceNumber
[0236]        ENDMETHOD referenceNumber?
[0237]
[0238]        METHOD lessThan?(aPublication : Publication) -
              >Boolean
[0239]        AS
[0240]          // Compare two Publications by reference number using
                    the operator < for
[0241]          // Strings.
[0242]
[0243]          IF theReferenceNumber < (SEND aPublication THE
              MESSAGE referenceNumber?) THEN
[0244]          RETURN TRUE
[0245]          ELSE
[0246]          RETURN FALSE
[0247]          ENDIF
[0248]        ENDMETHOD lessThan?
[0249]
[0250]        METHOD isOnLoan? ->Boolean
[0251]        AS
[0252]          // Deliver the private property onLoan to a client.
```

```
[0253]
[0254]        RETURN onLoan
[0255]     ENDMETHOD isOnLoan?
[0256]
[0257]     METHOD setOnLoan (aValue : Boolean)
[0258]     AS
[0259]       // Set the private property onLoan to the parameter of
                the operation.
[0260]
[0261]        SEND onLoan THE MESSAGE assign (aValue)
[0262]     ENDMETHOD setOnLoan
[0263]
[0264] ENDCLASS Publication
[0265]
[0266]
[0267] //
[0268] //   CLASS Library
[0269] //
[0270] //   REVISION HISTORY
[0271] //
[0272] //       VERSION NUMBER 1.0
[0273] //
[0274] //       DATE 8 September 1995
[0275] //
[0276] //       AUTHOR K Barclay / J Savage
[0277] //
[0278] //       PURPOSE First release
[0279] //
[0280] //
[0281] //       VERSION NUMBER 1.1
[0282] //
[0283] //       DATE 9 September 1995
[0284] //
[0285] //       AUTHOR K Barclay / J Savage
[0286] //
[0287] //       PURPOSE Support for Users.
[0288] //
[0289] //   DESCRIPTION
[0290] //
[0291] //       An instance of this class acts as the Library object
                that holds
[0292] //       Publications that can be added or displayed. Users
                can borrow
[0293] //       and return Publications from the Library.
[0294] //
[0295] //
[0296] CLASS Library
[0297] WITH
[0298] PUBLIC INTERFACE
[0299]   Library
[0300]   Library (aName : String)
[0301]   addUser (aUser : User LINK)
[0302]   addOnePublication (aPublication : Publication LINK
            INOUT)
[0303]   returnOnePublication (aReferenceNumber : String)
```

```
[0304]    borrowOnePublication?(aReferenceNumber:String)
          ->Publication LINK
[0305]    displayLoanStock?
[0306]    displayBorrowedStock?
[0307]    displayUsers?
[0308]  PROTECTED INTERFACE
[0309]    NONE
[0310]  PRIVATE IMPLEMENTATION
[0311]    REPRESENTATION
[0312]      theName:String
[0313]    AGGREGATIONS
[0314]      thePublications:POrderedCollection[Publication
          LINK]
[0315]    ASSOCIATIONS
[0316]      theBorrowers:POrderedCollection[User LINK]  INVERSE
          OF theLender
[0317]    DEFINITIONS
[0318]      METHOD Library
[0319]      AS
[0320]        //Default container.
[0321]
[0322]        //Set the private property theName to the value of an
              empty String.
[0323]        SEND theName THE MESSAGE initialise("")
[0324]
[0325]        //Set the aggregation components container
              thePublications and the
[0326]        //associates container the Borrowers to sensible
              values.
[0327]        SEND thePublications THE MESSAGE
              initialise(DEFAULTSIZE, MANAGED)
[0328]        SEND theBorrowers THE MESSAGE
              initialise(DEFAULTSIZE, UNMANAGED)
[0329]      ENDMETHOD Library
[0330]
[0331]      METHOD Library(aName:String)
[0332]      AS
[0333]        //Parameterised constructor.
[0334]
[0335]        //Set the private property theName to the value of the
              actual parameter.
[0336]        SEND theName THE MESSAGE initialise(aName)
[0337]
[0338]        //Set the aggregation components container
              thePublications and the
[0339]        //associates container the Borrowers to sensible
              values.
[0340]        SEND thePublications THE MESSAGE
              initialise(DEFAULTSIZE, MANAGED)
[0341]        SEND theBorrowers THE MESSAGE
              initialise(DEFAULTSIZE, UNMANAGED)
[0342]      ENDMETHOD Library
[0343]
[0344]      METHOD addUser(aUser:User LINK)
```

```
[0345]    AS
[0346]      // Add a User to the Library.
[0347]
[0348]      IF aUser != NIL THEN
[0349]        SEND theBorrowers THE MESSAGE add (aUser)
[0350]      ENDIF
[0351]    ENDMETHOD addUser
[0352]
[0353]    METHOD addOnePublication (aPublication : Publication
          LINK INOUT)
[0354]    AS
[0355]      // Add a Publication to the Library.
[0356]
[0357]      IF aPublication != NIL THEN
[0358]        SEND aPublication THE MESSAGE setOnLoan (FALSE)
[0359]        SEND thePublications THE MESSAGE add (aPublication)
[0360]      ENDIF
[0361]    ENDMETHOD addOnePublication
[0362]
[0363]    METHOD returnOnePublication (aReferenceNumber
          : String)
[0364]    AS
[0365]      // Take charge of a Publication returned by a client.
[0366]
[0367]      FOREACH aPublication : Publication LINK IN
          thePublications DO
[0368]        IF (SEND aPublication THE MESSAGE
          referenceNumber?) ==aReferenceNumber THEN
[0369]        SEND aPublication THE MESSAGE setOnLoan (FALSE)
[0370]        RETURN
[0371]        ENDIF
[0372]      ENDFOREACH
[0373]    ENDMETHOD returnOnePublication
[0374]
[0375]    METHOD borrowOnePublication? (aReferenceNumber
          : String) ->Publication LINK
[0376]    AS
[0377]      // Deliver a Publication with a specified reference
            number to a client.
[0378]
[0379]      FOREACH aPublication : Publication LINK IN
          thePublications DO
[0380]        IF (SEND aPublication THE MESSAGE
          referenceNumber?) ==aReferenceNumber
[0381]          AND (SEND aPublication THE MESSAGE isOnLoan?) ==
            FALSE THEN
[0382]        SEND aPublication THE MESSAGE setOnLoan (TRUE)
[0383]        RETURN aPublication
[0384]        ENDIF
[0385]      ENDFOREACH
[0386]
[0387]      RETURN NIL
[0388]    ENDMETHOD borrowOnePublication?
[0389]
```

```
[0390]    METHOD displayLoanStock?
[0391]    AS
[0392]      // Output to the screen details of Publications
                 available for loan.
[0393]
[0394]    SEND theScreen THE MESSAGE insert ("\nCurrent Loan
          Stock:\t")
[0395]    SEND theScreen THE MESSAGE insert (theName)
[0396]    SEND theScreen THE MESSAGE insert ("\n")
[0397]
[0398]    FOREACH aPublication : Publication LINK IN
          thePublications DO
[0399]      IF (SEND aPublication THE MESSAGE isOnLoan?) ==
           FALSE THEN
[0400]        SEND aPublication THE MESSAGE display?
[0401]      ENDIF
[0402]    ENDFOREACH
[0403]    SEND theScreen THE MESSAGE insert ("\n")
[0404]
[0405]      // If required the screen may be held with the
                 following sentences.
[0406]      // INSTANCE theResponse : String ("")
[0407]      // SEND theScreen THE MESSAGE insert ("\n\tType a
                 character to continue > ")
[0408]      // SEND theKeyboard THE MESSAGE extract (theResponse)
[0409]      //
[0410]      // Similarly the screen may be held if these sentences
                 are embedded in the FOREACH
[0411]      // control sentence immediately after the message
                 display?
[0412]    ENDMETHOD displayLoanStock?
[0413]
[0414]    METHOD displayBorrowedStock?
[0415]    AS
[0416]      // Output to the screen details of Publications out on
                 loan.
[0417]
[0418]    SEND theScreen THE MESSAGE insert ("\Borrowed
          Stock:\t")
[0419]    SEND theScreen THE MESSAGE insert (theName)
[0420]    SEND theScreen THE MESSAGE insert ("\n")
[0421]
[0422]    FOREACH aPublication : Publication LINK IN
          thePublications DO
[0423]      IF ( SEND aPublication THE MESSAGE isOnLoan?) ==
           TRUE THEN
[0424]        SEND aPublication THE MESSAGE display?
[0425]      ENDIF
[0426]    ENDFOREACH
[0427]    SEND theScreen THE MESSAGE insert ("\n")
[0428]
[0429]      // If required the screen may be held with the
                 following sentences.
[0430]      // INSTANCE theResponse : String ("")
```

```
[0431]        // SEND theScreen THE MESSAGE insert ("\n\tType a
                  character to continue > ")
[0432]        // SEND theKeyboard THE MESSAGE extract (theResponse)
[0433]        //
[0434]        // Similarly the screen may be held if these sentences
                  are embedded in the FOREACH
[0435]        // control sentence immediately after the message
                  display?
[0436]     ENDMETHOD displayBorrowedStock?
[0437]
[0438]     METHOD displayUsers?
[0439]     AS
[0440]        // Output to the screen details of Users and the
                  Publications they have out
[0441]        // on loan.
[0442]
[0443]     SEND theScreen THE MESSAGE insert ("\nUsers:\n")
[0444]     FOREACH aUser : User LINK IN theBorrowers DO
[0445]       SEND theScreen THE MESSAGE insert (SEND aUser THE
                MESSAGE name?)
[0446]       SEND theScreen THE MESSAGE insert ("\n")
[0447]       SEND aUser THE MESSAGE displayPublications?
[0448]     ENDFOREACH
[0449]     SEND theScreen THE MESSAGE insert ("\n")
[0450]
[0451]        // If required the screen may be held with the
                  following sentences.
[0452]        // INSTANCE theResponse : String ("")
[0453]        // SEND theScreen THE MESSAGE insert ("\n\tType a
                  character to continue > ")
[0454]        // SEND theKeyboard THE MESSAGE extract (theResponse)
[0455]
[0456]      ENDMETHOD displayUsers?
[0457]
[0458] ENDCLASS Library
[0459]
[0460]
[0461] //
[0462] //   CLASS Application
[0463] //
[0464] //   REVISION HISTORY
[0465] //
[0466] //      VERSION NUMBER 1.0
[0467] //
[0468] //      DATE 8 September 1995
[0469] //
[0470] //      AUTHOR K Barclay / J Savage
[0471] //
[0472] //      PURPOSE First release
[0473] //
[0474] //
[0475] //      VERSION NUMBER 2.0
[0476] //
[0477] //      DATE 9 September 1995
```

```
[0478]  //
[0479]  //      AUTHOR K Barclay / J Savage
[0480]  //
[0481]  //      PURPOSE Support for Users of the Library and the use
                of a private
[0482]  //                              operation for initialisation.
[0483]  //
[0484]  //
[0485]  //   DESCRIPTION
[0486]  //
[0487]  //      An instance of this class provides the top-level
                control of the system.
[0488]  //
[0489]  //      One Library and several Users are created with
                dynamic duration as
[0490]  //      they are associates.
[0491]  //
[0492]  //      Publications are created with dynamic duration as
                we intend using
[0493]  //      the polymorphic effect.
[0494]  //
[0495]  CLASS Application
[0496]  WITH
[0497]  PUBLIC INTERFACE
[0498]    Application
[0499]    run
[0500]  PROTECTED INTERFACE
[0501]    NONE
[0502]  PRIVATE IMPLEMENTATION
[0503]    REPRESENTATION
[0504]      initialiseLibrary (aLibrary : Library LINK INOUT)
[0505]    AGGREGATIONS NONE
[0506]    ASSOCIATIONS NONE
[0507]    DEFINITIONS
[0508]      METHOD Application
[0509]      AS
[0510]        // Default constructor.
[0511]
[0512]        // Although there is nothing to do it is good practice
                  to have an explicit
[0513]        // default constructor.
[0514]      ENDMETHOD Application
[0515]
[0516]      METHOD run
[0517]      AS
[0518]        // Top-level control messages.
[0519]
[0520]        // Create a Library with dynamic duration.
[0521]        INSTANCE theLibrary : Library LINK ("Dunning
                Library")
[0522]
[0523]        // Initialise the Library.
[0524]        SEND me THE MESSAGE initialiseLibrary (theLibrary)
[0525]
```

```
[0526]        //Create two Users with dynamic duration.
[0527]        INSTANCE u1 : User LINK ("Ken", "21 High Street")
[0528]        INSTANCE u2 : User LINK ("John", "42 Croft Square")
[0529]
[0530]        //Configure the architecture.
[0531]        SEND theLibrary THE MESSAGE addUser (u1)
[0532]        SEND theLibrary THE MESSAGE addUser (u2)
[0533]        SEND u1 THE MESSAGE addLibrary (theLibrary)
[0534]        SEND u2 THE MESSAGE addLibrary (theLibrary)
[0535]
[0536]        //Display the Users.
[0537]        SEND theLibrary THE MESSAGE displayUsers?
[0538]
[0539]        //Borrow four Publications.
[0540]        SEND theLibrary THE MESSAGE displayLoanStock?
[0541]        SEND u1 THE MESSAGE borrowOnePublication ("AA1")
[0542]        SEND u1 THE MESSAGE borrowOnePublication ("BB2")
[0543]        SEND u2 THE MESSAGE borrowOnePublication ("CC3")
[0544]        SEND u2 THE MESSAGE borrowOnePublication ("EE5")
[0545]
[0546]        //Display the results.
[0547]        SEND theLibrary THE MESSAGE displayLoanStock?
[0548]        SEND theLibrary THE MESSAGE displayBorrowedStock?
[0549]        SEND theLibrary THE MESSAGE displayUsers?
[0550]
[0551]        //Return two Publications.
[0552]        SEND u1 THE MESSAGE returnOnePublication
[0553]        SEND u2 THE MESSAGE returnOnePublication
[0554]
[0555]        //Display the results
[0556]        SEND theLibrary THE MESSAGE displayLoanStock?
[0557]        SEND theLibrary THE MESSAGE displayBorrowedStock?
[0558]        SEND theLibrary THE MESSAGE displayUsers?
[0559]    ENDMETHOD run
[0560]
[0561]    METHOD initialiseLibrary (aLibrary : Library LINK
           INOUT)
[0562]    AS
[0563]        //Private operation to help initialise the system.
[0564]
[0565]        //Create three Book and one Map object with dynamic
               duration.
[0566]        INSTANCE b1 : Book LINK ("C++ Problem Solving and
           Programming",
[0567]                              "Prentice Hall", Date (1, 1, 1994),
                                        "AA1", "Barclay", 1)
[0568]        INSTANCE b2 : Book LINK ("Object Oriented Modelling
           and Design",
[0569]                              "Prentice Hall", Date (2, 2, 1994),
                                    "BB2", "Rumbaugh et al.", 2)
[0570]        INSTANCE b3 : Book LINK ("Object Oriented Design",
[0571]                                    "Benjamin Cummings",
                              Date (3, 3, 1994), "CC3", "Booch", 1)
```

```
[0572]         INSTANCE b4 : Book LINK("Object Oriented System
               Design",
[0573]                         "Prentice Hall", Date(4,4,1994),
                                           "DD4", "Yourdon", 1)
[0574]
[0575]         INSTANCE m1 : Map LINK("Burgundy", "Michelin",
[0576]                    Date(5,5,1994), "EE5", "Michelin", 5)
[0577]
[0578]         // Add LINKs to Books and Maps to the Library.
[0579]         SEND aLibrary THE MESSAGE addOnePublication(b1)
[0580]         SEND aLibrary THE MESSAGE addOnePublication(b2)
[0581]         SEND aLibrary THE MESSAGE addOnePublication(b3)
[0582]         SEND aLibrary THE MESSAGE addOnePublication(b4)
[0583]         SEND aLibrary THE MESSAGE addOnePublication(m1)
[0584]
[0585]      ENDMETHOD initialiseLibrary
[0586]
[0587]   ENDCLASS Application
[0588]
[0589]
[0590]   //
[0591]   //   CLASS Book
[0592]   //
[0593]   //   REVISION HISTORY
[0594]   //
[0595]   //      VERSION NUMBER 1.0
[0596]   //
[0597]   //      DATE 8 September 1995
[0598]   //
[0599]   //      AUTHOR K Barclay / J Savage
[0600]   //
[0601]   //      PURPOSE First release
[0602]   //
[0603]   //   DESCRIPTION
[0604]   //
[0605]   //      An instance of this class acts a Book that is held by
               a Library and
[0606]   //      Users.
[0607]   //
[0608]   CLASS Book
[0609]     SPECIALISATION OF Publication
[0610]   WITH
[0611]   PUBLIC INTERFACE
[0612]     Book
[0613]     Book(aTitle : String, aPublisher : String, aDate : Date,
               aReferenceNumber : String, anAuthor : String, anEdition
               : Integer)
[0614]     display?                                    REDEFINED
[0615]   PROTECTED INTERFACE
[0616]     NONE
[0617]   PRIVATE IMPLEMENTATION
[0618]     REPRESENTATION
[0619]       theAuthor : String
[0620]       theEdition : Integer
```

```
[0621]    AGGREGATIONS NONE
[0622]    ASSOCIATIONS NONE
[0623]    DEFINITIONS
[0624]      METHOD Book
[0625]      AS
[0626]        // Default constructor.
[0627]
[0628]        // Initialise the Publication representation
                   entries.
[0629]        SEND SUPERCLASS Publication THE MESSAGE initialise
[0630]
[0631]        // Set the unique Book representation entries to
                   sensible values.
[0632]        SEND theAuthor THE MESSAGE initialise("")
[0633]        SEND theEdition THE MESSAGE initialise(1)
[0634]      ENDMETHOD Book
[0635]
[0636]      METHOD Book(aTitle : String, aPublisher : String, aDate
                 : Date, aReferenceNumber : String, anAuthor : String,
                 anEdition : Integer)
[0637]      AS
[0638]        // Parameterised constructor.
[0639]
[0640]        // Initialise the Publication representation
                   entries to the corresponding
[0641]        // parameters of the constructor.
[0642]        SEND SUPERCLASS Publication THE MESSAGE
                 initialise(aTitle, aPublisher,
[0643]                                    aDate, aReferenceNumber)
[0644]
[0645]        // Set the unique Book representation entries to the
                   corresponding
[0646]        // parameters of the constructor.
[0647]        SEND theAuthor THE MESSAGE initialise(anAuthor)
[0648]        SEND theEdition THE MESSAGE initialise(anEdition)
[0649]      ENDMETHOD Book
[0650]
[0651]      METHOD display?
[0652]      AS
[0653]        // Output to the screen relevant details for a Book.
[0654]
[0655]        SEND theScreen THE MESSAGE insert("Book[")
[0656]        SEND me THE MESSAGE displayPublicationPart?
[0657]        SEND theScreen THE MESSAGE insert(theAuthor)
[0658]        SEND theScreen THE MESSAGE insert(", ")
[0659]        SEND theScreen THE MESSAGE insert(theEdition)
[0660]        SEND theScreen THE MESSAGE insert("]\n")
[0661]      ENDMETHOD display?
[0662]
[0663] ENDCLASS Book
[0664]
[0665]
[0666] //
[0667] //   CLASS Map
```

```
[0668]  //
[0669]  //   REVISION HISTORY
[0670]  //
[0671]  //      VERSION NUMBER 1.0
[0672]  //
[0673]  //      DATE 8 September 1995
[0674]  //
[0675]  //      AUTHOR K Barclay / J Savage
[0676]  //
[0677]  //      PURPOSE First release
[0678]  //
[0679]  //   DESCRIPTION
[0680]  //
[0681]  //      An instance of this class acts a Map that is held by
                a Library and
[0682]  //      Users.
[0683]  //
[0684]  CLASS Map
[0685]    SPECIALISATION OF Publication
[0686]  WITH
[0687]  PUBLIC INTERFACE
[0688]    Map
[0689]    Map(aTitle : String, aPublisher : String, aDate : Date,
            aReferenceNumber : String, aSeriesName : String,
            aSheetNumber : Integer)
[0690]    display?                                    REDEFINED
[0691]  PROTECTED INTERFACE
[0692]    NONE
[0693]  PRIVATE IMPLEMENTATION
[0694]    REPRESENTATION
[0695]      theSeriesName : String
[0696]      theSheetNumber : Integer
[0697]  AGGREGATIONS NONE
[0698]  ASSOCIATIONS NONE
[0699]  DEFINITIONS
[0700]    METHOD Map
[0701]    AS
[0702]      // Default constructor.
[0703]
[0704]      // Initialise Publication representation entries.
[0705]      SEND SUPERCLASS Publication THE MESSAGE initialise
[0706]
[0707]      // Set the unique Map representation entries to
              sensible values.
[0708]      SEND theSeriesName THE MESSAGE initialise("")
[0709]      SEND theSheetNumber THE MESSAGE initialise(0)
[0710]    ENDMETHOD Map
[0711]
[0712]    METHOD Map(aTitle : String, aPublisher : String, aDate
            : Date, aReferenceNumber : String, aSeriesName
            : String, aSheetNumber : Integer)
[0713]    AS
[0714]      // Parameterised constructor.
[0715]
```

```
[0716]        // Initialise the Publication representation
                 entries to corresponding
[0717]        // parameters of the constructor.
[0718]        SEND SUPERCLASS Publication THE MESSAGE
                 initialise(aTitle, aPublisher, aDate,
[0719]        aReferenceNumber)
[0720]
[0721]        // Set the unique Map representation entries to
                 corresponding
[0722]        // parameters of the constructor.
[0723]        SEND theSeriesName THE MESSAGE
                 initialise(aSeriesName)
[0724]        SEND theSheetNumber THE MESSAGE
                 initialise(aSheetNumber)
[0725]    ENDMETHOD Map
[0726]
[0727]    METHOD display?
[0728]    AS
[0729]      // Output to the screen relevant details of a Map.
[0730]
[0731]      SEND theScreen THE MESSAGE insert("Map[")
[0732]      SEND me THE MESSAGE displayPublicationPart?
[0733]      SEND theScreen THE MESSAGE insert(theSeriesName)
[0734]      SEND theScreen THE MESSAGE insert(", ")
[0735]      SEND theScreen THE MESSAGE insert(theSheetNumber)
[0736]      SEND theScreen THE MESSAGE insert("]\n")
[0737]    ENDMETHOD display?
[0738]
[0739] ENDCLASS Map
[0740]
[0741]
[0742]
```

E.5 Chapter 8, version 3 of the Library system

```
[0001] //.
[0002] //.
[0003] //.  ROME Copyright (c) Richard McMahon. 1993, 1994.
[0004] //.  Generated On January 6, 1996 At 3:33:27.03 pm
[0005]
[0006]
[0007]
[0008] //. -- Class Definitions: -----------------
[0009]
[0010] //
[0011] // CLASS User
[0012] //
[0013] // REVISION HISTORY
[0014] //
[0015] //      VERSION NUMBER 1.0
[0016] //
```

```
[0017]  //      DATE 8 September 1995
[0018]  //
[0019]  //      AUTHOR K Barclay / J Savage
[0020]  //
[0021]  //      PURPOSE First release
[0022]  //
[0023]  //
[0024]  //  DESCRIPTION
[0025]  //
[0026]  //      An instance of this class acts as a User that can
                borrow and return
[0027]  //      Publications from/to a Library. A User can also
                display Publications out
[0028]  //      on loan.
[0029]  //
[0030]  CLASS User
[0031]  WITH
[0032]  PUBLIC INTERFACE
[0033]    User
[0034]    User (aName : String, anAddress : String)
[0035]    addLibrary (aLibrary : Library LINK)
[0036]    borrowOnePublication (aReferenceNumber : String)
[0037]    returnOnePublication
[0038]    name? ->String?
[0039]    lessThan? (aUser : User) ->Boolean
[0040]    displayPublications?
[0041]  PROTECTED INTERFACE
[0042]    NONE
[0043]  PRIVATE IMPLEMENTATION
[0044]    REPRESENTATION
[0045]      theName : String
[0046]      theAddress : String
[0047]    AGGREGATIONS
[0048]      thePublications : POrderedCollection [Publication
            LINK]
[0049]    ASSOCIATIONS
[0050]      theLender : Library LINK INVERSE OF theBorrowers
[0051]    DEFINITIONS
[0052]      METHOD User
[0053]      AS
[0054]        // Default constructor
[0055]
[0056]        // Set the representation entries to sensible values.
[0057]      SEND theName THE MESSAGE initialise ("")
[0058]      SEND theAddress THE MESSAGE initialise ("")
[0059]
[0060]        // Set the associate theLender and the aggregate
                components container
[0061]        // thePublications to sensible values.
[0062]      SEND theLender THE MESSAGE initialise (NIL)
[0063]      SEND thePublications THE MESSAGE
            initialise (DEFAULTSIZE, UNMANAGED)
[0064]      ENDMETHOD User
[0065]
```

```
[0066]    METHOD User (aName : String, anAddress : String)
[0067]    AS
[0068]      // Parameterised constructor.
[0069]
[0070]      // Set the representation entries to the
                corresponding parameters of
[0071]      // the constructor.
[0072]      SEND theName THE MESSAGE initialise (aName)
[0073]      SEND theAddress THE MESSAGE initialise (anAddress)
[0074]
[0075]      // Set the associate, theLender and the aggregate
                components container
[0076]      // thePublications to sensible values.
[0077]      SEND theLender THE MESSAGE initialise (NIL)
[0078]      SEND thePublications THE MESSAGE
                initialise (DEFAULTSIZE, UNMANAGED)
[0079]    ENDMETHOD User
[0080]
[0081]    METHOD addLibrary (aLibrary : Library LINK)
[0082]    AS
[0083]      // Establish a LINK with a Library.
[0084]
[0085]      SEND theLender THE MESSAGE assign (aLibrary)
[0086]    ENDMETHOD addLibrary
[0087]
[0088]    METHOD borrowOnePublication (aReferenceNumber
          : String)
[0089]    AS
[0090]      // Borrow a Publication with a specified reference
                number from the Library.
[0091]
[0092]      INSTANCE thePublication : Publication LINK
[0093]        (SEND theLender THE MESSAGE
                          borrowOnePublication? (aReference
                                                    Number))
[0094]
[0095]      IF thePublication != NIL THEN
[0096]        SEND thePublications THE MESSAGE
                addFirst (thePublication)
[0097]      ENDIF
[0098]    ENDMETHOD borrowOnePublication
[0099]
[0100]    METHOD returnOnePublication
[0101]    AS
[0102]      // Return a Publication to the Library.
[0103]
[0104]      INSTANCE thePublication : Publication LINK
[0105]              (SEND thePublications THE MESSAGE first?)
[0106]      SEND theLender THE MESSAGE returnOnePublication
[0107]                        (SEND thePublication THE MESSAGE
                                        referenceNumber?)
[0108]      SEND thePublications THE MESSAGE removeLast
[0109]    ENDMETHOD returnOnePublication
[0110]
```

```
[0111]    METHOD name? ->String
[0112]    AS
[0113]      // Deliver the private property theName to a client.
[0114]
[0115]      RETURN theName
[0116]    ENDMETHOD name?
[0117]
[0118]    METHOD lessThan? (aUser :User) ->Boolean
[0119]    AS
[0120]      // Compare two Users by name using the operator < for
               Strings.
[0121]
[0122]      IF (SEND aUser THE MESSAGE name?) < theName THEN
[0123]        RETURN TRUE
[0124]      ELSE
[0125]        RETURN FALSE
[0126]      ENDIF
[0127]    ENDMETHOD lessThan?
[0128]
[0129]    METHOD displayPublications?
[0130]    AS
[0131]      // Output to the screen details of Publications out on
               loan together with the
[0132]      // User's name.
[0133]
[0134]      SEND theScreen THE MESSAGE insert ("\nPublications
             borrowed by ")
[0135]      SEND theScreen THE MESSAGE insert (theName)
[0136]      SEND theScreen THE MESSAGE insert ("\n")
[0137]
[0138]      IF (SEND thePublications THE MESSAGE isEmpty?) ==
           FALSE THEN
[0139]        FOREACH aPublication :Publication LINK IN
             thePublications DO
[0140]          SEND aPublication THE MESSAGE display?
[0141]        ENDFOREACH
[0142]      ELSE
[0143]        SEND theScreen THE MESSAGE insert ("\tNo
             publications on loan. \n")
[0144]      ENDIF
[0145]
[0146]      // If required the screen may be held with the
               following sentences.
[0147]      // INSTANCE theResponse :String ("")
[0148]      // SEND theScreen THE MESSAGE insert ("\n\tType a
               character to continue > ")
[0149]      // SEND theKeyboard THE MESSAGE extract (theResponse)
[0150]      //
[0151]      // Similarly the screen may be held if these sentences
               are embedded in the FOREACH
[0152]      // control sentence immediately after the message
               display?
[0153]    ENDMETHOD displayPublications?
[0154]
```

```
[0155]  ENDCLASS User
[0156]
[0157]
[0158]  //
[0159]  //  CLASS Publication
[0160]  //
[0161]  //  REVISION HISTORY
[0162]  //
[0163]  //     VERSION NUMBER 1.0
[0164]  //
[0165]  //     DATE 8 September 1995
[0166]  //
[0167]  //     AUTHOR K Barclay / J Savage
[0168]  //
[0169]  //     PURPOSE First release.
[0170]  //
[0171]  //  DESCRIPTION
[0172]  //
[0173]  //     This class acts as a basis for the construction of
                all other Publications.
[0174]  //     As such it guarantees a common interface.
[0175]  //
[0176]  ABSTRACT CLASS Publication
[0177]  WITH
[0178]  PUBLIC INTERFACE
[0179]    Publication
[0180]    Publication(aTitle : String, aPublisher : String,
                aPublicationDate : Date, aReferenceNumber : String)
[0181]    display?                                  DEFERRED
[0182]    referenceNumber? ->String
[0183]    lessThan?(aPublication : Publication) ->Boolean
[0184]    isOnLoan? ->Boolean
[0185]    setOnLoan(aValue : Boolean)
[0186]  PROTECTED INTERFACE
[0187]    displayPublicationPart?
[0188]  PRIVATE IMPLEMENTATION
[0189]    REPRESENTATION
[0190]      theTitle : String
[0191]      thePublisher : String
[0192]      thePublicationDate : Date
[0193]      theReferenceNumber : String
[0194]      onLoan : Boolean
[0195]    AGGREGATIONS NONE
[0196]    ASSOCIATIONS NONE
[0197]    DEFINITIONS
[0198]      METHOD Publication
[0199]      AS
[0200]        // Default constructor
[0201]
[0202]        // Set the representation entries to sensible values.
[0203]        SEND theTitle THE MESSAGE initialise("")
[0204]        SEND thePublisher THE MESSAGE initialise("")
[0205]        SEND thePublicationDate THE MESSAGE initialise(Date
                (1,1,1900))
```

```
[0206]        SEND theReferenceNumber THE MESSAGE
              initialise("000")
[0207]        SEND onLoan THE MESSAGE initialise(FALSE)
[0208]     ENDMETHOD Publication
[0209]
[0210]     METHOD Publication(aTitle :String, aPublisher
           :String, aPublicationDate :Date, aReferenceNumber
           :String)
[0211]     AS
[0212]       //Parameterised constructor.
[0213]
[0214]       //Set the representation entries to the
                 corresponding parameters of the
[0215]       //constructor.
[0216]       SEND theTitle THE MESSAGE initialise(aTitle)
[0217]       SEND thePublisher THE MESSAGE
              initialise(aPublisher)
[0218]       SEND thePublicationDate THE MESSAGE
              initialise(aPublicationDate)
[0219]       SEND theReferenceNumber THE MESSAGE
              initialise(aReferenceNumber)
[0220]       SEND onLoan THE MESSAGE initialise(FALSE)
[0221]     ENDMETHOD Publication
[0222]
[0223]     METHOD displayPublicationPart?
[0224]     AS
[0225]       //Output to the screen relevent details of the
                 Publication.
[0226]
[0227]       SEND theScreen THE MESSAGE insert(theTitle)
[0228]       SEND theScreen THE MESSAGE insert(", ")
[0229]       SEND theScreen THE MESSAGE
              insert(theReferenceNumber)
[0230]       SEND theScreen THE MESSAGE insert(", ")
[0231]     ENDMETHOD displayPublicationPart?
[0232]
[0233]     METHOD referenceNumber? ->String
[0234]     AS
[0235]       //Deliver the private property theReferenceNumber
                 to a client.
[0236]
[0237]       RETURN theReferenceNumber
[0238]     ENDMETHOD referenceNumber?
[0239]
[0240]     METHOD lessThan?(aPublication :Publication) -
           >Boolean
[0241]     AS
[0242]       //Compare two Publications by reference number using
                 the operator < for
[0243]       //Strings.
[0244]
[0245]       IF theReferenceNumber < (SEND aPublication THE
           MESSAGE referenceNumber?) THEN
[0246]         RETURN TRUE
```

```
[0247]        ELSE
[0248]          RETURN FALSE
[0249]        ENDIF
[0250]      ENDMETHOD lessThan?
[0251]
[0252]      METHOD isOnLoan? ->Boolean
[0253]      AS
[0254]        // Deliver the private property onLoan to a client.
[0255]
[0256]        RETURN onLoan
[0257]      ENDMETHOD isOnLoan?
[0258]
[0259]      METHOD setOnLoan(aValue : Boolean)
[0260]      AS
[0261]        // Set the private property onLoan to the parameter of
                 the operation.
[0262]
[0263]        SEND onLoan THE MESSAGE assign(aValue)
[0264]      ENDMETHOD setOnLoan
[0265]
[0266] ENDCLASS Publication
[0267]
[0268]
[0269] //
[0270] //   CLASS Article
[0271] //
[0272] //   REVISION HISTORY
[0273] //
[0274] //       VERSION NUMBER 1.0
[0275] //
[0276] //       DATE 8 September 1995
[0277] //
[0278] //       AUTHOR K Barclay / J Savage
[0279] //
[0280] //       PURPOSE First release.
[0281] //
[0282] //   DESCRIPTION
[0283] //
[0284] //       An instance of this class acts an Article that is
                 part of a Periodical.
[0285] //
[0286] CLASS Article
[0287] WITH
[0288] PUBLIC INTERFACE
[0289]    Article
[0290]    Article(aTitle : String, anAuthor : String)
[0291]    title? ->String
[0292]    lessThan(anArticle : Article) ->Boolean
[0293]    display?
[0294] PROTECTED INTERFACE
[0295]    NONE
[0296] PRIVATE IMPLEMENTATION
[0297]    REPRESENTATION
[0298]      theTitle : String
```

```
[0299]      theAuthor : String
[0300]   AGGREGATIONS NONE
[0301]   ASSOCIATIONS NONE
[0302]   DEFINITIONS
[0303]    METHOD Article
[0304]    AS
[0305]      // Default constructor.
[0306]
[0307]
[0308]      // Set the representation entries to sensible values.
[0309]      SEND theTitle THE MESSAGE initialise("")
[0310]      SEND theAuthor THE MESSAGE initialise("")
[0311]    ENDMETHOD Article
[0312]
[0313]    METHOD Article(aTitle : String, anAuthor : String)
[0314]    AS
[0315]      // Parameterised constructor.
[0316]
[0317]      // Set the representation entries to the
                 corresponding parameters of the
[0318]      // constructor.
[0319]      SEND theTitle THE MESSAGE initialise(aTitle)
[0320]      SEND theAuthor THE MESSAGE initialise(anAuthor)
[0321]    ENDMETHOD Article
[0322]
[0323]    METHOD title? ->String
[0324]    AS
[0325]      // Deliver the private property theTitle to a client.
[0326]
[0327]      RETURN theTitle
[0328]    ENDMETHOD title?
[0329]
[0330]    METHOD lessThan(anArticle : Article) - >Boolean
[0331]    AS
[0332]      // Compare two Articles by title using the operator <
                 for Strings.
[0333]
[0334]      IF theTitle < (SEND anArticle THE MESSAGE title?) THEN
[0335]        RETURN TRUE
[0336]      ELSE
[0337]        RETURN FALSE
[0338]      ENDIF
[0339]    ENDMETHOD lessThan
[0340]
[0341]    METHOD display?
[0342]    AS
[0343]      // Output the relevant Article details to the screen.
[0344]
[0345]      SEND theScreen THE MESSAGE insert("\n ")
[0346]      SEND theScreen THE MESSAGE insert(theTitle)
[0347]      SEND theScreen THE MESSAGE insert(", ")
[0348]      SEND theScreen THE MESSAGE insert(theAuthor)
[0349]
[0350]    ENDMETHOD display?
```

```
[0351]
[0352]  ENDCLASS Article
[0353]
[0354]
[0355]  //
[0356]  //  CLASS Library
[0357]  //
[0358]  //  REVISION HISTORY
[0359]  //
[0360]  //      CLASS Library
[0361]  //
[0362]  //  REVISION HISTORY
[0363]  //
[0364]  //      VERSION NUMBER 1.0
[0365]  //
[0366]  //      DATE 8 September 1995
[0367]  //
[0368]  //      AUTHOR K Barclay / J Savage
[0369]  //
[0370]  //      PURPOSE First release.
[0371]  //
[0372]  //
[0373]  //      VERSION NUMBER 1.1
[0374]  //
[0375]  //      DATE 9 September 1995
[0376]  //
[0377]  //      AUTHOR K Barclay / J Savage
[0378]  //
[0379]  //      PURPOSE Support for Users.
[0380]  //
[0381]  //  DESCRIPTION
[0382]  //
[0383]  //      An instance of this class acts as the Library object
               that holds
[0384]  //      Publications that can be added or displayed. Users
               can borrow
[0385]  //      and return Publications from/to the Library.
[0386]  //
[0387]  CLASS Library
[0388]  WITH
[0389]  PUBLIC INTERFACE
[0390]    Library
[0391]    Library(aName : String)
[0392]    addUser(aUser : User LINK)
[0393]    addOnePublication(aPublication : Publication LINK
          INOUT)
[0394]    returnOnePublication(aReferenceNumber : String)
[0395]    borrowOnePublication?(aReferenceNumber : String)
          ->Publication LINK
[0396]    displayLoanStock?
[0397]    displayBorrowedStock?
[0398]    displayUsers?
[0399]  PROTECTED INTERFACE
[0400]    NONE
[0401]  PRIVATE IMPLEMENTATION
```

```
[0402]    REPRESENTATION
[0403]      theName : String
[0404]    AGGREGATIONS
[0405]      thePublications : POrderedCollection[Publication
          LINK]
[0406]    ASSOCIATIONS
[0407]      theBorrowers : PSortedCollection[User LINK]  INVERSE
          OF theLender
[0408]    DEFINITIONS
[0409]      METHOD Library
[0410]      AS
[0411]        // Default container.
[0412]
[0413]        // Set the private property theName to the value of an
              empty String.
[0414]        SEND theName THE MESSAGE initialise("")
[0415]
[0416]        // Set the aggregation components container
              thePublications and the
[0417]        // associates container theBorrowers to sensible
              values.
[0418]        SEND thePublications THE MESSAGE
          initialise(DEFAULTSIZE, MANAGED)
[0419]        SEND theBorrowers THE MESSAGE
          initialise(DEFAULTSIZE, UNMANAGED)
[0420]      ENDMETHOD Library
[0421]
[0422]      METHOD Library(aName : String)
[0423]      AS
[0424]        // Parameterised constructor.
[0425]
[0426]        // Set the private property theName to the value of the
              actual parameter.
[0427]        SEND theName THE MESSAGE initialise(aName)
[0428]
[0429]        // Set the aggregation components container
              thePublications and the
[0430]        // associates container theBorrowers to sensible
              values.
[0431]        SEND thePublications THE MESSAGE
          initialise(DEFAULTSIZE, MANAGED)
[0432]        SEND theBorrowers THE MESSAGE
          initialise(DEFAULTSIZE, UNMANAGED)
[0433]      ENDMETHOD Library
[0434]
[0435]      METHOD addUser(aUser : User LINK)
[0436]      AS
[0437]        // Add a User to the Library.
[0438]
[0439]        IF aUser != NIL THEN
[0440]          SEND theBorrowers THE MESSAGE add(aUser)
[0441]        ENDIF
[0442]      ENDMETHOD addUser
[0443]
```

```
[0444]    METHOD addOnePublication(aPublication :Publication
          LINK INOUT)
[0445]    AS
[0446]      // Add a Publication to the Library.
[0447]
[0448]      IF aPublication != NIL THEN
[0449]        SEND aPublication THE MESSAGE setOnLoan(FALSE)
[0450]        SEND thePublications THE MESSAGE add(aPublication)
[0451]      ENDIF
[0452]    ENDMETHOD addOnePublication
[0453]
[0454]    METHOD returnOnePublication(aReferenceNumber
          :String)
[0455]    AS
[0456]      // Return a Publication with a specified reference
             number to the Library.
[0457]
[0458]      FOREACH aPublication :Publication LINK IN
          thePublications DO
[0459]        IF (SEND aPublication THE MESSAGE
             referenceNumber?) ==aReferenceNumber THEN
[0460]        SEND aPublication THE MESSAGE setOnLoan(FALSE)
[0461]        RETURN
[0462]        ENDIF
[0463]      ENDFOREACH
[0464]    ENDMETHOD returnOnePublication
[0465]
[0466]    METHOD borrowOnePublication?(aReferenceNumber
          :String) ->Publication LINK
[0467]    AS
[0468]      // Deliver a Publication with a specified reference
             number to a client.
[0469]
[0470]      FOREACH aPublication :Publication LINK IN
          thePublications DO
[0471]        IF (SEND aPublication THE MESSAGE
             referenceNumber?) ==aReferenceNumber AND (SEND
             aPublication THE MESSAGE isOnLoan?) ==FALSE THEN
[0472]        SEND aPublication THE MESSAGE setOnLoan(TRUE)
[0473]        RETURN aPublication
[0474]        ENDIF
[0475]      ENDFOREACH
[0476]
[0477]      RETURN NIL
[0478]    ENDMETHOD borrowOnePublication?
[0479]
[0480]    METHOD displayLoanStock?
[0481]    AS
[0482]      // Output to the screen details of Publications
             available for loan.
[0483]
[0484]      SEND theScreen THE MESSAGE insert("\nLoan
          Stock:\n")
```

```
[0485]      FOREACH aPublication :Publication LINK IN
            thePublications DO
[0486]       IF (SEND aPublication THE MESSAGE isOnLoan?) ==
             FALSE THEN
[0487]        SEND aPublication THE MESSAGE display?
[0488]       ENDIF
[0489]      ENDFOREACH
[0490]      SEND theScreen THE MESSAGE insert ("\n")
[0491]
[0492]      // If required the screen may be held with the
                following sentences.
[0493]      // INSTANCE theResponse :String("")
[0494]      // SEND theScreen THE MESSAGE insert ("\n\tType a
                character to continue > ")
[0495]      // SEND theKeyboard THE MESSAGE extract (theResponse)
[0496]      //
[0497]      // Similarly the screen may be held if these sentences
                are embedded in the FOREACH
[0498]      // control sentence immediately after the message
                display?
[0499]      ENDMETHOD displayLoanStock?
[0500]
[0501]      METHOD displayBorrowedStock?
[0502]      AS
[0503]       // Output to the screen details of Publications out on
                loan.
[0504]
[0505]      SEND theScreen THE MESSAGE insert ("\nBorrowed
            Stock:\n")
[0506]      FOREACH aPublication :Publication LINK IN
            thePublications DO
[0507]       IF (SEND aPublication THE MESSAGE isOnLoan?) ==TRUE
             THEN
[0508]        SEND aPublication THE MESSAGE display?
[0509]       ENDIF
[0510]      ENDFOREACH
[0511]      SEND theScreen THE MESSAGE insert ("\n")
[0512]
[0513]      // If required the screen may be held with the
                following sentences.
[0514]      // INSTANCE theResponse :String("")
[0515]      // SEND theScreen THE MESSAGE insert ("\n\tType a
                character to continue > ")
[0516]      // SEND theKeyboard THE MESSAGE extract (theResponse)
[0517]      //
[0518]      // Similarly the screen may be held if these sentences
                are embedded in the FOREACH
[0519]      // control sentence immediately after the message
                display?
[0520]      ENDMETHOD displayBorrowedStock?
[0521]
[0522]      METHOD displayUsers?
[0523]      AS
[0524]       // Output to the screen details of Users and the
```

```
[0525]          // Publications they have out loan.
[0526]
[0527]          SEND theScreen THE MESSAGE insert ("\nUsers:\n")
[0528]          FOREACH aUser :User LINK IN theBorrowers DO
[0529]            SEND theScreen THE MESSAGE insert (SEND aUser THE
                  MESSAGE name?)
[0530]            SEND theScreen THE MESSAGE insert ("\n")
[0531]            SEND aUser THE MESSAGE displayPublications?
[0532]          ENDFOREACH
[0533]          SEND theScreen THE MESSAGE insert ("\n")
[0534]
[0535]          // If required the screen may be held with the
                  following sentences.
[0536]          // INSTANCE theResponse :String("")
[0537]          // SEND theScreen THE MESSAGE insert ("\n\tType a
                  character to continue > ")
[0538]          // SEND theKeyboard THE MESSAGE extract (theResponse)
[0539]        ENDMETHOD displayUsers?
[0540]
[0541] ENDCLASS Library
[0542]
[0543]
[0544] //
[0545] //   CLASS Application
[0546] //
[0547] //   REVISION HISTORY
[0548] //
[0549] //       VERSION NUMBER 1.0
[0550] //
[0551] //       DATE 8 September 1995
[0552] //
[0553] //       AUTHOR K Barclay / J savage
[0554] //
[0555] //       PURPOSE First release.
[0556] //
[0557] //
[0558] //       VERSION NUMBER 2.0
[0559] //
[0560] //       DATE 9 September 1995
[0561] //
[0562] //       AUTHOR K Barclay / J Savage
[0563] //
[0564] //       PURPOSE Support for Users of the Library.
[0565] //
[0566] //
[0567] //       VERSION NUMBER 3.0
[0568] //
[0569] //       DATE 10 September 1995
[0570] //
[0571] //       AUTHOR J Savage / K Barclay
[0572] //
[0573] //       PURPOSE Addition of Periodicals.
[0574] //
[0575] //
```

```
[0576]  //   DESCRIPTION
[0577]  //
[0578]  //       An instance of this class provides the top-level
                 control of the system.
[0579]  //
[0580]  //       One Library and several Users are created with
                 dynamic duration as
[0581]  //       they are associates.
[0582]  //
[0583]  //       Publications are created with dynamic duration as
                 we intend using
[0584]  //       the polymorphic effect.
[0585]  //
[0586]  CLASS Application
[0587]  WITH
[0588]  PUBLIC INTERFACE
[0589]   Application
[0590]   run
[0591]  PROTECTED INTERFACE
[0592]    NONE
[0593]  PRIVATE IMPLEMENTATION
[0594]    REPRESENTATION
[0595]     initialiseLibrary(aLibrary :Library LINK INOUT)
[0596]   AGGREGATIONS NONE
[0597]   ASSOCIATIONS NONE
[0598]    DEFINITIONS
[0599]    METHOD Application
[0600]    AS
[0601]     //Default constructor.
[0602]
[0603]     //Although there is nothing to do it is good practice
              to have an explicit
[0604]     //default constructor. The alternative is to assume
              that the implementation
[0605]     //language will supply one.
[0606]    ENDMETHOD Application
[0607]
[0608]    METHOD run
[0609]    AS
[0610]     //Top-level control messages.
[0611]
[0612]     //Create a Library with dynamic duration.
[0613]     INSTANCE theLibrary :Library LINK ("Dunning
              Library")
[0614]
[0615]     //Initialise the Library.
[0616]     SEND me THE MESSAGE initialiseLibrary(theLibrary)
[0617]
[0618]     //Create two Users with dynamic duration.
[0619]     INSTANCE u1 :User LINK ("Ken", "21 High Street")
[0620]     INSTANCE u2 :User LINK ("John", "42 Croft Square")
[0621]
[0622]     //Configure the architecture.
[0623]     SEND theLibrary THE MESSAGE addUser(u1)
```

```
[0624]        SEND theLibrary THE MESSAGE addUser (u2)
[0625]        SEND u1 THE MESSAGE addLibrary (theLibrary)
[0626]        SEND u2 THE MESSAGE addLibrary (theLibrary)
[0627]
[0628]        // Display the Users.
[0629]        SEND theLibrary THE MESSAGE displayUsers?
[0630]
[0631]        // Borrow five Publications.
[0632]        SEND theLibrary THE MESSAGE displayLoanStock?
[0633]        SEND u1 THE MESSAGE borrowOnePublication ("AA1")
[0634]        SEND u1 THE MESSAGE borrowOnePublication ("BB2")
[0635]        SEND u2 THE MESSAGE borrowOnePublication ("CC3")
[0636]        SEND u2 THE MESSAGE borrowOnePublication ("EE5")
[0637]        SEND u1 THE MESSAGE borrowOnePublication ("GG7")
[0638]
[0639]        // Display the results
[0640]        SEND theLibrary THE MESSAGE displayLoanStock?
[0641]        SEND theLibrary THE MESSAGE displayBorrowedStock?
[0642]        SEND theLibrary THE MESSAGE displayUsers?
[0643]
[0644]        // Return two Publications.
[0645]        SEND u1 THE MESSAGE returnOnePublication
[0646]        SEND u2 THE MESSAGE returnOnePublication
[0647]
[0648]        // Display the results
[0649]        SEND theLibrary THE MESSAGE displayLoanStock?
[0650]        SEND theLibrary THE MESSAGE displayBorrowedStock?
[0651]        SEND theLibrary THE MESSAGE displayUsers?
[0652]    ENDMETHOD run
[0653]
[0654]    METHOD initialiseLibrary (aLibrary : Library LINK
          INOUT)
[0655]    AS
[0656]      // Private operation to help initialise the Library.
[0657]
[0658]        // Create four Book and one Map objects with dynamic
              duration.
[0659]        INSTANCE b1 : Book LINK ("C++ Problem Solving and
              Programming",
[0660]                            "Prentice Hall", Date (1, 1, 1994),
                                            "AA1", "Barclay", 1)
[0661]        INSTANCE b2 : Book LINK ("Object Oriented Modelling
              and Design",
[0662]                            "Prentice Hall", Date (2, 2, 1994),
                                       "BB2", "Rumbaugh et al.", 2)
[0663]        INSTANCE b3 : Book LINK ("Object Oriented Design",
[0664]                                       "Benjamin Cummings",
                                  Date (3, 3, 1994), "CC3", "Booch", 1)
[0665]        INSTANCE b4 : Book LINK ("Object Oriented System
              Design",
[0666]                            "Prentice Hall", Date (4, 4, 1994),
                                            "DD4", "Yourdon", 1)
[0667]
[0668]        INSTANCE m1 : Map LINK ("Burgundy", "Michelin",
```

```
[0669]                             Date(5,5,1994), "EE5","Michelin",5)
[0670]
[0671]        // Add LINKs to four Books and one Map to the Library.
[0672]        SEND aLibrary THE MESSAGE addOnePublication(b1)
[0673]        SEND aLibrary THE MESSAGE addOnePublication(b2)
[0674]        SEND aLibrary THE MESSAGE addOnePublication(b3)
[0675]        SEND aLibrary THE MESSAGE addOnePublication(b4)
[0676]        SEND aLibrary THE MESSAGE addOnePublication(m1)
[0677]
[0678]        // Create two Periodical objects with dynamic
                  duration.
[0679]        INSTANCE per1 :Periodical LINK("Journal of Object
              Oriented Programming",
[0680]                            "SIGS Publications Inc.",
                          Date(1,3,1994), "FF6", "R Weiner")
[0681]        INSTANCE per2 :Periodical LINK("The C++ Report",
              "SIGS Publications Inc.",
[0682]                            Date(1,7,1992), "GG7", "S Lippman")
[0683]
[0684]        // Create four Articles with dynamic duration.
[0685]        INSTANCE a1 :Article LINK("Guide to OO Training and
              Mentoring Services",
[0686]                                      "H Newling")
[0687]        INSTANCE a2 :Article LINK("The Life of an Object
              Model",
[0688]                                      "J Rumbaugh")
[0689]        INSTANCE a3 :Article LINK("Using C++ Effectively",
              "S Myers")
[0690]        INSTANCE a4 :Article LINK("Crossing Paradigms : A
              Pilgrim's Journey from C to C++",
[0691]                                      "F Tavaakkolian")
[0692]
[0693]        // Add the Articles to their corresponding
                  Periodicals.
[0694]        SEND per1 THE MESSAGE addOneArticle(a1)
[0695]        SEND per1 THE MESSAGE addOneArticle(a2)
[0696]        SEND per2 THE MESSAGE addOneArticle(a3)
[0697]        SEND per2 THE MESSAGE addOneArticle(a4)
[0698]
[0699]        // Add two Periodicals to the Library.
[0700]        SEND aLibrary THE MESSAGE addOnePublication(per1)
[0701]        SEND aLibrary THE MESSAGE addOnePublication(per2)
[0702]    ENDMETHOD initialiseLibrary
[0703]
[0704] ENDCLASS Application
[0705]
[0706]
[0707] //
[0708] // CLASS Book
[0709] //
[0710] // REVISION HISTORY
[0711] //
[0712] //    VERSION NUMBER 1.0
[0713] //
```

```
[0714]  //      DATE 8 September 1995
[0715]  //
[0716]  //      AUTHOR K Barclay / J Savage
[0717]  //
[0718]  //      PURPOSE First release
[0719]  //
[0720]  //DESCRIPTION
[0721]  //
[0722]  //      An instance of this class acts a Book that is held by
                a Library and
[0723]  //      Users.
[0724]  //
[0725]  CLASS Book
[0726]    SPECIALISATION OF Publication
[0727]  WITH
[0728]  PUBLIC INTERFACE
[0729]    Book
[0730]    Book (aTitle : String, aPublisher : String, aDate : Date,
          aReferenceNumber : String, anAuthor : String, anEdition
          : Integer)
[0731]  display?                                      REDEFINED
[0732]  PROTECTED INTERFACE
[0733]    NONE
[0734]  PRIVATE IMPLEMENTATION
[0735]    REPRESENTATION
[0736]      theAuthor : String
[0737]      theEdition : Integer
[0738]    AGGREGATIONS NONE
[0739]    ASSOCIATIONS NONE
[0740]    DEFINITIONS
[0741]      METHOD Book
[0742]      AS
[0743]        // Default constructor.
[0744]
[0745]        // Initialise the Publication representation
                  entries.
[0746]        SEND SUPERCLASS Publication THE MESSAGE initialise
[0747]
[0748]        // Set the unique Book representation entries to
                  sensible values.
[0749]        SEND theAuthor THE MESSAGE initialise ("")
[0750]        SEND theEdition THE MESSAGE initialise (1)
[0751]      ENDMETHOD Book
[0752]
[0753]      METHOD Book (aTitle : String, aPublisher : String, aDate
            : Date, aReferenceNumber : String, anAuthor : String,
            anEdition : Integer)
[0754]      AS
[0755]        // Parameterised constructor.
[0756]
[0757]        // Initialise Publication representation entries to
                  the corresponding
[0758]        // parameters of the constructor.
```

```
[0759]        SEND SUPERCLASS Publication THE MESSAGE
              initialise(aTitle, aPublisher,
[0760]                                    aDate, aReferenceNumber)
[0761]
[0762]      // Set the unique Book representation entries to the
               corresponding
[0763]      // parameters of the constructor.
[0764]        SEND theAuthor THE MESSAGE initialise(anAuthor)
[0765]        SEND theEdition THE MESSAGE initialise(anEdition)
[0766]      ENDMETHOD Book
[0767]
[0768]      METHOD display?
[0769]      AS
[0770]        // Output relevant Book details to the screen.
[0771]
[0772]        SEND theScreen THE MESSAGE insert("Book[")
[0773]        SEND me THE MESSAGE displayPublicationPart?
[0774]        SEND theScreen THE MESSAGE insert(theAuthor)
[0775]        SEND theScreen THE MESSAGE insert(", ")
[0776]        SEND theScreen THE MESSAGE insert(theEdition)
[0777]        SEND theScreen THE MESSAGE insert("]\n")
[0778]      ENDMETHOD display?
[0779]
[0780] ENDCLASS Book
[0781]
[0782]
[0783] //
[0784] // CLASS Map
[0785] //
[0786] // REVISION HISTORY
[0787] //
[0788] //      VERSION NUMBER 1.0
[0789] //
[0790] //      DATE 8 September 1995
[0791] //
[0792] //      AUTHOR K Barclay / J Savage
[0793] //
[0794] //      PURPOSE First release
[0795] //
[0796] // DESCRIPTION
[0797] //
[0798] //      An instance of this class acts a Map that is held by
               a Library and
[0799] //      Users.
[0800] //
[0801] CLASS Map
[0802]   SPECIALISATION OF Publication
[0803] WITH
[0804] PUBLIC INTERFACE
[0805]   Map
[0806]   Map(aTitle : String, aPublisher : String, aDate : Date,
           aReferenceNumber : String, aSeriesName : String,
           aSheetNumber : Integer)
[0807]   display?                                     REDEFINED
```

```
[0808]  PROTECTED INTERFACE
[0809]    NONE
[0810]  PRIVATE IMPLEMENTATION
[0811]    REPRESENTATION
[0812]      theSeriesName : String
[0813]      theSheetNumber : Integer
[0814]    AGGREGATIONS NONE
[0815]    ASSOCIATIONS NONE
[0816]    DEFINITIONS
[0817]      METHOD Map
[0818]      AS
[0819]        // Default constructor.
[0820]
[0821]        // Initialise the Publication representation
                  entries.
[0822]        SEND SUPERCLASS Publication THE MESSAGE initialise
[0823]
[0824]        // Set the unique Map representation entries to
                  sensible values.
[0825]        SEND theSeriesName THE MESSAGE initialise("")
[0826]        SEND theSheetNumber THE MESSAGE initialise(0)
[0827]      ENDMETHOD Map
[0828]
[0829]      METHOD Map(aTitle : String, aPublisher : String, aDate
              : Date, aReferenceNumber : String, aSeriesName
              : String, aSheetNumber : Integer)
[0830]      AS
[0831]        // Parameterised constructor.
[0832]
[0833]        // Initialise the Publication representation
                  entries to the corresponding
[0834]        // parameters of the constructor.
[0835]        SEND SUPERCLASS Publication THE MESSAGE
              initialise(aTitle, aPublisher,
[0836]                                      aDate, aReferenceNumber)
[0837]
[0838]        // Set the unique Map representation entries to the
                  corresponding
[0839]        // parameters of the constructor.
[0840]        SEND theSeriesName THE MESSAGE
              initialise(aSeriesName)
[0841]        SEND theSheetNumber THE MESSAGE
              initialise(aSheetNumber)
[0842]      ENDMETHOD Map
[0843]
[0844]      METHOD display?
[0845]      AS
[0846]        // Output relevant details of a Map to the screen.
[0847]
[0848]        SEND theScreen THE MESSAGE insert("Map[")
[0849]        SEND me THE MESSAGE displayPublicationPart?
[0850]        SEND theScreen THE MESSAGE insert(theSeriesName)
[0851]        SEND theScreen THE MESSAGE insert(", ")
[0852]        SEND theScreen THE MESSAGE insert(theSheetNumber)
```

```
[0853]        SEND theScreen THE MESSAGE insert ("]\n")
[0854]        ENDMETHOD display?
[0855]
[0856] ENDCLASS Map
[0857]
[0858]
[0859] //
[0860] // CLASS Perodical
[0861] //
[0862] // REVISION HISTORY
[0863] //
[0864] //     VERSION NUMBER 1.0
[0865] //
[0866] //     DATE 8 September 1995
[0867] //
[0868] //     AUTHOR K Barclay / J Savage
[0869] //
[0870] //     PURPOSE First release
[0871] //
[0872] // DESCRIPTION
[0873] //
[0874] //     An instance of this class acts a Periodical that is
               held by a Library and
[0875] //     Users.
[0876] //
[0877] CLASS Periodical
[0878]    SPECIALISATION OF Publication
[0879] WITH
[0880] PUBLIC INTERFACE
[0881]    Periodical
[0882]    Periodical(aTitle :String, aPublisher :String,
               aPublicationDate :Date, aReferenceNumber :String,
               anEditor :String)
[0883]    addOneArticle(anArticle :Article LINK INOUT)
[0884]    display?                                    REDEFINED
[0885] PROTECTED INTERFACE
[0886]    NONE
[0887] PRIVATE IMPLEMENTATION
[0888]    REPRESENTATION
[0889]      theEditor :String
[0890]    AGGREGATIONS
[0891]      theArticles :POrderedCollection[Article LINK]
[0892]    ASSOCIATIONS NONE
[0893]    DEFINITIONS
[0894]      METHOD Periodical
[0895]      AS
[0896]        // Default constructor.
[0897]
[0898]        // Initialise the Publication representation
                 entries.
[0899]        SEND SUPERCLASS Publication THE MESSAGE initialise
[0900]
[0901]        // Initialise the unique Periodical representation
                 entries to sensible values.
```

```
[0902]     SEND theEditor THE MESSAGE initialise("")
[0903]     SEND theArticles THE MESSAGE
           initialise(DEFAULTSIZE, MANAGED)
[0904]   ENDMETHOD Periodical
[0905]
[0906]   METHOD Periodical(aTitle :String, aPublisher
         :String, aPublicationDate :Date, aReferenceNumber
         :String, anEditor :String)
[0907]   AS
[0908]     // Parameterised constructor.
[0909]
[0910]     // Initialise the Publication representation
              entries to the corresponding
[0911]     // parameters of the constructor.
[0912]     SEND SUPERCLASS Publication THE MESSAGE
           initialise(aTitle, aPublisher,
[0913]                    aPublicationDate, aReferenceNumber)
[0914]
[0915]     // Initialise the unique Periodical representation
              entries to the corresponding
[0916]     // parameters of the constructor.
[0917]     SEND theEditor THE MESSAGE initialise(anEditor)
[0918]     SEND theArticles THE MESSAGE
           initialise(DEFAULTSIZE, MANAGED)
[0919]   ENDMETHOD Periodical
[0920]
[0921]   METHOD addOneArticle(anArticle :Article LINK INOUT)
[0922]   AS
[0923]     // Add an Article to the Periodical.
[0924]
[0925]     IF anArticle != NIL THEN
[0926]       SEND theArticles THE MESSAGE add(anArticle)
[0927]     ENDIF
[0928]   ENDMETHOD addOneArticle
[0929]
[0930]   METHOD display?
[0931]   AS
[0932]     // Output relevant details of a Periodical to the
              screen.
[0933]
[0934]     SEND theScreen THE MESSAGE insert("Periodical [")
[0935]     SEND me THE MESSAGE displayPublicationPart?
[0936]     SEND theScreen THE MESSAGE insert(theEditor)
[0937]     SEND theScreen THE MESSAGE insert("\n    with
           Articles:")
[0938]
[0939]     FOREACH anArticle :Article LINK IN theArticles DO
[0940]       SEND anArticle THE MESSAGE display?
[0941]     ENDFOREACH
[0942]
[0943]     SEND theScreen THE MESSAGE insert("]\n")
[0944]
[0945]     // If required the screen may be held with the
              following sentences.
```

```
[0946]        // INSTANCE theResponse : String("")
[0947]        // SEND theScreen THE MESSAGE insert("\n\tType a
                  character to continue > ")
[0948]        // SEND theKeyboard THE MESSAGE extract(theResponse)
[0949]        //
[0950]        // Similarly the screen may be held if these sentences
                  are embedded in the FOREACH
[0951]        // control sentence immediately after the message
                  display?
[0952]      ENDMETHOD display?
[0953]
[0954]  ENDCLASS Periodical
[0955]
[0956]
[0957]
```

Appendix F

C++ program listings

Chapter 6

Program 6.2

```
//////////////////////////////////////////////////////////
//
//          main
// ROME Copyright (c) Richard McMahon. 1993, 1994.
// ROME Copyright (c) Ken Barclay 1995.
// Generated On December 29, 1995 At 5:05:04.08 pm
//
//////////////////////////////////////////////////////////

#include "ccstring.h"
#include "application.h"

int main()
{
  Application    app;
  app.run();

  return 0;
}

//-- End Implementation ------------------------------------

//////////////////////////////////////////////////////////
//
//          application.h
// ROME Copyright (c) Richard McMahon. 1993, 1994.
// ROME Copyright (c) Ken Barclay 1995.
// Generated On December 29, 1995 At 5:05:04.08 pm
//
//////////////////////////////////////////////////////////

#ifndef APPLICATION
  #define APPLICATION
```

```
#include "loom.h"
#include "ccstring.h"


class Application {
public:          // PUBLIC INTERFACE
                 Application(void);
   void          run(void);

};

#endif

//-- End Specification ---------------------------------------


///////////////////////////////////////////////////////////
//
//           application.cpp
// ROME Copyright (c) Richard McMahon. 1993, 1994.
// ROME Copyright (c) Ken Barclay 1995.
// Generated On December 29, 1995 At 5:05:04.08 pm
//
///////////////////////////////////////////////////////////

#include "Car.h"
#include "Person.h"
#include "Application.h"



Application::Application(void)
{
}

void
Application::run(void)
{
  //
  // Make two instances
  //
  Car* renault = new Car("Renault", "Safrane");
  Person* ken = new Person("Ken Barclay");
  //
  // Assign the car to ken
  //
  ken->setVehicleLink(renault);
  //
  // Now see the effect
  //
  cout << ken->name();
  cout << " owns: ";
  cout << ken->carMake();
```

```
    cout << "\n";
}


//-- End Implementation --------------------------------------


///////////////////////////////////////////////////////////
//
//              car.h
// ROME Copyright (c) Richard McMahon. 1993, 1994.
// ROME Copyright (c) Ken Barclay 1995.
// Generated On December 29, 1995 At 5:05:04.08 pm
//
///////////////////////////////////////////////////////////

#ifndef CAR
  #define CAR

  #include "loom.h"
  #include "ccstring.h"


  class Car {
  public:          // PUBLIC INTERFACE
                   Car(const CString& aMake, const CString& aModel);
    CString        make(void) const;
    CString        model(void) const;

  private:         // REPRESENTATION
    CString        theMake;
    CString        theModel;

  };

#endif

//-- End Specification ---------------------------------------


///////////////////////////////////////////////////////////
//
//              car.cpp
// ROME Copyright (c) Richard McMahon. 1993, 1994.
// ROME Copyright (c) Ken Barclay 1995.
// Generated On December 29, 1995 At 5:05:04.08 pm
//
///////////////////////////////////////////////////////////

#include "Car.h"


Car::Car(const CString& aMake, const CString&   aModel)
  : theMake(aMake),
```

```
      theModel(aModel)
{

}

CString
Car::make(void) const
{
  return theMake;
}

CString
Car::model(void) const
{
  return theModel;
}



//-- End Implementation -------------------------------------


////////////////////////////////////////////////////////////
//
//            person.h
// ROME Copyright (c) Richard McMahon. 1993, 1994.
// ROME Copyright (c) Ken Barclay 1995.
// Generated On December 29, 1995 At 5:05:04.08 pm
//
////////////////////////////////////////////////////////////

#ifndef PERSON
  #define PERSON

  #include "loom.h"
  #include "ccstring.h"

  class Car;        // forward references

  class Person {
  public:        // PUBLIC INTERFACE
              Person(const CString& aName);
    CString       name(void) const;
    CString       carMake(void) const;
    void          setVehicleLink(Car* aCar);

  private:       // REPRESENTATION
    CString       theName;

  private:       // ASSOCIATION
    Car*          theVehicle;

  };
```

```
#endif

//-- End Specification -------------------------------------

////////////////////////////////////////////////////////////
//
//          person.cpp
// ROME Copyright (c) Richard McMahon. 1993, 1994.
// ROME Copyright (c) Ken Barclay 1995.
// Generated On December 29, 1995 At 5:05:04.08 pm
//
////////////////////////////////////////////////////////////

#include "Car.h"
#include "Person.h"

Person::Person(const CString& aName)
  : theName(aName),
    theVehicle(NULL)
{

}

CString
Person::name(void) const
{
  return theName;
}

CString
Person::carMake(void) const
{
  return theVehicle->make();
}

void
Person::setVehicleLink(Car* aCar)
{
  theVehicle = aCar;
}

//-- End Implementation ------------------------------------
```

Program 6.3

```
////////////////////////////////////////////////////////////
//
//          main
// ROME Copyright (c) Richard McMahon. 1993, 1994.
// ROME Copyright (c) Ken Barclay 1995.
// Generated On December 29, 1995 At 5:08:18.24 pm
//
////////////////////////////////////////////////////////////
```

```
#include "ccstring.h"
#include "application.h"

int main()
{
  Application    app;
  app.run();

  return 0;
}

//-- End Implementation -----------------------------------


/////////////////////////////////////////////////////////
//
//          application.h
// ROME Copyright (c) Richard McMahon. 1993, 1994.
// ROME Copyright (c) Ken Barclay 1995.
// Generated On December 29, 1995 At 5:08:18.24 pm
//
/////////////////////////////////////////////////////////

#ifndef APPLICATION
  #define APPLICATION

  #include "loom.h"
  #include "ccstring.h"


  class Application {
  public:       // PUBLIC INTERFACE
                Application(void);
    void        run(void);

  };

#endif

//-- End Specification ------------------------------------


/////////////////////////////////////////////////////////
//
//          application.cpp
// ROME Copyright (c) Richard McMahon. 1993, 1994.
// ROME Copyright (c) Ken Barclay 1995.
// Generated On December 29, 1995 At 5:08:18.24 pm
//
/////////////////////////////////////////////////////////

#include "Company.h"
#include "ccstring.h"
#include "Employee.h"
```

```
#include "Application.h"


Application::Application(void)
{
}

void
Application::run(void)
{
  //
  // First create an organisation
  //
  Company co("Napier");
  //
  // Now read some staff name/salary pairs ending with the unique
  // name "ZZZ". Establish new Employees with these values and hire
  // them.
  //
  CString staffName = "";
  Integer staffSalary = 0;
  cout << "Enter staff list:\n";
  cin >> staffName;
  cin >> staffSalary;
  while(staffName != "ZZZ") {
    Employee* emp = new Employee(staffName, staffSalary);
    co.hire(emp);
    cin >> staffName;
    cin >> staffSalary;
  }
  //
  // Now see how much the salaries cost.
  //
  cout << "Staff bill for ";
  cout << co.name();
  cout << " is ";
  cout << co.salaryBill();
  cout << "\n";
}


//-- End Implementation -----------------------------------


///////////////////////////////////////////////////////////
//
//              employee.h
// ROME Copyright (c) Richard McMahon. 1993, 1994.
// ROME Copyright (c) Ken Barclay 1995.
// Generated On December 29, 1995 At 5:08:18.24 pm
//
///////////////////////////////////////////////////////////

#ifndef EMPLOYEE
```

```
#define EMPLOYEE

#include "loom.h"
#include "ccstring.h"


class Employee {
public:          // PUBLIC INTERFACE
                            Employee (const CString& aName,
                                    const Integer& aSalary);
  CString          name (void) const;
  Integer          salary (void) const;
  Logical          lessThan (const Employee& anEmployee)
                   const;
  Integer          hashValue (void) const;

private:         // REPRESENTATION
  CString          theName;
  Integer          theSalary;

};

#endif

//-- End Specification -------------------------------------
////////////////////////////////////////////////////////////
//
//            employee.cpp
// ROME Copyright (c) Richard McMahon. 1993, 1994.
// ROME Copyright (c) Ken Barclay 1995.
// Generated On December 29, 1995 At 5:08:18.24 pm
//
////////////////////////////////////////////////////////////

#include "Employee.h"


Employee::Employee (const CString& aName,
   const Integer& aSalary)
  : theName (aName),
    theSalary (aSalary)
{

}

CString
Employee::name (void) const
{
  return theName;
}

Integer
```

```
Employee::salary(void) const
{
  return theSalary;
}

Logical
Employee::lessThan(const Employee& anEmployee) const
{
  CString anEmployeeName = anEmployee.name();
  if(theName < anEmployeeName) {
    return LTRUE;
  } else {
    return LFALSE;
  }
}

Integer
Employee::hashValue(void) const
{
  return theName.hashValue();
}


//-- End Implementation ------------------------------------


////////////////////////////////////////////////////////////
//
//            company.h
// ROME Copyright (c) Richard McMahon. 1993, 1994.
// ROME Copyright (c) Ken Barclay 1995.
// Generated On December 29, 1995 At 5:08:18.30 pm
//
////////////////////////////////////////////////////////////

#ifndef COMPANY
  #define COMPANY

  #include "loom.h"
  #include "ccstring.h"
  #include "pset.h"

  class Employee; 11 // forward references

  class Company {
  public:        // PUBLIC INTERFACE
                    Company(const CString& aName);
    CString         name(void) const;
    void            hire(Employee* anEmployee);
    Logical         hasEmployee(const CString& aName) const;
    Integer         salaryBill(void) const;

  private:       // REPRESENTATION
    CString         theName;
```

```
    private:         // AGGREGATION
      PSet< Employee* >          theEmployees;

    };

#endif

//-- End Specification ------------------------------------

//////////////////////////////////////////////////////////
//
//              company.cpp
// ROME Copyright (c) Richard McMahon. 1993, 1994.
// ROME Copyright (c) Ken Barclay 1995.
// Generated On December 29, 1995 At 5:08:18.30 pm
//
//////////////////////////////////////////////////////////

#include "Employee.h"
#include "Company.h"


Company::Company(const CString& aName)
  : theName(aName),
    theEmployees(DEFAULTSIZE, MANAGED)
{

}

CString
Company::name(void) const
{
  return theName;
}

void
Company::hire(Employee* anEmployee)
{
  theEmployees.add(anEmployee);
}

Logical
Company::hasEmployee(const CString& aName) const
{
  PIterator< Employee* >    empIterator(theEmployees);
  while( empIterator.isExhausted() == LFALSE ) {
    Employee* emp = empIterator.selection();
    CString empName = emp->name();
    if (empName == aName) {
      return LTRUE;
    }
    empIterator.advance();
  }
```

```
    return LFALSE;
}

Integer
Company::salaryBill(void) const
{
  Integer totalSalary = 0;
  PIterator< Employee* > empIterator(theEmployees);
  while( empIterator.isExhausted() == LFALSE ) {
    Employee* emp = empIterator.selection();
    Integer empSalary = emp->salary();
    totalSalary = totalSalary+empSalary;
    empIterator.advance();
  }
  return totalSalary;
}


//-- End Implementation ------------------------------------
```

Program 6.4

```
////////////////////////////////////////////////////////
//
//            main
// ROME Copyright (c) Richard McMahon. 1993, 1994.
// ROME Copyright (c) Ken Barclay 1995.
// Generated On December 29, 1995 At 5:12:11.78 pm
//
////////////////////////////////////////////////////////

#include "ccstring.h"
#include "application.h"

int main()
{
  Application    app;
  app.run();
  return 0;
}

//-- End Implementation ------------------------------------


////////////////////////////////////////////////////////
//
//            application.h
// ROME Copyright (c) Richard McMahon. 1993, 1994.
// ROME Copyright (c) Ken Barclay 1995.
// Generated On December 29, 1995 At 5:12:11.78 pm
//
////////////////////////////////////////////////////////
```

```
#ifndef APPLICATION
  #define APPLICATION

  #include "loom.h"
  #include "ccstring.h"


  class Application {
  public:          // PUBLIC INTERFACE
    void             run(void);

  };

#endif

//-- End Specification ------------------------------------


/////////////////////////////////////////////////////////////
//
//          application.cpp
// ROME Copyright (c) Richard McMahon. 1993, 1994.
// ROME Copyright (c) Ken Barclay 1995.
// Generated On December 29, 1995 At 5:12:11.78 pm
//
/////////////////////////////////////////////////////////////

#include "Company.h"
#include "Employee.h"
#include "Employment.h"
#include "Application.h"

void
Application::run(void)
{
  //
  // First, create some employing organisation
  //
  Company* napier = new Company("Napier");
  //
  // Then establish some people who might work for the company.
  //
  Employee* john = new Employee("John Savage");
  Employee* ken = new Employee("Ken Barclay");
  Employee* jessie = new Employee("Jessie Kennedy");
  Employee* lesley = new Employee("Lesley Beddie");
  //
  // Now give john and ken a job with Napier
  //
  Employment* johnsJob =
    new Employment("Lecturer", 1000, napier, john);
  Employment* kensJob =
    new Employment("Systems Manager", 800, napier, ken);
  napier->addEmployment(johnsJob);
```

```
john->addEmployment(johnsJob);
napier->addEmployment(kensJob);
ken->addEmployment(kensJob);
//
// And see the effect
//
napier->displayEmployees();
//
// Give jessie two jobs with napier
//
Employment* jessiesFirstJob =
  new Employment("Part Time Lecturer", 500, napier, jessie);
  Employment* jessiesSecondJob =
  new Employment("Part Time Research Assistant", 300, napier,
  jessie);
napier->addEmployment(jessiesFirstJob);
napier->addEmployment(jessiesSecondJob);
jessie->addEmployment(jessiesFirstJob);
jessie->addEmployment(jessiesSecondJob);
napier->displayEmployees();
}


//-- End Implementation ------------------------------------


//////////////////////////////////////////////////////////
//
//          company.h
// ROME Copyright (c) Richard McMahon. 1993, 1994.
// ROME Copyright (c) Ken Barclay 1995.
// Generated On December 29, 1995 At 5:12:11.78 pm
//
//////////////////////////////////////////////////////////

#ifndef COMPANY
  #define COMPANY

  #include "loom.h"
  #include "ccstring.h"
  #include "pordcol.h"

  class Employment;  // forward references

  class Company {
  public:        // PUBLIC INTERFACE
                 Company(const CString& aName);
    void         addEmployment(Employment* anEmployment);
    void         displayEmployees(void) const;

  private:       // REPRESENTATION
    CString          theName;

  private:       // ASSOCIATION
```

```
      POrderedCollection< Employment* > thePosts;
                                      // INVERSE OF theEmployer


  };

#endif

//-- End Specification ------------------------------------



//////////////////////////////////////////////////////////
//
//            company.cpp
// ROME Copyright (c) Richard McMahon. 1993, 1994.
// ROME Copyright (c) Ken Barclay 1995.
// Generated On December 29, 1995 At 5:12:11.84 pm
//
//////////////////////////////////////////////////////////

#include "Employment.h"
#include "Company.h"



Company::Company(const CString& aName)
  : theName(aName),
    thePosts(DEFAULTSIZE, UNMANAGED)
{

}

void
Company::addEmployment(Employment* anEmployment)
{
  thePosts.add(anEmployment);
}

void
Company::displayEmployees(void) const
{
  cout << theName;
  cout << "\n------\n";
  PIterator< Employment* > employmentIterator(thePosts);
  while( employmentIterator.isExhausted() == LFALSE ) {
    Employment* employment = employmentIterator.selection();
    employment->display();
    employmentIterator.advance();
  }
  cout << "\n\n";
}



//-- End Implementation ------------------------------------
```

```
//////////////////////////////////////////////////////////
//
//           employee.h
// ROME Copyright (c) Richard McMahon. 1993, 1994.
// ROME Copyright (c) Ken Barclay 1995.
// Generated On December 29, 1995 At 5:12:11.78 pm
//
//////////////////////////////////////////////////////////

#ifndef EMPLOYEE
 #define EMPLOYEE

 #include "loom.h"
 #include "ccstring.h"
 #include "pordcol.h"

 class Employment;  // forward references

 class Employee {
 public:         // PUBLIC INTERFACE
               Employee (const CString& aName);
   void        addEmployment (Employment* anEmployment);
   CString     name (void) const;

 private:        // REPRESENTATION
   CString       theName;

 private:        // ASSOCIATION
   POrderedCollection< Employment* >  theJobs;
                                       //INVERSE OF theEmployee

 };

#endif

//-- End Specification -------------------------------------

//////////////////////////////////////////////////////////
//
//           employee.cpp
// ROME Copyright (c) Richard McMahon. 1993, 1994.
// ROME Copyright (c) Ken Barclay 1995.
// Generated On December 29, 1995 At 5:12:11.78 pm
//
//////////////////////////////////////////////////////////

#include "Employment.h"
#include "Employee.h"


Employee::Employee (const CString& aName)
 : theName (aName),
   theJobs (DEFAULTSIZE, UNMANAGED)
{
```

```
}

void
Employee::addEmployment(Employment* anEmployment)
{
  theJobs.add(anEmployment);
}
CString
Employee::name(void) const
{
  return theName;
}

//-- End Implementation ------------------------------------

////////////////////////////////////////////////////////////
//
//          employment.h
// ROME Copyright (c) Richard McMahon. 1993, 1994.
// ROME Copyright (c) Ken Barclay 1995.
// Generated On December 29, 1995 At 5:12:11.78 pm
//
////////////////////////////////////////////////////////////

#ifndef EMPLOYMENT
  #define EMPLOYMENT

  #include "loom.h"
  #include "ccstring.h"

  class Company;          // forward references
  class Employee;

  class Employment {
  public:          // PUBLIC INTERFACE
    Employment(const CString& aJobTitle, const Integer& aSalary,
                  Company* anEmployer, Employee* anEmployee);
    CString     jobTitle(void) const;
    Logical     lessThan(const Employment& anEmployment) const;
    void        display(void) const;

  private:          // REPRESENTATION
    CString          theJobTitle;
    Integer          theSalary;

  private:          // ASSOCIATION
    Company*    theEmployer;   // INVERSE OF thePosts
    Employee*   theEmployee;   // INVERSE OF theJobs

  };

#endif

//-- End Specification ------------------------------------
```

```
//////////////////////////////////////////////////////////
//
//          employment.cpp
// ROME Copyright (c) Richard McMahon. 1993, 1994.
// ROME Copyright (c) Ken Barclay 1995.
// Generated On December 29, 1995 At 5:12:11.78 pm
//
//////////////////////////////////////////////////////////

#include "Company.h"
#include "Employee.h"
#include "Employment.h"


Employment::Employment(const CString& aJobTitle,
   const Integer& aSalary, Company* anEmployer,
   Employee* anEmployee)
 :theJobTitle(aJobTitle),
   theSalary(aSalary),
   theEmployer(anEmployer),
   theEmployee(anEmployee)
{

}

CString
Employment::jobTitle(void) const
{
  return theJobTitle;
}

Logical
   Employment::lessThan(const Employment& anEmployment) const
{
  CString anEmploymentTitle = anEmployment.jobTitle();
  if(theJobTitle < anEmploymentTitle) {
    return LTRUE;
  } else {
    return LFALSE;
  }
}

void
Employment::display(void) const
{
  cout << theEmployee->name();
  cout << ": ";
  cout << theJobTitle;
  cout << ", ";
  cout << theSalary;
  cout << "\n";
}

//-- End Implementation -------------------------------------
```

Chapter 9

Program 9.2

```
/////////////////////////////////////////////////////////
//
//          main
// ROME Copyright (c) Richard McMahon. 1993, 1994.
// ROME Copyright (c) Ken Barclay 1995.
// Generated On January 2, 1996 At 4:20:06.63 pm
//
/////////////////////////////////////////////////////////

#include "ccstring.h"
#include "application.h"

int main()
{
  Application    app;
  app.run();

  return 0;
}


//-- End Implementation ------------------------------------


/////////////////////////////////////////////////////////
//
//          application.h
// ROME Copyright (c) Richard McMahon. 1993, 1994.
// ROME Copyright (c) Ken Barclay 1995.
// Generated On January 2, 1996 At 4:20:06.63 pm
//
/////////////////////////////////////////////////////////

#ifndef APPLICATION
  #define APPLICATION

  #include "loom.h"
  #include "ccstring.h"


  //
  // #include "company.h"
  // #include "employee.h"
  // #include "manager.h"
  //

  class Application {
  public:        // PUBLIC INTERFACE
               Application(void);
    void          run(void);
```

```
  public:
    virtual CString          className(void) const;
                                                //POLYMORPHIC


  };

#endif

//-- End Specification -------------------------------------


///////////////////////////////////////////////////////////
//
//          application.cpp
// ROME Copyright (c) Richard McMahon. 1993, 1994.
// ROME Copyright (c) Ken Barclay 1995.
// Generated On January 2, 1996 At 4:20:06.63 pm
//
///////////////////////////////////////////////////////////

#include "Company.h"
#include "Employee.h"
#include "ccstring.h"
#include "Manager.h"
#include "Application.h"


//
//  #include "company.h"
//  #include "employee.h"
//  #include "manager.h"
//


Application::Application(void)
{
}
void
Application::run(void)
{
    //
    // Prepare a list of Employee and Manager objects, all of whom are
    //    employed by the Company object known as Napier. From the
    //    staff list determine the total Company salary bill.
    //
    Company co("Napier");
    Employee* newEmployee = 0;
    CString name = "";
    CString title = "";
    Integer salary = 0;
    Integer budget = 0;
    Integer day = 0;
    Integer month = 0;
    Integer year = 0;
    CString status = "";
```

```
      cout << "Employee type (ZZZ, EMP or MAN): ";
      cin >> status;
      while(status != "ZZZ") {
        if(status == "EMP") {
          cout << "Enter employee's name: ";
          cin >> name;
          cout << "Enter employee's date of birth: ";
          cin >> day;
          cin >> month;
          cin >> year;
          cout << "Enter employee's job title and salary: ";
          cin >> title;
          cin >> salary;
          Employee* emp =
            new Employee(name, CDate(day, month, year), title,
            salary);
          newEmployee = emp;
        } else {
          cout << "Enter manager's name: ";
          cin >> name;
          cout << "Enter manager's date of birth: ";
          cin >> day;
          cin >> month;
          cin >> year;
          cout << "Enter manager's job title, salary and budget: ";
          cin >> title;
          cin >> salary;
          cin >> budget;
          Manager* man =
            new Manager(name, CDate(day, month, year), title, salary,
            budget);
          newEmployee = man;
        }
        co.hire(newEmployee);
        cout << "Employee type (ZZZ, EMP or MAN): ";
        cin >> status;
      }
      cout << "Salary bill for: ";
      cout << co.name();
      cout << " is ";
      cout << co.salaryBill();
      cout << "\n";
    }


    CString
    Application::className(void) const
                                                    // POLYMORPHIC
    {
      return "Application";
    }



    //-- End Implementation ---------------------------------------
```

```
/////////////////////////////////////////////////////////
//
//           person.h
// ROME Copyright (c) Richard McMahon. 1993, 1994.
// ROME Copyright (c) Ken Barclay 1995.
// Generated On January 2, 1996 At 4:20:06.63 pm
//
/////////////////////////////////////////////////////////

#ifndef PERSON
  #define PERSON

  #include "loom.h"
  #include "ccstring.h"
  #include "ccdate.h"
  class Person {
  public:        // PUBLIC INTERFACE
                    Person(const CString& aName,
                               const CDate& aDateOfBirth);
    CString         name(void) const;
    Integer         age(void) const;

  private:       // REPRESENTATION
    CString         theName;
    CDate           theDateOfBirth;

  public:
    virtual CString     className(void) const;
                                            //POLYMORPHIC

  };

#endif

//-- End Specification ------------------------------------


/////////////////////////////////////////////////////////
//
//           person.cpp
// ROME Copyright (c) Richard McMahon. 1993, 1994.
// ROME Copyright (c) Ken Barclay 1995.
// Generated On January 2, 1996 At 4:20:06.63 pm
//
/////////////////////////////////////////////////////////

#include "Person.h"


Person::Person(const CString& aName, const CDate&
  aDateOfBirth)
  : theName(aName),
    theDateOfBirth(aDateOfBirth)
{
```

```
}

CString
Person::name(void) const
{
  return theName;
}

Integer
Person::age(void) const
{
  //
  // Simplistic algorithm, taking no account of months or days
  // within the month.
  //
  CDate today;
  Integer todayYear = today.year();
  Integer dobYear = theDateOfBirth.year();
  return todayYear - dobYear;
}


CString
Person::className(void) const                       // POLYMORPHIC
{
  return "Person";
}


//-- End Implementation -------------------------------------


////////////////////////////////////////////////////////////
//
//          employee.h
// ROME Copyright (c) Richard McMahon. 1993, 1994.
// ROME Copyright (c) Ken Barclay 1995.
// Generated On January 2, 1996 At 4:20:06.63 pm
//
////////////////////////////////////////////////////////////

#ifndef EMPLOYEE
  #define EMPLOYEE

  #include "loom.h"
  #include "Person.h"
  #include "ccstring.h"
  #include "ccdate.h"
  class Employee : public Person {
  public:        // PUBLIC INTERFACE
    Employee(const CString& aName, const CDate& aDateOfBirth,
    const CString& aJobTitle, const Integer& aSalary);
    CString         jobTitle(void) const;
```

```
   Integer          salary(void) const;
   Logical          lessThan(const Employee& anEmployee) const;

 private:           // REPRESENTATION
   CString              theJobTitle;
   Integer              theSalary;

 public:
   virtual CString   className(void) const;
                                           // POLYMORPHIC

 };

#endif

//-- End Specification -------------------------------------

/////////////////////////////////////////////////////////
//
//            employee.cpp
// ROME Copyright (c) Richard McMahon. 1993, 1994.
// ROME Copyright (c) Ken Barclay 1995.
// Generated On January 2, 1996 At 4:20:06.63 pm
//
/////////////////////////////////////////////////////////

#include "Employee.h"


Employee::Employee(const CString& aName,
          const CDate& aDateOfBirth,
    const CString& aJobTitle, const Integer& aSalary)
  : Person(aName, aDateOfBirth),
    theJobTitle(aJobTitle),
    theSalary(aSalary)
{
}

CString
Employee::jobTitle(void) const
{
  return theJobTitle;
}

Integer
Employee::salary(void) const
{
  return theSalary;
}

Logical
Employee::lessThan(const Employee& anEmployee) const
{
```

```
    CString jobName = anEmployee.jobTitle();
    if(theJobTitle < jobName) {
      return LTRUE;
    } else {
      return LFALSE;
    }
}


CString
Employee::className(void) const                      // POLYMORPHIC
{
  return "Employee";
}

//-- End Implementation -------------------------------------

//////////////////////////////////////////////////////////////
//
//              manager.h
// ROME Copyright (c) Richard McMahon. 1993, 1994.
// ROME Copyright (c) Ken Barclay 1995.
// Generated On January 2, 1996 At 4:20:06.63 pm
//
//////////////////////////////////////////////////////////////

#ifndef MANAGER
  #define MANAGER

  #include "loom.h"
  #include "Employee.h"
  #include "ccstring.h"
  #include "ccdate.h"


  class Manager : public Employee {
  public:         // PUBLIC INTERFACE
    Manager(const CString& aName, const CDate& aDateOfBirth,
            const CString& aJobTitle, const Integer& aSalary,
            const Integer& aBudget);
    Integer            budget(void) const;

  private:        // REPRESENTATION
    Integer            theBudget;

  public:
    virtual CString    className(void) const;
                                               // POLYMORPHIC

  };

#endif
```

```
//-- End Specification ----------------------------------------


////////////////////////////////////////////////////////////
//
//            manager.cpp
// ROME Copyright (c) Richard McMahon. 1993, 1994.
// ROME Copyright (c) Ken Barclay 1995.
// Generated On January 2, 1996 At 4:20:06.63 pm
//
////////////////////////////////////////////////////////////

#include "Manager.h"


Manager::Manager(const CString& aName,
                 const CDate& aDateOfBirth,
                 const CString& aJobTitle,
                 const Integer& aSalary,
                 const Integer& aBudget)
        : Employee(aName, aDateOfBirth, aJobTitle, aSalary),
          theBudget(aBudget)
{

}

Integer
Manager::budget(void) const
{
  return theBudget;
}


CString
Manager::className(void) const      // POLYMORPHIC
{
  return "Manager";
}


//-- End Implementation ---------------------------------------


////////////////////////////////////////////////////////////
//
//            company.h
// ROME Copyright (c) Richard McMahon. 1993, 1994.
// ROME Copyright (c) Ken Barclay 1995.
// Generated On January 2, 1996 At 4:20:06.63 pm
//
////////////////////////////////////////////////////////////

#ifndef COMPANY
  #define COMPANY
```

```
#include "loom.h"
#include "ccstring.h"
#include "pordcol.h"

class Employee;          // forward references


//
// A Company has a one-to-many association with Employee
//  objects. Using the principle of substitutability these may
//  be either vanilla Employee objects or Manager objects which
//  are specialised kinds of the former.
//
//

class Company {
public:          // PUBLIC INTERFACE
                 Company (const CString& aName);
  CString        name (void) const;
  void           hire (Employee* anEmployee);
  Integer        salaryBill (void) const;

private:         // REPRESENTATION
  CString              theName;

private:         // ASSOCIATION
  POrderedCollection< Employee* >                    theEmployees;

public:
  virtual CString      className (void) const;   // POLYMORPHIC

};

#endif

//-- End Specification -------------------------------------


////////////////////////////////////////////////////////////
//
//             company.cpp
// ROME Copyright (c) Richard McMahon. 1993, 1994.
// ROME Copyright (c) Ken Barclay 1995.
// Generated On January 2, 1996 At 4:20:06.63 pm
//
////////////////////////////////////////////////////////////

#include "Employee.h"
#include "Company.h"


//
// A Company has a one-to-many association with Employee objects.
//  Using the principle of substitutability these may be either
//  vanilla Employee objects or Manager objects which are
//  specialised kinds of the former.
```

```
//
//

Company::Company(const CString& aName)
  : theName(aName),
    theEmployees(DEFAULTSIZE, MANAGED)
{

}

CString
Company::name(void) const
{
  return theName;
}

void
Company::hire(Employee* anEmployee)
{
  theEmployees.add(anEmployee);
}

Integer
Company::salaryBill(void) const
{
  Integer totalSalary = 0;
  PIterator< Employee* > empIterator(theEmployees);
  while( empIterator.isExhausted() == LFALSE ) {
    Employee* emp = empIterator.selection();
    Integer empSalary = emp->salary();
    totalSalary = totalSalary+empSalary;
    empIterator.advance();
  }
  return totalSalary;
}

CString
Company::className(void) const       // POLYMORPHIC
{
  return "Company";
}

//-- End Implementation ------------------------------------
```

Program 9.3

```
/////////////////////////////////////////////////////////////
//
//            main
// ROME Copyright (c) Richard McMahon. 1993, 1994.
// ROME Copyright (c) Ken Barclay 1995.
// Generated On January 2, 1996 At 4:31:37.76 pm
//
/////////////////////////////////////////////////////////////
```

```
#include "ccstring.h"
#include "application.h"

int main()
{
  Application  app;
  app.run();

  return 0;
}

//-- End Implementation -------------------------------------


///////////////////////////////////////////////////////////
//
//          application.h
// ROME Copyright (c) Richard McMahon. 1993, 1994.
// ROME Copyright (c) Ken Barclay 1995.
// Generated On January 2, 1996 At 4:31:37.76 pm
//
///////////////////////////////////////////////////////////

#ifndef APPLICATION
  #define APPLICATION

  #include "loom.h"
  #include "ccstring.h"


  class Application {
  public:        // PUBLIC INTERFACE
                 Application(void);
    void         run(void);

  public:
    virtual CString    className(void) const;
                                             // POLYMORPHIC

  };

#endif

//-- End Specification --------------------------------------


///////////////////////////////////////////////////////////
//
//          application.cpp
// ROME Copyright (c) Richard McMahon. 1993, 1994.
// ROME Copyright (c) Ken Barclay 1995.
// Generated On January 2, 1996 At 4:31:37.76 pm
//
///////////////////////////////////////////////////////////
```

```
#include "Employee.h"
#include "Manager.h"
#include "Manager.h"
#include "Employee.h"
#include "Application.h"


Application::Application(void)
{
}

void
Application::run(void)
{
  //
  // Demonstrate the effect of a redefined function and static
binding.
  //
  Employee e1("Ken Barclay", CDate(2, 2, 1974),
                                    "Systems Manager", 1000);
  Manager m1("John Savage", CDate(1, 1, 1973),
                                    "Lecturer", 1200, 1000);
  Manager* m2 =
    new Manager("Jessie Kennedy", CDate(3, 3, 1975),
                                    "Senior Lecturer", 1600, 1500);
  Employee* e2 = m2;
  e1.display();
  m1.display();
  e2->display();
}


CString
Application::className(void) const
                                                    //POLYMORPHIC

{
  return "Application";
}


//-- End Implementation -------------------------------------


/////////////////////////////////////////////////////////////
//
//              person.h
// ROME Copyright (c) Richard McMahon. 1993, 1994.
// ROME Copyright (c) Ken Barclay 1995.
// Generated On January 2, 1996 At 4:31:37.76 pm
//
/////////////////////////////////////////////////////////////

#ifndef PERSON
  #define PERSON
```

```
#include "loom.h"
#include "ccstring.h"
#include "ccdate.h"

class Person{
public:          //PUBLIC INTERFACE
    Person(const CString& aName, const CDate& aDateOfBirth);
  CString          name(void) const;
  Integer          age(void) const;

private:         //REPRESENTATION
  CString          theName;
  CDate            theDateOfBirth;

public:
  virtual CString       className(void) const;
                                            // POLYMORPHIC

};

#endif

//-- End Specification -----------------------------------


/////////////////////////////////////////////////////////
//
//           person.cpp
// ROME Copyright (c) Richard McMahon. 1993, 1994.
// ROME Copyright (c) Ken Barclay 1995.
// Generated On January 2, 1996 At 4:31:37.76 pm
//
/////////////////////////////////////////////////////////

#include "Person.h"


Person::Person(const CString& aName, const CDate& aDateOfBirth)
  : theName(aName),
    theDateOfBirth(aDateOfBirth)
{

}

CString
Person::name(void) const
{
  return theName;
}

Integer
Person::age(void) const
```

```
{
  //
  // Simplistic algorithm, taking no account of
  //   months or days within the month.
  //
  CDate today;
  Integer todayYear = today.year();
  Integer dobYear = theDateOfBirth.year();
  return todayYear - dobYear;
}


CString
Person::className(void) const      // POLYMORPHIC
{
  return "Person";
}


//-- End Implementation ------------------------------------


/////////////////////////////////////////////////////////
//
//              employee.h
// ROME Copyright (c) Richard McMahon. 1993, 1994.
// ROME Copyright (c) Ken Barclay 1995.
// Generated On January 2, 1996 At 4:31:37.76 pm
//
/////////////////////////////////////////////////////////

#ifndef EMPLOYEE
  #define EMPLOYEE

  #include "loom.h"
  #include "Person.h"
  #include "ccstring.h"
  #include "ccdate.h"

  class Employee : public Person {
  public:        // PUBLIC INTERFACE
    Employee(const CString& aName, const CDate& aDateOfBirth,
    const CString& aJobTitle, const Integer& aSalary);
    CString            jobTitle(void) const;
    Integer            salary(void) const;
    void               display(void) const;

    private:       // REPRESENTATION
      CString            theJobTitle;
      Integer            theSalary;

    public:
      virtual CString      className(void) const;
```

// POLYMORPHIC

```cpp
  };

#endif

//-- End Specification ------------------------------------

///////////////////////////////////////////////////////////
//
//              employee.cpp
// ROME Copyright (c) Richard McMahon. 1993, 1994.
// ROME Copyright (c) Ken Barclay 1995.
// Generated On January 2, 1996 At 4:31:37.76 pm
//
///////////////////////////////////////////////////////////

#include "Employee.h"

Employee::Employee(const CString& aName,
                   const CDate& aDateOfBirth,
                   const CString& aJobTitle,
                   const Integer& aSalary)
  : Person(aName, aDateOfBirth),
    theJobTitle(aJobTitle),
    theSalary(aSalary)
{

}

CString
Employee::jobTitle(void) const
{
  return theJobTitle;
}

Integer
Employee::salary(void) const
{
  return theSalary;
}

void
Employee::display(void) const
{
  cout << this->Person::name();
  cout << ": ";
  cout << theJobTitle;
  cout << "\n";
}


CString
```

```
Employee::className(void) const      // POLYMORPHIC
{
  return "Employee";
}


//-- End Implementation ------------------------------------


////////////////////////////////////////////////////////////
//
//           manager.h
// ROME Copyright (c) Richard McMahon. 1993, 1994.
// ROME Copyright (c) Ken Barclay 1995.
// Generated On January 2, 1996 At 4:31:37.76 pm
//
////////////////////////////////////////////////////////////

#ifndef MANAGER
  #define MANAGER
  #include "loom.h"
  #include "Employee.h"
  #include "ccstring.h"
  #include "ccdate.h"

  class Manager : public Employee {
  public:          // PUBLIC INTERFACE
    Manager(const CString& aName, const CDate& aDateOfBirth,
            const CString& aJobTitle, const Integer& aSalary,
            const Integer& aBudget);
  Integer            budget(void) const;
  void               display(void) const;

  private:         // REPRESENTATION
    Integer            theBudget;

  public:
    virtual CString    className(void) const;
                                               // POLYMORPHIC

  };

#endif

//-- End Specification ------------------------------------

////////////////////////////////////////////////////////////
//
//           manager.cpp
// ROME Copyright (c) Richard McMahon. 1993, 1994.
// ROME Copyright (c) Ken Barclay 1995.
// Generated On January 2, 1996 At 4:31:37.76 pm
//
////////////////////////////////////////////////////////////
```

```
#include "Manager.h"


Manager::Manager(const CString& aName, const CDate&
aDateOfBirth, const CString& aJobTitle, const Integer& aSalary,
const Integer& aBudget)
: Employee(aName, aDateOfBirth, aJobTitle, aSalary),
theBudget(aBudget)
{

}

Integer
Manager::budget(void) const
{
  return theBudget;
}

void
Manager::display(void) const
{
  cout << this->Person::name();
  cout << ": ";
  cout << theBudget;
  cout << "\n";
}


CString
Manager::className(void) const        // POLYMORPHIC
{
  return "Manager";
}


//-- End Implementation --------------------------------------
```

Program 9.4

```
///////////////////////////////////////////////////////
//
//           main
// ROME Copyright (c) Richard McMahon. 1993, 1994.
// ROME Copyright (c) Ken Barclay 1995.
// Generated On January 2, 1996 At 4:39:58.52 pm
//
///////////////////////////////////////////////////////

#include "ccstring.h"
#include "application.h"

int main()
{
```

```
  Application    app;
  app.run();

  return 0;
}

//-- End Implementation -------------------------------------


//////////////////////////////////////////////////////////////
//
//          application.h
// ROME Copyright (c) Richard McMahon. 1993, 1994.
// ROME Copyright (c) Ken Barclay 1995.
// Generated On January 2, 1996 At 4:39:58.52 pm
//
//////////////////////////////////////////////////////////////

#ifndef APPLICATION
  #define APPLICATION

  #include "loom.h"
  #include "ccstring.h"


  class Application {
  public:        // PUBLIC INTERFACE
                 Application(void);
    void             run(void);

  public:
    virtual CString      className(void) const;
                                          // POLYMORPHIC

  };

#endif

//-- End Specification ---------------------------------------


//////////////////////////////////////////////////////////////
//
//          application.cpp
// ROME Copyright (c) Richard McMahon. 1993, 1994.
// ROME Copyright (c) Ken Barclay 1995.
// Generated On January 2, 1996 At 4:39:58.52 pm
//
//////////////////////////////////////////////////////////////

#include "Employee.h"
#include "Manager.h"
#include "Manager.h"
#include "Employee.h"
```

```
#include "Application.h"

Application::Application(void)
{
}

void
Application::run(void)
{
  //
  // Demonstrate the effect of a redefined function
  //   and dynamic binding.
  //
  Employee e1("Ken Barclay", CDate(2, 2, 1974),
    "Systems Manager", 1000);
  Manager m1("John Savage", CDate(1, 1, 1973), "Lecturer",
    1200, 1000);
  Manager* m2 =
    new Manager("Jessie Kennedy", CDate(3, 3, 1975),
    "Senior Lecturer", 1600, 1500);
  Employee* e2 = m2;
  e1.display();
  m1.display();
  e2->display();
}


CString
Application::className(void) const
                                                    //POLYMORPHIC
{
  return "Application";
}

//-- End Implementation ---------------------------------------
/////////////////////////////////////////////////////////////
//
//            person.h
// ROME Copyright (c) Richard McMahon. 1993, 1994.
// ROME Copyright (c) Ken Barclay 1995.
// Generated On January 2, 1996 At 4:39:58.52 pm
//
/////////////////////////////////////////////////////////////

#ifndef PERSON
  #define PERSON

  #include "loom.h"
  #include "ccstring.h"
  #include "ccdate.h"


  class Person {
  public:          // PUBLIC INTERFACE
```

```
                         Person(const CString& aName,
                                   const CDate& aDateOfBirth);
     CString              name(void) const;
     Integer              age(void) const;

   private:          //REPRESENTATION
     CString            theName;
     CDate              theDateOfBirth;

   public:
     virtual CString         className(void) const;
                                              //POLYMORPHIC

   };

#endif


//--End Specification -------------------------------------


///////////////////////////////////////////////////////
//
//            person.cpp
//ROME Copyright (c) Richard McMahon. 1993, 1994.
//ROME Copyright (c) Ken Barclay 1995.
//Generated On January 2, 1996 At 4:39:58.52 pm
//
///////////////////////////////////////////////////////

#include "Person.h"

Person::Person(const CString& aName,
                                const CDate& aDateOfBirth)
  : theName(aName),
    theDateOfBirth(aDateOfBirth)
{

}

CString
Person::name(void) const
{
  return theName;
}

Integer
Person::age(void) const
{
  //
  //Simplistic algorithm, taking no account of months or days
  //within the month.
  //
  CDate today;
```

```
    Integer todayYear = today.year();
    Integer dobYear = theDateOfBirth.year();
    return todayYear - dobYear;
}


CString
Person::className(void) const       // POLYMORPHIC
{
  return "Person";
}

//-- End Implementation -------------------------------------

//////////////////////////////////////////////////////////////
//
//              employee.h
// ROME Copyright (c) Richard McMahon. 1993, 1994.
// ROME Copyright (c) Ken Barclay 1995.
// Generated On January 2, 1996 At 4:39:58.52 pm
//
//////////////////////////////////////////////////////////////


#ifndef EMPLOYEE
  #define EMPLOYEE

  #include "loom.h"
  #include "Person.h"
  #include "ccstring.h"
  #include "ccdate.h"


  class Employee : public Person {
  public:         // PUBLIC INTERFACE
    Employee(const CString& aName, const CDate& aDateOfBirth,
             const CString& aJobTitle, const Integer& aSalary);
    CString          jobTitle(void) const;
    Integer          salary(void) const;
    virtual void       display(void) const;
                                              //POLYMORPHIC

  private:        // REPRESENTATION
    CString          theJobTitle;
    Integer          theSalary;

  public:
    virtual CString        className(void) const;
                                              // POLYMORPHIC

  };

#endif
```

```
//-- End Specification ---------------------------------------

//////////////////////////////////////////////////////////////
//
//            employee.cpp
// ROME Copyright (c) Richard McMahon. 1993, 1994.
// ROME Copyright (c) Ken Barclay 1995.
// Generated On January 2, 1996 At 4:39:58.52 pm
//
//////////////////////////////////////////////////////////////

#include "Employee.h"


Employee::Employee(const CString& aName,
                                    const CDate& aDateOfBirth,
   const CString& aJobTitle, const Integer& aSalary)
  : Person(aName, aDateOfBirth),
    theJobTitle(aJobTitle),
    theSalary(aSalary)
{

}

CString
Employee::jobTitle(void) const
{
  return theJobTitle;
}

Integer
Employee::salary(void) const
{
  return theSalary;
}

void
Employee::display(void) const         // POLYMORPHIC
{
  cout << this->Person::name();
  cout << ": ";
  cout << theJobTitle;
  cout << "\n";
}


CString
Employee::className(void) const        // POLYMORPHIC
{
  return "Employee";
}


//-- End Implementation --------------------------------------
```

```
////////////////////////////////////////////////////////
//
//          manager.h
// ROME Copyright (c) Richard McMahon. 1993, 1994.
// ROME Copyright (c) Ken Barclay 1995.
// Generated On January 2, 1996 At 4:39:58.52 pm
//
////////////////////////////////////////////////////////

#ifndef MANAGER
 #define MANAGER

 #include "loom.h"
 #include "Employee.h"
 #include "ccstring.h"
 #include "ccdate.h"


 class Manager : public Employee {
 public:         // PUBLIC INTERFACE
   Manager (const CString& aName, const CDate& aDateOfBirth,
            const CString& aJobTitle, const Integer& aSalary,
            const Integer& aBudget);
   Integer          budget(void) const;
   virtual void     display(void) const;
                                                // REDEFINED


 private:        // REPRESENTATION
   Integer          theBudget;

 public:
   virtual CString        className(void) const;
                                                // POLYMORPHIC

 };

#endif

//-- End Specification ------------------------------------


////////////////////////////////////////////////////////
//
//          manager.cpp
// ROME Copyright (c) Richard McMahon. 1993, 1994.
// ROME Copyright (c) Ken Barclay 1995.
// Generated On January 2, 1996 At 4:39:58.52 pm
//
////////////////////////////////////////////////////////

#include "Manager.h"

Manager::Manager(const CString& aName,
                              const CDate& aDateOfBirth,
```

```
                      const CString& aJobTitle, const Integer& aSalary,
                                             const Integer& aBudget):
Employee(aName, aDateOfBirth, aJobTitle, aSalary),
                                        theBudget(aBudget)
{

}

Integer
Manager::budget(void) const
{
  return theBudget;
}

void
Manager::display(void) const        // REDEFINED
{
  cout << this->Person::name();
  cout << ": ";
  cout << theBudget;
  cout << "\n";
}



CString
Manager::className(void) const     // POLYMORPHIC
{
  return "Manager";
}


//-- End Implementation --------------------------------------
```

Program 9.5

```
////////////////////////////////////////////////////////////
//
//             main
// ROME Copyright (c) Richard McMahon. 1993, 1994.
// ROME Copyright (c) Ken Barclay 1995.
// Generated On January 2, 1996 At 4:56:53.37 pm
//
////////////////////////////////////////////////////////////

#include "ccstring.h"
#include "application.h"

int main()
{
  Application  app;
  app.run();
```

```
        return 0;
}

//-- End Implementation -------------------------------------


///////////////////////////////////////////////////////////
//
//          application.h
// ROME Copyright (c) Richard McMahon. 1993, 1994.
// ROME Copyright (c) Ken Barclay 1995.
// Generated On January 2, 1996 At 4:56:53.37 pm
//
///////////////////////////////////////////////////////////

#ifndef APPLICATION
  #define APPLICATION
  #include "loom.h"
  #include "ccstring.h"


  //
  //  #include "company.h"
  //  #include "salesemployee.h"
  //  #include "salesmanager.h"
  //

  class Application {
  public:        // PUBLIC INTERFACE
                   Application(void);
    void           run(void);

  public:
    virtual CString      className(void) const;
                                              // POLYMORPHIC

  };

#endif

//-- End Specification --------------------------------------


///////////////////////////////////////////////////////////
//
//          application.cpp
// ROME Copyright (c) Richard McMahon. 1993, 1994.
// ROME Copyright (c) Ken Barclay 1995.
// Generated On January 2, 1996 At 4:56:53.37 pm
//
///////////////////////////////////////////////////////////

#include "Company.h"
#include "SalesEmployee.h"
```

```
#include "ccstring.h"
#include "SalesManager.h"
#include "Application.h"

//   care: operating environment filenames may be case sensitive!
// #include "company.h"
// #include "salesemployee.h"
// #include "salesmanager.h"
//


Application::Application(void)
{
}

void
Application::run(void)
{
  //
  // Prepare a list of Employee and Manager objects,
  //   all of whom are employed by the Company object
  //   known as Napier. From the staff list of the
  //   company produce a printout of the sales achieved
  //   by each employee.
  //
  Company co("Napier");
  SalesEmployee* newEmployee = 0;
  CString name = "";
  CString title = "";
  Integer salary = 0;
  Integer sales = 0;
  Integer target = 0;
  Integer budget = 0;
  Integer day = 0;
  Integer month = 0;
  Integer year = 0;
  CString status = "";
  cout << "Employee type (ZZZ, EMP or MAN): ";
  cin >> status;
  while(status != "ZZZ") {
    if(status == "EMP") {
      cout << "Enter employee's name: ";
      cin >> name;
      cout << "Enter employee's date of birth: ";
      cin >> day;
      cin >> month;
      cin >> year;
      cout << "Enter employee's job title, salary and sales: ";
      cin >> title;
      cin >> salary;
      cin >> sales;

      SalesEmployee* emp =
      new SalesEmployee(name, CDate(day, month, year), title,
                                              salary, sales);
```

```
                newEmployee = emp;
         }else{
          cout << "Enter manager's name: ";
          cin >> name;
          cout << "Enter manager's date of birth: ";
          cin >> day;
          cin >> month;
          cin >> year;
          cout << "Enter manager's job title, salary, sales and
                   budget: ";
          cin >> title;
          cin >> salary;
          cin >> sales;
          cin >> target;
          SalesManager* man =
                       new SalesManager(name, CDate(day, month, year),
                                        title, salary, sales, target);
          newEmployee = man;
         }
         co.hire(newEmployee);
         cout << "Employee type (ZZZ, EMP or MAN): ";
         cin >> status;
      }
      co.salesReport();
   }


   CString
   Application::className(void) const
                                                   //POLYMORPHIC
   {
      return "Application";
   }



   //-- End Implementation --------------------------------------


   ///////////////////////////////////////////////////////////////
   //
   //            person.h
   // ROME Copyright (c) Richard McMahon. 1993, 1994.
   // ROME Copyright (c) Ken Barclay 1995.
   // Generated On January 2, 1996 At 4:56:53.43 pm
   //
   ///////////////////////////////////////////////////////////////

   #ifndef PERSON
    #define PERSON

    #include "loom.h"
    #include "ccstring.h"
```

```
#include "ccdate.h"


class Person {
public:         // PUBLIC INTERFACE
                                Person (const CString& aName,
                                   const CDate& aDateOfBirth);

  CString             name (void) const;
  Integer             age (void) const;

private:        // REPRESENTATION
  CString           theName;
  CDate             theDateOfBirth;

public:
  virtual CString       className (void) const;
                                          // POLYMORPHIC
};

#endif

//-- End Specification -------------------------------------

/////////////////////////////////////////////////////////////
//
//              person.cpp
// ROME Copyright (c) Richard McMahon. 1993, 1994.
// ROME Copyright (c) Ken Barclay 1995.
// Generated On January 2, 1996 At 4:56:53.43 pm
//
/////////////////////////////////////////////////////////////

#include "Person.h"


Person::Person (const CString& aName, const CDate& aDateOfBirth)
  : theName (aName),
    theDateOfBirth (aDateOfBirth)
{

}

CString
Person::name (void) const
{
  return theName;
}

Integer
Person::age (void) const
{
  //
  // Simplistic algorithm, taking no account of
  // months or days within the month.
```

```
//
CDate today;
Integer todayYear = today.year();
Integer dobYear = theDateOfBirth.year();
return todayYear - dobYear;
}


CString
Person::className(void) const      // POLYMORPHIC
{
  return "Person";
}


//-- End Implementation -------------------------------------


/////////////////////////////////////////////////////////
//
//          salesemployee.h
// ROME Copyright (c) Richard McMahon. 1993, 1994.
// ROME Copyright (c) Ken Barclay 1995.
// Generated On January 2, 1996 At 4:56:53.43 pm
//
/////////////////////////////////////////////////////////

#ifndef SALESEMPLOYEE
  #define SALESEMPLOYEE

  #include "loom.h"
  #include "Person.h"
  #include "ccstring.h"
  #include "ccdate.h"


  class SalesEmployee : public Person {
  public:          // PUBLIC INTERFACE
    SalesEmployee(const CString& aName, const CDate&
    aDateOfBirth,
              const CString& aJobTitle, const Integer& aSalary,
              const Integer& aSales);
    CString          jobTitle(void) const;
    Integer          salary(void) const;
    Logical          lessThan(const SalesEmployee&
                          anEmployee) const;
    virtual void     displaySales(void) const;
                                                // POLYMORPHIC
    Integer          sales(void) const;

  private:         // REPRESENTATION
    CString          theJobTitle;
    Integer          theSalary;
```

```
    Integer              theAchievedSales;

  public:
    virtual CString       className(void) const;
                                              // POLYMORPHIC
  };

#endif

//-- End Specification -------------------------------------

/////////////////////////////////////////////////////////
//
//          salesemployee.cpp
// ROME Copyright (c) Richard McMahon. 1993, 1994.
// ROME Copyright (c) Ken Barclay 1995.
// Generated On January 2, 1996 At 4:56:53.43 pm
//
/////////////////////////////////////////////////////////

#include "SalesEmployee.h"


SalesEmployee::SalesEmployee(const CString& aName,
               const CDate& aDateOfBirth,
               const CString& aJobTitle,
               const Integer& aSalary, const Integer& aSales)
  : Person(aName, aDateOfBirth),
    theJobTitle(aJobTitle),
    theSalary(aSalary),
    theAchievedSales(aSales)
{

}

CString
SalesEmployee::jobTitle(void) const
{
  return theJobTitle;
}

Integer
SalesEmployee::salary(void) const
{
  return theSalary;
}

Logical
SalesEmployee::lessThan(const SalesEmployee&  anEmployee)
const
{
  CString jobName = anEmployee.jobTitle();
  if(theJobTitle < jobName) {
```

```
    return LTRUE;
  } else {
    return LFALSE;
  }
}


void
SalesEmployee::displaySales(void) const
                                                      //POLYMORPHIC
{
  cout << this->Person::name();
  cout << ": ";
  cout << theAchievedSales;
  cout << "\n";
}

Integer
SalesEmployee::sales(void) const
{
  return theAchievedSales;
}


CString
SalesEmployee::className(void) const
                                                      //POLYMORPHIC
{
  return "SalesEmployee";
}


//-- End Implementation ------------------------------------


////////////////////////////////////////////////////////////
//
//            salesmanager.h
// ROME Copyright (c) Richard McMahon. 1993, 1994.
// ROME Copyright (c) Ken Barclay 1995.
// Generated On January 2, 1996 At 4:56:53.43 pm
//
////////////////////////////////////////////////////////////

#ifndef SALESMANAGER
  #define SALESMANAGER

  #include "loom.h"
  #include "SalesEmployee.h"
  #include "ccstring.h"
  #include "ccdate.h"


  class SalesManager : public SalesEmployee {
  public:          // PUBLIC INTERFACE
```

```
    SalesManager(const CString& aName, const CDate&
                aDateOfBirth, const CString&
                aJobTitle, const Integer& aSalary,
                const Integer& aSales, const Integer& aTarget);
  virtual void    displaySales(void) const;
                                                    //REDEFINED

 private:           // REPRESENTATION
   Integer          theSalesTarget;

 public:
   virtual CString     className(void) const;
                                                    // POLYMORPHIC

 };

#endif

//-- End Specification ------------------------------------


///////////////////////////////////////////////////////////
//
//          salesmanager.cpp
//ROME Copyright (c) Richard McMahon. 1993, 1994.
//ROME Copyright (c) Ken Barclay 1995.
//Generated On January 2, 1996 At 4:56:53.43 pm
//
///////////////////////////////////////////////////////////

#include "SalesManager.h"


SalesManager::SalesManager(const CString& aName,
                const CDate& aDateOfBirth,
                const CString& aJobTitle,
                const Integer& aSalary, const Integer& aSales,
                const Integer& aTarget)
     : SalesEmployee(aName, aDateOfBirth, aJobTitle, aSalary,
                                                    aSales),
   theSalesTarget(aTarget)
{

}

void
SalesManager::displaySales(void) const
                                                    // REDEFINED
{
  cout << this->Person::name();
  cout << ": ";
  cout << this->SalesEmployee::sales();
  cout << ": ";
  cout << theSalesTarget;
```

```
    cout << "\n";
}


CString
SalesManager::className(void) const
                                                        //POLYMORPHIC
{
  return "SalesManager";
}


//-- End Implementation -------------------------------------


////////////////////////////////////////////////////////////
//
//                company.h
// ROME Copyright (c) Richard McMahon. 1993, 1994.
// ROME Copyright (c) Ken Barclay 1995.
// Generated On January 2, 1996 At 4:56:53.43 pm
//
////////////////////////////////////////////////////////////

#ifndef COMPANY
 #define COMPANY

 #include "loom.h"
 #include "ccstring.h"
 #include "pordcol.h"

 class SalesEmployee;                          // forward references

 //
 // A Company has a one-to-many association with
 //   Employee objects. Using the principle of
 //   substitutability these may be either vanilla
 //   Employee objects or Manager objects which are
 //   specialised kinds of the former.
 //
 //

 class Company {
 public:        // PUBLIC INTERFACE
                                 Company(const CString& aName);
   CString       name(void) const;
   void          hire(SalesEmployee* anEmployee);
   void          salesReport(void) const;

 private:       // REPRESENTATION
   CString            theName;

 private:       // ASSOCIATION
   POrderedCollection< SalesEmployee* > theEmployees;
```

```
  public:
    virtual CString      className (void) const;
                                                   // POLYMORPHIC


  };

#endif

//-- End Specification -------------------------------------

////////////////////////////////////////////////////////////
//
//            company.cpp
// ROME Copyright (c) Richard McMahon. 1993, 1994.
// ROME Copyright (c) Ken Barclay 1995.
// Generated On January 2, 1996 At 4:56:53.43 pm
//
////////////////////////////////////////////////////////////

#include "SalesEmployee.h"
#include "Company.h"

//
// A Company has a one-to-many association with
//   Employee objects. Using the principle of
//   substitutability these may be either vanilla
//   Employee objects or Manager objects which are
//   specialised kinds of the former.
//
//

Company::Company (const CString& aName)
  : theName (aName),
    theEmployees (DEFAULTSIZE, MANAGED)
{

}

CString
Company::name (void) const
{
  return theName;
}

void
Company::hire (SalesEmployee* anEmployee)
{
  theEmployees.add (anEmployee);
}

void
Company::salesReport (void) const
{
  cout << "Sales report for: ";
```

```
    cout << theName;
    cout << "\n";
    PIterator< SalesEmployee* > empIterator(theEmployees);
    while( empIterator.isExhausted() == LFALSE ) {
      SalesEmployee* emp = empIterator.selection();
      emp->displaySales();
      empIterator.advance();
    }
}

CString
Company::className(void) const    // POLYMORPHIC
{
  return "Company";
}


//-- End Implementation ------------------------------------
```

Program 9.6

```
//////////////////////////////////////////////////////////
//
//            main
// ROME Copyright (c) Richard McMahon. 1993, 1994.
// ROME Copyright (c) Ken Barclay 1995.
// Generated On January 2, 1996 At 7:01:09.73 pm
//
//////////////////////////////////////////////////////////

#include "ccstring.h"
#include "application.h"

int main()
{
  Application    app;
  app.run();

  return 0;
}

//-- End Implementation ------------------------------------

//////////////////////////////////////////////////////////
//
//            application.h
// ROME Copyright (c) Richard McMahon. 1993, 1994.
// ROME Copyright (c) Ken Barclay 1995.
// Generated On January 2, 1996 At 7:01:09.73 pm
//
//////////////////////////////////////////////////////////
```

```
#ifndef APPLICATION
  #define APPLICATION

  #include "loom.h"
  #include "ccstring.h"


  class Application {
  public:        // PUBLIC INTERFACE
                   Application(void);
    void           run(void);

  public:
    virtual CString          className(void) const;
                                         // POLYMORPHIC


  };

#endif

//-- End Specification -------------------------------------

///////////////////////////////////////////////////////////
//
//          application.cpp
// ROME Copyright (c) Richard McMahon. 1993, 1994.
// ROME Copyright (c) Ken Barclay 1995.
// Generated On January 2, 1996 At 7:01:09.73 pm
//
///////////////////////////////////////////////////////////

#include "Company.h"
#include "ccstring.h"
#include "Sales.h"
#include "Manager.h"
#include "Application.h"


Application::Application(void)
{
}

void
Application::run(void)
{
  Company organisation("Napier");
  CString name = "";
  Integer day = 0;
  Integer month = 0;
  Integer year = 0;
  Integer sales = 0;
  Integer target = 0;
  CString managerName = "";
```

```cpp
        CString status = "";
        ifstream dataFile("p06.dat");
        dataFile >> status;
        while(status != "ZZZ") {
          if(status == "SAL") {
            dataFile >> name;
            dataFile >> day;
            dataFile >> month;
            dataFile >> year;
            dataFile >> sales;
            dataFile >> managerName;
            Sales* salesEmployee =
              new Sales(name, CDate(day, month, year), sales);
            organisation.appointSales(salesEmployee,
              managerName);
          } else {
            dataFile >> name;
            dataFile >> day;
            dataFile >> month;
            dataFile >> year;
            dataFile >> target;
            Manager* salesManager =
              new Manager(name, CDate(day, month, year), target);
            organisation.appointManager(salesManager);
          }
          dataFile >> status;
        }
        organisation.salesReport();
      }

      CString
      Application::className(void) const // POLYMORPHIC
      {
        return "Application";
      }

      //-- End Implementation -------------------------------------


      /////////////////////////////////////////////////////////
      //
      //              person.h
      // ROME Copyright (c) Richard McMahon. 1993, 1994.
      // ROME Copyright (c) Ken Barclay 1995.
      // Generated On January 2, 1996 At 7:01:09.73 pm
      //
      /////////////////////////////////////////////////////////

      #ifndef PERSON
        #define PERSON

        #include "loom.h"
        #include "ccstring.h"
        #include "ccdate.h"
```

```
   class Person {
   public:          // PUBLIC INTERFACE
Person (const CString& aName, const
                                        CDate& aDateOfBirth);

    CString            name (void) const;
    Integer            age (void) const;

   private:          // REPRESENTATION
     CString           theName;
     CDate             theDateOfBirth;

   public:
     virtual CString    className (void) const;
                                        // POLYMORPHIC

   };

#endif

//-- End Specification --------------------------------------

//////////////////////////////////////////////////////////
//
//              person.cpp
// ROME Copyright (c) Richard McMahon. 1993, 1994.
// ROME Copyright (c) Ken Barclay 1995.
// Generated On January 2, 1996 At 7:01:09.73 pm
//
//////////////////////////////////////////////////////////
#include "Person.h"


Person::Person (const CString& aName, const CDate& aDateOfBirth)
  : theName (aName),
    theDateOfBirth (aDateOfBirth)
{

}

CString
Person::name (void) const
{
  return theName;
}

Integer
Person::age (void) const
{
  //
  // Simplistic algorithm, taking no account of months or days
  // within the month.
  //
  CDate today;
```

```
    Integer todayYear = today.year();
    Integer dobYear = theDateOfBirth.year();
    return todayYear - dobYear;
}


CString
Person::className(void) const                      // POLYMORPHIC
{
  return "Person";
}



//-- End Implementation -------------------------------------------


////////////////////////////////////////////////////////////////
//
//            employee.h
// ROME Copyright (c) Richard McMahon. 1993, 1994.
// ROME Copyright (c) Ken Barclay 1995.
// Generated On January 2, 1996 At 7:01:09.73 pm
//
////////////////////////////////////////////////////////////////

#ifndef EMPLOYEE
 #define EMPLOYEE

 #include "loom.h"
 #include "Person.h"
 #include "ccstring.h"
 #include "ccdate.h"


 class Employee : public Person {   // ABSTRACT
 public:          // PUBLIC INTERFACE
  Employee(const CString& aName, const CDate& aDateOfBirth,
           const CString& aJobTitle, const Integer& aSalary);
  Logical      lessThan(const Employee& anEmployee) const;
  virtual void  displaySales(void) const = 0;
                                                   // DEFERRED

  protected:        // PROTECTED INTERFACE
   CString           jobTitle(void) const;
   Integer           salary(void) const;

  private:          // REPRESENTATION
   CString           theJobTitle;
   Integer           theSalary;

  public:
   virtual CString    className(void) const;
```

// POLYMORPHIC

```cpp
  };

#endif

//-- End Specification ------------------------------------

//////////////////////////////////////////////////////////
//
//            employee.cpp
// ROME Copyright (c) Richard McMahon. 1993, 1994.
// ROME Copyright (c) Ken Barclay 1995.
// Generated On January 2, 1996 At 7:01:09.73 pm
//
//////////////////////////////////////////////////////////

#include "Employee.h"

Employee::Employee(const CString& aName,
                   const CDate& aDateOfBirth,
                   const CString& aJobTitle,
                   const Integer& aSalary)
  : Person(aName, aDateOfBirth),
    theJobTitle(aJobTitle),
    theSalary(aSalary)
{

}

CString
Employee::jobTitle(void) const
{
  return theJobTitle;
}

Integer
Employee::salary(void) const
{
  return theSalary;
}

Logical
Employee::lessThan(const Employee& anEmployee)     const
{
  CString jobName = anEmployee.jobTitle();
  if(theJobTitle < jobName) {
    return LTRUE;
  } else {
    return LFALSE;
  }
}
CString
```

```
Employee::className(void) const    // POLYMORPHIC
{
  return "Employee";
}
```

```
//-- End Implementation ------------------------------------
```

```
///////////////////////////////////////////////////////////
//
//              sales.h
// ROME Copyright (c) Richard McMahon. 1993, 1994.
// ROME Copyright (c) Ken Barclay 1995.
// Generated On January 2, 1996 At 7:01:09.79 pm
//
///////////////////////////////////////////////////////////
```

```
#ifndef SALES
  #define SALES

  #include "loom.h"
  #include "Employee.h"
  #include "ccstring.h"
  #include "ccdate.h"


  class Sales : public Employee {
  public:          // PUBLIC INTERFACE
    Sales(const CString& aName, const CDate& aDateOfBirth,
          const Integer& aSales);
    Integer      sales(void) const;
    virtual void displaySales(void) const;
                                              // REDEFINED
    Logical      lessThan(const Sales& aSales) const;

  private:         // REPRESENTATION
    Integer      theAchievedSales;

  public:
    virtual CString  className(void) const;
                                              // POLYMORPHIC

  };
#endif
```

```
//-- End Specification ------------------------------------
```

```
////////////////////////////////////////////////////////
//
//            sales.cpp
// ROME Copyright (c) Richard McMahon. 1993, 1994.
// ROME Copyright (c) Ken Barclay 1995.
// Generated On January 2, 1996 At 7:01:09.79 pm
//
////////////////////////////////////////////////////////

#include "Sales.h"

Sales::Sales(const CString& aName, const CDate& aDateOfBirth,
                    const Integer& aSales)
      : Employee(aName, aDateOfBirth, "Sales Assistant", 1500),
    theAchievedSales(aSales)
{

}

Integer
Sales::sales(void) const
{
  return theAchievedSales;
}

void
Sales::displaySales(void) const                        // REDEFINED
{
  cout << this->Employee::name();
  cout << "[";
  cout << this->Employee::jobTitle();
  cout << "]";
  cout << theAchievedSales;
  cout << "\n";
}

Logical
Sales::lessThan(const Sales& aSales) const
{
  Integer achievedSales = aSales.sales();
  if (theAchievedSales < achievedSales) {
    return LTRUE;
  } else {
    return LFALSE;
  }
}

CString
Sales::className(void) const                           // POLYMORPHIC
{
  return "Sales";
}

//-- End Implementation -------------------------------------
```

```
///////////////////////////////////////////////////////
//
//            manager.h
// ROME Copyright (c) Richard McMahon. 1993, 1994.
// ROME Copyright (c) Ken Barclay 1995.
// Generated On January 2, 1996 At 7:01:09.79 pm
//
///////////////////////////////////////////////////////

#ifndef MANAGER
 #define MANAGER

 #include "loom.h"
 #include "Employee.h"
 #include "ccstring.h"
 #include "ccdate.h"
 #include "pordcol.h"

 class Sales;                                // forward references

 class Manager : public Employee {
 public:         // PUBLIC INTERFACE
   Manager (const CString& aName, const CDate& aDateOfBirth,
                              const Integer& aTarget);

   virtual void     displaySales (void) const;
                                          // REDEFINED
   void             appointTeamMember (Sales* aSalesPerson);

 private:        // REPRESENTATION
   Integer          theSalesTarget;

 private:        // ASSOCIATION
   POrderedCollection< Sales* >     theSalesTeam;

 public:
   virtual CString    className (void) const;
                                          // POLYMORPHIC

 };

#endif

//-- End Specification ----------------------------------


///////////////////////////////////////////////////////
//
//            manager.cpp
// ROME Copyright (c) Richard McMahon. 1993, 1994.
// ROME Copyright (c) Ken Barclay 1995.
// Generated On January 2, 1996 At 7:01:09.79 pm
//
///////////////////////////////////////////////////////
```

```
#include "Sales.h"
#include "Manager.h"


Manager::Manager(const CString& aName, const CDate&
                       aDateOfBirth, const Integer& aTarget)
   : Employee(aName, aDateOfBirth, "Sales Executive", 2000),
   theSalesTarget(aTarget),
   theSalesTeam(DEFAULTSIZE, UNMANAGED)
{

}

void
Manager::displaySales(void) const                      // REDEFINED
{
  Integer totalSales = 0;
  PIterator< Sales* > salesMemberIterator(theSalesTeam);
  while( salesMemberIterator.isExhausted() ==LFALSE ) {
    Sales* salesMember = salesMemberIterator.selection();
    Integer salesAmount = salesMember->sales();
    totalSales = totalSales+salesAmount;
    salesMemberIterator.advance();
  }
  cout << this->Person::name();
  cout << "[";
  cout << this->Employee::jobTitle();
  cout << "]";
  cout << totalSales;
  cout << ": ";
  cout << theSalesTarget;
  cout << "\n";
}

void
Manager::appointTeamMember(Sales* aSalesPerson)
{
  theSalesTeam.add(aSalesPerson);
}


CString
Manager::className(void) const                         // POLYMORPHIC
{
  return "Manager";
}


//-- End Implementation -----------------------------------
```

```
/////////////////////////////////////////////////////////////
//
//            company.h
//ROME Copyright (c) Richard McMahon. 1993, 1994.
//ROME Copyright (c) Ken Barclay 1995.
//Generated On January 2, 1996 At 7:01:09.79 pm
//
/////////////////////////////////////////////////////////////

#ifndef COMPANY
 #define COMPANY

 #include "loom.h"
 #include "ccstring.h"
 #include "pordcol.h"

 class Sales;        // forward references
 class Manager;
 class Employee;

 //
 // A Company has a one-to-many association with
 //  Employee objects. Using the principle of
 //  substitutability these may be either vanilla
 //  Employee objects or Manager objects which are
 //  specialised kinds of the former.
 //
 //

 class Company {
 public:        // PUBLIC INTERFACE
Company (const CString& aName);
   CString    name (void) const;
   void       appointSales (Sales* aSalesPerson,
                                   const CString& aManager);
   void       appointManager (Manager* aManager);
   void       salesReport (void) const;

 private:        // REPRESENTATION
   CString        theName;

 private:        // ASSOCIATION
   POrderedCollection< Employee* >  theEmployees;

 public:
   virtual CString        className (void) const;
                                               // POLYMORPHIC

 };

#endif

//-- End Specification -----------------------------------------
```

```
///////////////////////////////////////////////////////
//
//           company.cpp
// ROME Copyright (c) Richard McMahon. 1993, 1994.
// ROME Copyright (c) Ken Barclay 1995.
// Generated On January 2, 1996 At 7:01:09.79 pm
//
///////////////////////////////////////////////////////

#include "Employee.h"
#include "Manager.h"
#include "Sales.h"
#include "Company.h"

//
// A Company has a one-to-many association with
//   Employee objects. Using the principle of
//   substitutability these may be either vanilla
//   Employee objects or Manager objects which are
//   specialised kinds of the former.
//
//


Company::Company(const CString& aName)
  : theName(aName),
    theEmployees(DEFAULTSIZE, MANAGED)
{

}

CString
Company::name(void) const
{
  return theName;
}

void
Company::appointSales(Sales* aSalesPerson,
                                const CString& aManager)
{
  PIterator< Employee* > empIterator(theEmployees);
  while( empIterator.isExhausted() == LFALSE ) {
    Employee* emp = empIterator.selection();
    CString empName = emp->name();
    if(aManager == empName) {
      Manager* managerEmployee = 0;
      managerEmployee = (Manager*)emp;
      theEmployees.add(aSalesPerson);
      managerEmployee->appointTeamMember(aSalesPerson);
      return;
    }
    empIterator.advance();
  }
```

```
    // NO such manager -- do nothing!

}

void
Company::appointManager(Manager* aManager)
{
  theEmployees.add(aManager);
}

void
Company::salesReport(void) const
{
  cout << "Sales report for: ";
  cout << theName;
  cout << "\n";
  cout << "================================\n";
  PIterator<Employee*> empIterator(theEmployees);
  while( empIterator.isExhausted() == LFALSE ) {
    Employee* emp = empIterator.selection();
    emp->displaySales();
    empIterator.advance();
  }
}



CString
Company::className(void) const                    // POLYMORPHIC
{
  return "Company";
}


//-- End Implementation ------------------------------------
```

Index

OBJECT-ORIENTED DESIGN WITH C++ TUTORIAL DISK

Ken Barclay and John Savage

Limited warranty

The program is provided as is without warranty of any kind, either expressed or implied, including but not limited to the implied warranties of merchantability and fitness for a particular purpose. The entire risk as to the quality and performance of the program is with you. Should the program prove defective, you assume the entire cost of all necessary servicing, repair, or correction.

Prentice Hall Europe (being the business name and imprint of International Book Distributors) does not warrant that the functions contained in the program will meet your requirements or that the operation of the program will be uninterrupted or error free. However, Prentice Hall Europe warrants the diskette(s) on which the program is furnished to be free from defects in the materials and workmanship under normal use for a period of ninety (90) days from the date of delivery to you evidenced by a copy of your receipt. The defective diskette must be returned to Prentice Hall Europe, Attention: Editorial, Computing, for this warranty to be effected.

Limitations of remedies

Prentice Hall Europe's entire liability and your exclusive remedy shall be:

(a) The replacement of the diskette(s) if you have met the conditions as described under Limited Warranty or

(b) A full refund if Prentice Hall Europe is unable to deliver a diskette free from defects in materials or workmanship.

In no event will Prentice Hall Europe be liable to you for any damages including any lost profits, lost savings, or other incidental or consequential damages arising out of the use or inability to use such program even if Prentice Hall Europe has been advised of the possibility of such damages or any claim by any other party.

General

You may not sublicense, assign, or transfer the limited warranties of the program except as expressly provided in this Agreement. Any attempt otherwise to sublicense, assign, or transfer any of the rights, duties, or obligations hereunder is void.

This agreement will be governed by the laws of Great Britain and Northern Ireland.

Should you have any questions concerning this agreement, you may contact Prentice Hall Europe by writing to:

Prentice Hall Europe
Campus 400
Maylands Avenue
Hemel Hempstead
Herts HP2 7EZ

By opening this package you acknowledge that you have read this agreement and understand it and agree to be bound by its terms and conditions. You further agree that it is the complete and exclusive statement of the agreement between us which supersedes any proposal or prior agreement, oral or written, and any other communication between us relating to the subject matter of this agreement.

ISBN 0–13–256371–1